Get the eBook FREE!

(PDF, ePub, Kindle, and liveBook all included)

We believe that once you buy a book from us, you should be able to read it in any format we have available. To get electronic versions of this book at no additional cost to you, purchase and then register this book at the Manning website.

Go to https://www.manning.com/freebook and follow the instructions to complete your pBook registration.

That's it!
Thanks from Manning!

Elixir in Action, Third Edition

Elixir in Action

THIRD EDITION

SAŠA JURIĆ

FOREWORD BY FRANCESCO CESARINI

MANNING

SHELTER ISLAND

For online information and ordering of this and other Manning books, please visit www.manning.com. The publisher offers discounts on this book when ordered in quantity. For more information, please contact

Special Sales Department
Manning Publications Co.
20 Baldwin Road
PO Box 761
Shelter Island, NY 11964
Email: orders@manning.com

Manning Publications Co.
20 Baldwin Road
PO Box 761
Shelter Island, NY 11964

Development editor:	Rebecca Johnson
Review editor:	Dunja Nikitović
Production editor:	Kathy Rossland
Copy editor:	Christian Berk
Proofreader:	Katie Tennant
Technical proofreader:	Marius Butuc
Typesetter:	Gordan Salinovic
Cover designer:	Marija Tudor

ISBN 9781633438514
Printed in the United States of America

To Renata, who never read this book,
and Lea, who doesn't even know it exists

brief contents

contents

foreword

Successful programming languages are invented to solve problems existing languages and tools do not address well. When I asked José Valim what problem he was trying to solve when creating Elixir, he responded that he wanted to bring the power of Erlang and the BEAM to other communities of programmers. He started with the web through the Phoenix framework, followed by successful inroads into the embedded and machine learning spaces. "What problem were you trying to solve?" is a question I have asked dozens of language inventors, with varied answers. José was the first, who, in his reply, said his focus was on the adoption of ideas, semantics, and runtime of another extremely powerful language, Erlang. He did it by approaching the problem with a different syntax, tools, and development approach.

What problems were Erlang co-inventors, Joe Armstrong, Robert Virding, and Mike Williams, trying to solve? They set out on a quest to understand how to better and more efficiently build and maintain scalable, fault-tolerant systems. These systems in the early '90s were typically associated with telecom switches, but soon, they became applicable to any piece of software connected to the internet. Their solution happened to be a programming language, even if they had not set out to invent one. Erlang ended up being used in major infrastructure projects at Cisco, Ericsson, Klarna, Goldman Sachs, T-Mobile, WhatsApp, and Amazon, alongside many other top companies. As more programming languages were added to the BEAM, Erlang and its runtime became an Ecosystem of languages today referred to as the Erlang ecosystem. Elixir is, without a doubt, the most popular of these languages.

So how does all of this relate to the book you are about to read? It is simple. To truly understand and embrace the power of Elixir, you need to understand both Erlang and OTP. I am not suggesting you go off and learn these languages but, instead, learn Elixir from someone who has used Erlang professionally for many years before making the transition. Saša Jurić, by explaining what makes Erlang special, shows you how to efficiently use Elixir. Explaining why Erlang works the way it does shows you the what and the how of Elixir. This is what differentiates *Elixir in Action* from all of the other books on the topic. I hope you enjoy it as much as I did, learning not only about a programming language but about the philosophy of the ecosystem as a whole.

Happy coding!

—Francesco Cesarini

Founder of Erlang Solutions;

Member of the team who worked on the R1 release of OTP;

Coauthor of *Erlang Programming* and *Designing for Scalability with Erlang/OTP*;

Founding member of the Erlang Ecosystem Foundation;

Senior lecturer at the University of Oxford

preface

In 2010, I was given the task of implementing a system to transmit frequent updates to a few thousand connected users in near-real time. My company at the time was mostly using Ruby on Rails, but I needed something more suitable for such a highly concurrent challenge. Following the suggestion of my CTO, I looked into Erlang, read some material, made a prototype, and performed a load test. I was impressed with the initial results and moved on to implement the whole thing in Erlang. A few months later, the system was shipped, and it's been doing its job ever since.

As time passed, I began to increasingly appreciate Erlang and the way it helped me manage such a complex system. Gradually, I came to prefer Erlang over the technologies I had used previously. I began to evangelize the language, first in my company and then at local events. Finally, at the end of 2012, I started the blog *The Erlangelist* (http://theerlangelist.com), where I aim to showcase the advantages of Erlang to programmers from OO backgrounds.

Because Erlang is an unusual language, I began experimenting with Elixir, hoping it would help me explain the beauty of Erlang in a way that would resonate with OO programmers. Despite the fact that it was at an early stage of development (at the time, it was at version 0.8), I was immediately impressed with Elixir's maturity and the way it integrated with Erlang. Soon, I started using Elixir to develop new features for my Erlang-based system.

A few months later, I was contacted by Michael Stephens of Manning Publications, who asked me if I was interested in writing a book about Elixir. At the time, two Elixir books were already in the making. After some consideration, I decided there was space for another book that would approach the topic from a different angle, focusing on Elixir concurrency and the OTP way of thinking. Writing the book took a lot of work, but it was a rewarding experience.

This is the third edition of the book, and it isn't radically different from the first or second ones. Rather, it focuses on bringing the book up to date with the latest developments in Elixir and Erlang, such as the new ways of working with application configuration and OTP releases.

At this point, *Elixir in Action* is again fully up to date and teaches you the most recent techniques for building software systems with Elixir. I hope you enjoy reading the book, learn a lot from it, and have a chance to apply your new knowledge in your work!

acknowledgments

Writing this book required a significant time investment, so, above all, I want to thank my wife, Renata, for her endless support and patience during those long hours and busy weekends.

I'd like to thank Manning for making this book happen. In particular, thanks go to Michael Stephens, for making the initial contact; Marjan Bace, for giving me a chance to write this book; Bert Bates, for pointing me in the right direction; Karen Miller and Rebecca Johnson, for keeping me on track; Aleksandar Dragosavljević and Dunja Niki-tović, for managing the review process; Kevin Sullivan and Vincent Nordhaus for over-seeing production; Tiffany Taylor, Andy Carroll, and Christian Berk, for transforming my "English" into proper English; and Candace Gillhoolley, Ana Romac, Christopher Kaufmann, and Radmila Ercegovac, for promoting the book.

The material in this book has been significantly improved thanks to great feedback from reviewers and early readers. Above all, I wish to thank Andrew Gibson for useful feedback and great insights as well as for rescuing me when I got stuck at the last hur-dle. I'd also like to thank Oleksii Sholik, Peter Minten, and Marius Butuc, who pro-vided excellent immediate technical feedback during the writing process.

A big thank you goes to all the technical reviewers: Al Rahimi, Alan Lenton, Ales-sandro Campeis, Alexander Zenger, Alexey Galiullin, Andrew Courter, Ariel Otilibili, Arun Kumar, Ashad Dean, Christoffer Fink, Christopher Bailey, Christopher Haupt, Clive Harber, Daniel Couper, Eoghan O'Donnell, Frederick Schiller, Gábor László Hajba, George Thomas, Heather Campbell, Ioannis Polyzos, Jeroen Benckhuijsen, Jim Amrhein, Johan Mattisson, Jorge Deflon, José Valim, Kosmas Chatzimichalis,

Laszlo Hegedus, Mafinar Khan, Mark Ryall, Mathias Polligkeit, Michael Piscatello, Mohsen Mostafa Jokar, Rahul Sinha, Riza Fahmi, Simon Hewitt, Simone Sguazza, Tijl Vercaemer, Tom Geudens, Tomer Elmalem, Ved Antani, and Yurii Bodarev.

I also wish to thank all the readers who bought and read the Manning Early Access Program (MEAP) version and provided useful comments. Thank you for taking the time to read my ramblings and for providing insightful feedback.

The people who gave us Elixir and Erlang, including the original inventors, core team members, and contributors, deserve a special mention. Thank you for creating such great products that make my job easier and more fun. Thank you, Francesco Cesarini, for the lovely foreword. Finally, special thanks go to all the members of the Elixir community; this is the nicest and friendliest developer community I've ever known!

about this book

Elixir is a modern functional programming language for building large-scale, distributed, fault-tolerant, scalable systems for the Erlang virtual machine (VM). Although the language is compelling in its own right, arguably, its biggest advantage is that it targets the Erlang platform.

Erlang was made to help developers deal with the challenge of high availability. Originally, the product was intended for developing telecommunication systems, but today, it's used in all kinds of domains, such as collaboration tools, online payment systems, real-time bidding systems, database servers, and multiplayer online games, to name only a few examples. If you're developing a system that must provide service to a multitude of users around the world, you'll want that system to function continuously without noticeable downtime, regardless of any software or hardware problems that occur at run time. Otherwise, significant and frequent outages will leave end users unhappy, and ultimately, they may seek alternative solutions. A system with frequent downtime is unreliable and unusable and, thus, fails to fulfill its intended purpose. Therefore, high availability becomes an increasingly important property—and Erlang can help you achieve that.

Elixir aims to modernize and improve the experience of developing Erlang-powered systems. The language is a compilation of features from various other languages, such as Erlang, Clojure, and Ruby. Furthermore, Elixir ships with a toolset that simplifies project management, testing, packaging, and documentation building. Arguably, Elixir lowers the entry barrier into the Erlang world and improves developer productivity. Having the Erlang runtime as the target platform means Elixir-based systems are able to use all the libraries from the Erlang ecosystem, including the battle-tested OTP framework that ships with Erlang.

Who should read this book

This book is a tutorial that will teach you how to build production-ready Elixir-based systems. It's not a complete reference on Elixir and Erlang—it doesn't cover every nuance of the language or every possible aspect of the underlying Erlang VM. It glosses over or skips many topics, such as floating-point precision, Unicode specifics, file I/O, unit testing, and more. Although they're relevant, such topics aren't this book's primary focus, and you can research them yourself when the need arises. Omitting or dealing quickly with these conventional topics gives us space to treat more interesting and unusual areas in greater detail. Concurrent programming and the way it helps bring scalability, fault tolerance, distribution, and availability to systems are the core topics of this book.

Some of the techniques covered in this book aren't discussed in full detail. I've omitted some fine-print nuances for the sake of brevity and focus. My goal is not to provide complete coverage but, rather, to teach you about the underlying principles and how each piece fits into the bigger picture. After finishing this book, you should find it simple to research and understand the remaining details on your own. To give you a push in the right direction, mentions of and links to further interesting topics appear throughout the book.

Because this book deals with upper-intermediate topics, there are some prerequisites you should meet before reading it. I've assumed you're a professional software developer with a couple of years of experience. The exact technology you're proficient in isn't relevant: it can be Java, C#, Ruby, C++, or another general-purpose programming language. Any experience in development of backend (server-side) systems is helpful.

You don't need to know anything about Erlang, Elixir, or other concurrent platforms. In particular, you don't need to know anything about functional programming. Elixir is a functional language, which, if you come from an OO background, may scare you a bit. As a long-time OO programmer, I can sincerely tell you not to worry. The underlying functional concepts in Elixir are relatively simple and should be easy to grasp. Of course, functional programming is significantly different from whatever you've seen in a typical OO language, and it takes some getting used to. But it's not rocket science, and if you're an experienced developer, you should have no problem understanding these concepts.

How this book is organized: A road map

The book is divided into three parts. Part 1 introduces the Elixir language, presents and describes its basic building blocks, and then treats common functional programming idioms in more detail:

- Chapter 1 provides a high-level overview of Erlang and Elixir and explains why those technologies are useful and what distinguishes them from other languages and platforms.
- Chapter 2 presents the main building blocks of Elixir, such as modules, functions, and the type system.

- Chapter 3 gives a detailed explanation of pattern matching and how it's used to deal with flow control.
- Chapter 4 explains how to build higher-level abstractions on top of immutable data structures.

Part 2 builds on these foundations and focuses on the Erlang concurrency model and its many benefits, such as scalability and fault-tolerance:

- Chapter 5 explains the Erlang concurrency model and presents basic concurrency primitives.
- Chapter 6 discusses generic server processes—building blocks of highly concurrent Elixir and Erlang systems.
- Chapter 7 demonstrates how to build a more involved concurrent system.
- Chapter 8 presents the idioms of error handling, with a special focus on errors and faults in concurrent systems.
- Chapter 9 provides an in-depth discussion of how to isolate all kinds of errors and minimize their impact in production.
- Chapter 10 discusses a couple of alternatives to generic server processes that are sometimes more appropriate for implementing parts of your system.

Part 3 deals with systems in production:

- Chapter 11 explains OTP applications, which are used to package reusable components.
- Chapter 12 discusses distributed systems, which can help you improve fault tolerance and scalability.
- Chapter 13 presents various ways of preparing an Elixir-based system for production, particularly focusing on OTP releases.

About the code

This book contains many examples of source code both in numbered listings and in line with normal text. In both cases, source code is formatted in a `fixed-width font` `like this` to separate it from ordinary text.

In some cases, the original source code has been reformatted; we've added line breaks and reworked indentation to accommodate the available page space in the book. Additionally, comments in the source code have been removed from the listings when the code is described in the text. Code annotations accompany many of the listings, highlighting important concepts.

You can get executable snippets of code from the liveBook (online) version of this book at https://livebook.manning.com/book/elixir-in-action-third-edition. The complete code for the examples in the book is available for download from the Manning website at https://www.manning.com/books/elixir-in-action-third-edition, and from GitHub at https://github.com/sasa1977/elixir-in-action/tree/3rd-edition.

liveBook discussion forum

Purchase of *Elixir in Action, Third Edition*, includes free access to liveBook, Manning's online reading platform. Using liveBook's exclusive discussion features, you can attach comments to the book globally or to specific sections or paragraphs. It's a snap to make notes for yourself, ask and answer technical questions, and receive help from the author and other users. To access the forum, go to https://livebook.manning.com/book/elixir-in-action-third-edition/discussion. You can also learn more about Manning's forums and the rules of conduct at https://livebook.manning.com/discussion.

Manning's commitment to our readers is to provide a venue where a meaningful dialogue between individual readers and between readers and the author can take place. It is not a commitment to any specific amount of participation on the part of the author, whose contribution to the forum remains voluntary (and unpaid). We suggest you try asking the author some challenging questions lest their interest stray! The forum and the archives of previous discussions will be accessible from the publisher's website as long as the book is in print.

about the author

 **SAŠA JURIĆ** is a developer with extensive experience implementing high-volume, concurrent, server-side systems—desktop and kiosk applications—using various programming languages, such as C#, Ruby, and JavaScript. For the past 14 years, his main professional focus has been on the BEAM languages, primarily Elixir. In recent years, he's been working as an Elixir mentor, helping teams adopt Elixir and use it in production. He occasionally blogs about Elixir and Erlang at https://www.theerlangelist.com/.

about the cover illustration

The figure on the cover of *Elixir in Action, Third Edition*, "A Russian Girl," is taken from a book by Thomas Jefferys, published between 1757 and 1772.

In those days, it was easy to identify where people lived and what their trade or station in life was just by their dress. Manning celebrates the inventiveness and initiative of the computer business with book covers based on the rich diversity of regional culture centuries ago, brought back to life by pictures from collections such as this one.

Part 1

Functional Elixir

The first part of the book is an introduction to Elixir as a functional language. We start by providing a high-level overview of Elixir and Erlang, discussing the goals and benefits of both technologies. In chapter 2, you'll learn about the basic building blocks of the Elixir language, such as modules, functions, and the type system. Chapter 3 details the treatment of pattern-matching and control-flow idioms. In chapter 4, you'll learn how to implement higher-level data abstractions with immutable data structures.

First steps *1*

This chapter covers

- An overview of Erlang
- The benefits of Elixir

This marks the beginning of your journey into the world of Elixir and Erlang, two efficient and useful technologies that can significantly simplify the development of large, scalable systems. Chances are, you're reading this book to learn about Elixir. But because Elixir is built on top of Erlang and depends heavily on it, you should first learn a bit about what Erlang is and the benefits it offers. So let's take a brief, high-level look at Erlang.

1.1 About Erlang

Erlang is a development platform for building scalable and reliable systems that constantly provide service with little or no downtime. This is a bold statement, but it's exactly what Erlang was made for. Conceived in the mid-1980s by Ericsson, a Swedish telecom giant, Erlang was driven by the needs of the company's own telecom systems, where properties like reliability, responsiveness, scalability, and constant availability were imperative. A telephone network should always operate regardless of the number of simultaneous calls, unexpected bugs, or hardware and software upgrades taking place.

Despite being originally built for telecom systems, Erlang is in no way specialized for this domain. It doesn't contain explicit support for programming telephones, switches, or other telecom devices. Instead, Erlang is a general-purpose development platform that provides special support for technical, nonfunctional challenges, such as concurrency, scalability, fault tolerance, distribution, and high availability.

In the late 1980s and early '90s, when most software was desktop-based, the need for high availability was limited to specialized systems, such as telecoms. Today, we face a much different situation: the focus is on the internet and the web, and most applications are driven and supported by a server system that processes requests, crunches data, and pushes relevant information to many connected clients. Today's popular systems are more about communication and collaboration; examples include social networks, content-management systems, on-demand multimedia, and multiplayer games.

These systems have some nonfunctional requirements in common. The system must be responsive, regardless of the number of connected clients. The effects of unexpected errors must be minimal, instead of affecting the entire system. It's acceptable if an occasional request fails due to a bug, but it's a major problem if the entire system to becomes completely unavailable. Ideally, the system should never crash or be taken down, not even during a software upgrade. It should always be up and running, providing service to its clients.

These goals might seem difficult to reach, but they're imperative when building systems that people depend on. Unless a system is responsive and reliable, it will eventually fail to fulfill its purpose. Therefore, when building server-side systems, it's essential to make the system constantly available.

This is the intended purpose of Erlang. High availability is explicitly supported via technical concepts, such as scalability, fault tolerance, and distribution. Unlike with most other modern development platforms, these concepts were the main motivation and driving force behind the development of Erlang. The Ericsson team, led by Joe Armstrong, spent a couple of years designing, prototyping, and experimenting before creating the development platform. Its uses may have been limited in the early '90s, but today, almost any system can benefit from it.

Erlang has recently gained more attention. It powers various large systems such as the WhatsApp messaging application, the Discord instant messaging platform, the RabbitMQ message queue, financial systems, and multiplayer backends, and has been doing so for three decades. It's truly a proven technology, both in time and scale. But what is the magic behind Erlang? Let's take a look at how Erlang can help you build highly available, reliable systems.

1.1.1 *High availability*

Erlang was specifically created to support the development of highly available systems—systems that are always online and provide service to their clients even when faced with unexpected circumstances. On the surface, this may seem simple, but as you probably know, many things can go wrong in production. To make systems work 24/7 without any downtime, you must first tackle some technical challenges:

- *Fault tolerance*—A system must keep working when something unforeseen happens. Unexpected errors occur, bugs creep in, components occasionally fail, network connections drop, or the entire machine where the system is running crashes. Whatever happens, you want to localize the effect of an error as much as possible, recover from the error, and keep the system running and providing service.

- *Scalability*—A system should be able to handle any possible load. Of course, you don't buy tons of hardware just in case the entire planet's population might start using your system someday, but you should be able to respond to a load increase by adding more hardware resources without any software intervention. Ideally, this should be possible without a system restart.

- *Distribution*—To make a system that never stops, you need to run it on multiple machines. This promotes the overall stability of the system: if a machine is taken down, another one can take over. Furthermore, this gives you the means to scale horizontally—you can address load increase by adding more machines to the system, thus adding work units to support the higher demand.

- *Responsiveness*—It goes without saying that a system should always be reasonably fast and responsive. Request handling shouldn't be drastically prolonged, even if the load increases or unexpected errors happen. In particular, occasional lengthy tasks shouldn't block the rest of the system or have a significant effect on performance.

- *Live update*—In some cases, you may want to push a new version of your software without restarting any servers. For example, in a telephone system, you don't want to disconnect established calls while you upgrade the software.

If you manage to handle these challenges, the system will truly become highly available and be able to constantly provide service to users, rain or shine.

Erlang provides tools to address these challenges—that's what it was built for. A system can gain all these properties and, ultimately, become highly available through the power of the Erlang concurrency model. Let's look at how concurrency works in Erlang.

1.1.2 Erlang concurrency

Concurrency is at the heart and soul of Erlang systems. Almost every nontrivial Erlang-based production system is highly concurrent. Even the programming language is sometimes called a *concurrency-oriented language*. Instead of relying on heavyweight threads and OS processes, Erlang takes concurrency into its own hands, as illustrated in figure 1.1.

The basic concurrency primitive is called an *Erlang process* (not to be confused with OS processes or threads), and typical Erlang systems run thousands, or even millions, of such processes. The Erlang virtual machine, called *Bogdan/Björn's Erlang Abstract Machine* (BEAM), uses its own schedulers to distribute the execution of processes over the available CPU cores, thus parallelizing execution as much as possible. The way processes are implemented provides many benefits.

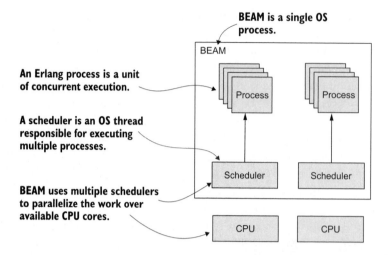

BEAM is a single OS process.

An Erlang process is a unit of concurrent execution.

A scheduler is an OS thread responsible for executing multiple processes.

BEAM uses multiple schedulers to parallelize the work over available CPU cores.

**Figure 1.1
Concurrency in the Erlang virtual machine**

FAULT TOLERANCE

Erlang processes are completely isolated from each other. They share no memory, and a crash of one process doesn't cause a crash of other processes. This helps you isolate the effect of an unexpected error. If something bad happens, it has only a local effect. Moreover, Erlang provides you with the means to detect a process crash and do something about it; typically, you start a new process in place of the crashed one.

SCALABILITY

Sharing no memory, processes communicate via asynchronous messages. This means there are no complex synchronization mechanisms, such as locks, mutexes, or semaphores. Consequently, the interaction between concurrent entities is much simpler to develop and understand.

Typical Erlang systems are divided into a large number of concurrent processes, which cooperate together to provide the complete service. The virtual machine can efficiently parallelize the execution of processes as much as possible. Because they can take advantage of all available CPU cores, this makes Erlang systems scalable.

DISTRIBUTION

Communication between processes works the same way regardless of whether these processes reside in the same BEAM instance or on two different instances on two separate, remote computers. Therefore, a typical, highly concurrent, Erlang-based system is automatically ready to be distributed over multiple machines. This, in turn, gives you the ability to scale out—to run a cluster of machines that share the total system load. Additionally, running on multiple machines makes the system truly resilient; if one machine crashes, others can take over.

RESPONSIVENESS

The runtime is specifically tuned to promote the overall responsiveness of the system. I've mentioned Erlang takes the execution of multiple processes into its own hands by employing dedicated schedulers that interchangeably execute many Erlang processes.

A scheduler is preemptive—it gives a small execution window to each process and then pauses it and runs another process. Because the execution window is small, a single long-running process can't block the rest of the system. Furthermore, I/O operations are internally delegated to separate threads, or a kernel-poll service of the underlying OS is used, if available. This means any process that waits for an I/O operation to finish won't block the execution of other processes.

Even garbage collection is specifically tuned to promote system responsiveness. Recall that processes are completely isolated and share no memory. This allows per-process garbage collection; instead of stopping the entire system, each process is individually collected, as needed. Such collections are much quicker and don't block the entire system for long periods of time. In fact, in a multicore system, it's possible for one CPU core to run a short garbage collection while the remaining cores are doing standard processing.

As you can see, concurrency is a crucial element in Erlang, and it's related to more than just parallelism. Owing to the underlying implementation, concurrency promotes fault tolerance, distribution, and system responsiveness. Typical Erlang systems run many concurrent tasks, using thousands or even millions of processes. This can be especially useful when you're developing server-side systems, which can often be implemented completely in Erlang.

1.1.3 Server-side systems

Erlang can be used in various applications and systems. There are examples of Erlang-based desktop applications, and it's often used in embedded environments. Its sweet spot, in my opinion, lies in server-side systems—systems that run on one or more servers and must serve many clients simultaneously. The term *server-side system* indicates that it's more than a simple server that processes requests. It's an entire system that, in addition to handling requests, must run various background jobs and manage some kind of server-wide in-memory state, as illustrated in figure 1.2.

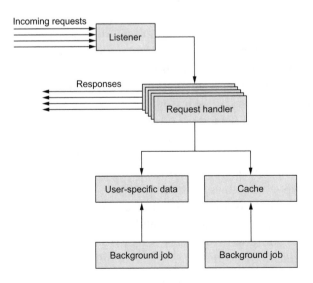

Figure 1.2 Server-side system

A server-side system is often distributed on multiple machines that collaborate to produce business value. You might place different components on different machines, and you also might deploy some components on multiple servers to achieve load balancing or support failover scenarios.

This is where Erlang can make your life significantly simpler. By providing you with primitives to make your code concurrent, scalable, and distributed, it allows you to implement the entire system completely in Erlang. Every component in figure 1.2 can be implemented as an Erlang process, which makes the system scalable, fault-tolerant, and easy to distribute. By relying on Erlang's error-detection and recovery primitives, you can further increase reliability and recover from unexpected errors.

Let's look at a real-life example. I've been involved professionally in the development of two web servers, both having similar technical needs: serving a multitude of clients, handling long-running requests, managing server-wide in-memory state, persisting data that must survive OS processes and machine restarts, and running background jobs. Table 1.1 lists the technologies used in each server.

Table 1.1   **Comparison of technologies used in two real-life web servers**

Technical requirement	Server A	Server B
HTTP server	NGINX and Phusion Passenger	Erlang
Request processing	Ruby on Rails	Erlang
Long-running requests	Go	Erlang
Server-wide state	Redis	Erlang
Persistable data	Redis and MongoDB	Erlang
Background jobs	cron, Bash scripts, and Ruby	Erlang
Service crash recovery	Upstart	Erlang

Server A is powered by various technologies, most of them well known in the community. There were specific reasons for using these technologies: each was introduced to resolve a shortcoming of those already present in the system. For example, Ruby on Rails handles concurrent requests in separate OS processes. We needed a way to share data between these different processes, so we introduced Redis. Similarly, MongoDB is used to manage persistent frontend data, most often user-related information. Thus, there's a rationale behind every technology used in server A, but the entire solution seems complex. It's not contained in a single project; the components are deployed separately, and it isn't trivial to start the entire system on a development machine. We had to develop a tool to help us start the system locally!

In contrast, server B accomplishes the same technical requirements while relying on a single technology, using platform features created specifically for these purposes and proven in large systems. Moreover, the entire server is a single project that runs inside a single BEAM instance—in production, it runs inside only one OS process, using a handful of OS threads. Concurrency is handled completely by the Erlang scheduler, and the system is scalable, responsive, and fault tolerant. Because it's implemented as a single project, the system is easier to manage, deploy, and run locally on the development machine.

It's important to notice that Erlang tools aren't always full-blown alternatives to mainstream solutions, such as web servers like NGINX, database servers like MongoDB, and in-memory key–value stores like Redis. But Erlang gives you options, making it possible to implement an initial solution using exclusively Erlang and resorting to alternative technologies when an Erlang solution isn't sufficient. This makes the entire system more homogeneous and, therefore, easier to develop and maintain.

It's also worth noting that Erlang isn't an isolated island. It can run in-process code written in languages such as C, C++, or Rust and can communicate with external components such as message queues, in-memory key–value stores, and external databases. Therefore, when opting for Erlang, you aren't deprived of using existing third-party technologies. Instead, you have the option of using them when they're called for rather than because your primary development platform doesn't give you a tool to solve your problems. Now that you know about Erlang's strengths and the areas in which it excels, let's take a closer look at what Erlang is.

1.1.4   The development platform

Erlang is more than a programming language. It's a full-blown development platform consisting of four distinct parts: the language, the virtual machine, the framework, and the tools.

Erlang the language is the primary way of writing code that runs in the Erlang virtual machine. It's a simple, functional language with basic concurrency primitives.

Source code written in Erlang is compiled into bytecode that's then executed in the BEAM. This is where the true magic happens. The virtual machine parallelizes your concurrent Erlang programs and takes care of process isolation, distribution, and the overall responsiveness of the system.

The standard part of the release is a framework called *Open Telecom Platform* (OTP). Despite its somewhat misleading name, the framework has nothing to do with telecom systems. It's a general-purpose framework that abstracts away many typical Erlang tasks, including the following:

- Concurrency and distribution patterns
- Error detection and recovery in concurrent systems
- Packaging code into libraries
- Systems deployment
- Live code updates

OTP is battle tested in many production systems and is such an integral part of Erlang that it's hard to draw a line between the two. Even the official distribution is called *Erlang/OTP*.

The tools are used for several typical tasks, such as compiling Erlang code, starting a BEAM instance, creating deployable releases, running the interactive shell, connecting to the running BEAM instance, and so on. Both BEAM and its accompanying tools are cross-platform. You can run them on most mainstream operating systems, such as Unix, Linux, and Windows. The entire Erlang distribution is open source, and you can find the source on the official site (https://www.erlang.org/) or on the Erlang GitHub repository (https://github.com/erlang/otp). Ericsson is still in charge of the development process and releases a new version once a year.

1.1.5   *Relationship to microservices*

Due to its concurrency model and how it is used to increase the availability of the system, Erlang is sometimes compared to microservices. So let's spend some time analyzing the similarities and differences between the two. For the purpose of this section, a service means a part of the system running in a separate OS process. Such a definition is oversimplified and very mechanical, but it's sufficient for our needs.

Splitting the system into multiple services can improve system fault tolerance and scalability. Because the system is powered by multiple OS processes, if one crashes, it will have a smaller effect on the entire system. Furthermore, the services can be spread out across multiple machines, which makes the system more resilient against hardware failures. Finally, running multiple instances of services makes the system horizontally scalable.

At first glance, it seems we can get all the benefits of Erlang by splitting the system into services, especially if we keep the services smaller in size and scope (i.e., microservices).

While it is true that there is some overlap between microservices and Erlang concurrency, it's worth pointing out that the latter leads to much more fine-grained concurrency. For example, in an online multiplayer game, you'd run at least one process per each participating player as well as per game session. This would improve the system responsiveness, provide the potential for vertical scalability, and increase fault tolerance.

You can't really simulate this with microservices alone because it would require too many OS processes. Instead, you'd typically have one service instance manage multiple activities. To improve the responsiveness and vertical scalability, you'd need to use a combination of nonblocking I/O and OS-level concurrency (e.g., run a few instances of the service on each machine). To improve fault tolerance, you'd need to reach for defensive coding, manually placing `try...catch` or similar constructs all over the code. The end result is more complicated code with inferior guarantees.

On the other hand, microservices offer some important benefits that are not easily achieved with BEAM. In particular, the ecosystem developed around the practice, including tools such as Docker and Kubernetes, significantly simplifies the operational tasks, such as deployment, horizontal scaling, and coarse-grained fault tolerance. In theory, you could get these benefits by using BEAM alone, but it would require a lot of low-level manual work.

Therefore, BEAM concurrency and microservices complement each other well, and they are often used together, in practice. Packaging a BEAM-powered service into a Docker container is possible and straightforward. Once the service is containerized, you can easily deploy it to some managed environment, such as a Kubernetes cluster.

Owing to its concurrency model, Erlang gives you a lot of flexibility when choosing your architecture, without forcing you to compromise the availability of the system. You can opt for a coarser-grained split, using only a few services aligned with the organization structure. In many cases, a plain monolith deployed to a PaaS, such as Heroku, Fly.io, or Gigalixir, will suffice. If that stops being the case, perhaps because the system grows in size and complexity, you can gradually move to the (micro)services architecture.

That concludes the story of Erlang. But if Erlang is so great, why do you need Elixir? The next section aims to answer this question.

1.2   About Elixir

Elixir is an alternative language for the Erlang virtual machine that allows you to write cleaner, more compact code that does a better job of revealing your intentions. You write programs in Elixir and run them normally in BEAM.

Elixir is an open source project, originally started by José Valim. Unlike Erlang, Elixir is more of a collaborative effort; presently, it has about 1,200 contributors. New features are frequently discussed on mailing lists, the GitHub issue tracker, and the #elixir-lang IRC channel on Libera.Chat (https://libera.chat/). José has the last word, but the entire project is a true open source collaboration, attracting an interesting mixture of seasoned Erlang veterans and talented young developers. The source code can be found on the GitHub repository at https://github.com/elixir-lang/elixir.

Elixir targets the Erlang runtime. The result of compiling the Elixir source code is BEAM-compliant bytecode files that can run in a BEAM instance and can normally cooperate with pure Erlang code—you can use Erlang libraries from Elixir, and vice versa. There's nothing you can do in Erlang that can't be done in Elixir, and usually, the Elixir code is as performant as its Erlang counterpart.

Elixir is semantically close to Erlang: many of its language constructs map directly to their Erlang counterparts. But Elixir provides some additional constructs that make it possible to radically reduce boilerplate and duplication. In addition, it tidies up some important parts of the standard libraries and provides some nice syntactic sugar and a uniform tool for creating and packaging systems. Everything you can do in Erlang is possible in Elixir, and vice versa, but in my experience, the Elixir solution is usually easier to develop and maintain.

Let's take a closer look at how Elixir improves on some Erlang features. We'll start with boilerplate and noise reduction.

1.2.1 *Code simplification*

One of the most important benefits of Elixir is its ability to radically reduce boilerplate and eliminate noise from code, which results in simpler code that's easier to write and maintain. Let's see what this means by contrasting Erlang and Elixir code.

A frequently used building block in Erlang concurrent systems is the server process. You can think of server processes as something like concurrent objects—they embed private state and can interact with other processes via messages. Being concurrent, different processes may run in parallel. Typical Erlang systems rely heavily on processes, running thousands, or even millions, of them.

The following example Erlang code implements a simple server process that adds two numbers.

Listing 1.1 Erlang-based server process that adds two numbers

```
-module(sum_server).
-behaviour(gen_server).

-export([
  start/0, sum/3,
  init/1, handle_call/3, handle_cast/2, handle_info/2, terminate/2,
  code_change/3
]).

start() -> gen_server:start(?MODULE, [], []).
sum(Server, A, B) -> gen_server:call(Server, {sum, A, B}).

init(_) -> {ok, undefined}.
handle_call({sum, A, B}, _From, State) -> {reply, A + B, State}.
handle_cast(_Msg, State) -> {noreply, State}.
handle_info(_Info, State) -> {noreply, State}.
terminate(_Reason, _State) -> ok.
code_change(_OldVsn, State, _Extra) -> {ok, State}.
```

Even without any knowledge of Erlang, this seems like a lot of code for something that only adds two numbers. To be fair, the addition is concurrent, but regardless, due to the large amount of code, it's hard to see the forest for the trees. It's definitely not immediately obvious what the code does. Moreover, it's difficult to write such code. Even after years of production-level Erlang development, I still can't write this without consulting the documentation or copying and pasting it from previously written code.

The problem with Erlang is that this boilerplate is almost impossible to remove, even if it's identical in most places (which, in my experience, is the case). The language provides almost no support for eliminating this noise. In all fairness, there is a way to reduce the boilerplate using a construct called *parse transform*, but it's clumsy and complicated to use. In practice, Erlang developers write their server processes using the preceding pattern.

Because server processes are an important and frequently used tool in Erlang, it's unfortunate that Erlang developers must constantly copy and paste this noise and work with it. Surprisingly, many people get used to it, probably due to the wonderful things BEAM does for them. It's often said that Erlang makes hard things easy and easy things hard. Still, the previous code leaves an impression that you should be able to do better.

Let's look at the Elixir version of the same server process.

Listing 1.2 Elixir-based server process that adds two numbers

```
defmodule SumServer do
  use GenServer

  def start do
    GenServer.start(__MODULE__, nil)
  end

  def sum(server, a, b) do
    GenServer.call(server, {:sum, a, b})
  end

  def handle_call({:sum, a, b}, _from, state) do
    {:reply, a + b, state}
  end
end
```

The Elixir version requires significantly less code and is, therefore, easier to read and maintain. Its intention is more clearly revealed, and it's less burdened with noise. And yet, it's as capable and flexible as the Erlang version. It behaves exactly the same at runtime and retains the complete semantics. There's nothing you can do in the Erlang version that's not possible in its Elixir counterpart.

Despite being significantly smaller, the Elixir version of a sum server process still feels somewhat noisy, given that all it does is add two numbers. The excess noise exists because Elixir retains a 1:1 semantic relation to the underlying Erlang library that's used to create server processes.

But Elixir gives you tools to further eliminate whatever you may regard as noise and duplication. For example, I've developed my own Elixir library, called *ExActor*, that makes the server process definition dense, as shown next.

Listing 1.3 Elixir-based server process

```
defmodule SumServer do
  use ExActor.GenServer

  defstart start

  defcall sum(a, b) do
    reply(a + b)
  end
end
```

The intention of this code should be obvious, even to developers with no previous Elixir experience. At run time, the code works almost exactly the same as the two previous versions. The transformation that makes this code behave like the previous examples happens at compile time. When it comes to the bytecode, all three versions are similar.

> **NOTE** I mention the ExActor library only to illustrate how much you can abstract away in Elixir. You won't use that library in this book because it's a third-party abstraction that hides important details of how server processes work. To completely take advantage of server processes, it's important that you understand what makes them tick, which is why in this book, you'll learn about lower-level abstractions. Once you understand how server processes work, you can decide for yourself whether you want to use ExActor to implement server processes.

This final implementation of the sum server process is powered by the Elixir macros facility. A *macro* is Elixir code that runs at compile time. Macros take an internal representation of your source code as input and can create alternative output. Elixir macros are inspired by Lisp and shouldn't be confused with C-style macros. Unlike C/C++ macros, which work with pure text, Elixir macros work on an *abstract syntax tree* (AST) structure, which makes it easier to perform nontrivial manipulations of the input code to obtain alternative output. Of course, Elixir provides helper constructs to simplify this transformation.

Let's take another look at how the sum operation is defined in listing 1.3:

```
defcall sum(a, b) do
  reply(a + b)
end
```

Notice the `defcall` at the beginning. There's no such keyword in Elixir. This is a custom macro that translates the given definition to something like the following:

```
def sum(server, a, b) do
  GenServer.call(server, {:sum, a, b})
end

def handle_call({:sum, a, b}, _from, state) do
  {:reply, a + b, state}
end
```

Because macros are written in Elixir, they're flexible and powerful, making it possible to extend the language and introduce new constructs that look like an integral part of the language. For example, the open source Ecto project, which aims to bring LINQ-style (https://learn.microsoft.com/en-us/dotnet/csharp/linq/) queries to Elixir, is also powered by Elixir macro support and provides an expressive query syntax that looks deceptively like part of the language:

```
from w in Weather,
  where: w.prcp > 0 or w.prcp == nil,
  select: w
```

Due to its macro support and smart compiler architecture, most of Elixir is written in Elixir. Language constructs like `if` and `unless` are implemented via Elixir macros. Only the smallest possible core is done in Erlang—everything else is then built on top of it in Elixir!

Elixir macros are something of a dark art, but they make it possible to flush out nontrivial boilerplate at compile time and extend the language with your own DSL-like constructs.

But Elixir isn't all about macros. Another worthy improvement is some seemingly simple syntactic sugar that makes functional programming much easier.

1.2.2   Composing functions

Both Erlang and Elixir are functional languages. They rely on immutable data and functions that transform data. One of the supposed benefits of this approach is that code is divided into many small, reusable, composable functions.

Unfortunately, the composability feature works clumsily in Erlang. Let's look at an adapted example from my own work. One piece of code I'm responsible for maintains an in-memory model and receives XML messages that modify the model. When an XML message arrives, the following actions must be completed:

- Apply the XML to the in-memory model.
- Process the resulting changes.
- Persist the model.

Here's an Erlang sketch of the corresponding function:

```
process_xml(Model, Xml) ->
  Model1 = update(Model, Xml),
  Model2 = process_changes(Model1),
  persist(Model2).
```

I don't know about you, but this doesn't look composable to me. Instead, it seems fairly noisy and error prone. The temporary variables `Model1` and `Model2` are introduced here only to take the result of one function and feed it to the next.

Of course, you could eliminate the temporary variables and inline the calls:

```
process_xml(Model, Xml) ->
  persist(
    process_changes(
      update(Model, Xml)
    )
  ).
```

This style, known as *staircasing*, is admittedly free of temporary variables, but it's clumsy and hard to read. To understand what goes on here, you have to manually parse it inside out.

Although Erlang programmers are more or less limited to such clumsy approaches, Elixir gives you an elegant way to chain multiple function calls together:

```
def process_xml(model, xml) do
  model
  |> update(xml)
  |> process_changes()
  |> persist()
end
```

The pipe operator |> takes the result of the previous expression and feeds it to the next one as the first argument. The resulting code is clean, contains no temporary variables, and reads like prose—top to bottom, left to right. Under the hood, this code is transformed at compile time to the staircased version. This is again possible because of Elixir's macro system.

The pipe operator highlights the power of functional programming. You treat functions as data transformations and then combine them in different ways to get the desired effect.

1.2.3 The big picture

There are many other areas where Elixir improves on the original Erlang approach. The API for standard libraries is cleaned up and follows some defined conventions. Syntactic sugar is introduced that simplifies typical idioms. A concise syntax for working with structured data is provided. String manipulation is improved, and the language has explicit support for Unicode manipulation. In the tooling department, Elixir provides a tool called *Mix* that simplifies common tasks, such as creating applications and libraries, managing dependencies, and compiling and testing code. In addition, a package manager called *Hex* (https://hex.pm/), which makes it simpler to package, distribute, and reuse dependencies, is available.

The list goes on and on, but instead of presenting each feature, I'd like to express a personal sentiment based on my own production experience. Personally, I find it much more pleasant to code in Elixir. The resulting code seems simpler, more readable, and less burdened with boilerplate, noise, and duplication. At the same time, you retain the complete runtime characteristics of pure Erlang code. You can also use all the available libraries from the Erlang ecosystem, both standard and third party.

1.3 Disadvantages

No technology is a silver bullet, and Erlang and Elixir are definitely no exceptions. Thus, it's worth mentioning some of their shortcomings.

1.3.1 Speed

Erlang is certainly not the fastest platform out there. If you look at various synthetic benchmarks on the internet, you usually won't see Erlang high on the list. Erlang programs are run in BEAM and, therefore, can't achieve the speed of machine-compiled languages, such as C and C++. But this isn't accidental or poor engineering on the part of the Erlang/OTP team.

The goal of the platform isn't to squeeze out as many requests per second as possible but to keep performance as predictable and within limits as possible. The level of performance your Erlang system achieves on a given machine shouldn't degrade significantly, meaning there shouldn't be unexpected system hiccups due to, for example, the garbage collector kicking in. Furthermore, as explained earlier, long-running BEAM processes don't block or significantly affect the rest of the system. Finally, as the load increases, BEAM can use as many hardware resources as are available. If the hardware capacity isn't enough, you can expect graceful system degradation—requests will take longer to process, but the system won't be paralyzed. This is due to the preemptive nature of the BEAM scheduler, which performs frequent context switches that keep the system ticking and favors short-running processes. And of course, you can address higher system demand by adding more hardware.

Nevertheless, intensive CPU computations aren't as performant as, for example, their C/C++ counterparts, so you may consider implementing such tasks in some other language and then integrating the corresponding component into your Erlang system. If most of your system's logic is heavily CPU bound, you should probably consider some other technology.

1.3.2 Ecosystem

The ecosystem built around Erlang isn't small, but it definitely isn't as large as that of some other languages. At the time of writing, a quick search on GitHub reveals about 20,000 Erlang-based repositories and about 45,000 Elixir repositories. In contrast, there are more than 1,500,000 Ruby-based repositories and almost 7,000,000 based on JavaScript.

You should be aware that your choice of libraries won't be as abundant as you may be used to, and in turn, you may end up spending extra time on something that would take minutes in other languages. If that happens, keep in mind all the benefits you get from Erlang. As I've explained, Erlang goes a long way toward making it possible to write fault-tolerant systems that can run for a long time with hardly any downtime. This is a significant challenge and a specific focus of the Erlang platform. Although it's admittedly unfortunate that the ecosystem isn't as robust as it could be, in my experience, Erlang's significant aid in solving hard problems makes it a useful tool. Of course, those difficult problems may not always be important. Perhaps you don't expect a high load or a system doesn't need to run constantly and be extremely fault tolerant. In such cases, you may want to consider some other technology stack with a more evolved ecosystem.

Summary

- Erlang is a technology for developing highly available systems that constantly provide service with little or no downtime. It has been battle tested in diverse, large systems for three decades.
- Elixir is a modern language that makes development for the Erlang platform much more pleasant. It helps organize code more efficiently and abstracts away boilerplate, noise, and duplication.

Building blocks

2

It's time to start learning about Elixir. This chapter presents the basic building blocks of the language, such as modules, functions, and the type system. This will be a somewhat lengthy, not particularly exciting, tour of language features, but the material presented here is important because it prepares the stage for exploring more interesting, higher-level topics.

Before starting, make sure you've installed Elixir version 1.15 and Erlang version 26. There are several ways to install Elixir, and it's best to follow the instructions from the official Elixir site at https://elixir-lang.org/install.html.

With that out of the way, let's start our tour of Elixir. The first thing you should know about is the interactive shell.

> **Detailed information**
>
> This book doesn't provide a detailed reference on any of the language or platform features. That would take up too much space, and the material would quickly become outdated. Here are some other references you can check out:
>
> - For an alternative syntax quick start, you should look at the Getting Started guide on the Elixir official site: https://mng.bz/NVRn.
> - A more detailed reference can be found in the online documentation: https://hexdocs.pm/elixir.
> - For specific questions, you can turn to the Elixir forum (https://elixirforum .com/) or the Slack channel (https://elixir-lang.slack.com/).
> - Finally, for many things, you'll need to look into the Erlang documentation: https:// www.erlang.org/doc. If you're not familiar with Erlang syntax, you may also need to read Elixir's crash course on Erlang (https://elixir-lang.org/crash-course.html).

2.1   *The interactive shell*

The simplest way to experiment and learn about a language's features is through the interactive shell. You can start the Elixir interactive shell from the command line by running the `iex` command:

```
$ iex
Erlang/OTP 26 [erts-14.0] [source] [64-bit] [smp:20:20] [ds:20:20:10]

Interactive Elixir (1.15.0) - press Ctrl+C to exit
  (type h() ENTER for help)

iex(1)>
```

Running `iex` starts an instance of BEAM and then an interactive Elixir shell inside it. Runtime information is printed, such as the Erlang and Elixir version numbers, and then the prompt is provided, so you can enter Elixir expressions:

```
iex(1)> 1 + 2      ⟵─── Elixir expression
3                 ⟵─┐
                    │ Result of the expression
```

After you type an expression, it's interpreted and executed. Its return value is then printed to the screen.

> **NOTE** Everything in Elixir is an expression that has a return value. This includes not only function calls but also constructs like `if` and `case`.

> **TIP** You'll use `iex` extensively throughout the book, especially in the initial chapters. The expression result often won't be particularly relevant, and it will be omitted to reduce noise. Regardless, keep in mind that each expression returns a result, and when you enter an expression in the shell, its result will be presented.

You can type practically anything that constitutes valid Elixir code, including relatively complicated multiline expressions:

```
iex(2)> 2 * (          | The expression
         3 + 1         | isn't finished.
       ) / 4    ⟵─────┐
2.0                    | The expression is finished, so it's evaluated.
```

Notice how the shell doesn't evaluate the expression until you finish it on the last line. In Elixir, you need no special characters, such as semicolons, to indicate the end of an expression. Instead, a line break indicates the end of an expression, if the expression is complete. Otherwise, the parser waits for additional input until the expression becomes complete. If you get stuck (e.g., if you miss a closing parenthesis), you can abort the entire expression with #iex:break written on a separate line:

```
iex(3)> 1 + (2
...(3)> #iex:break
** (TokenMissingError) iex:1: incomplete expression

iex(3)>
```

The quickest way to leave the shell is to press Ctrl-C twice. Doing so brutally kills the OS process and all background jobs that are executing. Because the shell is mostly used for experimenting and shouldn't be used to run real production systems, it's usually fine to terminate it this way. But if you want a more polite way of stopping the system, you can invoke System.stop.

> **NOTE** There are several ways to start Elixir and the Erlang runtime as well as to run your Elixir programs. You'll learn a bit about all of them by the end of this chapter. In the first part of this book, you'll mostly work with the iex shell because it's a simple and efficient way of experimenting with the language.

You can do many things with the shell, but most often, you'll use it to enter expressions and inspect their results. You can research for yourself what else can be done in the shell. Basic help can be obtained with the h command:

```
iex(3)> h
```

Entering this in the shell will output an entire screen of iex-related instructions. You can also look for the documentation of the IEx module, which is responsible for the shell's workings:

```
iex(4)> h IEx
```

You can find the same help in the online documentation at https://hexdocs.pm/iex.

Now that you have a basic tool with which to experiment, you are ready to research the features of the language. You'll start with variables.

2.2   *Working with variables*

Elixir is a dynamic programming language, which means you don't explicitly declare a variable or its type. Instead, the variable type is determined by whatever data it contains at the moment. In Elixir terms, assignment is called *binding*. When you initialize a variable with a value, the variable is bound to that value:

```
iex(1)> monthly_salary = 10000    ◁—— Binds a variable
10000    ◁————
              └—— The result of the last expression
```

Each expression in Elixir has a result. In the case of the = operator, the result is whatever is on the right side of the operator. After the expression is evaluated, the shell prints this result to the screen.

Now, you can reference the variable:

```
                              ┌—— The expression that returns
iex(2)> monthly_salary   ◁————┘   the value of the variable
10000   ◁————
             └—— The value of the variable
```

The variable can, of course, be used in complex expressions:

```
iex(3)> monthly_salary * 12
120000
```

In Elixir, a variable name always starts with a lowercase alphabetic character or an underscore. After that, any combination of alphanumeric characters and underscores is allowed. The prevalent convention is to use only lowercase ASCII letters, digits, and underscores:

```
valid_variable_name
also_valid_1
validButNotRecommended
NotValid
```

Variable names can also end with the question mark (?) or exclamation mark (!) characters:

```
valid_name?
also_ok!
```

Variables can be rebound to a different value:

```
iex(1)> monthly_salary = 10000    ◁—— Sets the initial value
10000

iex(2)> monthly_salary    ◁—— Verifies the value
10000
```

```
iex(3)> monthly_salary = 11000      ⟵——— Rebinds the variable
11000

iex(4)> monthly_salary      ⟵——— Verifies the effect of rebinding
11000
```

Rebinding doesn't mutate the existing memory location. It reserves new memory and reassigns the symbolic name to the new location.

> **NOTE** You should always keep in mind that data is immutable. Once a memory location is occupied with data, it can't be modified until it's released. But variables can be rebound, which makes them point to a different memory location. Thus, variables are mutable, but the data they point to is immutable.

Elixir is a garbage-collected language, which means you don't have to manually release memory. When a variable goes out of scope, the corresponding memory is eligible for garbage collection and will be released sometime in the future, when the garbage collector cleans up the memory.

2.3 Organizing your code

Being a functional language, Elixir relies heavily on functions. Due to the immutable nature of the data, a typical Elixir program consists of many small functions. You'll witness this in chapters 3 and 4, as you start using some typical functional idioms. Multiple functions can be further organized into modules.

2.3.1 Modules

A *module* is a collection of functions, somewhat like a namespace. Every Elixir function must be defined inside a module.

Elixir comes with a standard library that provides many useful modules. For example, the IO module can be used to complete various I/O operations. The puts function from the IO module can be used to print a message to the screen:

```
                                         ┌ Calls the puts function
                                         │ of the IO module
iex(1)> IO.puts("Hello World!")   ⟵——┘
Hello World!   ⟵
  ⌐⟶ :ok                          └ The IO.puts function prints to the screen.
│
Return value of IO.puts
```

As you can see in the example, to call a function of a module you use the syntax `ModuleName.function_name(args)`.

To define your own module, you use the `defmodule` expression. Inside the module, you define functions using the `def` expression. Listing 2.1 demonstrates the definition of a module.

Listing 2.1   Defining a module (geometry.ex)

```
defmodule Geometry do          ⊲—— Starts a module definition
  def rectangle_area(a, b) do
    a * b                        Function definition
  end
end    ⊲—
            Ends a module definition
```

There are two ways you can use this module. First, you can copy and paste this definition directly into `iex`—as mentioned, almost anything can be typed into the shell. A second way is to tell `iex` to interpret the file while starting:

```
$ iex geometry.ex
```

Using either method yields the same effect. The code is compiled, and the resulting module is loaded into the runtime and can be used from the shell session. Let's try it:

```
$ iex geometry.ex

iex(1)> Geometry.rectangle_area(6, 7)     ⊲—— Invokes the function
42    ⊲—
            Function result
```

That was simple! You created a `Geometry` module, loaded it into a shell session, and used it to compute the area of a rectangle.

> **NOTE** As you may have noticed, the filename has the .ex extension. This is a common convention for Elixir source files.

In the source code, a module must be defined in a single file. A single file may contain several module definitions:

```
defmodule Module1 do
  ...
end

defmodule Module2 do
  ...
end
```

A module name must follow certain rules. It starts with an uppercase letter and is usually written in camel case style. A module name can consist of alphanumeric characters, underscores, and the dot (.) character. Dots are often used to organize modules hierarchically:

```
defmodule Geometry.Rectangle do
  ...
end

defmodule Geometry.Circle do
  ...
end
```

You can also nest module definitions:

```
defmodule Geometry do
  defmodule Rectangle do
    ...
  end
  ...
end
```

The inner module can be referenced with `Geometry.Rectangle`.

Note that there is nothing special about the dot character. It's just one of the allowed characters in a module name. The compiled version doesn't record any hierarchical relations between the modules.

This is typically used to organize the modules in some meaningful hierarchy that is easier to navigate when reading the code. Additionally, this informal scoping can eliminate possible name clashes. For example, consider two libraries, one implementing a JSON encoder and another implementing an XML encoder. If both libraries defined the module called `Encoder`, you couldn't use them both in the same project. However, if the modules are called `Json.Encoder` and `Xml.Encoder`, then the name clash is avoided. For this reason, it's customary to add some common prefix to all module names in a project. Usually, the application or library name is used for this purpose.

2.3.2 *Functions*

A function must always be a part of a module. Function names follow the same conventions as variables: they start with a lowercase letter or underscore character and are followed by a combination of alphanumerics and underscores.

As with variables, function names can end with the `?` and `!` characters. The `?` character is often used to indicate a function that returns either `true` or `false`. Placing the `!` character at the end of the name indicates a function that may raise a runtime error. Both of these are conventions, rather than rules, but it's best to follow them and respect the community style.

Functions can be defined using the `def` macro:

```
defmodule Geometry do
  def rectangle_area(a, b) do      ⟵——— Function declaration
    ...          ⟵┐
  end             │ Function body
end
```

The definition starts with the `def` expression and is followed by the function name, argument list, and body enclosed in a do...end block. Because you're dealing with a dynamic language, there are no type specifications for arguments.

> **NOTE** Notice that `defmodule` and `def` aren't referred to as keywords. That's because they're not! Instead, these are examples of Elixir *macros*. You don't need to worry about how this works yet; it's explained a bit later in this chapter. If it helps, you can think of `def` and `defmodule` as keywords, but be aware this isn't exactly true.

If a function has no arguments, you can omit the parentheses:

```
defmodule Program do
  def run do
    ...
  end
end
```

What about the return value? Recall that in Elixir, everything that has a return value is an expression. The return value of a function is the return value of its last expression. There's no explicit return in Elixir.

> **NOTE**   Given that there's no explicit return, you might wonder how complex functions work. This will be covered in detail in chapter 3, where you'll learn about branching and conditional logic. The general rule is to keep functions short and simple, which makes it easy to compute the result and return it from the last expression.

You saw an example of returning a value in listing 2.1, but let's repeat it here:

```
defmodule Geometry do
  def rectangle_area(a, b) do     Calculates the area and
    a * b                ◁————    returns the result
  end
end
```

You can now verify this. Start the shell again, and then try the `rectangle_area` function:

```
$ iex geometry.ex

iex(1)> Geometry.rectangle_area(3, 2)   ◁——— Calls the function
6            ◁————
                     Function return value
```

If a function body consists of a single expression, you can use a condensed form and define it in a single line:

```
defmodule Geometry do
  def rectangle_area(a, b), do: a * b
end
```

To call a function defined in another module, use the module name followed by the function name:

```
iex(1)> Geometry.rectangle_area(3, 2)
6
```

Of course, you can always store the function result to a variable:

```
iex(2)> area = Geometry.rectangle_area(3, 2)    <┐  Calls the function
6                                                   │  and stores its result

iex(3)> area    <───  Verifies the variable content
6
```

Parentheses are optional in Elixir, so you can omit them:

```
iex(4)> Geometry.rectangle_area 3, 2
6
```

Personally, I find that omitting parentheses makes the code ambiguous, so my advice is to always include them when calling a function.

Using a code formatter

Starting with version 1.6, Elixir ships with a code formatter, which you can use to format your code in a consistent style and avoid worrying about lower-level style decisions, such as layouts or parentheses usage.

For example, after formatting the following code snippet

```
defmodule Client
do
def run do
Geometry.rectangle_area 3,2
end
end
```

you'll end up with this nice-looking code:

```
defmodule Client do
  def run do
    Geometry.rectangle_area(3, 2)
  end
end
```

You can format your code with the `mix format` task (https://hexdocs.pm/mix/Mix.Tasks.Format.html), or install a formatter extension in your editor of choice.

If a function being called resides in the same module, you can omit the module prefix:

```
defmodule Geometry do
  def rectangle_area(a, b) do
    a * b
  end

  def square_area(a) do
    rectangle_area(a, a)    <───  Calls to a function in the same module
  end
end
```

Given that Elixir is a functional language, you'll often need to combine functions, passing the result of one function as the argument to the next one. Elixir comes with a built-in operator, |>, called the *pipe operator,* that does exactly this:

```
iex(5)> -5 |> abs() |> Integer.to_string() |> IO.puts()
5
```

This code is transformed at compile time into the following:

```
iex(6)> IO.puts(Integer.to_string(abs(-5)))
5
```

More generally, the pipe operator places the result of the previous call as the first argument of the next call. So the following code

```
prev(arg1, arg2) |> next(arg3, arg4)
```

is translated at compile time to this:

```
next(prev(arg1, arg2), arg3, arg4)
```

Arguably, the pipeline version is more readable because the sequence of execution is read from left to right. The pipe operator looks especially elegant in source files, where you can lay out the pipeline over multiple lines:

```
-5                        ◁────┐  Starts with –5
|> abs()                   ◁──── Calculates the abs value
|> Integer.to_string()  ◁────┐
┌─▷ |> IO.puts()              Converts to a string
Prints to the console
```

Multiline pipeline in the shell

If you paste the previous pipeline chain into an `iex` session, you'll notice that each intermediate result is printed to the console:

```
iex(1)> -5
-5                           ◁──┐

iex(2)> |> abs()
5                            ◁──┤
                                 │  Prints the result
iex(3)> |> Integer.to_string()   │  of each step
"5"                          ◁──┤

iex(4)> |> IO.puts()
5                            ◁──┘
```

Recall that `iex` evaluates the Elixir expression as soon as it is complete and valid. In this example, each line completes a valid Elixir expression, such as `-5` or `-5 |> abs()`, and therefore, each intermediate result is printed.

2.3.3 Function arity

Arity describes the number of arguments a function receives. A function is uniquely identified by its containing module, name, and arity. Take a look at the following function:

```
defmodule Rectangle do
  def area(a, b) do      <──── Function with two arguments
    ...
  end
end
```

The function `Rectangle.area` receives two arguments, so it's said to be a function of arity 2. In the Elixir world, this function is often called `Rectangle.area/2`, where `/2` denotes the function's arity.

Why is this important? Because two functions with the same name but different arities are two different functions, as the following example demonstrates.

Listing 2.2 Functions with the same name but different arities (arity_demo.ex)

```
defmodule Rectangle do
  def area(a), do: area(a, a)      <──── Rectangle.area/1

  def area(a, b), do: a * b        <──── Rectangle.area/2
end
```

Load this module into the shell, and try the following:

```
iex(1)> Rectangle.area(5)
25

iex(2)> Rectangle.area(5,6)
30
```

As you can see, these two functions act completely differently. The name might be overloaded, but the arities differ, so we talk about them as two distinct functions, each with its own implementation.

It usually makes no sense for different functions with the same name to have completely different implementations. More commonly, a lower-arity function delegates to a higher-arity function, providing some default arguments. This is what happens in listing 2.2, where `Rectangle.area/1` delegates to `Rectangle.area/2` .

Let's look at another example.

Listing 2.3 Same-name functions, different arities, and default params (arity_calc.ex)

```
defmodule Calculator do            Calculator.add/1 delegates
  def add(a), do: add(a, 0)    <── to Calculator.add/2.
  def add(a, b), do: a + b     <──
end                                Calculator.add/2 contains the implementation.
```

Again, a lower-arity function is implemented in terms of a higher-arity one. This pattern is so frequent that Elixir allows you to specify defaults for arguments by using the \\ operator followed by the argument's default value:

```
defmodule Calculator do                    Defining a default
  def add(a, b \\ 0), do: a + b      ◁──┘  value for argument b
end
```

This definition generates two functions exactly as in listing 2.3.

You can set the defaults for any combination of arguments:

```
defmodule MyModule do                      Setting defaults for
  def fun(a, b \\ 1, c, d \\ 2) do   ◁──┘  multiple arguments
    a + b + c + d
  end
end
```

Always keep in mind that default values generate multiple functions of the same name with different arities. The previous code generates three functions, `MyModule.fun/2`, `MyModule.fun/3`, and `MyModule.fun/4`, with the following implementations:

```
def fun(a, c), do: fun(a, 1, c, 2)
def fun(a, b, c), do: fun(a, b, c, 2)
def fun(a, b, c, d), do: a + b + c + d
```

Because arity distinguishes multiple functions of the same name, it's not possible to have a function accept a variable number of arguments. There's no counterpart of C's … or JavaScript's `arguments`.

2.3.4 *Function visibility*

When you define a function using the `def` macro, the function is made public—it can be called by anyone else. In Elixir terminology, it's said that the function is *exported*. You can also use the `defp` macro to make the function private. A private function can be used only inside the module it's defined in. The following example demonstrates this.

Listing 2.4   A module with a public and a private function (private_fun.ex)

```
defmodule TestPrivate do             Public function
  def double(a) do          ◁──┘
    sum(a, a)         ◁─┐
  end                    Calls the private function

  defp sum(a, b) do    ◁─┐
    a + b                  Private function
  end
end
```

The module `TestPrivate` defines two functions. The function `double` is exported and can be called from outside. Internally, it relies on the private function `sum` to do its work.

Let's try this in the shell. Load the module, and do the following:

```
iex(1)> TestPrivate.double(3)
6

iex(2)> TestPrivate.sum(3, 4)
** (UndefinedFunctionError) function TestPrivate.sum/2
...
```

As you can see, the private function can't be invoked outside the module.

2.3.5 *Imports and aliases*

Calling functions from another module can sometimes be cumbersome because you need to reference the module name. If your module often calls functions from another module, you can import that other module into your own. Importing a module allows you to call its public functions without prefixing them with the module name:

```
defmodule MyModule do
  import IO          ⟵──── Imports the module

  def my_function do
    puts "Calling imported function."   ⟵──── You can use puts instead of IO.puts.
  end
end
```

Of course, you can import multiple modules. In fact, the standard library's `Kernel` module is automatically imported into every module. `Kernel` contains functions that are often used, so automatic importing makes them easier to access.

> **NOTE** You can see what functions are available in the Kernel module by looking in the online documentation at https://hexdocs.pm/elixir/Kernel.html.

Another expression, `alias`, makes it possible to reference a module under a different name:

```
defmodule MyModule do
  alias IO, as: MyIO   ⟵──── Creates an alias for IO

  def my_function do
    MyIO.puts("Calling imported function.")   ⟵──── Calls a function using the alias
  end
end
```

Aliases can be useful if a module has a long name. For example, if your application is heavily divided into a deeper module hierarchy, it can be cumbersome to reference modules via fully qualified names. Aliases can help with this. For example, let's say you have a `Geometry.Rectangle` module. You can alias it in your client module and use a shorter name:

```
defmodule MyModule do
  alias Geometry.Rectangle, as: Rectangle     ◁─── Sets up an alias to a module

  def my_function do
    Rectangle.area(...)    ◁─── Calls a module function using the alias
  end
end
```

In the preceding example, the alias of `Geometry.Rectangle` is the last part in its name. This is the most common use of `alias`, so Elixir allows you to skip the `as` option in this case:

```
defmodule MyModule do
  alias Geometry.Rectangle          ◁─── Sets up an alias to a module

  def my_function do
    Rectangle.area(...)     ◁─── Calls a module function using the alias
  end
end
```

Aliases can help you reduce some noise, especially if you call functions from a long-named module many times.

2.3.6   *Module attributes*

The purpose of module attributes is twofold: they can be used as compile-time constants, and you can register any attribute, which can then be queried at run time. Let's look at an example.

The following module provides basic functions for working with circles:

```
iex(1)> defmodule Circle do
          @pi 3.14159    ◁─── Defines a module attribute

          def area(r), do: r*r*@pi        ◁─── Uses a module attribute
          def circumference(r), do: 2*r*@pi
        end

iex(2)> Circle.area(1)
3.14159

iex(3)> Circle.circumference(1)
6.28318
```

Notice how you define a module directly in the shell. This is permitted and makes it possible to experiment without storing any files on disk.

The important thing about the `@pi` constant is that it exists only during the compilation of the module, when the references to it are inlined.

Moreover, an attribute can be registered, which means it will be stored in the generated binary and can be accessed at run time. Elixir registers some module attributes by default. For example, the attributes `@moduledoc` and `@doc` can be used to provide documentation for modules and functions:

```
defmodule Circle do
  @moduledoc "Implements basic circle functions"
  @pi 3.14159

  @doc "Computes the area of a circle"
  def area(r), do: r*r*@pi

  @doc "Computes the circumference of a circle"
  def circumference(r), do: 2*r*@pi
end
```

To try this, however, you need to generate a compiled file. Here's a quick way to do it. Save this code to the circle.ex file somewhere, and then run `elixirc circle.ex`. This will generate the file Elixir.Circle.beam. Next, start the `iex` shell from the same folder. You can now retrieve the attribute at run time:

```
iex(1)> Code.fetch_docs(Circle)
{:docs_v1, 2, :elixir, "text/markdown",
 %{"en" => "Implements basic circle functions"}, %{},
 [
   {{:function, :area, 1}, 5, ["area(r)"],
    %{"en" => "Computes the area of a circle"}, %{}},
   {{:function, :circumference, 1}, 8, ["circumference(r)"],
    %{"en" => "Computes the circumference of a circle"}, %{}}
 ]}
```

Notably, other tools from the Elixir ecosystem know how to work with these attributes. For example, you can use the help feature of `iex` to see the module's documentation:

```
iex(2)> h Circle   ←——————  Module documentation

                                Circle

Implements basic circle functions

iex(3)> h Circle.area   ←——————  Function documentation
                         def area(r)

Computes the area of a circle
```

Furthermore, you can use the `ex_doc` tool (see https://hexdocs.pm/ex_doc) to generate HTML documentation for your project. This is the way Elixir documentation is produced, and if you plan to build more complex projects, especially something that will be used by many different clients, you should consider using `@moduledoc` and `@doc`.

The underlying point is that registered attributes can be used to attach meta information to a module, which can then be used by other Elixir (and even Erlang) tools. There are many other preregistered attributes, and you can also register your own custom attributes. Take a look at the documentation for the `Module` module (https://hexdocs.pm/elixir/Module.html) for more details.

TYPE SPECIFICATIONS

Type specifications (often called *typespecs*) are another important feature based on attributes. These allow you to provide type information for your functions, which can later be analyzed with a static analysis tool called `dialyzer` (https://www.erlang.org/doc/man/dialyzer.html).

Here's how we can extend the `Circle` module to include typespecs:

```
defmodule Circle do
  @pi 3.14159

  @spec area(number) :: number     <───── Type specification for area/1
  def area(r), do: r*r*@pi

  @spec circumference(number) :: number     <───── Type specification for circumference/1
  def circumference(r), do: 2*r*@pi
end
```

Here, you use the `@spec` attribute to indicate that both functions accept and return a number.

Typespecs provide a way to compensate for the lack of a static type system. This can be useful in conjunction with the `dialyzer` tool to perform static analysis of your programs. Furthermore, typespecs allow you to better document your functions. Remember that Elixir is a dynamic language, so function inputs and outputs can't be easily deduced by looking at the function's signature. Typespecs can help significantly with this, and I can attest that it's much easier to understand someone else's code when typespecs are provided.

For example, look at the typespec for the Elixir function `List.insert_at/3`:

```
@spec insert_at(list, integer, any) :: list
```

Even without looking at the code or reading the docs, you can reasonably guess that this function inserts a term of any type (third argument) to a list (first argument) at a given position (second argument) and returns a new list.

You won't be using typespecs in this book, mostly to keep the code as short as possible. But if you plan to build more complex systems, my advice is to seriously consider using typespecs. You can find a detailed reference in the official docs at https://hexdocs.pm/elixir/typespecs.html.

2.3.7 Comments

Comments in Elixir start with the # character, which indicates that the rest of the line is a comment:

```
# This is a comment
a = 3.14 # so is this
```

Block comments aren't supported. If you need to comment multiple lines, prefix each one with the # character.

At this point, we're done with the basics of functions and modules. You're now aware of the primary code-organization techniques. With that out of our way, it's time to look at the Elixir type system.

2.4 Understanding the type system

At its core, Elixir uses the Erlang type system. Consequently, integration with Erlang libraries is usually simple. The type system itself is reasonably simple, but if you're coming from a classical object-oriented language, you'll find it significantly different from what you're used to. This section covers basic Elixir types and discusses some implications of immutability. To begin, let's look at numbers.

2.4.1 Numbers

Numbers can be integers or floats, and they work mostly as you'd expect:

```
iex(1)> 3        ◁──── Integer
3

iex(2)> 0xFF     ◁──── Integer written in hex
255

iex(3)> 3.14     ◁──── Float
3.14

iex(4)> 1.0e-2   ◁──── Float, exponential notation
0.01
```

Standard arithmetic operators are supported:

```
iex(5)> 1 + 2 * 3
7
```

The division operator / works differently than you might expect. It always returns a float value:

```
iex(6)> 4/2
2.0

iex(7)> 3/2
1.5
```

To perform integer division or calculate the remainder, you can use auto-imported `Kernel` functions:

```
iex(8)> div(5,2)
2

iex(9)> rem(5,2)
1
```

To add syntactic sugar, you can use the underscore character as a visual delimiter:

```
iex(10)> 1_000_000
1000000
```

There's no upper limit on an integer's size, and you can use arbitrarily large numbers:

```
iex(11)> 99999999999999999999999999999999999999999999999999999999999999
99999999999999999999999999999999999999999999999999999999999999
```

If you're worried about memory size, it's best to consult the official Erlang memory guide at http://mng.bz/QREv. An integer takes up as much space as needed to accommodate the number, whereas a float occupies either 32 or 64 bits, depending on the build architecture of the virtual machine. Floats are internally represented in IEEE 754-1985 (binary precision) format.

2.4.2 Atoms

Atoms are literally named constants. They're similar to symbols in Ruby or enumerations in C/C++. Atom constants start with a colon character followed by a combination of alphanumerics and/or underscore characters:

```
:an_atom
:another_atom
```

It's possible to use spaces in the atom name with the following syntax:

```
:"an atom with spaces"
```

An atom consists of two parts: the *text* and the *value*. The atom text is whatever you put after the colon character. At run time, this text is kept in the *atom table*. The value is the data that goes into the variable, and it's merely a reference to the atom table.

This is exactly why atoms are best used for named constants. They're efficient in both memory and performance. When you say

```
variable = :some_atom
```

the variable doesn't contain the entire text—only a reference to the atom table. Therefore, memory consumption is low, the comparisons are fast, and the code is still readable.

ALIASES

There's another syntax for atom constants. You can omit the beginning colon and start with an uppercase character:

```
AnAtom
```

This is called an *alias*, and at compile time, it's transformed into `:"Elixir.AnAtom"`. We can easily check this in the shell:

```
iex(1)> AnAtom == :"Elixir.AnAtom"
true
```

When you use an alias, the compiler implicitly adds the `Elixir.` prefix to its text and generates the atom. But if an alias already contains the `Elixir.` prefix, it's not added. Consequently, the following also works:

```
iex(2)> AnAtom == Elixir.AnAtom
true
```

You may recall from earlier that you can also use aliases to give alternate names to modules:

```
iex(3)> alias IO, as: MyIO

iex(4)> MyIO.puts("Hello!")
Hello!
```

It's no accident that the term *alias* is used for both things. When you write `alias IO, as: MyIO`, you instruct the compiler to transform `MyIO` into `IO`. Resolving this further, the final result emitted in the generated binary is `:Elixir.IO`. Therefore, with an alias set up, the following also holds:

```
iex(5)> MyIO == Elixir.IO
true
```

All of this may seem strange, but it has an important underlying purpose. Aliases support the proper resolution of modules. This will be discussed at the end of the chapter when we revisit modules and look at how they're loaded at run time.

ATOMS AS BOOLEANS

It may come as a surprise that Elixir doesn't have a dedicated Boolean type. Instead, the atoms `:true` and `:false` are used. As syntactic sugar, Elixir allows you to reference these atoms without the starting colon character:

```
iex(1)> :true == true
true

iex(2)> :false == false
true
```

The term *Boolean* is still used in Elixir to denote an atom that has a value of either `:true` or `:false`. The standard logical operators work with Boolean atoms:

```
iex(1)> true and false
false

iex(2)> false or true
true

iex(3)> not false
true

iex(4)> not :an_atom_other_than_true_or_false
** (ArgumentError) argument error
```

Always keep in mind that a Boolean is just an atom that has a value of true or false.

NIL AND TRUTHY VALUES

Another special atom is :nil, which works somewhat similarly to null from other languages. You can reference nil without a colon:

```
iex(1)> nil == :nil
true
```

The atom nil plays a role in Elixir's additional support for *truthiness*, which works similarly to the way it's used in mainstream languages, such as C/C++ and Ruby. The atoms nil and false are treated as *falsy* values, whereas everything else is treated as a *truthy* value.

This property can be used with Elixir's short-circuit operators ||, &&, and !. The operator || returns the first expression that isn't falsy:

```
iex(1)> nil || false || 5 || true
5
```

Because both nil and false are falsy expressions, the number 5 is returned. Notice that subsequent expressions won't be evaluated at all. If all expressions evaluate to a falsy value, the result of the last expression is returned.

The operator && returns the second expression but only if the first expression is truthy. Otherwise, it returns the first expression without evaluating the second one:

```
iex(1)> true && 5
5

iex(2)> false && 5
false

iex(3)> nil && 5
nil
```

Short-circuiting can be used for elegant operation chaining. For example, if you need to fetch a value from cache, a local disk, or a remote database, you can do something like this:

```
read_cached() || read_from_disk() || read_from_database()
```

Similarly, you can use the operator && to ensure certain conditions are met:

```
database_value = connection && read_data(connection)
```

In both examples, short-circuit operators make it possible to write concise code without resorting to complicated nested conditional expressions.

2.4.3   *Tuples*

Tuples are something like untyped structures, or records, and they're most often used to group a fixed number of elements together. The following snippet defines a tuple consisting of a person's name and age:

```
iex(1)> person = {"Bob", 25}
{"Bob", 25}
```

To extract an element from the tuple, you can use the Kernel.elem/2 function, which accepts a tuple and the zero-based index of the element. Recall that the Kernel module is auto-imported, so you can call elem instead of Kernel.elem:

```
iex(2)> age = elem(person, 1)
25
```

To modify an element of the tuple, you can use the Kernel.put_elem/3 function, which accepts a tuple, a zero-based index, and the new value of the field in the given position:

```
iex(3)> put_elem(person, 1, 26)
{"Bob", 26}
```

The function put_elem doesn't modify the tuple. It returns the new version, keeping the old one intact. Recall that data in Elixir is immutable, so you can't do an in-memory modification of a value. You can verify that the previous call to put_elem didn't change the person variable:

```
iex(4)> person
{"Bob", 25}
```

So how can you use the put_elem function, then? You need to store its result to another variable:

```
iex(5)> older_person = put_elem(person, 1, 26)
{"Bob", 26}

iex(6)> older_person
{"Bob", 26}
```

Recall that variables can be rebound, so you can also do the following:

```
iex(7)> person = put_elem(person, 1, 26)
{"Bob", 26}
```

By doing this, you've effectively rebound the `person` variable to the new memory location. The old location isn't referenced by any other variable, so it's eligible for garbage collection.

> **NOTE** You may wonder if this approach is memory efficient. In most cases, there will be little data copying, and the two variables will share as much memory as possible. This will be explained later in this section, when we discuss immutability.

Tuples are most appropriate for grouping a small, fixed number of elements together. When you need a dynamically sized collection, you can use lists.

2.4.4   Lists

In Erlang, *lists* are used to manage dynamic, variable-sized collections of data. The syntax deceptively resembles arrays from other languages:

```
iex(1)> prime_numbers = [2, 3, 5, 7]
[2, 3, 5, 7]
```

Lists may look like arrays, but they work like singly linked lists. To do something with the list, you must traverse it. Therefore, most of the operations on lists have an O(n) complexity, including the `Kernel.length/1` function, which iterates through the entire list to calculate its length:

```
iex(2)> length(prime_numbers)
4
```

> ### List utility functions
>
> There are many operations you can complete with lists, but this section mentions only a couple of the most basic ones. For a detailed reference, see the documentation for the `List` module (https://hexdocs.pm/elixir/List.html). There are also many helpful services in the `Enum` module (https://hexdocs.pm/elixir/Enum.html).
>
> The `Enum` module deals with many different enumerable structures and is not limited to lists. The concept of enumerables will be explained in detail in chapter 4, when we discuss protocols.

To get an element of a list, you can use the `Enum.at/2` function:

```
iex(3)> Enum.at(prime_numbers, 3)
7
```

`Enum.at` is again an O(n) operation: it iterates from the beginning of the list to the desired element. Lists are never a good fit when direct access is called for. For those purposes, tuples, maps, or a higher-level data structure is appropriate.

You can check whether a list contains a particular element with the help of the `in` operator:

```
iex(4)> 5 in prime_numbers
true

iex(5)> 4 in prime_numbers
false
```

To manipulate lists, you can use functions from the `List` module. For example, `List.replace_at/3` modifies the element at a certain position:

```
iex(6)> List.replace_at(prime_numbers, 0, 11)
[11, 3, 5, 7]
```

As was the case with tuples, the modifier doesn't mutate the variable but returns the modified version of it, which you need to store to another variable:

```
iex(7)> new_primes = List.replace_at(prime_numbers, 0, 11)
[11, 3, 5, 7]
```

Or you can rebind to the same one:

```
iex(8)> prime_numbers = List.replace_at(prime_numbers, 0, 11)
[11, 3, 5, 7]
```

You can insert a new element at the specified position with the `List.insert_at/3` function:

```
iex(9)> List.insert_at(prime_numbers, 3, 13)      ◁──┐  Inserts a new element
[11, 3, 5, 13, 7]                                      at the fourth position
```

To append to the end, you can use a negative value for the insert position:

```
iex(10)> List.insert_at(prime_numbers, -1, 13)   ◁──┐  The value of –1 indicates that
[11, 3, 5, 7, 13]                                      the element should be appended
                                                       to the end of the list.
```

Like most list operations, modifying an arbitrary element has a complexity of O(n). In particular, appending to the end is expensive because it always takes *n* steps, with *n* being the length of the list.

In addition, the dedicated operator ++ is available. It concatenates two lists:

```
iex(11)> [1, 2, 3] ++ [4, 5]
[1, 2, 3, 4, 5]
```

Again, the complexity is O(n), with *n* being the length of the left list (the one you're appending to). In general, you should avoid adding elements to the end of a list. Lists are most efficient when new elements are pushed to the top or popped from it. To understand why, let's look at the recursive nature of lists.

RECURSIVE LIST DEFINITION

An alternative way of looking at lists is to think of them as recursive structures. A list can be represented by a pair (head, tail), where *head* is the first element of the list and *tail* "points" to the (head, tail) pair of the remaining elements, as illustrated in figure 2.1.

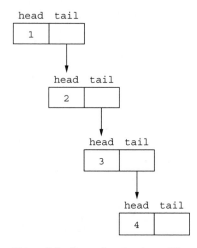

Figure 2.1   Recursive structure of the list [1, 2, 3, 4]

If you're familiar with Lisp, then you know this concept as *cons cells*. In Elixir, there's a special syntax to support recursive list definition:

```
a_list = [head | tail]
```

head can be any type of data, whereas tail is itself a list. If tail is an empty list, it indicates the end of the entire list.

Let's look at some examples:

```
iex(1)> [1 | []]
[1]

iex(2)> [1 | [2 | []]]
[1, 2]

iex(3)> [1 | [2]]
[1, 2]

iex(4)> [1 | [2, 3, 4]]
[1, 2, 3, 4]
```

This is just another syntactical way of defining lists, but it illustrates what a list is. It's a pair with two values: a head and a tail, with the tail being itself a list.

The following snippet is a canonical recursive definition of a list:

```
iex(1)> [1 | [2 | [3 | [4 | []]]]]
[1, 2, 3, 4]
```

Of course, nobody wants to write expressions like this one. But it's important that you're always aware that, internally, lists are recursive structures of (head, tail) pairs.

To get the head of the list, you can use the hd function. The tail can be obtained by calling the tl function:

```
iex(1)> hd([1, 2, 3, 4])
1

iex(2)> tl([1, 2, 3, 4])
[2, 3, 4]
```

Both operations are O(1) because they amount to reading one or the other value from the (head, tail) pair.

> **NOTE** For the sake of completeness, it should be mentioned that the tail doesn't need to be a list. It can be any type. When the tail isn't a list, it's said that the list is improper, and most of the standard list manipulations won't work. Improper lists have some special uses, but we won't deal with them in this book.

Once you know the recursive nature of the list, it's simple and efficient to push a new element to the top of the list:

```
iex(1)> a_list = [5, :value, true]
[5, :value, true]

iex(2)> new_list = [:new_element | a_list]
[:new_element, 5, :value, true]
```

Construction of the `new_list` is an O(1) operation, and no memory copying occurs—the tail of the `new_list` is the `a_list`. To understand how this works, let's discuss the internal details of immutability a bit.

2.4.5 *Immutability*

As has been mentioned before, Elixir data can't be mutated. Every function returns the new, modified version of the input data. You must take the new version into another variable or rebind it to the same symbolic name. In any case, the result resides in another memory location. The modification of the input will result in some data copying, but generally, most of the memory will be shared between the old and new versions. Let's take a closer look at how this works.

MODIFYING TUPLES

Let's start with tuples. A modified tuple is always a complete, shallow copy of the old version. Consider the following code (see figure 2.2):

```
a_tuple = {a, b, c}
new_tuple = put_elem(a_tuple, 1, b2)
```

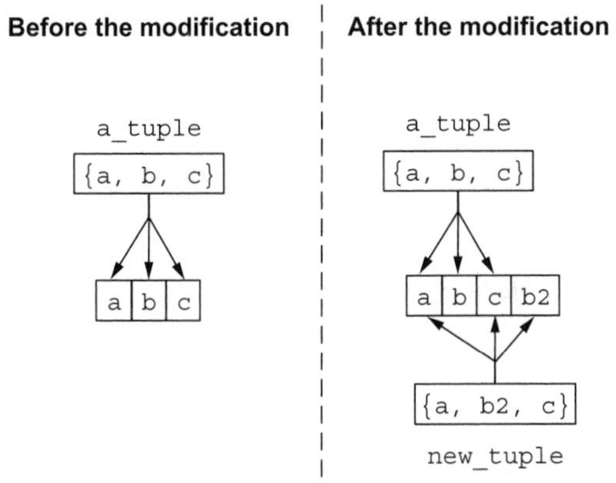

Before the modification | **After the modification**

Figure 2.2 **Modifying a tuple creates a shallow copy of it.**

The variable `new_tuple` will contain a shallow copy of `a_tuple`, differing only in the second element.

Both tuples reference variables `a` and `c`, and whatever is in those variables is shared (and not duplicated) between both tuples. `new_tuple` is a shallow copy of the original `a_tuple`.

What happens if you rebind a variable? In this case, after rebinding, the variable `a_tuple` references another memory location. The old location of `a_tuple` isn't accessible and is available for garbage collection. The same holds for the variable `b` referenced by the old version of the tuple, as illustrated in figure 2.3.

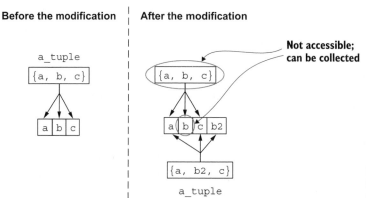

Figure 2.3   **Rebinding a tuple makes the old data garbage collectible.**

Keep in mind that tuples are always copied, but the copying is shallow. Lists, however, have different properties.

MODIFYING LISTS

When you modify the *n*th element of a list, the new version will contain shallow copies of the first *n* − 1 elements followed by the modified element. After that, the tails are completely shared, as illustrated in figure 2.4.

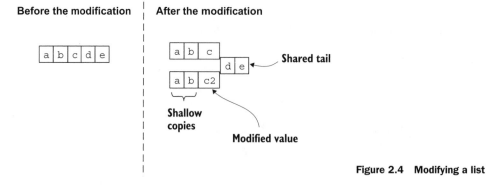

Figure 2.4   **Modifying a list**

This is precisely why adding elements to the end of a list is expensive. To append a new element at the tail, you must iterate and (shallow) copy the entire list. In contrast, pushing an element to the top of a list doesn't copy anything, which makes it the least expensive operation, as illustrated in figure 2.5.

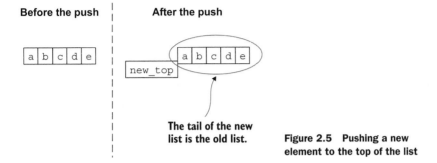

Figure 2.5   Pushing a new element to the top of the list

In this case, the new list's tail *is* the previous list. This is often used in Elixir programs when iteratively building lists. In such cases, it's best to push consecutive elements to the top, and then, after the list is constructed, reverse the entire list in a single pass.

BENEFITS

Immutability may seem strange, and you may wonder about its purpose. There are two important benefits of immutability: side-effect-free functions and data consistency.

Given that data can't be mutated, you can treat most functions as side-effect-free transformations. They take an input and return a result. More complicated programs are written by combining simpler transformations:

```
def complex_transformation(data) do
  data
  |> transformation_1(...)
  |> transformation_2(...)
  ...
  |> transformation_n(...)
end
```

This code relies on the previously mentioned pipe operator that chains two functions together, feeding the result of the previous call as the first argument of the next call.

Side-effect-free functions are easier to analyze, understand, and test. They have well-defined inputs and outputs. When you call a function, you can be sure no variable will be implicitly changed. Whatever the function does, you must take its result and do something with it.

> **NOTE**   Elixir isn't a pure functional language, so functions may still have side effects. For example, a function may write something to a file and issue a database or network call, which causes it to produce a side effect. But you can be certain that a function won't modify the value of any variable.

The implicit consequence of immutable data is the ability to hold all versions of a data structure in the program. This, in turn, makes it possible to perform atomic in-memory operations. Let's say you have a function that performs a series of transformations:

```
def complex_transformation(original_data) do
  original_data
  |> transformation_1(...)
  |> transformation_2(...)
  ...
end
```

This code starts with the original data and passes it through a series of transformations, each one returning the new, modified version of the input. If something goes wrong, the `complex_transformation` function can return `original_data`, which will effectively roll back all of the transformations performed in the function. This is possible because none of the transformations modify the memory occupied by `original_data`.

This concludes our look at basic immutability theory. It may still be unclear how to properly use immutable data in more complex programs. This topic will be revisited in chapter 4, where we'll deal with higher-level data structures.

2.4.6 *Maps*

A map is a key–value store, where keys and values can be any term. Maps have dual usage in Elixir. They're used to power dynamically sized key–value structures, but they're also used to manage simple records—a couple of well-defined named fields bundled together. Let's take a look at these cases separately.

DYNAMICALLY SIZED MAPS

An empty map can be created with the `%{}` expression:

```
iex(1)> empty_map = %{}
```

A map with some values can be created with the following syntax:

```
iex(2)> squares = %{1 => 1, 2 => 4, 3 => 9}
```

You can also prepopulate a map with the `Map.new/1` function. The function takes an enumerable where each element is a tuple of size 2 (a pair):

```
iex(3)> squares = Map.new([{1, 1}, {2, 4}, {3, 9}])
%{1 => 1, 2 => 4, 3 => 9}
```

To fetch a value at the given key, you can use the following approach:

```
iex(4)> squares[2]
4

iex(5)> squares[4]
nil
```

In the second expression, you get `nil` because no value is associated with the given key.

A similar result can be obtained with `Map.get/3`. On the surface, this function behaves like `[]`. However, `Map.get/3` allows you to specify the default value, which is returned if the key isn't found. If this default isn't provided, `nil` will be returned:

```
iex(6)> Map.get(squares, 2)
4

iex(7)> Map.get(squares, 4)
nil

iex(8)> Map.get(squares, 4, :not_found)
:not_found
```

Notice that in the last expression, you don't precisely know whether there's no value under the given key or the value is `:not_found`. If you want to precisely distinguish between these cases, you can use `Map.fetch/2`:

```
iex(9)> Map.fetch(squares, 2)
{:ok, 4}

iex(10)> Map.fetch(squares, 4)
:error
```

As you can see, in the successful case, you'll get a value in the shape of `{:ok, value}`. This format makes it possible to precisely detect the case when the key isn't present.

Sometimes you want to proceed only if the key is in the map and raise an exception otherwise. This can be done with the `Map.fetch!/2` function:

```
iex(11)> Map.fetch!(squares, 2)
4

iex(12)> Map.fetch!(squares, 4)
** (KeyError) key 4 not found in: %{1 => 1, 2 => 4, 3 => 9}
    (stdlib) :maps.get(4, %{1 => 1, 2 => 4, 3 => 9})
```

To store a new element to the map, you can use `Map.put/3`:

```
iex(13)> squares = Map.put(squares, 4, 16)
%{1 => 1, 2 => 4, 3 => 9, 4 => 16}

iex(14)> squares[4]
16
```

There are many other helpful functions in the `Map` module, such as `Map.update/4` or `Map.delete/2`. You can look into the official module documentation at https://hexdocs .pm/elixir/Map.html. Additionally, a map is also enumerable, which means all the functions from the `Enum` module can work with maps.

STRUCTURED DATA

Maps are the go-to type for managing key–value data structures of an arbitrary size. However, they're also frequently used in Elixir to combine a couple of fields into a single structure. This use case somewhat overlaps that of tuples, but it provides the advantage of allowing you to access fields by name.

Let's look at an example. In the following snippet, you'll create a map that represents a single person:

```
iex(1)> bob = %{:name => "Bob", :age => 25, :works_at => "Initech"}
```

If keys are atoms, you can write this so that it's slightly shorter:

```
iex(2)> bob = %{name: "Bob", age: 25, works_at: "Initech"}
```

To retrieve a field, you can use the [] operator:

```
iex(3)> bob[:works_at]
"Initech"

iex(4)> bob[:non_existent_field]
nil
```

Atom keys again receive special syntax treatment. The following snippet fetches a value stored under the :age key:

```
iex(5)> bob.age
25
```

With this syntax, you'll get an error if you try to fetch a nonexistent field:

```
iex(6)> bob.non_existent_field
** (KeyError) key :non_existent_field not found
```

To change a field value, you can use the following syntax:

```
iex(7)> next_years_bob = %{bob | age: 26}
%{age: 26, name: "Bob", works_at: "Initech"}
```

This syntax can be used to change multiple attributes as well:

```
iex(8)> %{bob | age: 26, works_at: "Initrode"}
%{age: 26, name: "Bob", works_at: "Initrode"}
```

However, you can only modify values that already exist in the map. This makes the update syntax a perfect choice for powering maps that represent structures. If you mistype the field name, you'll get an immediate runtime error:

```
iex(9)> %{bob | works_in: "Initech"}
** (KeyError) key :works_in not found
```

Using maps to hold structured data is a frequent pattern in Elixir. The common pattern is to provide all the fields while creating the map, using atoms as keys. If the value for some field isn't available, you can set it to `nil`. Such a map, then, always has all the fields. You can modify the map with the update expression and fetch a desired field with the `a_map.some_field` expression.

Of course, such data is still a map, so you can also use the functions from the `Map` module, such as `Map.put/3` or `Map.fetch/2`. However, these functions are usually suitable for cases in which maps are used to manage a dynamic key–value structure.

2.4.7   *Binaries and bitstrings*

A binary is a chunk of bytes. You can create binaries by enclosing the byte sequence between << and >> operators. The following snippet creates a three-byte binary:

```
iex(1)> <<1, 2, 3>>
<<1, 2, 3>>
```

Each number represents the value of the corresponding byte. If you provide a byte value greater than 255, it's truncated to the byte size:

```
iex(2)> <<256>>
<<0>>

iex(3)> <<257>>
<<1>>

iex(4)> <<512>>
<<0>>
```

You can specify the size of each value and, thus, tell the compiler how many bits to use for that particular value:

```
iex(5)> <<257::16>>
<<1, 1>>
```

This expression places the number 257 into 16 bits of consecutive memory space. The output indicates that you use 2 bytes, both with a value of 1. This is due to the binary representation of 257, which, in 16-bit form, is written 00000001 00000001.

The size specifier is in bits and need not be a multiplier of 8. The following snippet creates a binary by combining two 4-bit values:

```
iex(6)> <<1::4, 15::4>>
<<31>>
```

The resulting value has 1 byte and is represented in the output using the normalized form 31 (0001 1111).

If the total size of all the values isn't a multiple of 8, the binary is called a *bitstring*—a sequence of bits:

```
iex(7)> <<1::1, 0::1, 1::1>>
<<5::size(3)>>
```

You can also concatenate two binaries or bitstrings with the operator <>:

```
iex(8)> <<1, 2>> <> <<3, 4>>
<<1, 2, 3, 4>>
```

There's much more that can be done with binaries, but for the moment, we'll put them aside. The most important thing you need to know about binaries is that they're consecutive sequences of bytes. Binaries play an important role in support for strings.

2.4.8   *Strings*

It may come as a surprise, but Elixir doesn't have a dedicated string type. Instead, strings are represented using either a binary or a list type.

BINARY STRINGS

The most common way to use strings is to specify them with the familiar double-quotes syntax:

```
iex(1)> "This is a string"
"This is a string"
```

The result is printed as a string, but underneath, it's a binary—nothing more than a consecutive sequence of bytes.

Elixir provides support for embedded string expressions. You can use #{} to place an Elixir expression in a string constant. The expression is immediately evaluated, and its string representation is placed at the corresponding location in the string:

```
iex(2)> "Embedded expression: #{3 + 0.14}"
"Embedded expression: 3.14"
```

Classical \ escaping works as you're used to:

```
iex(3)> "\r \n \" \\"
```

And strings don't need to finish on the same line:

```
iex(4)> "
        This is
        a multiline string
        "
```

Elixir provides another syntax for declaring strings, or *sigils*. In this approach, you enclose the string inside ~s():

```
iex(5)> ~s(This is also a string)
"This is also a string"
```

Sigils can be useful if you want to include quotes in a string:

```
iex(6)> ~s("Do... or do not. There is no try." -Master Yoda)
"\"Do... or do not. There is no try.\" -Master Yoda"
```

There's also an uppercase version ~S that doesn't handle interpolation or escape characters (\):

```
iex(7)> ~S(Not interpolated #{3 + 0.14})
"Not interpolated \#{3 + 0.14}"

iex(8)> ~S(Not escaped \n)
"Not escaped \\n"
```

Finally, there's a special *heredocs* syntax, which supports better formatting for multiline strings. Heredocs strings start with a triple double-quote. The ending triple double-quote must be on its own line:

```
iex(9)> """
        Heredoc must end on its own line """
        """
"Heredoc must end on its own line \"\"\"\n"
```

Because strings are binaries, you can concatenate them with the <> operator:

```
iex(10)> "String" <> " " <> "concatenation"
"String concatenation"
```

Many helper functions are available for working with binary strings. Most of them reside in the String module (https://hexdocs.pm/elixir/String.html).

CHARACTER LISTS

A *character list* (also called a *charlist*) is a list in which each element is an integer code point of the corresponding character. For example, the letters ABC could be represented as the list [65, 66, 67]:

```
iex(1)> IO.puts([65, 66, 67])
ABC
```

You can also create the list with the ~c sigil:

```
iex(2)> IO.puts(~c"ABC")
ABC
```

Another option is to use single quotes:

```
iex(3)> IO.puts('ABC')
ABC
```

Starting with Elixir 1.15, the recommended method is to use ~c. The Elixir formatter converts single quotes into a sigil equivalent. In addition, character lists are printed in the shell using the ~c syntax:

```
iex(4)> ~c"ABC"
~c"ABC"

iex(5)> [65, 66, 67]
~c"ABC"

iex(6)> 'ABC'
~c"ABC"
```

Character lists aren't compatible with binary strings. Most of the operations from the String module won't work with character lists. In general, you should prefer binary strings over character lists.

Occasionally, some functions work only with character lists. This mostly happens with pure Erlang libraries. In this case, you can convert a binary string to a character list version, using the String.to_charlist/1 function:

```
iex(7)> String.to_charlist("ABC")
~c"ABC"
```

To convert a character list to a binary string, you can use List.to_string/1:

```
iex(8)> List.to_string(~c"ABC")
"ABC"
```

In general, you should prefer binary strings as much as possible, using character lists only when some third-party library (most often written in pure Erlang) requires it.

2.4.9   *First-class functions*

In Elixir, a function is a first-class citizen, which means it can be assigned to a variable. Here, assigning a function to a variable doesn't mean calling the function and storing its result to a variable. Instead, the function definition itself is assigned, and you can use the variable to call the function.

Let's look at some examples. To create a function variable, you can use the fn expression:

```
iex(1)> square = fn x ->
          x * x
        end
```

The variable `square` now contains a function that computes the square of a number. Because the function isn't bound to a global name, it's also called an *anonymous* function or *lambda*.

Notice that the list of arguments isn't enclosed in parentheses. Technically, you can use parentheses here, but the prevalent convention, also enforced by the Elixir formatter, is to omit parentheses. In contrast, a list of arguments to a named function should be enclosed in parentheses. At first glance, this looks inconsistent, but there's a good reason for this convention, which will be explained in chapter 3.

You can call this function by specifying the variable name followed by a dot (`.`) and the arguments:

```
iex(2)> square.(5)
25
```

> **NOTE** You may wonder why the dot operator is needed here. In this context, its purpose is to make the code more explicit. When you encounter a `square.(5)` expression in the source code, you know an anonymous function is being invoked. In contrast, the expression `square(5)` is invoking a named function defined somewhere else in the module. Without the dot operator, you'd need to parse the surrounding code to understand whether you're calling a named or an anonymous function.

Because functions can be stored in a variable, they can be passed as arguments to other functions. This is often used to allow clients to parameterize generic logic. For example, the function `Enum.each/2` implements the generic iteration—it can iterate over anything enumerable, such as lists. The function `Enum.each/2` takes two arguments: an enumerable and a one-arity lambda (an anonymous function that accepts one argument). It iterates through the enumerable and calls the lambda for each element. The clients provide the lambda to specify what they want to do with each element.

The following snippet uses `Enum.each` to print each value of a list to the screen:

```
iex(3)> print_element = fn x -> IO.puts(x) end     ⟵── Defines the lambda
iex(4)> Enum.each(
          [1, 2, 3],
          print_element     ⟵── Passes the lambda to Enum.each
        )
```

```
1
2     Output printed
3     by the lambda
```

```
:ok     ⟵── Return value of Enum.each
```

Of course, you don't need a temp variable to pass the lambda to `Enum.each`:

```
iex(5)> Enum.each(
          [1, 2, 3],
          fn x -> IO.puts(x) end     ⟵── Passes the lambda directly
```

```
        )
```

```
1
2
3
```

Notice how the lambda simply forwards all arguments to IO.puts, doing no other meaningful work. For such cases, Elixir makes it possible to directly reference the function and have a more compact lambda definition. Instead of writing fn x -> IO.puts(x) end, you can write &IO.puts/1.

The & operator, also known as the *capture* operator, takes the full function quali-fier—a module name, a function name, and an arity—and turns that function into a lambda that can be assigned to a variable. You can use the capture operator to simplify the call to Enum.each:

```
iex(6)> Enum.each(
          [1, 2, 3],
          &IO.puts/1      <———— Passes the lambda that delegates to IO.puts
        )
```

The capture operator can also be used to shorten the lambda definition, making it pos-sible to omit explicit argument naming. For example, you can change this definition

```
iex(7)> lambda = fn x, y, z -> x * y + z end
```

into a more compact form:

```
iex(8)> lambda = &(&1 * &2 + &3)
```

This snippet creates a three-arity lambda. Each argument is referred to via the &n placeholder, which identifies the *n*th argument of the function. You can call this lambda like any other:

```
iex(9)> lambda.(2, 3, 4)
10
```

The return value 10 amounts to $2 \times 3 + 4$, as specified in the lambda definition.

CLOSURES

A lambda can reference any variable from the outside scope:

```
iex(1)> outside_var = 5
5
```

```
iex(2)> my_lambda = fn ->          Lambda references a variable
  IO.puts(outside_var)      <——|   from the outside scope.
end
```

```
iex(3)> my_lambda.()
5
```

As long as you hold the reference to `my_lambda`, the variable `outside_var` is also accessible. This is also known as *closure*; by holding a reference to a lambda, you indirectly hold a reference to all variables it uses, even if those variables are from the external scope.

A closure always captures a specific memory location. Rebinding a variable doesn't affect the previously defined lambda that references the same symbolic name:

```
iex(1)> outside_var = 5                                      Lambda captures the current
iex(2)> lambda = fn -> IO.puts(outside_var) end   ◁───┘      location of outside_var.
iex(3)> outside_var = 6        ◁───┐
iex(4)> lambda.()                    │ Rebinding doesn't affect the closure.
5
```

Proof the closure isn't affected

The preceding code illustrates another important point. Normally, after you have rebound `outside_var` to the value `6`, the original memory location would be eligible for garbage collection. But because the `lambda` function captures the original location (the one that holds the number 5) and you're still referencing that lambda, the original location isn't available for garbage collection.

2.4.10 Other built-in types

There are a couple of types I still haven't presented. We won't deal with them in depth, but they're worth mentioning for the sake of completeness:

- A *reference* is an almost unique piece of information in a BEAM instance. It's generated by calling `Kernel.make_ref/0` (or `make_ref`). According to the Elixir documentation, a reference will reoccur after approximately 2^{82} calls. But if you restart a BEAM instance, reference generation starts from the beginning, so its uniqueness is guaranteed only during the lifetime of the BEAM instance.
- A *process identifier* (PID) is used to identify an Erlang process. PIDs are important when cooperating between concurrent tasks, and you'll learn about them in chapter 5 when we discuss Erlang processes.
- The *port identifier* is important when using ports. It's a mechanism used in Erlang to talk to the outside world. File I/O and communication with external programs are done through ports. Ports are outside the scope of this book.

With that, we've covered all the basic data types. As you can see, Elixir has a simple type system, consisting of only a handful of data types.

Of course, higher-level types are also available, which build on these basic types to provide additional functionality. Let's look at some of the most important types that ship with Elixir.

2.4.11 Higher-level types

The aforementioned built-in types are inherited from the Erlang world. After all, Elixir code runs on BEAM, so its type system is heavily influenced by the Erlang foundations. But on top of these basic types, Elixir provides some higher-level abstractions.

The ones most frequently used are `Range`, `Keyword`, `MapSet`, `Date`, `Time`, `NaiveDateTime`, and `DateTime`. Let's examine each of them.

RANGE

A *range* is an abstraction that allows you to represent a range of numbers. Elixir even provides special syntax for defining ranges:

```
iex(1)> range = 1..2
```

You can ask whether a number falls in the range by using the `in` operator:

```
iex(2)> 2 in range
true

iex(3)> -1 in range
false
```

Ranges are enumerable, so functions from the `Enum` module know how to work with them. Earlier, you encountered `Enum.each/2`, which iterates through an enumerable. The following example uses this function with a range to print the first three natural numbers:

```
iex(4)> Enum.each(
          1..3,
          &IO.puts/1
        )

1
2
3
```

Range isn't a special type. Internally, it's represented as a map that contains range boundaries. Therefore, a range memory footprint is small and constant, regardless of the number of elements it represents. A million-number range is still just a small map. For more information on ranges, see the documentation for the `Range` module (https://hexdocs.pm/elixir/Range.html).

KEYWORD LISTS

A *keyword* list is a special case of a list, where each element is a two-element tuple, and the first element of each tuple is an atom. The second element can be of any type. Let's look at an example:

```
iex(1)> days = [{:monday, 1}, {:tuesday, 2}, {:wednesday, 3}]
```

Elixir supports a slightly shorter syntax for defining a keyword list:

```
iex(2)> days = [monday: 1, tuesday: 2, wednesday: 3]
```

Both expressions yield the same result: a list of pairs. Arguably, the second is a bit more elegant.

Keyword lists are often used for small-size key–value structures, where keys are atoms. Many useful functions are available in the `Keyword` module (https://hexdocs.pm/elixir/Keyword.html). For example, you can use `Keyword.get/2` to fetch the value for a key:

```
iex(3)> Keyword.get(days, :monday)
1

iex(4)> Keyword.get(days, :noday)
nil
```

Just as with maps, you can use the operator `[]` to fetch a value:

```
iex(5)> days[:tuesday]
2
```

Don't let that fool you, though. Because you're dealing with a list, the complexity of a lookup operation is O(n).

Keyword lists are most often useful for allowing clients to pass an arbitrary number of optional arguments. For example, the result of the function `IO.inspect`, which prints a string representation of a term to the console, can be controlled by providing additional options through a keyword list:

```
iex(6)> IO.inspect([100, 200, 300])        Default behavior
[100, 200, 300]

iex(7)> IO.inspect([100, 200, 300], [width: 3])
[100,                                      Passes additional
 200,                                      options
 300]
```

In fact, this pattern is so frequent that Elixir allows you to omit the square brackets if the last argument is a keyword list:

```
iex(8)> IO.inspect([100, 200, 300], width: 3, limit: 1)
[100,
 ...]
```

Notice that, in this example, you're still sending two arguments to `IO.inspect/2`: a list of numbers and a two-element keyword list. But this snippet demonstrates how to simulate optional arguments. You can accept a keyword list as the last argument of your function and make that argument default to an empty list:

```
def my_fun(arg1, arg2, opts \\ []) do
  ...
end
```

Your clients can then pass options via the last argument. Of course, it's up to you to check the contents in the `opts` argument and perform some conditional logic depending on what the caller has sent you.

You may wonder if it's better to use maps instead of keywords for optional arguments. A keyword list can contain multiple values for the same key. Additionally, you can control the ordering of keyword list elements—something that isn't possible with maps. Finally, many functions in standard libraries of Elixir and Erlang take their options as keyword lists. It's best to stick to the existing convention and accept optional parameters via keyword lists.

MapSet

A `MapSet` is the implementation of a set—a store of unique values, where a value can be of any type. Let's look at some examples:

```
iex(1)> days = MapSet.new([:monday, :tuesday, :wednesday])   ◁──── Creates a MapSet instance
MapSet.new([:monday, :tuesday, :wednesday])

iex(2)> MapSet.member?(days, :monday)   ◁──── Verifies the presence of the existing element
true

iex(3)> MapSet.member?(days, :noday)   ◁──── Verifies the presence of a nonexisting element
false

iex(4)> days = MapSet.put(days, :thursday)   ◁──── Puts a new element in the MapSet
MapSet.new([:monday, :tuesday, :wednesday, :thursday])
```

As you can see, you can manipulate the set using the function from the `MapSet` module. For a detailed reference, refer to the official documentation at https://hexdocs.pm/elixir/MapSet.html.

A `MapSet` is also an enumerable, so you can pass it to functions from the `Enum` module:

```
iex(5)> Enum.each(days, &IO.puts/1)
monday
thursday
tuesday
wednesday
```

As you can tell from the output, `MapSet` doesn't preserve the ordering of the items.

Times and dates

Elixir has a few modules for working with date and time types: `Date`, `Time`, `DateTime`, and `NaiveDateTime`.

A date can be created with the `~D` sigil. The following example creates a date that represents January 31, 2023:

```
iex(1)> date = ~D[2023-01-31]
~D[2023-01-31]
```

Once you've created the date, you can retrieve its individual fields:

```
iex(2)> date.year
2023

iex(3)> date.month
1
```

Similarly, you can represent a time with the ~T sigil, by providing hours, minutes, seconds, and microseconds:

```
iex(1)> time = ~T[11:59:12.00007]

iex(2)> time.hour
11

iex(3)> time.minute
59
```

There are also some useful functions available in the modules Date (https://hexdocs .pm/elixir/Date.html) and Time (https://hexdocs.pm/elixir/Time.html).

In addition to these two types, you can work with DateTime's using the NaiveDateTime and DateTime modules. The naive version can be created with the ~N sigil:

```
iex(1)> naive_datetime = ~N[2023-01-31 11:59:12.000007]

iex(2)> naive_datetime.year
2023

iex(3)> naive_datetime.hour
11
```

The DateTime module can be used to work with datetimes and supports time zones. A UTC datetime instance can be created using the ~U sigil:

```
iex(1)> datetime = ~U[2023-01-31 11:59:12.000007Z]

iex(2)> datetime.year
2023

iex(3)> datetime.hour
11

iex(4)> datetime.time_zone
"Etc/UTC"
```

You can refer to the reference documentation, available at https://hexdocs.pm/ elixir/NaiveDateTime.html and https://hexdocs.pm/elixir/DateTime.html, for more details on working with these types.

2.4.12 IO lists

An IO list is a special sort of list that's useful for incrementally building output that will be forwarded to an I/O device, such as a network or a file. Each element of an IO list must be one of the following:

- An integer in the range of 0 to 255
- A binary
- An IO list

In other words, an IO list is a deeply nested structure in which leaf elements are plain bytes (or binaries, which are again a sequence of bytes). For example, here's "Hello, world!" represented as a convoluted IO list:

```
iex(1)> iolist = [[[~c"He"], "llo,"], " worl", "d!"]
```

Notice how you can combine character lists and binary strings into a deeply nested list.

Many I/O functions can work directly and efficiently with such data. For example, you can print this structure to the screen:

```
iex(2)> IO.puts(iolist)
Hello, world!
```

Under the hood, the structure is flattened, and you can see the human-readable output. You'll get the same effect if you send an IO list to a file or a network socket.

IO lists are useful when you need to incrementally build a stream of bytes. Lists usually aren't effective in this case because appending to a list is an $O(n)$ operation. In contrast, appending to an IO list is $O(1)$ because you can use nesting. Here's a demonstration of this technique:

```
iex(3)> iolist = []              ◁─────── Initializes an IO list
iolist = [iolist, "This"]
iolist = [iolist, " is"]          Multiple appends
iolist = [iolist, " an"]          to an IO list
iolist = [iolist, " IO list."]

[[[[[], "This"], " is"], " an"], " IO list."]   ◁─────── Final IO list
```

Here, you append to an IO list by creating a new list with two elements: a previous version of the IO list and the suffix that's appended. Each such operation is $O(1)$, so this is performant. And, of course, you can send this data to an IO function:

```
iex(4)> IO.puts(iolist)
This is an IO list.
```

This concludes our initial tour of the type system. We've covered most of the basics, and we'll expand on them throughout the book, as the need arises. Next, it's time to learn a bit about Elixir operators.

2.5 *Operators*

You've been using various operators throughout this chapter, and in this section, we'll take a systematic look at the ones most commonly used in Elixir. Most of the operators are defined in the `Kernel` module, and you can refer to the module documentation for a detailed description.

Let's start with arithmetic operators. These include the standard +, -, *, and / operators, and they work mostly as you'd expect, with the exception that the division operator always returns a float, as explained when we were dealing with numbers earlier in this chapter.

The comparison operators are more or less similar to what you're used to. They're listed in table 2.1.

Table 2.1 Comparison operators

Operator	Description
===, !==	Strict equality/inequality
==, !=	Weak equality/inequality
<, >, >=, <=	Less than, greater than, less than or equal, greater than or equal

The only thing we need to discuss here is the difference between strict and weak equality. This is relevant only when comparing integers to floats:

```
iex(1)> 1 == 1.0      ⟵——— Weak equality
true

iex(2)> 1 === 1.0     ⟵——— Strict equality
false
```

Logical operators work on Boolean atoms. You saw them earlier in the discussion of atoms, but I'll repeat them once more: `and`, `or`, and `not`.

Unlike logical operators, short-circuit operators work with the concept of truthiness: the atoms `false` and `nil` are treated as falsy, and everything else is treated as truthy. The `&&` operator returns the first expression if it's falsy; otherwise, it returns the second expression. The `||` operator returns the first expression if it's truthy; otherwise, it returns the second expression. The unary operator `!` returns `false` if the value is truthy; otherwise, it returns `true`.

The operators presented here aren't the only ones available (e.g., you've also seen the pipe operator `|>`). But these are the most common ones, so it is worth mentioning them in one place. You can find the detailed information on operators at https://hexdocs.pm/elixir/operators.html.

Many operators are functions

Many operators in Elixir are actually functions. For example, instead of calling `a+b`, you can call `Kernel.+(a,b)`. Of course, no one would ever want to write this kind of code, but operator functions have a benefit when turned into anonymous functions. For example, you can create a two-arity lambda that sums two numbers by calling `&Kernel.+/2` or the shorter `&+/2`. Such lambdas can then be used with various enumeration and stream functions, as covered in chapter 3.

We've almost completed our initial tour of the language. One thing remains: Elixir macros.

2.6   *Macros*

Macros are one of the most important features Elixir brings to the table that are unavailable in plain Erlang. They make it possible to perform powerful code transformations at compile time, thus reducing boilerplate and providing elegant, mini-DSL expressions.

Macros are a fairly complex subject, and it would take a small book to treat them extensively. Because this book is more oriented toward runtime and BEAM, and macros are a somewhat advanced feature that should be used sparingly, I won't provide a detailed treatment. But you should have a general idea of how macros work because many Elixir features are powered by them.

A *macro* consists of Elixir code that can change the semantics of the input code. A macro is always called at compile time; it receives the parsed representation of the input Elixir code, and it has the opportunity to return an alternative version of that code.

Let's clear this up with an example. `unless` (an equivalent of `if not`) is a simple macro provided by Elixir:

```
unless some_expression do
  block_1
else
  block_2
end
```

`unless` isn't a special keyword. It's a macro (meaning an Elixir function) that transforms the input code into something like this:

```
if some_expression do
  block_2
else
  block_1
end
```

Such a transformation isn't possible with C-style macros because the code of the expression can be arbitrarily complex and deeply nested. But in Elixir macros (which are heavily inspired by Lisp), you already work on a parsed source representation, so you'll have access to the expression and both blocks in separate variables.

The end effect is that many parts of Elixir are written in Elixir with the help of macros. This includes the `unless` and `if` expressions as well as `defmodule` and `def`. Whereas other languages usually use keywords for such features, in Elixir, they're built on top of a much smaller language core.

The main point to take away is that macros are compile-time code transformers. Whenever I note that something is a macro, the underlying implication is that it runs at compile time and produces alternative code.

> **Special forms**
>
> The Elixir compiler treats some language constructs in a special way. Such constructs are called *special forms* (https://mng.bz/lVM2). Some examples include the capture syntax `&(...)`, `for` comprehension (presented in chapter 3), `receive` expression (chapter 5), and `try` blocks (chapter 8).

For details, you may want to look at the official meta-programming guide (https://mng.bz/BAd1). Meanwhile, we're done with our initial tour of the Elixir language. But before we finish this chapter, we should discuss some important aspects of the underlying runtime.

2.7 Understanding the runtime

As has been mentioned, the Elixir runtime is a BEAM instance. Once the compiling is done and the system is started, Erlang takes control. It's important to be familiar with some details of the virtual machine, so you can understand how your systems work. First, let's look at the significance of modules in the runtime.

2.7.1 Modules and functions in the runtime

Regardless of how you start the runtime, an OS process for the BEAM instance is started, and everything runs inside that process. This is true even when you're using the `iex` shell. If you need to find this OS process, you can look it up under the name `beam`.

Once the system is started, you run some code, typically by calling functions from modules. How does the runtime access the code? The VM keeps track of all modules loaded in-memory. When you call a function from a module, BEAM first checks whether the module is loaded. If it is, the code of the corresponding function is executed. Otherwise, the VM tries to find the compiled module file—the bytecode—on the disk and then load it and execute the function.

> **NOTE** The previous description reveals that each compiled module resides in a separate file. A compiled module file has the extension .beam (for Bogdan/Björn's Erlang Abstract Machine). The name of the file corresponds to the module name.

MODULE NAMES AND ATOMS

Let's recall how modules are defined:

```
defmodule Geometry do
  ...
end
```

Also recall from the discussion about atoms that `Geometry` is an alias that corresponds to `:"Elixir.Geometry"`, as demonstrated in the following snippet:

```
iex(1)> Geometry == :"Elixir.Geometry"
true
```

This isn't an accident. When you compile the source containing the `Geometry` module, the file generated on the disk is named Elixir.Geometry.beam, regardless of the name of the input source file. In fact, if multiple modules are defined in a single source file, the compiler will produce multiple .beam files that correspond to those modules. You can try this by calling the Elixir compiler (`elixirc`) from the command line:

```
$ elixirc source.ex
```

Here, the file source.ex defines a couple of modules. Assuming there are no syntax errors, you'll see multiple .beam files generated on the disk.

In the runtime, module names are aliases, and as I said, aliases are atoms. The first time you call the function of a module, BEAM tries to find the corresponding file on the disk. The VM looks for the file in the current folder and then in the code paths.

When you start BEAM with Elixir tools (e.g., `iex`), some code paths are predefined for you. You can add additional code paths by providing the `-pa` switch:

```
$ iex -pa my/code/path -pa another/code/path
```

You can check which code paths are used at run time by calling the Erlang function `:code.get_path`.

If the module is loaded, the runtime doesn't search for it on the disk. This can be used when starting the shell, to autoload modules:

```
$ iex my_source.ex
```

This command compiles the source file and then immediately loads all generated modules. Notice that in this case, .beam files aren't saved to disk. The `iex` tool performs an in-memory compilation.

Similarly, you can define modules in the shell:

```
iex(1)> defmodule MyModule do          ◁────┐  In-memory bytecode generation
            def my_fun, do: :ok              │  and loading of a module
          end

iex(2)> MyModule.my_fun
:ok
```

Again, the bytecode isn't saved to the disk in this case.

PURE ERLANG MODULES

You've already seen how to call a function from a pure (non-Elixir) Erlang module. Let's talk a bit about this syntax:

```
:code.get_path          ◁────────┐  Calls the get_path function of
                                     the pure Erlang :code module
```

In Erlang, modules also correspond to atoms. Somewhere on the disk is a file named code.beam that contains the compiled code of the `:code` module. Erlang uses simple filenames, which is the reason for this call syntax. But the rules are the same as with Elixir modules. In fact, Elixir modules are nothing more than Erlang modules with fancier names (e.g., `Elixir.MyModule`).

You can create modules with simple names in Elixir (although this isn't recommended):

```
defmodule :my_module do
  ...
end
```

Compiling the source file that contains such a definition will generate my_module.beam on the disk.

The important thing to remember from this discussion is that at run time, module names are atoms. And somewhere on the disk is an xyz.beam file, where *xyz* is the expanded form of an alias (e.g., `Elixir.MyModule` when the module is named `MyModule`).

DYNAMICALLY CALLING FUNCTIONS

Somewhat related to this discussion is the ability to dynamically call functions at run time. This can be done with the help of the `Kernel.apply/3` function:

```
iex(1)> apply(IO, :puts, ["Dynamic function call."])
Dynamic function call.
```

`Kernel.apply/3` receives three arguments: the module atom, the function atom, and the list of arguments passed to the function. Together, these three arguments, often called *module, function, arguments* (MFA), contain all the information needed to call an exported (public) function. `Kernel.apply/3` can be useful when you need to make a runtime decision about which function to call.

2.7.2   *Starting the runtime*

There are several ways to start BEAM. So far, you've been using `iex`, and you'll continue to do so for some time. But let's quickly look at all the possible ways to start the runtime.

INTERACTIVE SHELL

When you start the shell, the BEAM instance is started underneath, and the Elixir shell takes control. The shell takes the input, *interprets* it, and prints the result.

It's important to be aware that input is interpreted because that means it won't be as performant as the compiled code. This is generally fine because you use the shell only to experiment with the language. However, you shouldn't try to measure performance directly from `iex`. On the other hand, modules are always compiled. Even if you define a module in the shell, it will be compiled and loaded in-memory, so there will be no performance hit.

RUNNING SCRIPTS

The `elixir` command can be used to run a single Elixir source file. Here's the basic syntax:

```
$ elixir my_source.ex
```

When you start this, the following actions take place:

1 The BEAM instance is started.
2 The file my_source.ex is compiled in-memory, and the resulting modules are loaded to the VM. No .beam file is generated on the disk.
3 Whatever code resides outside of a module is interpreted.
4 Once everything is finished, BEAM is stopped.

This is generally useful for running scripts. In fact, it's recommended for such a script to have an .exs extension, with the trailing *s* indicating it's a script.

The following listing shows a simple Elixir script.

> **Listing 2.5   Elixir script (script.exs)**

```
defmodule MyModule do
  def run do
    IO.puts("Called MyModule.run")
  end
end                        ┌─ Code outside of a module
                           │  is executed immediately.
MyModule.run      ◁────────┘
```

You can execute this script from the command line:

```
$ elixir script.exs
```

This call first does the in-memory compilation of the `MyModule` module and then calls `MyModule.run`. After the call to `MyModule.run` finishes, the BEAM instance is stopped.

If you don't want a BEAM instance to terminate, you can provide the `--no-halt` parameter:

```
$ elixir --no-halt script.exs
```

This is most often useful if your main code (outside a module) starts concurrent tasks that perform all the work. In this situation, your main call finishes as soon as the concurrent tasks are started, and BEAM is immediately terminated (and no work is done). Providing the `--no-halt` option keeps the entire system alive and running.

THE MIX TOOL

The `mix` tool is used to manage projects made up of multiple source files. Whenever you need to build a production-ready system, `mix` is your best option.

To create a new Mix project, you can call the `mix new project_name` from the command line:

```
$ mix new my_project
```

This creates a new folder, named my_project, containing a few subfolders and files. You can change to the my_project folder and compile the entire project:

```
$ cd my_project
$ mix compile

$ mix compile
Compiling 1 file (.ex)
Generated my_project app
```

The compilation goes through all the files from the lib folder and places the resulting .beam files in the ebin folder.

You can execute various `mix` commands on the project. For example, the generator created the module `MyProject` with the single function `hello/0`. You can invoke it with `mix run`:

```
$ mix run -e "IO.puts(MyProject.hello())"
world
```

The generator also create a couple of tests, which can be executed with `mix test`:

```
$ mix test
..

Finished in 0.03 seconds
2 tests, 0 failures
```

Regardless of how you start the Mix project, it ensures the ebin folder (where the .beam files are placed) is in the load path, so the VM can find your modules.

You'll use `mix` a lot once you start creating more complex systems. For now, there's no need to go into any more detail.

Summary

- Elixir code is divided into modules and functions.
- Elixir is a dynamic language. The type of a variable is determined by the value it holds.
- Data is immutable—it can't be modified. A function can return the modified version of the input that resides in another memory location. The modified version shares as much memory as possible with the original data.
- The most important primitive data types are numbers, atoms, and binaries.
- There is no Boolean type. Instead, the atoms `true` and `false` are used.
- There is no nullability. The atom `nil` can be used for this purpose.
- There is no string type. Instead, you can use either binaries (recommended) or lists (when needed).
- The built-in complex types are tuples, lists, and maps. Tuples are used to group a small, fixed-size number of fields. Lists are used to manage variable-size collections. A map is a key–value data structure.
- `Range`, keyword lists, `MapSet`, `Date`, `Time`, `NaiveDateTime`, and `DateTime` are abstractions built on top of the existing built-in types.
- Functions are first-class citizens.
- Module names are atoms (or aliases) that correspond to .beam files on the disk.
- There are multiple ways of starting programs: `iex`, `elixir`, and the `mix` tool.

Control flow 3

This chapter covers

- Understanding pattern matching
- Working with multiclause functions
- Using conditional expressions
- Working with loops

Now that you're familiar with Elixir's basic building blocks, it's time to look at some typical low-level idioms of the language. In this chapter, we'll deal with conditionals and loops. As you'll see, these work differently than in many imperative languages.

Classical conditional constructs, such as `if` and `case`, are often replaced with *multiclause* functions, and there are no loop statements, such as `while`. However, you can still solve problems of arbitrary complexity in Elixir, and the resulting code is no more complicated than a typical object-oriented solution.

All this may sound a bit radical, which is why conditionals and loops receive detailed treatment in this chapter. But before we start discussing branching and looping, you need to learn about the important underlying mechanism: pattern matching.

3.1   *Pattern matching*

As mentioned in chapter 2, the = operator isn't an assignment. In the expression a = 1, we bind the variable a to the value 1. The = operator is called the *match operator*, and the assignment-like expression is an example of *pattern matching*.

Pattern matching is an important concept in Elixir. It's a feature that makes manipulations with complex variables (e.g., tuples and lists) a lot easier. Less obviously, it allows you to write elegant, declarative-like conditionals and loops. You'll see what this means by the end of the chapter; in this section, we'll look at the basic mechanical workings of pattern matching.

Let's begin by looking at the match operator.

3.1.1   *The match operator*

So far, you've seen the most basic use of the match operator:

```
iex(1)> person = {"Bob", 25}
```

We treated this as something akin to an assignment, but in reality, something more complex is going on here. At run time, the left side of the = operator is matched to the right side. The left side is called a *pattern*, whereas on the right side, there is an expression that evaluates to an Elixir term.

In the example, you match the variable person to the right-side term {"Bob", 25}. A variable always matches the right-side term, and it becomes *bound* to the value of that term. This may seem a bit theoretical, so let's look at a slightly more complex use of the match operator that involves tuples.

3.1.2   *Matching tuples*

The following example demonstrates basic pattern matching of tuples:

```
iex(1)> {name, age} = {"Bob", 25}
```

This expression assumes that the right-side term is a tuple of two elements. When the expression is evaluated, the variables name and age are bound to the corresponding elements of the tuple. You can now verify that these variables are correctly bound:

```
iex(2)> name
"Bob"

iex(3)> age
25
```

This feature is useful when you call a function that returns a tuple and you want to bind individual elements of that tuple to separate variables. The following example calls the Erlang function :calendar.local_time/0 to get the current date and time:

```
iex(4)> {date, time} = :calendar.local_time()
```

The date and time are also tuples, which you can further decompose as follows:

```
iex(5)> {year, month, day} = date
iex(6)> {hour, minute, second} = time
```

What happens if the right side doesn't correspond to the pattern? The match fails and an error is raised:

```
iex(7)> {name, age} = "can't match"
** (MatchError) no match of right hand side value: "can't match"
```

> **NOTE** We haven't yet covered the error-handling mechanisms—they'll be discussed in chapter 8. For now, suffice it to say that raising an error works somewhat like the classical exception mechanisms in mainstream languages. When an error is raised, control is immediately transferred to code somewhere up the call chain, which catches the error (assuming such code exists).

Finally, it's worth noting that, just like any other expression, the match expression also returns a value. The result of a match expression is always the right-side term you're matching against:

```
iex(8)> {name, age} = {"Bob", 25}       ⟵——— Match expression
{"Bob", 25}       ⟵————┐
                        └ Result of the match expression
```

3.1.3 *Matching constants*

Matching isn't confined to destructuring tuple elements to individual variables. Surprisingly enough, even constants are allowed on the left side of the match expression:

```
iex(1)> 1 = 1
1
```

Recall that the match operator = tries to match the right-side term to the left-side pattern. In the example, you try to match the pattern 1 to the term 1. Obviously, this succeeds, and the result of the entire expression is the right-side term. This example doesn't have much practical benefit, but it illustrates that you can place constants to the left of =, which proves = is not an assignment operator.

Constants are much more useful in compound matches. For example, tuples are sometimes used to group various fields of a record. The following snippet creates a tuple that holds a person's name and age:

```
iex(2)> person = {:person, "Bob", 25}
```

The first element is a constant atom :person, which you use to denote that this tuple represents a person. Later, you can rely on this knowledge and retrieve individual attributes of the person:

```
iex(3)> {:person, name, age} = person
{:person, "Bob", 25}
```

Here, you expect the right-side term to be a three-element tuple, with its first element having a value of :person. After the match, the remaining elements of the tuple are bound to the variables name and age, which you can easily verify:

```
iex(4)> name
"Bob"

iex(5)> age
25
```

This is a common idiom in Elixir. Many functions from Elixir and Erlang return either {:ok, result} or {:error, reason}. For example, imagine your system relies on a configuration file and expects it to always be available. You can read the file contents with the help of the File.read/1 function:

```
{:ok, contents} = File.read("my_app.config")
```

In this single line of code, three distinct things happen:

1 An attempt to open and read the file my_app.config takes place.
2 If the attempt succeeds, the file contents are extracted to the variable contents.
3 If the attempt fails, an error is raised. This happens because the result of File.read is a tuple in the form {:error, reason}, so the match to {:ok, contents} fails.

By using constants in patterns, you tighten the match, ensuring some part of the right side has a specific value.

3.1.4 *Variables in patterns*

Whenever a variable name exists in the left-side pattern, it always matches the corresponding right-side term. Additionally, the variable is bound to the term it matches.

Occasionally, we aren't interested in a value from the right-side term, but we still need to match on it. For example, let's say you want to get the current time of day. You can use the function :calendar.local_time/0, which returns a tuple: {date, time}. But you aren't interested in a date, so you don't want to store it to a separate variable. In such cases, you can use the *anonymous variable* (_):

```
iex(1)> {_, time} = :calendar.local_time()
iex(2)> time

{20, 44, 18}
```

When it comes to matching, the anonymous variable works just like a named variable: it matches any right-side term. But the value of the term isn't bound to any variable.

You can also add a descriptive name after the underscore character:

```
iex(1)> {_date, time} = :calendar.local_time()
```

The _date is regarded as an anonymous variable because its name starts with an underscore. Technically speaking, you could use that variable in the rest of the program, but the compiler will emit a warning.

Patterns can be arbitrarily nested. Taking the example further, let's say you only want to retrieve the current hour of the day:

```
iex(3)> {_, {hour, _, _}} = :calendar.local_time()

iex(4)> hour
20
```

A variable can be referenced multiple times in the same pattern. In the following expressions, you expect an RGB triplet with the same number for each component:

```
iex(5)> {amount, amount, amount} = {127, 127, 127}          Matches a tuple with
{127, 127, 127}                                             three identical elements

iex(6)> {amount, amount, amount} = {127, 127, 1}
** (MatchError) no match of right hand side value: {127, 127, 1}
```
Fails because the tuple elements aren't identical

Occasionally, you'll need to match against the contents of the variable. For this purpose, the *pin operator* (^) is provided. This is best explained with an example:

```
iex(7)> expected_name = "Bob"               Matches anything and then binds
"Bob"                                       to the expected_name variable

iex(8)> {^expected_name, _} = {"Bob", 25}
{"Bob", 25}                                        Matches to the content of
                                                   the expected_name variable
iex(9)> {^expected_name, _} = {"Alice", 30}
** (MatchError) no match of right hand side value: {"Alice", 30}
```

Using ^expected_name in patterns indicates you expect the *value* of the variable expected_name to be in the appropriate position in the right-side term. In this example, it would be the same as if you used the hardcoded pattern ({"Bob", _} = ...). Therefore, the first match succeeds, but the second fails.

Notice that the pin operator doesn't bind the variable. You expect that the variable is already bound to a value, and you try to match against that value.

3.1.5 Matching lists

List matching works similarly to tuples. The following example decomposes a three-element list:

```
iex(1)> [first, second, third] = [1, 2, 3]
[1, 2, 3]
```

And of course, the previously mentioned pattern techniques work as well:

```
[1, second, third] = [1, 2, 3]
[first, first, first] = [1, 1, 1]
[first, second, _ ] = [1, 2, 3]
[^first, second, _ ] = [1, 2, 3]
```

The first element must be 1.

All elements must have the same value.

You don't care about the third
element, but it must be present.

The first element must have the
same value as the variable first.

Matching lists is more often done by relying on their recursive nature. Recall from chapter 2 that each nonempty list is a recursive structure that can be expressed in the form `[head | tail]`. You can use pattern matching to put each of these two elements into separate variables:

```
iex(3)> [head | tail] = [1, 2, 3]
[1, 2, 3]

iex(4)> head
1

iex(5)> tail
[2, 3]
```

If you need only one element of the `[head, tail]` pair, you can use the anonymous variable. Here's an inefficient way of calculating the smallest element in the list:

```
iex(6)> [min | _] = Enum.sort([3,2,1])

iex(7)> min
1
```

First, you sort the list, and then, with the pattern `[min | _]`, you take only the head of the (sorted) list. Note that this could also be done with the `hd` function mentioned in chapter 2. In fact, in this case, `hd` would be more elegant. The pattern `[head | _]` is more useful when pattern-matching function arguments, as you'll see in section 3.2.

3.1.6   *Matching maps*

To match a map, the following syntax can be used:

```
iex(1)> %{name: name, age: age} = %{name: "Bob", age: 25}
%{age: 25, name: "Bob"}

iex(2)> name
"Bob"

iex(3)> age
25
```

When matching a map, the left-side pattern doesn't need to contain all the keys from the right-side term:

```
iex(4)> %{age: age} = %{name: "Bob", age: 25}

iex(5)> age
25
```

You may be wondering about the purpose of such a partial-matching rule. Maps are frequently used to represent structured data. In such cases, you're often interested in only some of the map's fields. For example, in the previous snippet, you just want to extract the age field, ignoring everything else. The partial-matching rule allows you to do exactly this.

Of course, a match will fail if the pattern contains a key that's not in the matched term:

```
iex(6)> %{age: age, works_at: works_at} = %{name: "Bob", age: 25}
** (MatchError) no match of right hand side value
```

3.1.7 *Matching bitstrings and binaries*

We won't deal with bitstrings and pure binaries much in this book, but it's worth mentioning some basic matching syntax. Recall that a *bitstring* is a chunk of bits, and a *binary* is a special case of a bitstring that's always aligned to the byte size.

To match a binary, you use syntax similar to creating one:

```
iex(1)> binary = <<1, 2, 3>>
<<1, 2, 3>>

iex(2)> <<b1, b2, b3>> = binary       ◁———— A binary match
<<1, 2, 3>>

iex(3)> b1
1

iex(4)> b2
2

iex(5)> b3
3
```

This example matches on a three-byte binary and extracts individual bytes to separate variables.

The following example takes the binary apart by taking its first byte into one variable and the rest of the binary into another:

```
iex(6)> <<b1, rest :: binary>> = binary
<<1, 2, 3>>

iex(7)> b1
```

```
1

iex(8)> rest
<<2, 3>>
```

`rest::binary` states that you expect an arbitrarily sized. You can even extract separate bits or groups of bits. The following example splits a single byte into two four-bit values:

```
iex(9)> <<a :: 4, b :: 4>> = << 155 >>
<< 155 >>

iex(10)> a
9

iex(11)> b
11
```

Pattern `a::4` states that you expect a four-bit value. In the example, you put the first four bits into variable `a` and the other four bits into variable `b`. Because the number 155 is represented as 10011011 in binary, you get values of `9` (1001 in binary) and `11` (1011 in binary).

Matching bitstrings and binaries is immensely useful when you're trying to parse packed binary content that comes from a file, an external device, or a network. In such situations, you can use binary matching to extract separate bits and bytes elegantly.

As mentioned, the examples in this book won't need this feature. Still, you should take note of binaries and pattern matching, in case the need arises at some point.

MATCHING BINARY STRINGS

Recall that strings are binaries, so you can use binary matches to extract individual bits and bytes from a string:

```
iex(13)> <<b1, b2, b3>> = "ABC"
"ABC"

iex(13)> b1
65

iex(14)> b2
66

iex(15)> b3
67
```

The variables `b1`, `b2`, and `b3` hold corresponding bytes from the string you matched on. This isn't very useful, especially if you're dealing with Unicode strings. Extracting individual characters is better done using functions from the `String` module.

A more useful pattern is to match the beginning of the string:

```
iex(16)> command = "ping www.example.com"
"ping www.example.com"

iex(17)> "ping " <> url = command     ⟵——— Matching the string
"ping www.example.com"

iex(18)> url
"www.example.com"
```

In this example, you construct a string that holds a `ping` command. When you write `"ping " <> url = command`, you state the expectation that a `command` variable is a binary string starting with `"ping "`. If this matches, the rest of the string is bound to the variable `url`.

3.1.8   *Compound matches*

You've already seen this, but let's make it explicit. Patterns can be arbitrarily nested, as in the following contrived example:

```
iex(1)> [_, {name, _}, _] = [{"Bob", 25}, {"Alice", 30}, {"John", 35}]
```

In this example, the term being matched is a list of three elements. Each element is a tuple representing a person, consisting of two fields: the person's name and age. The match extracts the name of the second person in the list.

Another interesting feature is match chaining. Before you see how that works, let's discuss match expressions in more detail.

A match expression has this general form:

```
pattern = expression
```

As you've seen in examples, you can place any expression on the right side:

```
iex(2)> a = 1 + 3
4
```

Let's break down what happens here:

1 The expression on the right side is evaluated.
2 The resulting value is matched against the left-side pattern.
3 Variables from the pattern are bound.
4 The result of the match expression is the result of the right-side term.

An important consequence of this is that match expressions can be chained:

```
iex(3)> a = (b = 1 + 3)
4
```

In this (not so useful) example, the following things happen:

1   The expression `1 + 3` is evaluated.
2   The result (4) is matched against the pattern `b`.
3   The result of the inner match (which is, again, 4) is matched against the pattern `a`.

Consequently, both `a` and `b` have the value `4`.

Parentheses are optional, and many developers omit them in this case:

```
iex(4)> a = b = 1 + 3
4
```

This yields the same result because the `=` operator is right-associative.

Now, let's look at a more useful example. Recall the function `:calendar.local_time/0`:

```
iex(5)> :calendar.local_time()
{{2023, 11, 11}, {21, 28, 41}}
```

Let's say you want to retrieve the function's total result (datetime) as well as the current hour of the day. Here's the way to do it in a single compound match:

```
iex(6)> date_time = {_, {hour, _, _}} = :calendar.local_time()
```

You can even swap the ordering. It still gives the same result (assuming you call it in the same second):

```
iex(7)> {_, {hour, _, _}} = date_time = :calendar.local_time()
```

In any case, you get what you wanted:

```
iex(8)> date_time
{{2023, 11, 11}, {21, 32, 34}}

iex(9)> hour
21
```

This works because the result of a pattern match is always the result of the term being matched (whatever is on the right side of the match operator). You can successively match against the result of that term and extract different parts you're interested in.

3.1.9   *General behavior*

We're almost done with basic pattern-matching mechanics. We've worked through a lot of examples, so let's try to formalize the behavior a bit.

The pattern-matching expression consists of two parts: the *pattern* (left side) and the *term* (right side). In a match expression, there is an attempt to match the term to the pattern.

If the match succeeds, all variables in the pattern are bound to the corresponding values from the term. The result of the entire expression is the entire term you matched. If the match fails, an error is raised.

Therefore, in a pattern-matching expression, you perform two different tasks:

- You assert your expectations about the right-side term. If these expectations aren't met, an error is raised.
- You bind some parts of the term to variables from the pattern.

Finally, it's worth mentioning that we haven't covered all possible patterns here. For the detailed reference, you can refer to the official documentation (https://mng.bz/dd6o).

The match operator = is just one example in which pattern matching can be used. Pattern matching powers many other kinds of expressions, and it's especially powerful when used in functions.

3.2 *Matching with functions*

The pattern-matching mechanism is used in the specification of function arguments. Recall the basic function definition:

```
def my_fun(arg1, arg2) do
  ...
end
```

The argument specifiers `arg1` and `arg2` are patterns, and you can use standard matching techniques.

Let's see this in action. As mentioned in chapter 2, tuples are often used to group related fields together. For example, if you do a geometry manipulation, you can represent a rectangle with a tuple, {a, b}, containing the rectangle's sides. The following listing shows a function that calculates a rectangle's area.

Listing 3.1 Pattern matching function arguments (rect.ex)

```
defmodule Rectangle do
  def area({a, b}) do      ⬅—— Matches a rectangle
    a * b
  end
end
```

Notice how you pattern-match the argument. The function `Rectangle.area/1` expects that its argument is a two-element tuple. It then binds corresponding tuple elements into variables and returns the result.

You can see whether this works from the shell. Start the shell, and then load the module:

```
$ iex rect.ex
```

Then try the function:

```
iex(1)> Rectangle.area({2, 3})
6
```

What happens here? When you call a function, the arguments you provide are matched against the patterns specified in the function definition. The function expects a two-element tuple and binds the tuple's elements to variables a and b.

When calling functions, the term being matched is the argument provided to the function call. The pattern you match against is the argument specifier—in this case, {a, b}.

Of course, if you provide anything that isn't a two-element tuple, an error will be raised:

```
iex(2)> Rectangle.area(2)
** (FunctionClauseError) no function clause matching in Rectangle.area/1
```

Pattern matching function arguments is an extremely useful tool. It underpins one of the most important features of Elixir: *multiclause functions*.

3.2.1 *Multiclause functions*

Elixir allows you to overload a function by specifying multiple clauses. A *clause* is a function definition specified by the def expression. If you provide multiple definitions of the same function with the same arity, it's said that the function has multiple clauses.

Let's see this in action. Extending the previous example, let's say you need to develop a Geometry module that can handle various shapes. You'll represent shapes with tuples and use the first element of each tuple to indicate which shape it represents:

```
rectangle = {:rectangle, 4, 5}
square = {:square, 5}
circle = {:circle, 4}
```

Given these shape representations, you can write the following function to calculate a shape's area.

Listing 3.2 Multiclause function (geometry.ex)

```
defmodule Geometry do
  def area({:rectangle, a, b}) do        ⟵——— First clause of area/1
    a * b
  end
```

```
  def area({:square, a}) do   ◁────── Second clause of area/1
    a * a
  end

  def area({:circle, r}) do   ◁────── Third clause of area/1
    r * r * 3.14
  end
end
```

As you can see, you provide three clauses of the same function. Depending on which argument you pass, the appropriate clause is called. Let's try this from the shell:

```
iex(1)> Geometry.area({:rectangle, 4, 5})
20

iex(2)> Geometry.area({:square, 5})
25

iex(3)> Geometry.area({:circle, 4})
50.24
```

When you call the function, the runtime goes through each of its clauses, in the order they're specified in the source code, and attempts to match the provided arguments. The first clause that successfully matches all arguments is executed.

Of course, if no clause matches, an error is raised:

```
iex(4)> Geometry.area({:triangle, 1, 2, 3})
** (FunctionClauseError) no function clause matching in Geometry.area/1
```

From the caller's perspective, a multiclause function is a single function. You can't directly reference a specific clause. Instead, you always work on the entire function. Recall from chapter 2 that you can create a function value with the capture operator, &:

```
&Module.fun/arity
```

If you capture `Geometry.area/1`, you capture all of its clauses:

```
iex(4)> fun = &Geometry.area/1     ◁────── Captures the entire function

iex(5)> fun.({:circle, 4})
50.24

iex(6)> fun.({:square, 5})
25
```

This proves that the function is treated as a whole, even if it consists of multiple clauses.

Sometimes, you'll want a function to return a term indicating a failure, rather than raising an error. You can introduce a *default* clause that always matches. Let's do this for the `area` function. The next listing adds a final clause that handles any invalid input.

Listing 3.3   Multiclause function (geometry_invalid_input.ex)

```
defmodule Geometry do
  def area({:rectangle, a, b}) do
    a * b
  end

  def area({:square, a}) do
    a * a
  end

  def area({:circle, r}) do
    r * r * 3.14
  end

  def area(unknown) do                    ◁─── Additional clause that handles invalid input
    {:error, {:unknown_shape, unknown}}
  end
end
```

If none of the first three clauses match, the final clause is called. This is because a variable pattern always matches the corresponding term. In this case, you return a two-element tuple, `{:error, reason}`, to indicate something has gone wrong.

   Try it from the shell:

```
iex(1)> Geometry.area({:square, 5})
25

iex(2)> Geometry.area({:triangle, 1, 2, 3})
{:error, {:unknown_shape, {:triangle, 1, 2, 3}}}
```

> **TIP**   For this to work correctly, it's important to place the clauses in the appropriate order. The runtime tries to select the clauses, using the order in the source code. If the `area(unknown)` clause were defined first, you'd always get the error result.

Notice that the `area(unknown)` clause works only for `area/1`. If you pass more than one argument, this clause won't be called. Recall from chapter 2 that functions differ in name and arity. Because functions with the same name but different arities are two different functions, there's no way to specify an `area` clause that's executed, regardless of how many arguments are passed.

   One final note: you should always group clauses of the same function together, instead of scattering them in various places in the module. If a multiclause function is spread all over the file, it becomes increasingly difficult to analyze the function's complete behavior. Even the compiler complains about this by emitting a compilation warning.

3.2.2 Guards

Let's say you want to write a function that accepts a number and returns an atom :negative, :zero, or :positive, depending on the number's value. This isn't possible with the simple pattern matching you've seen so far. Elixir gives you a solution for this in the form of guards.

Guards are an extension of the basic pattern-matching mechanism. They allow you to state additional broader expectations that must be satisfied for the entire pattern to match.

A guard can be specified by providing the when clause after the arguments list. This is best illustrated via an example. The following code tests whether a given number is positive, negative, or zero.

Listing 3.4 Using guards (test_num.ex)

```
defmodule TestNum do
  def test(x) when x < 0 do
    :negative
  end

  def test(x) when x == 0 do
    :zero
  end

  def test(x) when x > 0 do
    :positive
  end
end
```

The guard is a logical expression that adds further conditions to the pattern. In this example, we have three clauses with the same pattern (x), that would normally always match. The additional guard refines the pattern, making sure the clause is invoked only if the given condition is satisfied, as demonstrated in this shell session:

```
iex(1)> TestNum.test(-1)
:negative

iex(2)> TestNum.test(0)
:zero

iex(3)> TestNum.test(1)
:positive
```

Surprisingly enough, calling this function with a nonnumber yields strange results:

```
iex(4)> TestNum.test(:not_a_number)
:positive
```

What gives? The explanation lies in the fact that Elixir terms can be compared with the operators < and >, even if they're not of the same type. In this case, the type ordering determines the result:

```
number < atom < reference < fun < port < pid <
  tuple < map < list < bitstring (binary)
```

A number is smaller than any other type, which is why `TestNum.test/1` always returns `:positive` if you provide a nonnumber. To fix this, you must extend the guard by testing whether the argument is a number.

Listing 3.5 Using guards (test_num2.ex)

```
defmodule TestNum do
  def test(x) when is_number(x) and x < 0 do
    :negative
  end

  def test(x) when x == 0 do
    :zero
  end

  def test(x) when is_number(x) and x > 0 do
    :positive
  end
end
```

This code uses the function `Kernel.is_number/1` to test whether the argument is a number. Now, `TestNum.test/1` raises an error if you pass a nonnumber:

```
iex(1)> TestNum.test(-1)
:negative

iex(2)> TestNum.test(:not_a_number)
** (FunctionClauseError) no function clause matching in TestNum.test/1
```

The set of operators and functions that can be called from guards is very limited. In particular, you may not call your own functions, and most of the other functions won't work. These are some examples of operators and functions allowed in guards:

- Comparison operators (==, !=, ===, !==, >, <, <=, and >=)
- Boolean operators (and and or) and negation operators (not and !)
- Arithmetic operators (+, -, *, and /)
- Type-check functions from the `Kernel` module (e.g., is_number/1, is_atom/1, and so on)

You can find the complete, up-to-date list at https://mng.bz/rjVJ.

In some cases, a function used in a guard may cause an error to be raised. For example, `length/1` makes sense only on lists. Imagine you have the following function, which calculates the smallest element of a nonempty list:

```
defmodule ListHelper do
  def smallest(list) when length(list) > 0 do
    Enum.min(list)
  end

  def smallest(_), do: {:error, :invalid_argument}
end
```

You may think that calling `ListHelper.smallest/1` with anything other than a list will raise an error, but this won't happen. If an error is raised from inside the guard, it won't be propagated, and the guard expression will return `false`. The corresponding clause won't match, but some other clause might.

In the preceding example, if you call `ListHelper.smallest(123)`, you'll get the following result: `{:error, :invalid_argument}`. This demonstrates that an error in the guard expression is internally handled.

3.2.3 *Multiclause lambdas*

Anonymous functions (lambdas) may also consist of multiple clauses. First, recall the basic way of defining and using lambdas:

```
iex(1)> double = fn x -> x * 2 end      ◁──── Defines a lambda

iex(2)> double.(3)                       ◁──── Calls a lambda
6
```

The general lambda syntax has the following shape:

```
fn
  pattern_1, pattern_2 ->
    ...
```
Executed if pattern_1 matches the first argument and pattern_2 matches the second argument

```
  pattern_3, pattern_4 ->
    ...
```
Executed if pattern_3 matches the first argument and pattern_4 matches the second argument

```
  ...
end
```

Let's see this in action by reimplementing the `test/1` function that inspects whether a number is positive, negative, or zero:

```
iex(3)> test_num =
          fn
            x when is_number(x) and x < 0 -> :negative
            x when x == 0 -> :zero
            x when is_number(x) and x > 0 -> :positive
          end
```

Notice there's no special ending terminator for a lambda clause. The clause ends when the new clause is started (in the form `pattern ->`) or the lambda definition is finished with `end`.

> **NOTE** Because all clauses of a lambda are listed under the same `fn` expression, the parentheses for each clause are omitted by convention. In contrast, each clause of a named function is specified in a separate `def` (or `defp`) expression. As a result, parentheses around named function arguments are recommended.

You can now test this lambda:

```
iex(4)> test_num.(-1)
:negative

iex(5)> test_num.(0)
:zero

iex(6)> test_num.(1)
:positive
```

Multiclause lambdas come in handy when using higher-order functions, as you'll see later in this chapter. But for now, we're done with the basic theory behind multiclause functions. They play an important role in conditional runtime branching, which is our next topic.

3.3 *Conditionals*

Elixir provides some standard ways of doing conditional branching, with expressions such as `if` and `case`. Multiclause functions can be used for this purpose as well. In this section, we'll cover all the branching techniques, starting with multiclause functions.

3.3.1 *Branching with multiclause functions*

You've already seen how to use conditional logic with multiclauses, but let's see it once more:

```
defmodule TestNum do
  def test(x) when x < 0, do: :negative
  def test(0), do: :zero
  def test(x), do: :positive
end
```

The three clauses constitute three conditional branches. In a typical imperative language, such as JavaScript, you could write something like the following:

```
function test(x) {
  if (x < 0) return "negative";
  if (x == 0) return "zero";
  return "positive";
}
```

Arguably, both versions are equally readable. But with multiclauses, you can reap all the benefits of pattern matching, such as branching, depending on the shape of the data. In the following example, a multiclause is used to test whether a given list is empty:

```
defmodule TestList do
  def empty?([]), do: true
  def empty?([_|_]), do: false
end
```

The first clause matches the empty list, whereas the second clause relies on the head | tail representation of a nonempty list.

By relying on pattern matching, you can implement polymorphic functions that do different things depending on the input type. The following example implements a function that doubles a variable. The function behaves differently depending on whether it's called with a number or a binary (string):

```
iex(1)> defmodule Polymorphic do
          def double(x) when is_number(x), do: 2 * x
          def double(x) when is_binary(x), do: x <> x
        end

iex(2)> Polymorphic.double(3)
6

iex(3)> Polymorphic.double("Jar")
"JarJar"
```

The power of multiclauses becomes evident in recursions. The resulting code seems declarative and is devoid of redundant ifs and returns. Here's a recursive implementation of a factorial, based on multiclauses:

```
iex(4)> defmodule Fact do
          def fact(0), do: 1
          def fact(n), do: n * fact(n - 1)
        end

iex(5)> Fact.fact(1)
1

iex(6)> Fact.fact(3)
6
```

A multiclause-powered recursion is also used as a primary building block for looping. This will be thoroughly explained in the next section, but here's a simple example. The following function sums all the elements of a list:

```
iex(7)> defmodule ListHelper do
          def sum([]), do: 0
          def sum([head | tail]), do: head + sum(tail)
```

```
      end

iex(8)> ListHelper.sum([])
0

iex(9)> ListHelper.sum([1, 2, 3])
6
```

The solution implements the sum by relying on the recursive definition of a list. The sum of an empty list is always 0, and the sum of a nonempty list equals the value of its head plus the sum of its tail.

Everything that can be done with classical branching expressions can be accomplished with multiclauses. However, the underlying pattern-matching mechanism can often be more expressive, allowing you to branch depending on values, types, and shapes of function arguments. In some cases, though, the code looks better with the classical, imperative style of branching. Let's look at the other branching expressions we have in Elixir.

3.3.2 *Classical branching expressions*

Multiclause solutions may not always be appropriate. Using them requires creating a separate function and passing the necessary arguments. Sometimes, it's simpler to use a classical branching expression in the function, and for such cases, the expressions `if`, `unless`, `cond`, and `case` are provided. These work roughly as you might expect, although there are a couple of twists. Let's look at each of them.

IF AND UNLESS

The `if` expression has a familiar syntax:

```
if condition do
  ...
else
  ...
end
```

This causes one or the other branch to execute, depending on the truthiness of the condition. If the condition is anything other than `false` or `nil`, you end up in the main branch; otherwise, the `else` part is called.

You can also condense this into a one-liner, much like a `def` expression:

```
if condition, do: something, else: another_thing
```

Recall that everything in Elixir is an expression that has a return value. The `if` expression returns the result of the executed block (that is, of the block's last expression). If the condition isn't met and the `else` clause isn't specified, the return value is the atom `nil`:

```
iex(1)> if 5 > 3, do: :one
:one

iex(2)> if 5 < 3, do: :one
nil

iex(3)> if 5 < 3, do: :one, else: :two
:two
```

Let's look at a more concrete example. The following code implements a max function that returns the larger of two elements (according to the semantics of the > operator):

```
def max(a, b) do
  if a >= b, do: a, else: b
end
```

The unless expression is also available, which is the equivalent of if not …. Consider the following if expression:

```
if result != :error, do: send_notification(...)
```

This can be also expressed as

```
unless result == :error, do: send_notification(...)
```

COND

The cond expression can be thought of as equivalent to an if-else-if pattern. It takes a list of expressions and executes the block of the first expression that evaluates to a truthy value:

```
cond do
  expression_1 ->
    ...

  expression_2 ->
    ...

  ...
end
```

The result of cond is the result of the corresponding executed block. If none of the conditions are satisfied, cond raises an error.

The cond expression is a good fit if there are more than two branching choices:

```
def call_status(call) do
  cond do
    call.ended_at != nil -> :ended
    call.started_at != nil -> :started
    true -> :pending                      ⟵——— Equivalent of a default clause
  end
end
```

In this example, you're computing the status of a call. If the `ended_at` field is populated, the call has ended. Otherwise, if the `started_at` field is populated, the call has started. If neither of these two fields is populated, the call is pending. Notice the final clause: (`true -> :pending`). Since the condition of this clause (`true`) is always satisfied, this effectively becomes the fallback clause that is invoked if none of the previously stated conditions in the `cond` expression are met.

CASE

The general syntax of `case` is as follows:

```
case expression do
  pattern_1 ->
    ...

  pattern_2 ->
    ...

  ...
end
```

The term *pattern* here indicates that it deals with pattern matching. In the `case` expression, the provided `expression` is evaluated, and then the result is matched against the given clauses. The first one that matches is executed, and the result of the corresponding block (its last expression) is the result of the entire `case` expression. If no clause matches, an error is raised.

The `case`-powered version of the `max` function would then look like this:

```
def max(a,b) do
  case a >= b do
    true -> a
    false -> b
  end
end
```

The `case` expression is most suitable if you don't want to define a separate multiclause function. Other than that, there are no differences between `case` and multiclause functions. In fact, the general `case` syntax can be directly translated into the multiclause approach:

```
defp fun(pattern_1), do: ...
defp fun(pattern_2), do: ...
...
```

This must be called using the `fun(expression)`.

You can specify the default clause by using the anonymous variable to match anything:

```
case expression do
  pattern_1 -> ...
  pattern_2 -> ...
  ...

  _ -> ...    ⟵——— The default clause that always matches
end
```

As you've seen, there are different ways of doing conditional logic in Elixir. Multiclauses offer a more declarative feel to branching, but they require you to define a separate function and pass all the necessary arguments to it. Classical expressions, like if and case, seem more imperative but can often prove simpler than the multiclause approach. Selecting an appropriate solution depends on the specific situation as well as your personal preferences.

3.3.3 *The with expression*

The final branching expression we'll discuss is the with expression, which can be very useful when you need to chain a couple of expressions and return the error of the first expression that fails. Let's look at a simple example.

Suppose you need to process registration data submitted by a user. The input is a map, with keys being strings ("login", "email", and "password"). Here's an example of one input map:

```
%{
  "login" => "alice",
  "email" => "some_email",
  "password" => "password",
  "other_field" => "some_value",
  "yet_another_field" => "...",
  ...
}
```

Your task is to normalize this map into a map that contains only the fields login, email, and password. Usually, if the set of fields is well defined and known up front, you can represent the keys as atoms. Therefore, for the given input, you can return the following structure:

```
%{login: "alice", email: "some_email", password: "password"}
```

However, some required field might not be present in the input map. In this case, you want to report the error, so your function can have two different outcomes. It can return either the normalized user map or an error. An idiomatic approach in such cases is to make the function return {:ok, some_result} or {:error, error_reason}. In this exercise, the successful result is the normalized user map, whereas the error reason is descriptive text.

Start by writing the helper functions for extracting each field:

```
defp extract_login(%{"login" => login}), do: {:ok, login}
defp extract_login(_), do: {:error, "login missing"}

defp extract_email(%{"email" => email}), do: {:ok, email}
defp extract_email(_), do: {:error, "email missing"}

defp extract_password(%{"password" => password}), do: {:ok, password}
defp extract_password(_), do: {:error, "password missing"}
```

Here, you're relying on pattern matching to detect the field's presence.

Now, you need to write the top-level `extract_user/1` function, which combines these three functions. Here's one way to do it with `case`:

```
def extract_user(user) do
  case extract_login(user) do
    {:error, reason} ->
      {:error, reason}

    {:ok, login} ->
      case extract_email(user) do
        {:error, reason} ->
          {:error, reason}

        {:ok, email} ->
          case extract_password(user) do
            {:error, reason} ->
              {:error, reason}

            {:ok, password} ->
              %{login: login, email: email, password: password}
          end
      end
  end
end
```

This is quite noisy, given that the code composes three functions. Each time you fetch something, you need to branch depending on the result, and you end up with three nested cases. In real life, you usually must perform many more validations, so the code can become quite nasty pretty quickly.

This is precisely where `with` can help you. The `with` special form allows you to use pattern matching to chain multiple expressions, verify that the result of each conforms to the desired pattern, and return the first unexpected result.

In its simplest form, `with` has the following shape:

```
with pattern_1 <- expression_1,
     pattern_2 <- expression_2,
     ...

do
  ...
end
```

You start from the top, evaluating the first expression and matching the result against the corresponding pattern. If the match succeeds, you move to the next expression. If all the expressions are successfully matched, you end up in the do block, and the result of the with expression is the result of the last expression in the do block.

If any match fails, however, with will not proceed to evaluate subsequent expressions. Instead, it will immediately return the result that couldn't be matched.

Let's look at an example:

```
iex(1)> with {:ok, login} <- {:ok, "alice"},
            {:ok, email} <- {:ok, "some_email"} do
        %{login: login, email: email}
      end

%{email: "some_email", login: "alice"}
```

Here, you go through two pattern matches to extract the login and the email. Then, the do block is evaluated. The result of the with expression is the last result of the expression in the do block. Superficially, this is no different from the following:

```
{:ok, login} = {:ok, "alice"}
{:ok, email} = {:ok, "email"}
%{login: login, email: email}
```

The benefit of with is that it returns the first term that fails to be matched against the corresponding pattern:

```
iex(2)> with {:ok, login} <- {:error, "login missing"},
            {:ok, email} <- {:ok, "email"} do
        %{login: login, email: email}
      end

{:error, "login missing"}
```

In your case, this is precisely what's needed. Armed with this new knowledge, refactor the top-level extract_user function.

Listing 3.6 with-based user extraction (user_extraction.ex)

```
def extract_user(user) do
  with {:ok, login} <- extract_login(user),
       {:ok, email} <- extract_email(user),
       {:ok, password} <- extract_password(user) do
    {:ok, %{login: login, email: email, password: password}}
  end
end
```

As you can see, this code is much shorter and clearer. You extract desired pieces of data, moving forward only if you succeed. If something fails, you return the first error.

Otherwise, you return the normalized structure. The complete implementation can be found in user_extraction.ex. Try it out:

```
$ iex user_extraction.ex

iex(1)> UserExtraction.extract_user(%{})
{:error, "login missing"}

iex(2)> UserExtraction.extract_user(%{"login" => "some_login"})
{:error, "email missing"}

iex(3)> UserExtraction.extract_user(%{
          "login" => "some_login",
          "email" => "some_email"
        })
{:error, "password missing"}

iex(4)> UserExtraction.extract_user(%{
          "login" => "some_login",
          "email" => "some_email",
          "password" => "some_password"
        })
{:ok, %{email: "some_email", login: "some_login",
  password: "some_password"}}
```

The with special form has a couple more features not presented here. I recommend studying it in more detail at https://mng.bz/VRxy.

This concludes our tour of the branching expressions in Elixir. Now, it's time to look at how you can perform loops and iterations.

3.4   *Loops and iterations*

Looping in Elixir works very differently than in mainstream languages. Constructs such as while and do...while aren't provided. Nevertheless, any serious program needs to do some kind of dynamic looping. So how do you go about it in Elixir? The principal looping tool in Elixir is *recursion*, so next, we'll take a detailed look at how to use it.

> **NOTE** Although recursion is the basic building block of any kind of looping, most production Elixir code uses it sparingly. That's because there are many higher-level abstractions that hide the recursion details. You'll learn about many of these abstractions throughout the book, but it's important to understand how recursion works in Elixir because most of the complex code is based on this mechanism.

> **NOTE** Most of the examples in this section deal with simple problems, such as calculating the sum of all the elements in a list—tasks Elixir allows you to do in an effective and elegant one-liner. The point of the examples, however, is to understand the different aspects of recursion-based processing on simple problems.

3.4.1 Iterating with recursion

Let's say you want to implement a function that prints the first n natural numbers (positive integers). Because there are no loops, you must rely on recursion. The basic approach is illustrated in the following listing.

Listing 3.7 **Printing the first n natural numbers (natural_nums.ex)**

```
defmodule NaturalNums do
  def print(1), do: IO.puts(1)

  def print(n) do
    print(n - 1)
    IO.puts(n)
  end
end
```

This code relies on recursion, pattern matching, and multiclause functions. If n is equal to 1, you print the number. Otherwise, you print the first $n - 1$ numbers and then the nth one.

Trying it in the shell gives satisfying results:

```
iex(1)> NaturalNums.print(3)
1
2
3
```

You may have noticed that the function won't work correctly if you provide a negative integer or a float. This could be resolved with additional guards and is left for you as an exercise.

The code in listing 3.7 demonstrates the basic way of doing a conditional loop. You specify a multiclause function, first providing the clauses that stop the recursion. This is followed by more general clauses that produce part of the result and call the function recursively.

Next, let's look at computing something in a loop and returning the result. You've already seen this example when dealing with conditionals, but let's repeat it. The following code implements a function that sums all the elements in a given list.

Listing 3.8 **Calculating the sum of a list (sum_list.ex)**

```
defmodule ListHelper do
  def sum([]), do: 0

  def sum([head | tail]) do
    head + sum(tail)
  end
end
```

This code looks very declarative:

1 The sum of all the elements of an empty list is 0.
2 The sum of all the elements of a nonempty list equals the list's head plus the sum of the list's tail.

Let's see it in action:

```
iex(1)> ListHelper.sum([1, 2, 3])
6

iex(2)> ListHelper.sum([])
0
```

You probably know from other languages that a function call will lead to a stack push and, therefore, will consume some memory. A very deep recursion might lead to a stack overflow and crash the entire program. This isn't necessarily a problem in Elixir because of the tail-call optimization.

3.4.2 *Tail function calls*

If the last thing a function does is call another function (or itself), you're dealing with a *tail call*:

```
def original_fun(...) do
  ...
  another_fun(...)     ⟵——— Tail call
end
```

Elixir (or, more precisely, Erlang) treats tail calls in a specific manner by performing a *tail-call optimization*. In this case, calling a function doesn't result in the usual stack push. Instead, something more like a goto or jump statement happens. You don't allocate additional stack space before calling the function, which, in turn, means the tail function call consumes no additional memory.

How is this possible? In the previous snippet, the last thing done in `original_fun` is calling `another_fun`. The final result of `original_fun` is the result of `another_fun`. This is why the compiler can safely perform the operation by jumping to the beginning of `another_fun` without doing additional memory allocation. When `another_fun` finishes, you return to whatever place `original_fun` was called from.

Tail calls are especially useful in recursive functions. A tail-recursive function—that is, a function that calls itself at the very end—can run virtually forever without consuming additional memory.

The following function is the Elixir equivalent of an endless loop:

```
def loop_forever(...) do
  ...
  loop_forever(...)
end
```

Because tail recursion doesn't consume additional memory, it's an appropriate solution for arbitrarily large iterations.

In the next listing, you'll convert the `ListHelper.sum/1` function to the tail-recursive version.

Listing 3.9 Tail-recursive sum of the first *n* natural numbers (sum_list_tc.ex)

```
defmodule ListHelper do
  def sum(list) do
    do_sum(0, list)
  end

  defp do_sum(current_sum, []) do
    current_sum
  end

  defp do_sum(current_sum, [head | tail]) do
    new_sum = head + current_sum
    do_sum(new_sum, tail)
  end
end
```

The first thing to notice is that you have two functions. The exported function `sum/1` is called by the module clients, and on the surface, it works just like before.

The recursion takes place in the private `do_sum/2` function, which is implemented as tail recursive. This is a two-clause function, and we'll analyze it clause by clause. The second clause is more interesting, so we'll start with it. Here it is in isolation:

```
defp do_sum(current_sum, [head | tail]) do        Computes the new
  new_sum = head + current_sum            ◁——————   value of the sum
  do_sum(new_sum, tail)      ◁——————
end                              Tail-recursive call
```

This clause expects two arguments: the nonempty list to operate on and the sum you've calculated so far (`current_sum`). It then calculates the new sum and calls itself recursively with the remainder of the list and the new sum. Because the call happens at the very end, the function is tail recursive, and the call consumes no additional memory.

The variable `new_sum` is introduced here just to make things more obvious. You could also inline the computation:

```
defp do_sum(current_sum, [head | tail]) do
  do_sum(head + current_sum, tail)
end
```

This function is still tail recursive because it calls itself at the very end.

The final thing to examine is the first clause of do_sum/2:

```
defp do_sum(current_sum, []) do
  current_sum
end
```

This clause is responsible for stopping the recursion. It matches on an empty list, which is the last step of the iteration. When you get here, there's nothing else to sum, so you return the accumulated result.

Finally, you have the function sum/1:

```
def sum(list) do
  do_sum(0, list)
end
```

This function is used by clients and is also responsible for initializing the value of the current_sum parameter that's passed recursively in do_sum.

You can think of tail recursion as a direct equivalent of a classical loop in imperative languages. The parameter current_sum is a classical accumulator: the value for which you incrementally add the result in each iteration step. The do_sum/2 function implements the iteration step and passes the accumulator from one step to the next. Elixir is an immutable language, so you need this trick to maintain the accumulated value throughout the loop. The first clause of do_sum/2 defines the ending point of the iteration and returns the accumulator value.

In any case, the tail-recursive version of the list sum is now working, so you can try it from the shell:

```
iex(1)> ListHelper.sum([1, 2, 3])
6

iex(2)> ListHelper.sum([])
0
```

As you can see, from the caller's point of view, the function works exactly the same way. Internally, you rely on the tail recursion and can, therefore, process arbitrarily large lists without requiring extra memory for this task.

Tail vs. non-tail recursion
Given the properties of tail recursion, you might think it's always a preferred approach for doing loops. If you need to run an infinite loop, tail recursion is the only way that will work. Otherwise, aim for the version that seems more readable. Additionally, non-tail recursion can often produce more elegant and concise code that sometimes even performs better than its tail-recursive counterpart.

RECOGNIZING TAIL CALLS

Tail calls can take different shapes. You've seen the most obvious case, but there are a couple of others. A tail call can also happen in a conditional expression:

```
def fun(...) do
  ...
  if something do
    ...
    another_fun(...)    ⊲——— Tail call
  end
end
```

The call to `another_fun` is a tail call because it's the last thing the function does. The same rule holds for `unless`, `cond`, `case`, and `with` expressions.

But the following code isn't a tail call:

```
def fun(...) do
  1 + another_fun(...)    ⊲——— Not a tail call
end
```

This is because the call to `another_fun` isn't the last thing done in the `fun` function. After `another_fun` finishes, you must increment its result by 1 to compute the final result of `fun`.

PRACTICING

All this may seem complicated, but it's not too hard. If you're coming from imperative languages, it's probably not what you're used to, and it will take some time to get accustomed to the recursive way of thinking combined with the pattern-matching facility. You may want to take some time to experiment with recursion yourself. Here are a couple of functions you can write for practice:

- A `list_len/1` function that calculates the length of a list
- A `range/2` function that takes two integers, `from` and `to`, and returns a list of all integer numbers in the given range
- A `positive/1` function that takes a list and returns another list that contains only the positive numbers from the input list

Try to write these functions first in the non-tail-recursive form, and then convert them to the tail-recursive version. If you get stuck, the solutions are provided in the recursion_practice.ex and recursion_practice_tc.ex files (for the tail-recursive versions).

Recursion is the basic looping technique, and no loop can be done without it. Still, you won't need to write explicit recursion all that often. Many typical tasks can be performed using higher-order functions.

3.4.3   *Higher-order functions*

A *higher-order function* is a type of function that takes one or more functions as its input or returns one or more functions (or both). The word *function* here refers to the function value.

You already made first contact with higher-order functions in chapter 2, when you used `Enum.each/2` to iterate through a list and print all of its elements. Let's recall how to do this:

```
iex(1)> Enum.each(
          [1, 2, 3],
          fn x -> IO.puts(x) end       Passing a function value
        )                               to another function
1
2
3
```

The function `Enum.each/2` takes an enumerable (in this case, a list) and a lambda. It iterates through the enumerable, calling the lambda for each of its elements. Because `Enum.each/2` takes a lambda as its input, it's called a *higher-order function*.

You can use `Enum.each/2` to iterate over enumerable structures without writing the recursion. Under the hood, `Enum.each/2` is powered by recursion; there's no other way to do loops and iterations in Elixir. However, the complexity of writing the recursion, repetitive code, and intricacies of tail recursion is hidden from you.

`Enum.each/2` is just one example of an iteration powered by a higher-order function. Elixir's standard library provides many other useful iteration helpers in the `Enum` module. You should spend some time researching the module documentation (https://hexdocs.pm/elixir/Enum.html). Here, we'll look at some of the most frequently used `Enum` functions.

> **Enumerables**
>
> Most functions from the `Enum` module work on *enumerables*. You'll learn what this means in chapter 4. For now, it's sufficient to know that an enumerable is a data structure for which a certain contract is implemented that makes that data structure suitable to be used by functions from the `Enum` module.
>
> Some examples of enumerables include lists, ranges, maps, and `MapSet`. It's also possible to turn your own data structures into enumerables, thus harnessing all the features of the `Enum` module.

One manipulation you'll often need is a one-to-one transformation of a list to another list. This is why `Enum.map/2` is provided. It takes an enumerable and a lambda that maps each element to another element. The following example doubles every element in the list:

```
iex(1)> Enum.map(
          [1, 2, 3],
          fn x -> 2 * x end
        )
[2, 4, 6]
```

Recall from chapter 2 that you can use the capture operator, &, to make the lambda definition a bit denser:

```
iex(2)> Enum.map(
          [1, 2, 3],
          &(2 * &1)
        )
```

The `&(...)` denotes a simplified lambda definition, where you use `&n` as a placeholder for the *n*th argument of the lambda.

Another useful function is `Enum.filter/2`, which can be used to extract only some elements of the list, based on certain criteria. The following snippet returns all odd numbers from a list:

```
iex(3)> Enum.filter(
          [1, 2, 3],
          fn x -> rem(x, 2) == 1 end
        )
[1, 3]
```

`Enum.filter/2` takes an enumerable and a lambda. It returns only those elements for which the lambda returns `true`.

Of course, you can use the capture syntax as well:

```
iex(3)> Enum.filter(
          [1, 2, 3],
          &(rem(&1, 2) == 1)
        )
[1, 3]
```

Let's play a bit more with `Enum`. Recall the example from section 3.3.3, where you used `with` to verify that the login, email, and password are submitted. In that example, you returned the first encountered error. Armed with this new knowledge, you can improve that code to report all missing fields immediately.

To briefly recap, your input is a map, and you need to fetch the keys `"login"`, `"email"`, and `"password"` and then convert them into a map in which keys are atoms. If a required field isn't provided, you need to report an error. In the previous version, you simply reported the first missing field. A better user experience would be to return a list of all missing fields.

This is something you can do easily with the help of `Enum.filter/2`. The idea is to iterate through the list of required fields and take only those fields that aren't present in the map. You can easily check for the presence of a key with the help of `Map.has_key?/2`. The sketch of the solution then looks like the next listing.

Listing 3.10   Reporting all missing fields (user_extraction_2.ex)

```
case Enum.filter(
        ["login", "email", "password"],       Filters the required fields
        &(not Map.has_key?(user, &1))    ◁——— Takes only missing fields
    ) do
  [] ->   ◁——— No field is missing.
    ...

  missing_fields ->   ◁——— Some fields are missing.
    ...
end
```

There are two possible outcomes of `Enum.filter/2`. If the result is an empty list, all the fields are provided, and you can extract the data. Otherwise, some fields are missing, and you need to report an error. The code for each branch is omitted here for the sake of brevity, but you can find the complete solution in user_extraction_2.ex.

REDUCE

The most versatile function from the `Enum` module is likely `Enum.reduce/3`, which can be used to transform an enumerable into anything. If you're coming from languages that support first-class functions, you may already know `reduce` under the name *inject* or *fold*.

Reducing is best explained with an example. You'll use `reduce` to sum all the elements in a list. Before doing it in Elixir, let's see how you could do this task in an imperative manner. Here's an imperative JavaScript example:

```
var sum = 0;                        ◁——— Initializes the sum
[1, 2, 3].forEach(function(element) {
  sum += element;                   ◁——— Accumulates the result
})
```

This is a standard imperative pattern. You initialize an accumulator (the variable `sum`) and then do some looping, adjusting the accumulator value in each step. After the loop is finished, the accumulator holds the final value.

In a functional language, you can't change the accumulator, but you can still calculate the result incrementally by using `Enum.reduce/3`. The function has the following shape:

```
Enum.reduce(
  enumerable,
  initial_acc,
  fn element, acc ->
    ...
  end
)
```

`Enum.reduce/3` takes an enumerable as its first argument. The second argument is the initial value for the accumulator—what you compute incrementally. The final argument is a lambda that's called for each element. The lambda receives the element from the enumerable and the current accumulator value. The lambda's task is to compute and return the new accumulator value. When the iteration is done, `Enum.reduce/3` returns the final accumulator value.

Let's use `Enum.reduce/3` to sum up elements in the list:

```
iex(4)> Enum.reduce(
          [1, 2, 3],      Sets the initial accumulator value
          0,        ◄─────
          fn element, sum -> sum + element end   ◄─┐  Incrementally updates
        )                                           │  the accumulator
6
```

That's all there is to it! Coming from an imperative background myself, it helps me to think of the lambda as the function that's called in each iteration step. Its task is to add a bit of the information to the result.

You may recall I mentioned that many operators are functions, and you can turn an operator into a lambda by calling `&+/2`, `&*/2`, and so on. This combines nicely with higher-order functions. For example, the sum example can be written in a more compact form:

```
iex(5)> Enum.reduce([1,2,3], 0, &+/2)
6
```

It's worth mentioning that there's a function, called `Enum.sum/1`, that works exactly like this snippet. The point of the sum example was to illustrate how to iterate through a collection and accumulate the result.

Let's work a bit more with `reduce`. The previous example works only if you pass a list that consists exclusively of numbers. If the list contains anything else, an error is raised (because the + operator is defined only for numbers). The next example can work on any type of list and sums only its numeric elements:

```
iex(6)> Enum.reduce(
                [1, "not a number", 2, :x, 3],
Multiclause     0,
    lambda ├──► fn                                        Matches numerical
                  element, sum when is_number(element) -> ◄─┘ elements
                    sum + element

                  _, sum ->
                    sum      ◄────── Matches anything else
                end
        )
```

This example relies on a multiclause lambda to obtain the desired result. If the element is a number, you add its value to the accumulated sum. Otherwise, you return whatever sum you have at the moment, effectively passing it unchanged to the next iteration step.

Personally, I tend to avoid writing elaborate lambdas. If there's a bit more logic in the anonymous function, it's a sign that it will probably look better as a distinct function. In the following snippet, the lambda code is pushed to a separate private function:

```
defmodule NumHelper do
  def sum_nums(enumerable) do
    Enum.reduce(enumerable, 0, &add_num/2)      Captures the add_num/2
  end                                           to lambda

  defp add_num(num, sum) when is_number(num), do: sum + num    Handles each
  defp add_num(_, sum), do: sum                                iteration step
end
```

This is more or less similar to the approach you saw earlier. This example moves the iteration step to the separate, private function `add_num/2`. When calling `Enum.reduce`, you pass the lambda that delegates to that function, using the capture operator `&`.

Notice how when capturing the function, you don't specify the module name. That's because `add_num/2` resides in the same module, so you can omit the module prefix. In fact, because `add_num/2` is private, you can't capture it with the module prefix.

This concludes our basic showcase of the `Enum` module. Be sure to review the other available functions because you'll find many useful helpers for simplifying loops, iterations, and manipulations of enumerables.

3.4.4 *Comprehensions*

The cryptic *comprehensions* name denotes another expression that can help you iterate and transform enumerables. The following example uses a comprehension to square each element of a list:

```
iex(1)> for x <- [1, 2, 3] do
          x*x
        end
```

The comprehension iterates through each element and runs the do…end block. The result is a list that contains all the results returned by the do…end block. In this basic form, `for` is no different from `Enum.map/2`.

Comprehensions have several other features, which often make them elegant compared to `Enum`-based iterations. For example, it's possible to perform nested iterations over multiple collections. The following example takes advantage of this feature to calculate a small multiplication table:

```
iex(2)> for x <- [1, 2, 3], y <- [1, 2, 3], do: {x, y, x*y}
[
  {1, 1, 1}, {1, 2, 2}, {1, 3, 3},
  {2, 1, 2}, {2, 2, 4}, {2, 3, 6},
  {3, 1, 3}, {3, 2, 6}, {3, 3, 9}
]
```

In this example, the comprehension performs a nested iteration, calling the provided block for each combination of input collections.

Just like functions from the `Enum` module, comprehensions can iterate through anything that's enumerable. For example, you can use ranges to compute a multiplication table for single-digit numbers:

```
iex(3)> for x <- 1..9, y <- 1..9, do: {x, y, x*y}
```

In the examples so far, the result of the comprehension has been a list, but comprehensions can return anything that's collectable. *Collectable* is an abstract term for a functional data type that can collect values. Some examples include lists, maps, `MapSet`, and file streams; you can even make your own custom type collectable (more on that in chapter 4).

In more general terms, a comprehension iterates through enumerables, calling the provided block for each value and storing the results in some collectable structure. Let's see this in action.

The following snippet makes a map that holds a multiplication table. Its keys are tuples of factors {x,y}, and the values contain products:

```
iex(4)> multiplication_table =
          for x <- 1..9,
              y <- 1..9,
              into: %{} do        ⟵──── Specifies the collectable
            {{x, y}, x*y}
          end

iex(5)> Map.get(multiplication_table, {7, 6})
42
```

Notice the `into` option, which specifies what to collect. In this case, it's an empty map `%{}` that will be populated with values returned from the `do` block. Notice how you return a `{factors, product}` tuple from the `do` block. You use this format because the map "knows" how to interpret it. The first element will be used as a key, and the second will be used as the corresponding value.

Another interesting comprehension feature is that you can specify filters. This enables you to skip some elements from the input. The following example computes a nonsymmetrical multiplication table for numbers x and y, where x is never greater than y:

```
iex(6)> multiplication_table =
          for x <- 1..9,
              y <- 1..9,
              x <= y,          ⟵──── Comprehension filter
              into: %{} do
            {{x, y}, x*y}
          end

iex(7)> Map.get(multiplication_table, {6, 7})
```

```
42
iex(8)> Map.get(multiplication_table, {7, 6})
nil
```

The comprehension filter is evaluated for each element of the input enumerable, prior to block execution. If the filter returns `true`, the block is called and the result is collected. Otherwise, the comprehension moves on to the next element.

As you can see, comprehensions are an interesting feature, allowing you to do some elegant transformations of the input enumerable. Although this can be done with `Enum` functions, most notably `Enum.reduce/3`, the resulting code is often more elegant when comprehensions are used. This is particularly true when you must perform a Cartesian product (cross join) of multiple enumerables or traverse a nested collection to produce a flat result.

> **NOTE** Comprehensions can also iterate through a binary. The syntax is somewhat different, and we won't treat it here. For more details, it's best to look at the official `for` documentation at https://mng.bz/xj2d.

3.4.5 *Streams*

A *stream* is a special kind of enumerable that can be useful for doing lazy composable operations over anything enumerable. To see what this means, let's look at one shortcoming of standard `Enum` functions.

Let's say you have a list of employees and need to print each one, prefixed by their position in the list:

```
1. Alice
2. Bob
3. John
...
```

This is fairly simple to perform by combining various `Enum` functions. For example, there's a function, `Enum.with_index/1`, that takes an enumerable and returns a list of tuples, where the first element of the tuple is a member from the input enumerable and the second element is its zero-based index:

```
iex(1)> employees = ["Alice", "Bob", "John"]
["Alice", "Bob", "John"]

iex(2)> Enum.with_index(employees)
[{"Alice", 0}, {"Bob", 1}, {"John", 2}]
```

You can now feed the result of `Enum.with_index/1` to `Enum.each/2` to get the desired output:

```
iex(3)> employees
        |> Enum.with_index()
        |> Enum.each(fn {employee, index} ->
```

```
        IO.puts("#{index + 1}. #{employee}")
    end)
```

```
1. Alice
2. Bob
3. John
```

Here, you rely on the pipe operator to chain together various function calls. This saves you from having to use intermediate variables and makes the code a bit cleaner.

So what's the problem with this code? The `Enum.with_index/1` function goes through the entire list to produce another list with tuples, and then `Enum.each` performs another iteration through the new list. It would be better if you could do both operations in a single pass without building another list. This is where streams can help.

Streams are implemented in the `Stream` module (https://hexdocs.pm/elixir/Stream.html), which, at first glance, looks similar to the `Enum` module, containing functions like `map`, `filter`, and `take`. These functions take any enumerable as an input and give back a stream: an enumerable with some special powers.

A *stream* is a lazy enumerable, which means it produces the actual result on demand. Let's look at what this means.

The following snippet uses a stream to double each element in a list:

```
iex(4)> stream = Stream.map([1, 2, 3], fn x -> 2 * x end)    ⟵ Creates the stream
```

```
#Stream<[enum: [1, 2, 3],            The result of Stream.map/2
    funs: [#Function<44.45151713/1 in Stream.map/2>]] >    is a stream.
```

Because a stream is a lazy enumerable, the iteration over the input list (`[1, 2, 3]`) and the corresponding transformation (multiplication by 2) haven't yet happened. Instead, you get the structure that describes the computation.

To make the iteration happen, you need to pass the stream to an `Enum` function, such as `each`, `map`, or `filter`. You can also use the `Enum.to_list/1` function, which converts any kind of enumerable into a list:

```
iex(5)> Enum.to_list(stream)        ⟵ At this point, stream iteration takes place.
[2, 4, 6]
```

`Enum.to_list/1` (and any other `Enum` function, for that matter) is an eager operation. It immediately starts iterating through the input and creates the result. In doing so, `Enum.to_list/1` requests the input enumerable to start producing values. This is why the output of the stream is created when you send it to an `Enum` function.

The laziness of streams goes beyond iterating the list on demand. Values are produced one by one when `Enum.to_list` requests another element. For example, you can use `Enum.take/2` to request only one element from the stream:

```
iex(6)> Enum.take(stream, 1)
[2]
```

Because `Enum.take/2` iterates only until it collects the desired number of elements, the input stream doubles only one element in the list. The others are never visited.

Returning to the example of printing employees, using a stream allows you to print employees in a single go. The change to the original code is simple enough. Instead of using `Enum.with_index/1`, you can rely on its lazy equivalent, `Stream.with_index/1`:

```
iex(7)> employees
        |> Stream.with_index()              ←——— Performs a lazy transformation
        |> Enum.each(fn {employee, index} ->
            IO.puts("#{index + 1}. #{employee}")
          end)

1. Alice
2. Bob
3. John
```

The output is the same, but the list iteration is done only once. This becomes increasingly useful when you need to compose several transformations of the same list. The following example takes the input list and only prints the square root of elements representing a nonnegative number, adding an indexed prefix at the beginning:

```
iex(1)> [9, -1, "foo", 25, 49]
        |> Stream.filter(&(is_number(&1) and &1 > 0))
        |> Stream.map(&{&1, :math.sqrt(&1)})
        |> Stream.with_index()
        |> Enum.each(fn {{input, result}, index} ->
            IO.puts("#{index + 1}. sqrt(#{input}) = #{result}")
          end)

1. sqrt(9) = 3.0
2. sqrt(25) = 5.0
3. sqrt(49) = 7.0
```

This code is dense, and it illustrates how concise you can be by relying only on functions as the abstraction tool. You start with the input list and filter only positive numbers. Next, you transform each such number into an {input_number, square_root} tuple. Then, you index the resulting tuples using `Stream.with_index/1`. Finally, you print the result.

Even though you stack multiple transformations, everything is performed in a single pass when you call `Enum.each`. In contrast, if you used `Enum` functions everywhere, you'd need to run multiple iterations over each intermediate list, which would incur a memory-usage penalty.

This lazy property of streams can prove useful for consuming a slow and potentially large enumerable input. A typical case is when you need to parse each line of a file. Relying on eager `Enum` functions means you must read the entire file into memory and then iterate through each line. In contrast, using streams makes it possible to read and immediately parse one line at a time. For example, the following function takes a filename and returns the list of all lines from that file that are longer than 80 characters:

```
def large_lines!(path) do
  File.stream!(path)
  |> Stream.map(&String.trim_trailing(&1, "\n"))
  |> Enum.filter(&(String.length(&1) > 80))
end
```

Here, you rely on the `File.stream!/1` function, which takes the path of a file and returns a stream of its lines. Because the result is a stream, the iteration through the file happens only when you request it. After `File.stream!` returns, no byte from the file has been read yet. Then, you remove the trailing newline character from each line, again in a lazy manner. Finally, you eagerly take only long lines, using `Enum.filter/2`. This is when the iteration happens. The consequence is that you never read the entire file in memory; instead, you work on each line individually.

> **NOTE** There are no special tricks in the Elixir compiler that allow these lazy enumerations. The real implementation is fairly involved, but the basic idea behind streams is simple and relies on anonymous functions. In a nutshell, to make a lazy computation, you need to return a lambda that performs the computation. This makes the computation lazy because you return its description rather than its result. When the computation needs to be materialized, the consumer code can call the lambda.

INFINITE STREAMS

So far, you've produced streams by transforming an existing collection with functions such as `Stream.map` or `Stream.filter`. Some functions from the `Stream` module allow you to create a stream from scratch.

One such function is `Stream.iterate/2`, which can be used to produce an infinite collection, where each element is calculated based on the previous one. For example, the following snippet builds an infinite stream of natural numbers:

```
iex(1)> natural_numbers = Stream.iterate(
      1,
      fn previous -> previous + 1 end
    )
```

We can feed this infinite collection to other `Enum` and `Stream` functions to produce a finite sequence. For example, to take the first 10 natural numbers, you can use `Enum.take/2`:

```
iex(2)> Enum.take(natural_numbers, 10)
[1, 2, 3, 4, 5, 6, 7, 8, 9, 10]
```

Another example is the function `Stream.repeatedly/1`, which repeatedly invokes the provided lambda to generate an element. In the following example, we'll use it to repeatedly read the user's input from the console, stopping when the user submits a blank input:

```
iex(3)> Stream.repeatedly(fn -> IO.gets("> ") end)
        |> Stream.map(&String.trim_trailing(&1, "\n"))
        |> Enum.take_while(&(&1 != ""))

> Hello
> World
>
["Hello", "World"]
```

The `Stream` module contains a few more functions that produce an infinite stream, such as `Stream.unfold/2` or `Stream.resource/3`. Take a look at the official documentation, discussed earlier in the section, for details.

PRACTICE EXERCISES

This style of coding takes some getting used to. You'll use the techniques presented here throughout the book, but you should try to write a couple such iterations yourself. The following are some exercise ideas that may help you get into the swing of things.

Using `large_lines!/1` as a model, write the following functions:

1 A `lines_lengths!/1` that takes a file path and returns a list of numbers, with each number representing the length of the corresponding line from the file.
2 A `longest_line_length!/1` that returns the length of the longest line in a file.
3 A `longest_line!/1` that returns the contents of the longest line in a file.
4 A `words_per_line!/1` that returns a list of numbers, with each number representing the word count in a file. Hint: To find the word count of a line, use `length(String.split(line))`.

Solutions are provided in the enum_streams_practice.ex file, but I strongly suggest you spend some time trying to crack these problems yourself.

Summary

- Pattern matching is a mechanism that attempts to match a term on the right side to the pattern on the left side. In the process, variables from the pattern are bound to corresponding subterms from the term. If a term doesn't match the pattern, an error is raised.
- Function arguments are patterns. The aim of calling a function is to match the provided values to the patterns specified in the function definition.
- Functions can have multiple clauses. The first clause that matches all the arguments is executed.
- For conditional branching, you can use multiclause functions and expressions such as `if`, `unless`, `cond`, `case`, and `with`.

- Recursion is the main tool for implementing loops. Tail recursion is used when you need to run an arbitrarily long loop.
- Higher-order functions make writing loops much easier. There are many useful generic iteration functions in the `Enum` module. Additionally, the `Stream` module makes it possible to implement lazy and composable iterations.
- Comprehensions can also be used to iterate, transform, filter, and join various enumerables.

Data abstractions 4

This chapter covers

- Abstracting with modules
- Working with hierarchical data
- Polymorphism with protocols

This chapter discusses building higher-level data structures. In any complex system, there will be a need for abstractions such as `Money`, `Date`, `Employee`, and `OrderItem`. These are all textbook examples of higher-level abstractions that usually aren't directly supported by the language and are instead written on top of built-in types.

In Elixir, such abstractions are implemented with pure, stateless modules. In this chapter, you'll learn how to create and work with your own abstractions.

In a typical object-oriented (OO) language, the basic abstraction building blocks are classes and objects. For example, there may be a `String` class that implements various string operations. Each string is then an instance of that class and can be manipulated by calling methods, as the following Ruby snippet illustrates:

```
"a string".upcase
```

This approach generally isn't used in Elixir. Being a functional language, Elixir promotes decoupling of data from the code. Instead of classes, you use modules, which are collections of functions. Instead of calling methods on objects, you explicitly call module functions and provide input data via arguments. The following snippet shows the Elixir way of uppercasing a string:

```
String.upcase("a string")
```

Another big difference from OO languages is that data is immutable. To modify data, you must call some function and take its result into a variable; the original data is left intact. The following examples demonstrate this technique:

```
iex(1)> list = []
[]

iex(2)> list = List.insert_at(list, -1, :a)
[:a]

iex(3)> list = List.insert_at(list, -1, :b)
[:a, :b]

iex(4)> list = List.insert_at(list, -1, :c)
[:a, :b, :c]
```

In these examples, you're constantly keeping the result of the last operation and feeding it to the next one.

The important thing to notice in both Elixir snippets is that the module is used as the abstraction over the data type. When you need to work with strings, you reach for the String module. When you need to work with lists, you use the List module.

String and List are examples of modules that are dedicated to a specific data type. They're implemented in pure Elixir, and their functions rely on the predefined format of the input data. String functions expect a binary string as the first argument, whereas List functions expect a list.

Additionally, *modifier functions* (the ones that transform the data) return data of the same type. The function String.upcase/1 returns a binary string, whereas List.insert_at/3 returns a list.

Finally, a module also contains *query functions* that return some piece of information from the data, such as String.length/1 and List.first/1. Such functions still expect an instance of the abstraction as the first argument, but they return another type of information.

The basic principles of abstraction in Elixir can be summarized as follows:

- A module is in charge of abstracting some behavior.
- The module's functions usually expect an instance of the abstraction as the first argument.
- Modifier functions return a modified version of the abstraction.
- Query functions return some other type of data.

Given these principles, it's fairly straightforward to create your own higher-level abstractions, as you'll see in the next section.

4.1   *Abstracting with modules*

Lists and strings are lower-level types, but higher-level abstractions are based on the previously stated principles. In fact, you already saw examples of a higher-level abstraction in chapter 2. For example, a `MapSet` module implements a set. `MapSet` is implemented in pure Elixir and can serve as a good template for designing an abstraction in Elixir.

Let's look at an example that uses `MapSet`:

```
iex(1)> days =                                    Creates an abstraction instance
          MapSet.new() |>  ◁————┘
          MapSet.put(:monday) |>
          MapSet.put(:tuesday)           Modifies the instance

iex(2)> MapSet.member?(days, :monday)    ◁———— Queries the instance
true
```

This approach more or less follows the principles stated earlier. The code is slightly simplified by using the pipe operator to chain operations together. This is possible because all the functions from the `MapSet` module take a set as the first argument. Such functions are pipe friendly and can be chained with the `|>` operator.

Notice the `new/0` function that creates a new instance of the abstraction. There's nothing special about this function, and it could have been given any name. Its only purpose is to create a new data structure you can work with.

Because `MapSet` is an abstraction, you, as a client of this module, don't concern yourself with its internal workings or its data structure. You call `MapSet` functions, keeping whatever result you get and passing that result back to functions from the same module.

> **NOTE** You may think that abstractions like `MapSet` are something like user-defined types. Although there are many similarities, module-based abstractions aren't proper data types, like the ones explained in chapter 2. Instead, they're implemented by composing built-in data types. For example, a `MapSet` instance is also a map, which you can verify by invoking `is_map(MapSet.new())`.

Given this template, let's try to build a simple abstraction.

4.1.1   *Basic abstraction*

The example in this section is a simple to-do list. The problem is, admittedly, not spectacular, but it's complex enough to give you something to work with while not being overly complicated. This will allow you to focus on techniques without spending too much time trying to grasp the problem itself.

The basic version of the to-do list will support the following features:

- Creating a new to-do list
- Adding new entries to the list
- Querying the list

Here's an example of the desired usage:

```
$ iex simple_todo.ex

iex(1)> todo_list =
          TodoList.new() |>
          TodoList.add_entry(~D[2023-12-19], "Dentist") |>
          TodoList.add_entry(~D[2023-12-20], "Shopping") |>
          TodoList.add_entry(~D[2023-12-19], "Movies")

iex(2)> TodoList.entries(todo_list, ~D[2023-12-19])
["Movies", "Dentist"]

iex(3)> TodoList.entries(todo_list, ~D[2023-12-18])
[]
```

This is fairly self-explanatory. You create an instance by calling `TodoList.new/0`, and then you add some entries. Finally, you execute some queries. The expression `~D[2023-12-19]`, as explained in section 2.4.11, creates a date (December 19, 2023), powered by the `Date` module.

As the chapter progresses, you'll add additional features and modify the interface slightly. You'll continue adding features throughout this book, and by the end, you'll have a fully working distributed web server that can manage a large number of to-do lists.

For now, let's start with this simple interface. First, you must decide on the internal data representation. In the preceding snippet, you can see that the primary use case is finding all entries for a single date. Therefore, using a map seems like a reasonable initial approach. You'll use dates as keys, with values being lists of entries for given dates. With this in mind, the implementation of the `new/0` function is straightforward.

Listing 4.1 Initializing a to-do list (simple_todo.ex)

```
defmodule TodoList do
  def new(), do: %{}
  ...
end
```

Next, you must implement the `add_entry/3` function. This function expects a to-do list (which you know is a map) and must add the entry to the list under a given key (date). Of course, it's possible that no entries for that date exist, so you need to cover that case as well. As it turns out, this can be done with a single call to the `Map.update/4` function.

Listing 4.2   Adding an entry (simple_todo.ex)

```
defmodule TodoList do
  ...
  def add_entry(todo_list, date, title) do
    Map.update(
      todo_list,
      date,
      [title],       ◁———|  Initial value
      fn titles -> [title | titles] end     ◁——— Updater function
    )
  end
  ...
end
```

The `Map.update/4` function receives a map, a key, an initial value, and an updater function. If no value exists for the given key, the initial value is used; otherwise, the updater function is called. The function receives the existing value and returns the new value for that key. In this case, you push the new entry to the top of the list. You may remember from chapter 2 that lists are most efficient when pushing new elements to the top. Therefore, you opt for a fast insertion operation but sacrifice ordering—more recently added entries are placed before the older ones in the list.

Finally, you need to implement the `entries/2` function, which returns all entries for a given date, or an empty list, if no task exists for that date. This is fairly straightforward, as you can see in the following listing.

Listing 4.3   Querying the to-do list (simple_todo.ex)

```
defmodule TodoList do
  ...
  def entries(todo_list, date) do
    Map.get(todo_list, date, [])
  end
end
```

You fetch a value for the given date from `todo_list`, which must be a map. The third argument to `Map.get/3` is a default value that's returned if a given key isn't present in the map.

4.1.2   Composing abstractions

Nothing stops you from creating one abstraction on top of another. In our initial take on the to-do list, there's an opportunity to move some of the code into a separate abstraction.

Examine the way you operate on a map, allowing multiple values to be stored under a single key and retrieving all values for that key. This code could be moved to a separate abstraction. Let's call this `MultiDict`, which is implemented in the next listing.

```
defmodule MultiDict do
  def new(), do: %{}

  def add(dict, key, value) do
    Map.update(dict, key, [value], &[value | &1])
  end

  def get(dict, key) do
    Map.get(dict, key, [])
  end
end
```

This is more or less a copy-and-paste of the initial to-do list implementation. The names are changed a bit, and you use the capture operator to shorten the updater lambda definition: `&[value | &1]`.

With this abstraction in place, the `TodoList` module becomes much simpler.

```
defmodule TodoList do
  def new(), do: MultiDict.new()

  def add_entry(todo_list, date, title) do
    MultiDict.add(todo_list, date, title)
  end

  def entries(todo_list, date) do
    MultiDict.get(todo_list, date)
  end
end
```

This is a classical separation of concerns, where you extract a distinct responsibility into a separate abstraction, and then create another abstraction on top of it. A distinct `MultiDict` abstraction is now readily available to be used in other places in code, if needed. Furthermore, you can extend `TodoList` with additional functions that are specific to to-do lists and which, therefore, don't belong to `MultiDict`.

The point of this refactoring is to illustrate that the code organization isn't radically different from an OO approach. You use different tools to create abstractions (modules and functions instead of classes and methods), but the general idea is the same.

4.1.3 Structuring data with maps

`TodoList` now supports the basic features. You can insert entries into the structure and get all entries for a given date, but the interface is somewhat clumsy. When adding a new entry, you must specify each field as a separate argument:

```
TodoList.add_entry(todo_list, ~D[2023-12-19], "Dentist")
```

If you want to extend an entry with another attribute—such as time—you must change the signature of the function, which will, in turn, break all the clients. Moreover, you must change every place in the implementation where this data is being propagated. An obvious solution to this problem is to, somehow, combine all entry fields as a single abstraction.

As explained in section 2.4.6, the most common way of doing this in Elixir is to use maps, with field names stored as keys of the atom type. The following snippet demonstrates how you can create and use an `entry` instance:

```
iex(1)> entry = %{date: ~D[2023-12-19], title: "Dentist"}

iex(2)> entry.date
~D[2023-12-19]

iex(3)> entry.title
"Dentist"
```

You can immediately adapt your code to represent entries with maps. As it turns out, this change is extremely simple. All you need to do is change the code of the `TodoList.add_entry` function to accept two arguments: a to-do list instance and a map that describes an entry. The new version is presented in the following listing.

Listing 4.6   Representing entries with maps (todo_entry_map.ex)

```
defmodule TodoList do
  ...
  def add_entry(todo_list, entry) do
    MultiDict.add(todo_list, entry.date, entry)
  end
  ...
end
```

That was simple! You assume an entry is a map and add it to `MultiDict`, using its date field as a key.

Let's see this in action. To add a new entry, clients now must provide a map:

```
iex(1)> todo_list = TodoList.new() |>
TodoList.add_entry(%{date: ~D[2023-12-19], title: "Dentist"})
```

The client code is obviously more verbose because it must provide field names. But because entries are now structured in a map, data retrieval is improved. The `TodoList.entries/2` function now returns complete entries, not just their titles:

```
iex(2)> TodoList.entries(todo_list, ~D[2023-12-19])
[%{date: ~D[2023-12-19], title: "Dentist"}]
```

The current implementation of `TodoList` relies on a map. This means that at run time, it's impossible to make a distinction between a map and a `TodoList` instance. In some situations, you may want to define and enforce a more precise structure definition. For such cases, Elixir provides a feature called *structs*.

4.1.4 Abstracting with structs

Let's say you need to deal with fractions in your program. A *fraction* is a part of a whole, represented in the form of a/b, where a and b are integers called a *numerator* and a *denominator*. Passing around these two values separately is noisy and error prone. Therefore, it makes sense to introduce a small abstraction to help working with fractions. The following snippet demonstrates how such an abstraction could be used:

```
$ iex fraction.ex

iex(1)> Fraction.new(1, 2)
        |> Fraction.add(Fraction.new(1, 4))
        |> Fraction.value()
0.75
```

Here, you sum one-half (1/2) and one-quarter (1/4) and return the numerical value of the resulting fraction. A fraction is created using Fraction.new/2 and is then passed to various other functions that know how to work with it.

How can you implement this? There are many approaches, such as relying on plain tuples or using maps. In addition, Elixir provides a facility called *structs*, which allows you to specify the abstraction structure up front and bind it to a module. Each module can define only one struct, which can then be used to create new instances and pattern-match on them.

A fraction has a well-defined structure, so you can use structs to specify and enforce data shape. Let's see this in action.

To define a struct, use the defstruct macro (https://hexdocs.pm/elixir/Kernel .html#defstruct/1).

> **Listing 4.7 Defining a structure (fraction.ex)**

```
defmodule Fraction do
  defstruct a: nil, b: nil
  ...
end
```

A keyword list provided to defstruct defines the struct's fields along with their initial values. You can now instantiate a struct using this special syntax:

```
iex(1)> one_half = %Fraction{a: 1, b: 2}
%Fraction{a: 1, b: 2}
```

Notice how a struct bears the name of the module it's defined in. There's a close relation between structs and modules. A struct may exist only in a module, and a single module can define only one struct.

Internally, a struct is a special kind of map. Therefore, individual fields are accessed just like maps:

```
iex(2)> one_half.a
1

iex(3)> one_half.b
2
```

The nice thing about structs is that you can pattern-match on them:

```
iex(4)> %Fraction{a: a, b: b} = one_half
%Fraction{a: 1, b: 2}

iex(5)> a
1

iex(6)> b
2
```

This makes it possible to assert that some variable is really a struct:

```
iex(6)> %Fraction{} = one_half          Successful
%Fraction{a: 1, b: 2}                    match

iex(7)> %Fraction{} = %{a: 1, b: 2}
** (MatchError) no match of right hand side value: %{a: 1, b: 2}
```

> A struct pattern doesn't match a map.

Here, you use a `%Fraction{}` pattern that matches any `Fraction` struct, regardless of its contents. Pattern matching with structs works much like it does with maps. This means in a pattern match, you need to specify only the fields you're interested in, ignoring all other fields.

Updating a struct works similarly to the way it works with maps:

```
iex(8)> one_quarter = %Fraction{one_half | b: 4}
%Fraction{a: 1, b: 4}
```

This code creates a new struct instance based on the original one (`one_half`), changing the value of the field `b` to 4.

The shape of the struct is defined at compile time. As a result, some errors can be caught by the Elixir compiler. For example, suppose we make a typo in the field name:

```
iex(9)> %Fraction{a: 1, d: 2}
** (KeyError) key :d not found
```

The struct doesn't specify the field `:d`, so the error is reported. In contrast, if you used a regular map, this code would succeed. However, the program would fail in a distant place with a nonobvious reason, which would make the error more difficult to debug.

It's worth noting that this error is reported at compile time. If you make the same mistake in a source file, the code won't even compile.

Armed with this knowledge, let's add some functionality to the `Fraction` abstraction. First, you need to provide the creation function.

Listing 4.8   Instantiating a fraction (fraction.ex)

```elixir
defmodule Fraction do
  ...
  def new(a, b) do
    %Fraction{a: a, b: b}
  end
  ...
end
```

This is a simple wrapper around the `%Fraction{}` syntax. It makes the client code clearer and less coupled with the fact that structs are used.

Next, implement a `Fraction.value/1` function that returns a float representation of the fraction.

Listing 4.9   Calculating the fraction value (fraction.ex)

```elixir
defmodule Fraction do
  ...

  def value(%Fraction{a: a, b: b}) do     ◁───── Matches a fraction
    a / b
  end


  ...
end
```

The `value/1` function matches a fraction, taking its fields into individual variables and using them to compute the final result. The benefit of pattern matching is that the input type is enforced. If you pass anything that isn't a fraction instance, you'll get a match error.

Instead of decomposing fields into variables, you could also use dot notation:

```elixir
def value(fraction) do
  fraction.a / fraction.b
end
```

This version is arguably clearer, but on the flip side, it accepts any map, not just `Fraction` structs, which might lead to subtle bugs. For example, suppose there's a `Rectangle` struct with the same fields. You could accidentally pass such a struct to this function, and instead of failing, the function would return some meaningless result.

One final thing to do is to implement the `add` function.

Listing 4.10   Adding two fractions (fraction.ex)

```
defmodule Fraction
  ...

  def add(%Fraction{a: a1, b: b1}, %Fraction{a: a2, b: b2}) do
    new(
      a1 * b2 + a2 * b1,
      b2 * b1
    )
  end

  ...
end
```

You can now test your fraction:

```
iex(1)> Fraction.new(1, 2)
        |> Fraction.add(Fraction.new(1, 4))
        |> Fraction.value()
0.75
```

The code works as expected. By representing fractions with a struct, you can provide the definition of your type, listing all fields and their default values. Furthermore, it's possible to distinguish struct instances from any other data type. This allows you to place %Fraction{} matches in function arguments, thus asserting that you only accept fraction instances.

STRUCTS VS. MAPS

You should always be aware that structs are simply maps, so they have the same characteristics with respect to performance and memory usage. But a struct instance receives special treatment. Some things that can be done with maps don't work with structs. For example, you can't call Enum functions on a struct:

```
iex(1)> one_half = Fraction.new(1, 2)

iex(2)> Enum.to_list(one_half)
** (Protocol.UndefinedError) protocol Enumerable not implemented for
  %Fraction{a: 1, b: 2}
```

Remember that a struct is a functional abstraction and should, therefore, behave according to the implementation of the module where it's defined. In the case of the Fraction abstraction, you must define whether Fraction is enumerable and, if so, in what way. If this isn't done, Fraction isn't an enumerable, so you can't call Enum functions on it.

In contrast, a plain map is an enumerable, so you can convert it to a list:

```
iex(3)> Enum.to_list(%{a: 1, b: 2})
[a: 1, b: 2]
```

On the other hand, because structs are maps, directly calling the Map functions works:

```
iex(4)> Map.to_list(one_half)
[__struct__: Fraction, a: 1, b: 2]
```

Notice the __struct__: Fraction bit. This key–value pair is automatically included in each struct. It helps Elixir distinguish structs from plain maps and perform proper runtime dispatches from within polymorphic generic code. You'll learn more about this later, when we describe protocols.

The __struct__ field has an important consequence for pattern matching. A struct pattern can't match a plain map:

```
iex(5)> %Fraction{a: a, b: b} = %{a: 1, b: 2}
** (MatchError) no match of right hand side value: %{a: 1, b: 2}
```

However, a plain map pattern can match a struct:

```
iex(5)> %{a: a, b: b} = %Fraction{a: 1, b: 2}
%Fraction{a: 1, b: 2}

iex(6)> a
1

iex(7)> b
2
```

This is due to the way pattern matching works with maps. Remember that all fields from the pattern must exist in the matched term. When matching a map to a struct pattern, this isn't the case because %Fraction{} contains the field struct, which isn't present in the map being matched.

The opposite works because you match a struct to the %{a: a, b: b} pattern. Because all these fields exist in the Fraction struct, the match is successful.

RECORDS

In addition to maps and structs, there's another way to structure data: *records*. This is a feature that lets you use tuples and still be able to access individual elements by name. Records can be defined using the defrecord and defrecordp macros from the Record module (https://hexdocs.pm/elixir/Record.html).

Given that they're essentially tuples, records should be faster than maps (although the difference usually isn't significant in the grand scheme of things). On the flip side, the usage is more verbose, and it's not possible to access fields by name dynamically.

Records are present mostly for historical reasons. Before maps were used, records were one of the main tools for structuring data. In fact, many libraries from the Erlang ecosystem use records as their interface. If you need to interface an Erlang library using a record defined in that library, you must import that record into Elixir and define it as a record. This can be done using the Record.extract/2 function in conjunction with the defrecord macro. This idiom isn't required often, so records won't be demonstrated here. Still, it may be useful to keep this information in the back of your mind and research it if the need arises.

4.1.5 *Data transparency*

The modules you've devised so far are abstractions because clients aren't aware of their implementation details. For example, as a client, you call `Fraction.new/2` to create an instance of the abstraction and then send that instance back to some other function from the same module.

But the entire data structure is always visible. As a client, you can obtain individual fraction values, even if this was not intended by the library developer.

It's important to be aware that data in Elixir is always transparent. Clients can read any information from your structs (and any other data type), and there's no easy way of preventing that. In that sense, encapsulation works differently than in typical OO languages. In Elixir, modules are in charge of abstracting the data and providing operations to manipulate and query that data, but the data is never hidden.

Let's verify this in a shell session:

```
$ iex todo_entry_map.ex                              To-do list with a single element

iex(1)> todo_list = TodoList.new() |>
          TodoList.add_entry(%{date: ~D[2023-12-19], title: "Dentist"})

%{~D[2023-12-19] => [%{date: ~D[2023-12-19], title: "Dentist"}]}   ◄─────┘
```

Looking at the return value, you can see the entire structure of the to-do list. From the output, you can immediately tell that the to-do list is powered by a map, and you can also find out details about how individual entries are kept.

Let's look at another example. A `MapSet` instance is also an abstraction, powered by the `MapSet` module and a corresponding struct. At first glance, this isn't visible:

```
iex(1)> mapset = MapSet.new([:monday, :tuesday])
MapSet.new([:monday, :tuesday])
```

Notice how the result of the expression is printed in a special way, using the `MapSet.new(…)` output. This is due to the inspection mechanism in Elixir: whenever a result is printed in the shell, the function `Kernel.inspect/1` is called to transform the structure into an inspected string. For each abstraction you build, you can override the default behavior and provide your own inspected format. This is exactly what `MapSet` does, and you'll learn how to do this for a type later in this chapter, when we discuss protocols.

Occasionally, you may want to see the pure data structure, without this decorated output. This can be useful when you're debugging, analyzing, or reverse engineering code. To do so, you can provide a special option to the `inspect` function:

```
iex(2)> IO.puts(inspect(mapset, structs: false))
%{__struct__: MapSet, map: %{monday: [], tuesday: []}, version: 2}
```

The output now reveals the complete structure of a date, and you can "see through" the MapSet abstraction. This demonstrates that data privacy can't be fully enforced in Elixir. Remember from chapter 2 that the only complex types are tuples, lists, and maps. Any other abstraction, such as MapSet or your own TodoList, will ultimately be built on top of these types.

The benefit of data transparency is that the data can be easily inspected, which can be useful for debugging purposes. But as a client of an abstraction, you shouldn't rely on its internal representation, even though it's visible to you. You shouldn't pattern-match on the internal structure or try to extract or modify individual parts of it because a proper abstraction, such as MapSet, doesn't guarantee what the data will look like. The only guarantee is that the module's functions will work if you send them a properly structured instance that you already received from that same module.

Sometimes, a module will publicly document some parts of its internal structure. Good examples of this are the date and time modules, such as Date, Time, and DateTime. Looking at the documentation, you'll see explicit mention that the corresponding data is represented as a structure using fields such as year, month, hour, and so on. In this case, the structure of the data is publicly documented, and you can freely rely on it.

One final thing you should know, related to data inspection, is the IO.inspect/1 function. This function prints the inspected representation of a structure to the screen and returns the structure itself. This is particularly useful when debugging a piece of code. Look at the following example:

```
iex(1)> Fraction.new(1, 4) |>
        Fraction.add(Fraction.new(1, 4)) |>
        Fraction.add(Fraction.new(1, 2)) |>
        Fraction.value()
1.0
```

This code relies on the pipe operator to perform a series of fraction operations. Let's say you want to inspect the entire structure after each step. You can easily insert the call to IO.inspect/1 after every line:

```
iex(2)> Fraction.new(1, 4) |>
        IO.inspect() |>
        Fraction.add(Fraction.new(1, 4)) |>
        IO.inspect() |>
        Fraction.add(Fraction.new(1, 2)) |>
        IO.inspect() |>
        Fraction.value()
```

```
%Fraction{a: 1, b: 4}        Output of each
%Fraction{a: 8, b: 16}       IO.inspect call
%Fraction{a: 32, b: 32}
```

This works because IO.inspect/1 prints the data structure and then returns that same data structure, unchanged. You can also take a look at the dbg macro (https://hexdocs.pm/elixir/Kernel.html#dbg/2), which is somewhat similar but provides more debugging features.

We're now done with the basic theory behind functional abstractions, but you'll practice some more by extending the to-do list.

4.2   *Working with hierarchical data*

In this section, you'll extend the TodoList abstraction to provide basic CRUD support. You already have the *C* and *R* parts resolved with the add_entry/2 and entries/2 functions, respectively. Now, you need to add support for updating and deleting entries. To do this, you must be able to uniquely identify each entry in the to-do list, so you'll begin by adding unique ID values to each entry.

4.2.1   *Generating IDs*

When adding a new entry to the list, you'll autogenerate its ID value, using incremental integers for IDs. To implement this, you have to do a couple of things:

- *Represent the to-do list as a struct.* You need to do this because the to-do list now has to keep two pieces of information: the entries collection and the ID value for the next entry.

- *Use the entry's ID as the key.* So far, when storing entries in a collection, you used the entry's date as the key. You'll change this and use the entry's ID instead. This will make it possible to quickly insert, update, and delete individual entries. You'll now have exactly one value per each key, so you won't need the MultiDict abstraction anymore.

Let's start implementing this. The code in the following listing contains the module and struct definitions.

Listing 4.11   TodoList **struct (todo_crud.ex)**

```
defmodule TodoList do
    defstruct next_id: 1, entries: %{}     ⟵—— Struct that describes the to-do list

    def new(), do: %TodoList{}     ⟵—— Creates a new instance
    ...
end
```

The to-do list will now be represented as a struct with two fields. The field next_id contains the ID value that will be assigned to the new entry while it's being added to the structure. The field entries is the collection of entries. As has been mentioned, you're now using a map, and the keys are entry ID values.

During the struct definition, the default values for the next_id and entries fields are immediately specified. Therefore, you don't have to provide these when creating a new instance. The new/0 function creates and returns an instance of the struct.

Next, it's time to reimplement the `add_entry/2` function. It has to do more work:

- Set the ID for the entry being added.
- Add the new entry to the collection.
- Increment the `next_id` field.

Here's the code.

Listing 4.12   Autogenerating ID values for new entries (todo_crud.ex)

```
defmodule TodoList do
  ...

  def add_entry(todo_list, entry) do
    entry = Map.put(entry, :id, todo_list.next_id)    ◁──── Sets the new entry's ID

    new_entries = Map.put(              Adds the new
      todo_list.entries,                entry to the
      todo_list.next_id,                entries list
      entry
    )

    %TodoList{todo_list |               Updates
      entries: new_entries,             the struct
      next_id: todo_list.next_id + 1
    }
  end

  ...
end
```

A lot happens here, so let's take each step, one at a time.

In the function body, you first update the entry's id value with the value stored in the `next_id` field. Notice how you use `Map.put/3` to update the entry map. The input map may not contain the id field, so you can't use the standard `%{entry | id: next_id}` technique, which only works if the id field is already present in the map. Once the entry is updated, you add it to the entries collection, keeping the result in the `new_entries` variable.

Finally, you must update the `TodoList` struct instance, setting its `entries` field to the `new_entries` collection and incrementing the `next_id` field. Essentially, you made a complex change in the struct, modifying multiple fields as well as the input entry (because you set its id field).

To the external caller, the entire operation will be atomic. Either everything will happen or, in case of an error, nothing at all. This is the consequence of immutability. The effect of adding an entry is visible to others only when the `add_entry/2` function finishes and its result is taken into a variable. If something goes wrong and you raise an error, the effect of any transformations won't be visible.

It's also worth repeating, as mentioned in chapter 2, that the new to-do list (the one returned by the `add_entry/2` function) will share as much memory as possible with the input to-do list.

With the `add_entry/2` function finished, you need to adjust the `entries/2` function. This will be more complicated because you changed the internal structure. Earlier, you kept a date-to-entries mapping. Now, entries are stored using `id` as the key, so you have to iterate through all the entries and return the ones that fall on a given date.

Listing 4.13   Filtering entries for a given date (todo_crud.ex)

```
defmodule TodoList do
  ...

  def entries(todo_list, date) do
    todo_list.entries
    |> Map.values()                                    <--- Takes the values
    |> Enum.filter(fn entry -> entry.date == date end) <--- Filters entries
  end                                                        for a given
                                                             date
  ...

end
```

This function first uses `Map.values/1` to take the entries from the `entries` map. Then, only the entries that fall on the given date are taken using `Enum.filter/2`.

You can check whether your new version of the to-do list works:

```
$ iex todo_crud.ex

iex(1)> todo_list = TodoList.new() |>
          TodoList.add_entry(%{date: ~D[2023-12-19], title: "Dentist"}) |>
          TodoList.add_entry(%{date: ~D[2023-12-20], title: "Shopping"}) |>
          TodoList.add_entry(%{date: ~D[2023-12-19], title: "Movies"})

iex(2)> TodoList.entries(todo_list, ~D[2023-12-19])
[
  %{date: ~D[2023-12-19], id: 1, title: "Dentist"},
  %{date: ~D[2023-12-19], id: 3, title: "Movies"}
]
```

This works as expected, and you can even see the ID value for each entry. Also note that the interface of the `TodoList` module is the same as the previous version. You've made a number of internal modifications, changed the data representation, and practically rewritten the entire module. And yet the module's clients don't need to be altered because you kept the same interface for your functions.

This is nothing revolutionary—it's a classical benefit of wrapping the behavior behind a properly chosen interface. However, it demonstrates how you can construct and reason about higher-level types when working with stateless modules and immutable data.

4.2.2   *Updating entries*

Now that your entries have ID values, you can add additional modifier operations. Let's implement the `update_entry` operation, which can be used to modify a single entry in the to-do list.

This function will accept an entry ID, and an updater lambda, which will be invoked to update the entry. This will work similarly to `Map.update`. The lambda will receive the original entry and return its modified version. To keep things simple, the function won't raise an error if the entry with a given ID doesn't exist.

The following snippet illustrates the usage. Here, you modify the date of an entry that has an ID value of 1:

```
iex(1)> TodoList.update_entry(
          todo_list,
          1,                              ID of the entry to be modified
          &Map.put(&1, :date, ~D[2023-12-20])
        )                                 Modifies an entry date
```

The implementation is presented in the following listing.

Listing 4.14   Updating an entry (todo_crud.ex)

```
defmodule TodoList do
  ...

  def update_entry(todo_list, entry_id, updater_fun) do
    case Map.fetch(todo_list.entries, entry_id) do
      :error ->                                    No entry—returns the unchanged list
        todo_list

      {:ok, old_entry} ->                          Entry exists—performs the update
        new_entry = updater_fun.(old_entry)        and returns the modified list
        new_entries = Map.put(todo_list.entries, new_entry.id, new_entry)
        %TodoList{todo_list | entries: new_entries}
    end
  end

  ...
end
```

Let's break down what happens here. First, you look up the entry with the given ID, using `Map.fetch/2`. The function will return `:error` if the entry doesn't exist and `{:ok, value}` otherwise.

In the first case, if the entry doesn't exist, you return the original version of the list. Otherwise, you have to call the updater lambda to get the modified entry. Then, you store the modified entry into the entries collection. Finally, you store the modified entries collection in the `TodoList` instance and return that instance.

4.2.3   Immutable hierarchical updates

You may not have noticed, but in the previous example, you performed a deep update of an immutable hierarchy. Let's break down what happens when you call `TodoList.update_entry(todo_list, id, updater_lambda)`:

1 You take the target entry into a separate variable.

2 You call the updater that returns the modified version of the entry to you.

3 You call `Map.put` to put the modified entry into the entries collection.

4 You return the new version of the to-do list, which contains the new entries collection.

Notice that steps 2, 3, and 4 are the ones in which you transform data. Each of these steps creates a new variable that contains the transformed data. In each subsequent step, you take this data and update its container, again by creating a transformed version of it.

This is how you work with immutable data structures. If you have hierarchical data, you can't directly modify part of it that resides deep in its tree. Instead, you must walk down the tree to the particular part that needs to be modified and then transform it and all of its ancestors. The result is a copy of the entire model (in this case, the to-do list). As mentioned, the two versions—new and previous—will share as much memory as possible.

PROVIDED HELPERS

Although the technique presented works, it may become cumbersome for deeper hierarchies. Remember that to update an element deep in the hierarchy, you must walk to that element and then update all of its parents. To simplify this, Elixir offers support for more elegant, deep, hierarchical updates.

Let's look at a basic example. Suppose the to-do list is represented as a simple map, where keys are IDs and values are plain maps consisting of fields. Let's create one instance of such a to-do list:

```
iex(1)> todo_list = %{
  1 => %{date: ~D[2023-12-19], title: "Dentist"},
  2 => %{date: ~D[2023-12-20], title: "Shopping"},
  3 => %{date: ~D[2023-12-19], title: "Movies"}
}
```

Now, let's say you change your mind and want to go to the theater instead of a movie. The original structure can be modified elegantly using the `Kernel.put_in/2` macro:

```
iex(2)> put_in(todo_list[3].title, "Theater")    ◁──── Hierarchical update

%{
  1 => %{date: ~D[2023-12-19], title: "Dentist"},
  2 => %{date: ~D[2023-12-20], title: "Shopping"},
  3 => %{date: ~D[2023-12-19], title: "Theater"}    ◁──── The entry title is updated.
}
```

What happened here? Internally, `put_in/2` does something similar to what you did. It walks recursively to the desired element, transforms it, and then updates all the parents. Notice that this is still an immutable operation, meaning the original structure is left intact, and you must assign the result to a variable.

To be able to do a recursive walk, put_in/2 needs to receive source data and a path to the target element. In the preceding example, the source is provided as todo_list and the path is specified as [3].title. The macro put_in/2 then walks down that path, rebuilding the new hierarchy on the way up.

It's also worth noting that Elixir provides similar alternatives for data retrieval and updates in the form of the get_in/2, update_in/2, and get_and_update_in/2 macros. The fact that these are macros means the path you provide is evaluated at compile time and can't be built dynamically.

If you need to construct paths at run time, there are equivalent functions that accept the data and path as separate arguments. For example, Elixir also includes the put_in/3 macro, which can be used as follows:

```
iex(3)> path = [3, :title]

iex(4)> put_in(todo_list, path, "Theater")   ◄─── Using a path constructed at runtime
```

Functions and macros, such as put_in, rely on the Access module, which allows you to work with key–value structures, such as maps. You can also make your own abstraction work with Access. You need to implement a couple of functions required by the Access contract, and then put_in and related macros and functions will know how to work with your own abstraction. Refer to the official Access documentation (https:// hexdocs.pm/elixir/Access.html) for more details.

EXERCISE: DELETING AN ENTRY

Your TodoList module is almost complete. You've already implemented create (add_entry/2), retrieve (entries/2), and update (update_entry/3) operations. The last thing to implement is the delete_entry/2 operation. This is straightforward, and it's left for you to do as an exercise. If you get stuck, the solution is provided in the source file todo_crud.ex.

4.2.4 Iterative updates

So far, you've been doing updates manually, one at a time. Now, it's time to implement iterative updates. Imagine you have a raw list describing the entries:

```
$ iex todo_builder.ex

iex(1)> entries = [
          %{date: ~D[2023-12-19], title: "Dentist"},
          %{date: ~D[2023-12-20], title: "Shopping"},
          %{date: ~D[2023-12-19], title: "Movies"}
        ]
```

Now, you want to create an instance of the to-do list that contains all of these entries:

```
iex(2)> todo_list = TodoList.new(entries)
```

It's obvious that the `new/1` function performs an iterative build of the to-do list. How can you implement such a function? As it turns out, this is simple.

Listing 4.15   Iteratively building the to-do list (todo_builder.ex)

```
defmodule TodoList do
  ...

  def new(entries \\ []) do
    Enum.reduce(
      entries,
      %TodoList{},              ◁───    Initial accumulator value
      fn entry, todo_list_acc ->    ◁───
        add_entry(todo_list_acc, entry)    Iteratively updates the accumulator
      end
    )
  end

  ...
end
```

To build the to-do list iteratively, you're relying on `Enum.reduce/3`. Recall from chapter 3 that `reduce` is used to transform something enumerable to anything else. In this case, you're transforming a raw list of `Entry` instances into an instance of the `TodoList` struct. Therefore, you call `Enum.reduce/3`, passing the input list as the first argument, the new structure instance as the second argument (the initial accumulator value), and the lambda that's called in each step.

The lambda is called for each entry in the input list. Its task is to add the entry to the current accumulator (`TodoList` struct) and return the new accumulator value. To do this, the lambda delegates to the already-present `add_entry/2` function, reversing the argument order. The arguments need to be reversed because `Enum.reduce/3` calls the lambda, passing the iterated element (entry) and accumulator (`TodoList` struct). In contrast, `add_entry` accepts a struct and an entry.

Notice that you can make the lambda definition more compact with the help of the capture operator:

```
def new(entries \\ []) do
  Enum.reduce(
    entries,
    %TodoList{},
    &add_entry(&2, &1)    ◁───    Reverses the order of arguments
  )                              and delegates to add_entry/2
end
```

Whether you use this version or the previous one is entirely based on your personal taste.

4.2.5   *Exercise: Importing from a file*

Now, it's time for you to practice a bit. In this exercise, you'll create a `TodoList` instance from a comma-separated file.

Assume you have a todos.csv file in the current folder. Each line in the file describes a single to-do entry:

```
2023-12-19,Dentist
2023-12-20,Shopping
2023-12-19,Movies
```

Your task is to create an additional module, `TodoList.CsvImporter`, that can be used to create a `TodoList` instance from the file contents:

```
iex(1)> todo_list = TodoList.CsvImporter.import("todos.csv")
```

To simplify the task, assume the file is always available and in the correct format. Also assume that the comma character doesn't appear in the entry title.

This is generally not hard to do, but it might require some cracking and experimenting. The following are a couple of hints that will lead you in the right direction.

First, create a single file with the following layout:

```
defmodule TodoList do
  ...
end

defmodule TodoList.CsvImporter do
  ...
end
```

Always work in small steps. Implement part of the calculation, and then print the result to the screen using `IO.inspect/1`. I can't stress enough how important this is. This task requires some data pipelining. Working in small steps will allow you to move gradually and verify that you're on the right track.

The general steps you should undertake are as follows:

1 Open a file and go through it, removing `\n` from each line. Hint: Use `File.stream!/1`, `Stream.map/2`, and `String.trim_trailing/2`. You did this in chapter 3, when we talked about streams, in the example where you filtered lines longer than 80 characters.

2 Using `Stream.map`, transform each line obtained from the previous step into a to-do list entry.

  a Convert the line into a `[date_string, title]` list, using `String.split/2`.

  b Convert the date string into a date, using `Date.from_iso8601!` (https://hexdocs.pm/elixir/Date.html#from_iso8601!/2).

  c Create the to-do list entry (a map in the shape of `%{date: date, title: title}`).

The output of step 2 is an enumerable that consists of to-do entries. Pass that enumerable to the `TodoList.new/1` function you recently implemented.

In each of these steps, you'll receive an enumerable as an input, transform each element, and pass the resulting enumerable forward to the next step. In the final step, the resulting enumerable is passed to the already implemented `TodoList.new/1`, and the to-do list is created.

If you work in small steps, it's harder to get lost. For example, you can start by opening a file and printing each line to the screen. Then, try to remove the trailing newline from each line and print them to the screen, and so on.

While transforming the data in each step, you can work with `Enum` functions or functions from the `Stream` module. It will probably be simpler to start with eager functions from the `Enum` module and get the entire thing to work. Then, try to replace as many of the `Enum` functions as possible with their `Stream` counterparts. Recall from chapter 3 that the `Stream` functions are lazy and composable, which can reduce the amount of intermediate memory required for the operation. If you get lost, the solution is provided in the todo_import.ex file.

In the meantime, we're almost done with our exploration of higher-level abstractions. The final topic we'll briefly discuss is the Elixir way of doing polymorphism.

4.3 *Polymorphism with protocols*

Polymorphism is a runtime decision about which code to execute, based on the nature of the input data. In Elixir, the basic (but not the only) way of doing this is by using the language feature called *protocols*.

Before discussing protocols, let's see them in action. You've already seen polymorphic code. For example, the entire `Enum` module is generic code that works on anything enumerable, as the following snippet illustrates:

```
Enum.each([1, 2, 3], &IO.inspect/1)
Enum.each(1..3, &IO.inspect/1)
Enum.each(%{a: 1, b: 2}, &IO.inspect/1)
```

Notice how you use the same `Enum.each/2` function, sending it different data structures: a list, range, and map. How does `Enum.each/2` know how to walk each structure? It doesn't. The code in `Enum.each/2` is generic and relies on a contract. This contract, called a *protocol*, must be implemented for each data type you wish to use with `Enum` functions. Next, let's learn how to define and use protocols.

4.3.1 *Protocol basics*

A *protocol* is a module in which you declare functions without implementing them. Consider it a rough equivalent of an OO interface. The generic logic relies on the protocol and calls its functions. Then, you can provide a concrete implementation of the protocol for different data types.

Let's look at an example. The protocol `String.Chars` is provided by the Elixir standard library and is used to convert data to a binary string. This is how the protocol is defined in the Elixir source:

```
defprotocol String.Chars do    ◁——— Definition of the protocol
  def to_string(term)    ◁———
end                        Declaration of protocol functions
```

This resembles the module definition, with the notable difference that functions are declared but not implemented.

Notice the first argument of the function (the `term`). At runtime, the type of this argument determines the implementation that's called. Let's see this in action. Elixir already implements the protocol for atoms, numbers, and some other data types, so you can issue the following calls:

```
iex(1)> String.Chars.to_string(1)
"1"

iex(2)> String.Chars.to_string(:an_atom)
"an_atom"
```

If the protocol isn't implemented for the given data type, an error is raised:

```
iex(3)> String.Chars.to_string(TodoList.new())
** (Protocol.UndefinedError) protocol String.Chars not implemented
```

Usually, you don't need to call the protocol function directly. More often, there's generic code that relies on the protocol. In the case of `String.Chars`, this is the auto-imported function `Kernel.to_string/1`:

```
iex(4)> to_string(1)
"1"

iex(5)> to_string(:an_atom)
"an_atom"

iex(6)> to_string(TodoList.new())
** (Protocol.UndefinedError) protocol String.Chars not implemented
```

As you can see, the behavior of `to_string/1` is exactly the same as that of `String.Chars.to_string/1`. This is because `Kernel.to_string/1` delegates to the `String.Chars` implementation.

In addition, you can send anything that implements `String.Chars` to `IO.puts/1`:

```
iex(7)> IO.puts(1)
1

iex(8)> IO.puts(:an_atom)
```

```
an_atom

iex(9)> IO.puts(TodoList.new())
** (Protocol.UndefinedError) protocol String.Chars not implemented
```

As you can see, an instance of the `TodoList` isn't printable because `String.Chars` isn't implemented for the corresponding type.

4.3.2   *Implementing a protocol*

How do you implement a protocol for a specific type? Let's refer to the Elixir source again. The following snippet implements `String.Chars` for integers:

```
defimpl String.Chars, for: Integer do
  def to_string(term) do
    Integer.to_string(term)
  end
end
```

You start the implementation by calling the `defimpl` macro. Then, you specify which protocol to implement and the corresponding data type. Finally, the do/end block contains the implementation of each protocol function. In the example, the implementation delegates to the existing standard library function `Integer.to_string/1`.

The `for:` `Type` part deserves some explanation. The type is an atom and can be any of following aliases: `Tuple`, `Atom`, `List`, `Map`, `BitString`, `Integer`, `Float`, `Function`, `PID`, `Port`, or `Reference`. These values correspond to built-in Elixir types.

In addition, the alias `Any` is allowed, which makes it possible to specify a fallback implementation. If a protocol isn't defined for a given type, an error will be raised, unless a fallback to `Any` is specified in the protocol definition and an `Any` implementation exists. Refer to the protocol documentation (https://hexdocs.pm/elixir/Protocol.html) for details.

Finally, and most importantly, the type can be any other arbitrary alias (but not a regular, simple atom):

```
defimpl String.Chars, for: SomeAlias do
  ...
end
```

This implementation will be called if the first argument of the protocol function is a struct defined in the corresponding module. For example, you can implement `String.Chars` for `TodoList` as follows:

```
iex(1)> defimpl String.Chars, for: TodoList do
          def to_string(_) do
            "#TodoList"
          end
        end
```

Now, you can pass a to-do list instance to `IO.puts/1`:

```
iex(2)> IO.puts(TodoList.new())
#TodoList
```

It's important to notice that the protocol implementation doesn't need to be part of any module. This has powerful consequences: you can implement a protocol for a type, even if you can't modify the type's source code. You can place the protocol implementation anywhere in your own code, and the runtime will be able to take advantage of it.

4.3.3 Built-in protocols

Elixir comes with some predefined protocols. It's best to consult the online documentation for the complete reference (https://hexdocs.pm/elixir), but let's mention some of the most important ones.

You've already seen `String.Chars`, which specifies the contract for converting data into a binary string. There's also the `List.Chars` protocol, which converts input data to a character string (a list of characters).

If you want to control how your structure is printed in the debug output (via the `inspect` function), you can implement the `Inspect` protocol.

Arguably, the most important protocol is `Enumerable`. By implementing it, you can make your data structure *enumerable*. This means you can use all the functions from the `Enum` and `Stream` modules for free! This is probably the best demonstration of protocol usefulness. Both `Enum` and `Stream` are generic modules that offer many useful functions, which can work on your custom data structures as soon as you implement the `Enumerable` protocol.

Closely related to enumeration is the `Collectable` protocol. Recall from chapter 3 that a collectable structure is one that you can repeatedly add elements to. A collectable can be used with comprehensions to collect results or with `Enum.into/2` to transfer elements of one structure (enumerable) to another (collectable).

And, of course, you can define your own protocols and implement them for any available data structure (your own or someone else's). See the `Kernel.defprotocol/2` documentation for more information.

COLLECTABLE TO-DO LIST

Let's look at a more involved example. You'll make your to-do list collectable so that you can use it as a comprehension target. This is a slightly more advanced example, so don't worry if you don't understand each detail in the first go.

To make the abstraction collectable, you must implement the corresponding protocol:

```
defimpl Collectable, for: TodoList do
  def into(original) do
    {original, &into_callback/2}      Returns the
  end                                 appender lambda
```

```
defp into_callback(todo_list, {:cont, entry}) do
  TodoList.add_entry(todo_list, entry)
end

defp into_callback(todo_list, :done), do: todo_list
defp into_callback(_todo_list, :halt), do: :ok
end
```

**Appender
implementation**

The exported function `into/1` is called by the generic code (e.g., comprehensions). Here, you provide the implementation that returns the appender lambda. This appender lambda is then repeatedly invoked by the generic code to append each element to your data structure.

The appender function receives a to-do list and an instruction hint. If you receive `{:cont, entry}`, you must add a new entry. If you receive `:done`, you return the list, which, at this point, contains all appended elements. Finally, `:halt` indicates that the operation has been canceled, and the return value is ignored.

Let's see this in action. Copy and paste the previous code into the shell, and then try the following:

```
iex(1)> entries = [
        %{date: ~D[2023-12-19], title: "Dentist"},
        %{date: ~D[2023-12-20], title: "Shopping"},
        %{date: ~D[2023-12-19], title: "Movies"}
      ]

iex(2)> Enum.into(entries, TodoList.new())    ◁──── Collecting into a TodoList
%TodoList{...}
```

By implementing the `Collectable` protocol, you essentially adapt the `TodoList` abstraction to any generic code that relies on that protocol, such as `Enum.into/2` or `for` comprehension.

Summary

- A module is used to create an abstraction. A module's functions create, manipulate, and query data. Clients can inspect the entire structure but shouldn't rely on its shape.
- Maps can be used to group different fields together in a single structure.
- Structs are special kinds of maps that allow you to define data abstractions related to a module.
- Polymorphism can be implemented with protocols. A protocol defines an interface that is used by the generic logic. You can then provide specific protocol implementations for a data type.

Part 2

Concurrent Elixir

Elixir is both a functional and a concurrent language. While the functional aspect allows you to organize your code, the concurrent aspect allows you to organize your runtime and improve the availability of your system. In this part of the book, you'll learn how concurrency works and how it can help you build reliable systems. We begin with an introduction to concurrency in BEAM in chapter 5. Building on this, in chapter 6, you'll learn about OTP and generic server processes, which can simplify the implementation of typical concurrent idioms. In chapter 7, you'll see an example of a more involved concurrent system. Then, in chapter 8, we present the basic error-detection mechanism, with a special focus on detecting errors in concurrent systems via supervisors. Going deeper, in chapter 9 you'll learn how to build supervision trees to minimize negative effects of errors. Finally, chapter 10 presents some alternatives to generic server processes and discusses the tradeoffs between different approaches.

Concurrency primitives

5

This chapter covers

- Understanding BEAM concurrency principles
- Working with processes
- Working with stateful server processes
- Run-time considerations

Now that you have sufficient knowledge of Elixir and functional programming idioms, we'll turn our attention to BEAM concurrency—a feature that plays a central role in Elixir's and Erlang's support for scalability, fault tolerance, and distribution. In this chapter, we'll start our tour of BEAM concurrency by looking at basic techniques and tools. Before we explore the lower-level details, we'll take a look at higher-level principles.

5.1 Concurrency in BEAM

Erlang is all about writing highly available systems—systems that run forever and are always able to meaningfully respond to client requests. To make your system highly available, you must tackle the following challenges:

- *Fault tolerance*—Minimize, isolate, and recover from the effects of run-time errors.
- *Scalability*—Handle a load increase by adding more hardware resources without changing or redeploying the code.
- *Distribution*—Run your system on multiple machines so that others can take over if one machine crashes.

If you address these challenges, your systems can constantly provide service with minimal downtime and failures.

Concurrency plays an important role in achieving high availability. In BEAM, the unit of concurrency is a *process*—a basic building block that makes it possible to build scalable, fault-tolerant, distributed systems.

> **NOTE**   A BEAM process shouldn't be confused with an OS process. As you're about to learn, BEAM processes are much lighter and cheaper than OS processes. Because this book deals mostly with BEAM, the term *process* in the remaining text refers to a BEAM process.

In production, a typical server system must handle many simultaneous requests from different clients, maintain a shared state (e.g., caches, user session data, and server-wide data), and run some additional background processing jobs. For the server to work normally, all of these tasks should run reasonably quickly and be reliable.

Because many tasks are pending simultaneously, it's imperative to execute them in parallel as much as possible, thus taking advantage of all available CPU resources. For example, it's extremely bad if the lengthy processing of one request blocks all other pending requests and background jobs. Such behavior can lead to a constant increase in the request queue, and the system can become unresponsive.

Moreover, tasks should be as isolated from each other as possible. You don't want an unhandled exception in one request handler to crash another unrelated request handler; a background job; or, especially, the entire server. You also don't want a crashing task to leave behind an inconsistent memory state, which might later compromise another task.

That's exactly what the BEAM concurrency model does for us. Processes help us run things in parallel, allowing us to achieve *scalability*—the ability to address a load increase by adding more hardware power, which the system automatically takes advantage of.

Processes also ensure isolation, which, in turn, gives us *fault tolerance*—the ability to localize and limit the effect of unexpected run-time errors that inevitably occur. If you can localize exceptions and recover from them, you can implement a system that truly never stops, even when unexpected errors occur.

In BEAM, a process is a concurrent thread of execution. Two processes run concurrently and may, therefore, run in parallel, assuming at least two CPU cores are available. Unlike OS processes or threads, BEAM processes are lightweight, concurrent entities handled by the VM, which uses its own scheduler to manage their concurrent execution.

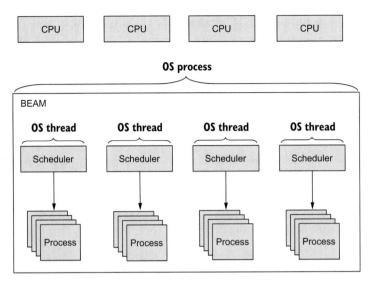

**Figure 5.1   BEAM as a single OS process, using a few threads to schedule
a large number of processes**

By default, BEAM uses as many schedulers as there are CPU cores available. For example, on a quad-core machine, four schedulers are used, as shown in figure 5.1.

Each scheduler runs in its own thread, and the entire VM runs in a single OS process. In figure 5.1, there's one OS process and four OS threads, and that's all you need to run a highly concurrent server system.

A scheduler is in charge of the interchangeable execution of processes. Each process gets an execution time slot; after the time is up, the running process is preempted, and the next one takes over.

Processes are light. It takes only a couple of microseconds to create a single process, and its initial memory footprint is a few kilobytes. By comparison, OS threads usually use a couple megabytes just for the stack. Therefore, you can create a large number of processes; the theoretical limit imposed by the VM is roughly 134 million!

This feature can be exploited in server-side systems to manage various tasks that should run simultaneously. Using a dedicated process for each task, you can take advantage of all available CPU cores and parallelize the work as much as possible.

Moreover, running tasks in different processes improves the server's reliability and fault tolerance. BEAM processes are completely isolated; they share no memory, and a crash of one process won't take down other processes. In addition, BEAM provides a means to detect a process crash and do something about it, such as restarting the crashed process. All this makes it easier to create systems that are more stable and can gracefully recover from unexpected errors, which will inevitably occur during production.

Finally, each process can manage some state and receive messages from other processes to manipulate or retrieve that state. As you saw in part 1 of this book, data in Elixir is immutable. To keep it alive, you need to hold on to it, constantly passing the result of one function to another. A process can be considered a container of this data—a place where an immutable structure is stored and kept alive for a longer time, possibly forever.

As you can see, there's more to concurrency than parallelization of the work. With this high-level view of BEAM processes in place, let's look at how you can create processes and work with them.

5.2 *Working with processes*

The benefits of processes are most obvious when you want to run something concurrently and parallelize the work as much as possible. For example, let's say you need to run a bunch of potentially long-running database queries. You could run those queries sequentially, one at a time, or you could try to run them concurrently, hoping that the total execution time will be reduced.

> **Concurrency vs. parallelism**
>
> It's important to realize that concurrency doesn't necessarily imply parallelism. Two concurrent programs have independent execution contexts, but this doesn't mean they will run in parallel. If you run two CPU-bound concurrent tasks and only have one CPU core, parallel execution can't happen. You can achieve parallelism by adding more CPU cores and relying on an efficient concurrent framework. But you should be aware that concurrency itself doesn't necessarily speed things up.

To keep things simple, we'll use a simulation of a long-running database query, presented in the following snippet:

```
iex(1)> run_query =
          fn query_def ->
            Process.sleep(2000)        Simulates a long-
            "#{query_def} result"      running query
          end
```

Here, the code sleeps for two seconds to simulate a long-running operation. When you call the `run_query` lambda, the shell is blocked until the lambda is done:

```
iex(2)> run_query.("query 1")

"query 1 result"        Two seconds later
```

Consequently, if you run five queries, it will take 10 seconds to get all the results:

```
iex(3)> Enum.map(
          1..5,
          fn index ->
            query_def = "query #{index}"
            run_query.(query_def)
          end
```

```
   )
```

```
["query 1 result", "query 2 result", "query 3 result"    ◁────── Ten seconds later
 "query 4 result", "query 5 result"]
```

Obviously, this is neither performant nor scalable. Assuming the queries are already optimized, the only thing you can do to try to make things faster is run the queries concurrently. This won't speed up individual queries, but the total time required to run all the queries should be reduced. In the BEAM world, to run something concurrently, you must create a separate process.

5.2.1   *Creating processes*

To create a process, you can use the auto-imported `spawn/1` function:

```
spawn(fn ->
  expression_1     │  Runs in the
  ...              │  new process
  expression_n     │
end)
```

The function `spawn/1` creates (spawns) a new process. The provided zero-arity lambda will run concurrently, in the spawned process. After the lambda finishes, the spawned process is stopped. As soon as the new process is spawned, `spawn/1` returns and the caller process can continue its execution.

You can try this to run the query concurrently:

```
iex(4)> spawn(fn ->
          query_result = run_query.("query 1")
          IO.puts(query_result)
        end)
#PID<0.48.0>    ◁────── Immediately returned

query 1 result  ◁────── Printed after 2 seconds
```

As you can see, the call to `spawn/1` returns immediately, and you can do something else in the shell while the query runs concurrently. Then, after 2 seconds, the result is printed to the screen.

The funny-looking `#PID<0.48.0>` that's returned by `spawn/1` is the identifier of the created process, often called a *PID*. This can be used to communicate with the process, as you'll see later in this chapter.

In the meantime, let's do some more experimenting with concurrent execution. First, you'll create a helper lambda that concurrently runs the query and prints the result:

```
iex(5)> async_query =
          fn query_def ->
            spawn(fn ->
              query_result = run_query.(query_def)
```

```
        IO.puts(query_result)
      end)
    end
```

```
iex(6)> async_query.("query 1")
#PID<0.52.0>
```

```
query 1 result   ⟵──── Two seconds later
```

This code demonstrates an important technique: passing data to the created process. Notice that `async_query` takes one argument and binds it to the `query_def` variable. This data is then passed to the newly created process via the closure mechanism. The inner lambda—the one that runs in a separate process—references the variable `query_def` from the outer scope. This results in cross-process data passing; the contents of `query_def` are passed from the main process to the newly created one. When it's passed to another process, the data is deep copied because two processes can't share any memory.

> **NOTE**   In BEAM, everything runs in a process. This also holds for the interactive shell. All expressions you enter in `iex` are executed in a single shell-specific process. In this example, the main process is the shell process.

Now that you have the `async_query` lambda in place, you can try to run five queries concurrently:

```
iex(7)> Enum.each(1..5, &async_query.("query #{&1}"))
:ok    ⟵───────
              | Returns immediately
query 1 result      |
query 2 result      |
query 3 result      | After 2
query 4 result      | seconds
query 5 result      |
```

As expected, the call to `Enum.each/2` now returns immediately (in the first sequential version, you had to wait 10 seconds for it to finish). Moreover, all the results are printed at practically the same time, 2 seconds later, which is a five-fold improvement over the sequential version. This happens because you run each computation concurrently.

For the same reason, the order of execution isn't deterministic. The output results can be printed in any order.

In contrast to the sequential version, the caller process doesn't get the result of the spawned processes. The processes run concurrently, each one printing the result to the screen. At the same time, the caller process runs independently and has no access to any data from the spawned processes. Remember, processes are completely independent and isolated.

Often, a simple "fire-and-forget" concurrent execution, where the caller process doesn't receive any notification from the spawned ones, will suffice. Sometimes, though, you'll want to return the result of the concurrent operation to the caller process. For this purpose, you can use the message-passing mechanism.

5.2.2 Message passing

In complex systems, you often need concurrent tasks to cooperate in some way. For example, you may have a main process that spawns multiple concurrent calculations, and then you may want to handle all the results in the main process.

Being completely isolated, processes can't use shared data structures to exchange knowledge. Instead, processes communicate via messages, as illustrated in figure 5.2.

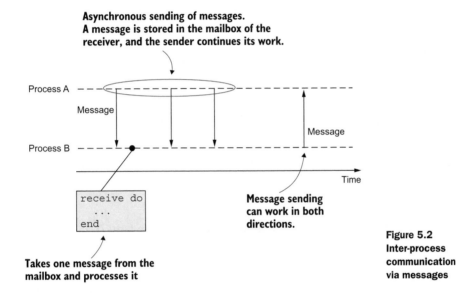

**Asynchronous sending of messages.
A message is stored in the mailbox of the
receiver, and the sender continues its work.**

Process A

Message

Process B

Time

```
receive do
    ...
end
```

**Takes one message from the
mailbox and processes it**

Message

**Message sending
can work in both
directions.**

**Figure 5.2
Inter-process
communication
via messages**

When process A wants process B to do something, it sends an asynchronous message to B. The content of the message is an Elixir term—anything you can store in a variable. Sending a message amounts to storing it into the receiver's mailbox. The caller then continues with its own execution, and the receiver can pull the message in at any time and process it in some way. Because processes can't share memory, a message is deep copied when it's sent.

The process mailbox is a FIFO queue limited only by the available memory. The receiver consumes messages in the order received, and a message can be removed from the queue only if it's consumed.

To send a message to a process, you need to have access to its process identifier (PID). Recall from the previous section that the PID of the newly created process is the result of the `spawn/1` function. In addition, you can obtain the PID of the current process by calling the auto-imported `self/0` function.

Once you have a receiver's PID, you can send it messages using the `Kernel.send/2` function:

```
send(pid, {:an, :arbitrary, :term})
```

The consequence of `send` is that a message is placed in the mailbox of the receiver. The caller process then continues running subsequent expressions.

On the receiver side, to pull a message from the mailbox, you must use the `receive` expression:

```
receive do
  pattern_1 -> do_something
  pattern_2 -> do_something_else
end
```

The `receive` expression works similarly to the `case` expression you saw in chapter 3. It tries to pull one message from the process mailbox, match it against any of the provided patterns, and run the corresponding code. You can easily test this by forcing the shell process to send messages to itself:

```
iex(1)> send(self(), "a message")    ⟵—— Sends the message

iex(2)> receive do
          message -> IO.inspect(message)          Receives the
        end                                        message

"a message"
```

If you want to handle a specific message, you can rely on pattern matching:

```
iex(3)> send(self(), {:message, 1})

iex(4)> receive do
          {:message, id} ->                   ⟵—— Pattern matches the message
            IO.puts("received message #{id}")
        end

received message 1
```

If there are no messages in the mailbox, `receive` waits indefinitely for a new message to arrive. The following call blocks the shell, and you need to manually terminate it:

```
iex(5)> receive do
          message -> IO.inspect(message)      The shell is blocked because
        end                               ⟵—— the process mailbox is empty.
```

The same thing happens if no message in the mailbox matches the provided patterns:

```
iex(1)> send(self(), {:message, 1})

iex(2)> receive do
```

```
{_, _, _} ->                    ⟵— This doesn't match the sent message.
    IO.puts("received")
end                             ⟵— The shell is blocked.
```

If you don't want `receive` to block, you can specify the `after` clause, which is executed if a message isn't received in a given time frame (in milliseconds):

```
iex(1)> receive do
          message -> IO.inspect(message)
        after
          5000 -> IO.puts("message not received")
        end
```

```
message not received    ⟵— Five seconds later
```

RECEIVE BEHAVIOR

Recall from chapter 3 that an error is raised when you can't pattern-match the given term. The `receive` expression is an exception to this rule. If a message doesn't match any of the provided clauses, it's put back into the process mailbox and the next message is processed.

The `receive` expression works as follows:

1 Take the first message from the mailbox.
2 Try to match it against any of the provided patterns, going from top to bottom.
3 If a pattern matches the message, run the corresponding code.
4 If no pattern matches, take the next message, and start from step 2.
5 If there are no more messages in the queue, wait for a new one to arrive. When a new message arrives, start from step 2.
6 If the `after` clause is specified and no message is matched in the given amount of time, run the code from the `after` block.

As you already know, each Elixir expression returns a value, and `receive` is no different. The result of `receive` is the result of the last expression in the appropriate clause:

```
iex(1)> send(self(), {:message, 1})

iex(2)> receive_result =
          receive do
            {:message, x} ->
              x + 2        ⟵— The result of receive
          end

iex(3)> IO.inspect(receive_result)
3
```

To summarize, `receive` tries to find the first (oldest) message in the process mailbox that can be matched against any of the provided patterns. If such a message is found, the corresponding code is executed. Otherwise, `receive` waits for such a message for a specified amount of time or indefinitely if the `after` clause isn't provided.

SYNCHRONOUS SENDING

The basic message-passing mechanism is the asynchronous "fire-and-forget" kind. A process sends a message and then continues to run, oblivious to what happens in the receiver. Sometimes, a caller needs some kind of response from the receiver. There's no special support for doing this. Instead, you must program both parties to cooperate using the basic asynchronous messaging facility.

The caller must include its own PID in the message contents and then wait for a response from the receiver:

```
send(pid, {self(), some_message})    ◁——— Includes caller PID in the message

receive do
  {:response, response} -> ...        ◁——— Waits for the response
end
```

The receiver uses the included PID to send the response to the caller:

```
receive do
  {caller_pid, message} ->
    response = ...                                        Sends the response
    send(caller_pid, {:response, response})   ◁———        to the caller
end
```

You'll see this in action a bit later, when we discuss server processes.

COLLECTING QUERY RESULTS

Let's try message passing with the concurrent queries developed in the previous section. In the previous attempt, you ran queries in separate processes and printed them to the screen from those processes. Let's recall how this works:

```
iex(1)> run_query =
          fn query_def ->
            Process.sleep(2000)
            "#{query_def} result"
          end

iex(2)> async_query =
          fn query_def ->
            spawn(fn ->
              query_result = run_query.(query_def)
              IO.puts(query_result)
            end)
          end
```

Now, instead of printing to the screen, let's collect all the results in the main process. First, you need to make the lambda send the query result to the caller process:

```
iex(3)> async_query =
          fn query_def ->                        Stores the PID of
            caller = self()        ◁———          the calling process
```

```
    spawn(fn ->
      query_result = run_query.(query_def)
      send(caller, {:query_result, query_result})
    end)
  end
```

Responds to the calling process

In this code, you first store the PID of the calling process to a distinct `caller` variable. This is necessary to allow the worker process (the one doing the calculation) to know the PID of the process that should receive the response.

Keep in mind that the result of `self/0` depends on the calling process. If you didn't store the result to the `caller` variable and you tried to `send(self(), …)` from the inner lambda, it would have no effect. The spawned process would send the message to itself because calling `self/0` returns the PID of the process that invoked the function.

The worker process can now use the `caller` variable to return the result of the calculation. The message is in the custom format `{:query_result, result}`. This makes it possible to distinguish between your messages and any others that might be sent to the caller process.

Now, you can start your queries:

```
iex(4)> Enum.each(1..5, &async_query.("query #{&1}"))
```

This runs all the queries concurrently, and the result is stored in the mailbox of the caller process. In this case, this is the shell (`iex`) process.

Notice that the caller process is neither blocked nor interrupted while receiving messages. Sending a message doesn't disturb the receiving process in any way. If the process is performing computations, it continues to do so. The only thing affected is the content of the receiving process's mailbox. Messages remain in the mailbox until they're consumed or the process terminates.

Let's get the results. First, you make a lambda that pulls one message from the mailbox and extracts the query result from it:

```
iex(5)> get_result =
          fn ->
            receive do
              {:query_result, result} -> result
            end
          end
```

Now, you can pull all the messages from the mailbox into a single list:

```
iex(6)> results = Enum.map(1..5, fn _ -> get_result.() end)
["query 3 result", "query 2 result", "query 1 result",
 "query 5 result", "query 4 result"]
```

Notice the use of `Enum.map/2`, which maps anything enumerable to a list of the same length. In this case, you create a range of size 5 and then map each element to the result of the `get_result` lambda. This works because you know there are five messages waiting for you. Otherwise, the loop would get stuck waiting for new messages to arrive.

It's also worth repeating that results arrive in a nondeterministic order. Because all computations run concurrently, it's not certain in which order they'll finish.

This is a simple implementation of a parallel map technique that can be used to process a large amount of work in parallel and then collect the results into a list. This idea can be expressed with a pipeline:

```
iex(7)> 1..5
        |> Enum.map(&async_query.("query #{&1}"))    <──┐  Starts concurrent
        |> Enum.map(fn _ -> get_result.() end)   <──┐   computations
```

Starts concurrent computations

Collects the results

5.3   *Stateful server processes*

Spawning processes to perform one-off tasks isn't the only use case for concurrency. In Elixir, it's common to create long-running processes that can serve various requests, sent in the form of messages. In addition, such processes may maintain some internal state—an arbitrary piece of data that may change over time.

We call such processes *stateful server processes*, and they are an important concept in Elixir and Erlang systems, so we'll spend some time exploring them.

5.3.1   *Server processes*

A *server process* is an informal name for a process that runs for a long time (or forever) and can handle various requests (messages). To make a process run forever, you must use endless tail recursion. You may remember from chapter 3 that tail calls receive special treatment. If the last thing a function does is call another function (or itself), a simple jump takes place instead of a stack push. Consequently, a function that always calls itself will run forever, without causing a stack overflow or consuming additional memory.

This can be used to implement a server process. You need to run the endless loop and wait for a message in each step of the loop. When the message is received, you handle it and then continue the loop. Let's try this by creating a server process that can run a query on demand.

The basic sketch of a long-running server process is provided in the following listing.

Listing 5.1   Long-running server process (database_server.ex)

```
defmodule DatabaseServer do
  def start do
    spawn(&loop/0)    <───── Starts the loop concurrently
  end

  defp loop do
    receive do
      ...
    end
```

Handles one message

```
    loop()      <——— Keeps the loop running
  end


  ...
end
```

`start/0` is the so-called *interface function* used by clients to start the server process. When `start/0` is called, it spawns the process that runs the `loop/0` function. This function powers the infinite loop of the process. The function waits for a message, handles it, and then calls itself, ensuring the process never stops.

Such implementation is what makes this process a server. Instead of actively running some computation, the process is mostly idle, waiting for the message (request) to arrive. It's worth noting that this loop isn't CPU intensive. Waiting for a message puts the process in a suspended state and doesn't waste CPU cycles.

Notice that functions in this module run in different processes. The function `start/0` is called by clients and runs in a client process. The private function `loop/0` runs in the server process. It's perfectly normal to have different functions from the same module running in different processes—there's no special relationship between modules and processes. A module is just a collection of functions, and these functions can be invoked in any process.

When implementing a server process, it usually makes sense to put all of its code in a single module. The functions of this module generally fall into two categories: interface and implementation. *Interface functions* are public and are executed in the caller process. They hide the details of process creation and the communication protocol. *Implementation functions* are usually private and run in the server process.

> **NOTE**   As was the case with classical loops, you typically won't need to code the recursion loop yourself. A standard abstraction called `GenServer` (generic server process) is provided, which simplifies the development of stateful server processes. The abstraction still relies on recursion, but this recursion is implemented in `GenServer`. You'll learn about this abstraction in chapter 6.

Let's look at the full implementation of the `loop/0` function.

Listing 5.2   Database server loop (database_server.ex)

```
defmodule DatabaseServer do
  ...

  defp loop do            | Awaits a message
    receive do    <——┘                          Runs the query and
      {:run_query, caller, query_def} ->         sends the response
        query_result = run_query(query_def)      to the caller
        send(caller, {:query_result, query_result})
    end
```

```
    loop()
  end

  defp run_query(query_def) do      <──── Query execution
    Process.sleep(2000)
    "#{query_def} result"
  end

  ...
end
```

This code reveals the communication protocol between the caller process and the database server. The caller sends a message in the format {:run_query, caller, query_def}. The server process handles such a message by executing the query and sending the query result back to the caller process.

Usually, you want to hide these communication details from clients. Clients shouldn't depend on knowing the exact structure of messages that must be sent or received. To hide this, it's best to provide a dedicated interface function. Let's introduce a function called run_async/2, which will be used by clients to request the operation—in this case, a query execution—from the server. This function makes the clients unaware of message-passing details; they just call run_async/2 and get the result. The implementation is given in the following listing.

Listing 5.3   Implementation of `run_async/2` (database_server.ex)

```
defmodule DatabaseServer do
  ...

  def run_async(server_pid, query_def) do
    send(server_pid, {:run_query, self(), query_def})
  end

  ...
end
```

The run_async/2 function receives the PID of the database server and a query you want to execute. It sends the appropriate message to the server and then does nothing else. Calling run_async/2 from the client requests the server process to run the query while the caller goes about its business.

Once the query is executed, the server sends a message to the caller process. To get this result, you need to add another interface function: get_result/0.

Listing 5.4   Implementation of `get_result/0` (database_server.ex)

```
defmodule DatabaseServer do
  ...

  def get_result do
```

```
    receive do
      {:query_result, result} -> result
    after
      5000 -> {:error, :timeout}
    end
  end


  ...
end
```

get_result/0 is called when the client wants to get the query result. Here, you use receive to get the message. The after clause ensures that you give up after some time passes (e.g., if something goes wrong during the query execution and a response never comes back).

The database server is now complete. Let's see how to use it:

```
iex(1)> server_pid = DatabaseServer.start()

iex(2)> DatabaseServer.run_async(server_pid, "query 1")
iex(3)> DatabaseServer.get_result()
"query 1 result"

iex(4)> DatabaseServer.run_async(server_pid, "query 2")
iex(5)> DatabaseServer.get_result()
"query 2 result"
```

Notice how you execute multiple queries in the same process. First, you run query 1, and then query 2. This proves the server process continues running after a message is received.

Because communication details are wrapped in functions, the client isn't aware of them. Instead, it communicates with the process with plain functions. Here, the server PID plays an important role. You receive the PID by calling DatabaseServer.start/0, and then you use it to issue requests to the server.

Of course, the request is handled asynchronously in the server process. After calling DatabaseServer.run_async/2, you can do whatever you want in the client (iex) process and collect the result when you need it.

SERVER PROCESSES ARE SEQUENTIAL

It's important to realize that a server process is internally sequential. It runs a loop that processes one message at a time. Thus, if you issue five asynchronous query requests to a single server process, they will be handled one by one, and the result of the last query will come after 10 seconds.

This is a good thing because it helps you reason about the system. A server process can be considered a synchronization point. If several actions need to happen synchronously, in a serialized manner, you can introduce a single process and forward all requests to that process, which handles the requests sequentially.

Of course, in this case, a sequential property is a problem. You want to run multiple queries concurrently to get the result as quickly as possible. What can you do about it?

Assuming the queries can be run independently, you can start a pool of server processes, and then for each query, you can somehow choose one of the processes from the pool and have that process run the query. If the pool is large enough and you divide the work uniformly across each worker in the pool, you'll parallelize the total work as much as possible.

Here's a basic sketch of how this can be done. First, create a pool of database-server processes:

```
iex(1)> pool = Enum.map(1..100, fn _ -> DatabaseServer.start() end)
```

Here, you create 100 database-server processes and store their PIDs in a list. You may think 100 processes is a lot, but recall that processes are lightweight. They take up a small amount of memory (~2 KB) and are created very quickly (in a few microseconds). Furthermore, because all of these processes wait for a message, they're effectively idle and don't waste CPU time.

Next, when you run a query, you need to decide which process will execute the query. The simplest way is to use the `:rand.uniform/1` function, which takes a positive integer n and returns a random number in the range 1..n. Taking advantage of this, the following expression distributes five queries over a pool of processes:

```
iex(2)> Enum.each(
          1..5,
          fn query_def ->                                    Selects a
            server_pid = Enum.at(pool, :rand.uniform(100) - 1)   random
            DatabaseServer.run_async(server_pid, query_def)      process
          end
        )
```

Runs a query on it — applies to `fn query_def ->` and `DatabaseServer.run_async(server_pid, query_def)`.

Note that this isn't efficient; you're using `Enum.at/2` to choose a random PID. Because you use a list to keep the processes, and a random lookup is an O(n) operation, selecting a random worker isn't very performant. You could do better if you used a map with process indexes as keys and PIDs as values. There are also several alternative approaches, such as using a round-robin approach. But for now, let's stick with this simple implementation.

Once you've queued the queries to the workers, you need to collect the responses. This is now straightforward, as illustrated in the following snippet:

```
iex(3)> Enum.map(1..5, fn _ -> DatabaseServer.get_result() end)
["5 result", "3 result", "1 result", "4 result", "2 result"]
```

Thanks to this, you get all the results much faster because queries are, again, executed concurrently.

5.3.2 *Keeping a process state*

Server processes open the possibility of keeping some kind of process-specific state. For example, when you talk to a database, you need to maintain a connection handle.

To keep state in the process, you can extend the `loop` function with additional argument(s). Here's a basic sketch:

```
def start do
  spawn(fn ->
    initial_state = ...          Initializes the state
    loop(initial_state)          during process creation
  end)                           Enters the loop with that state
end

defp loop(state) do
  ...
  loop(state)      Keeps the state during the loop
end
```

Let's use this technique to extend the database server with a connection. In this example, you'll use a random number as a simulation of the connection handle. First, you need to initialize the connection while the process starts, as demonstrated in the following listing.

> **Listing 5.5 Initializing the process state (stateful_database_server.ex)**

```
defmodule DatabaseServer do
  ...

  def start do
    spawn(fn ->
      connection = :rand.uniform(1000)
      loop(connection)
    end)
  end

  ...
end
```

Here, you open the connection and then pass the corresponding handle to the `loop` function. In real life, instead of generating a random number, you'd use a database client library (e.g., ODBC) to open the connection.

Next, you need to modify the `loop` function.

> **Listing 5.6 Using the connection while querying (stateful_database_server.ex)**

```
defmodule DatabaseServer do
  ...

  defp loop(connection) do
```

```
    receive do
      {:run_query, from_pid, query_def} ->
        query_result = run_query(connection, query_def)      ◁─┐  Uses the
        send(from_pid, {:query_result, query_result})           connection while
      end                                                        running the query

    loop(connection)      ◁─┐  Keeps the connection
  end                        in the loop argument
  defp run_query(connection, query_def) do
    Process.sleep(2000)
    "Connection #{connection}: #{query_def} result"
  end

  ...
end
```

The `loop` function takes the state (connection) as the first argument. Every time the loop is resumed, the function passes on the state to itself, so it is available in the next step.

Additionally, you must extend the `run_query` function to use the connection while querying the database. The connection handle (in this case, a number) is included in the query result.

With this, your stateful database server is complete. Notice that you didn't change the interface of its public functions, so the usage remains the same as it was. Let's see how it works:

```
iex(1)> server_pid = DatabaseServer.start()

iex(2)> DatabaseServer.run_async(server_pid, "query 1")
iex(3)> DatabaseServer.get_result()
"Connection 753: query 1 result"

iex(4)> DatabaseServer.run_async(server_pid, "query 2")
iex(5)> DatabaseServer.get_result()
"Connection 753: query 2 result"
```

The results for different queries are executed using the same connection handle, which is kept internally in the process loop and is completely invisible to other processes.

5.3.3   *Mutable state*

So far, you've seen how to keep constant process-specific state. It doesn't take much to make this state mutable. Here's the basic idea:

```
defp loop(state) do
  new_state =            ◁─┐  Computes the new state
    receive do              based on the message
      msg1 ->
        ...
```

```
    msg2 ->
      ...
  end

  loop(new_state)      ⟵——— Loops with the new state
end
```

This is a standard, stateful server technique in Elixir. The process determines the new state while handling the message. Then, the loop function calls itself with the new state, which, effectively, changes the state. The next received message operates on the new state.

From the outside, stateful processes are mutable. By sending messages to a process, a caller can affect its state and the outcome of subsequent requests handled in that server. In that sense, sending a message is an operation with possible side effects. Still, the server relies on immutable data structures. A state can be any valid Elixir variable, ranging from simple numbers to complex data abstractions, such as TodoList (which you built in chapter 4).

Let's see this in action. You'll start with a simple example: a stateful calculator process that keeps a number as its state. Initially, the state of the process is 0, and you can manipulate it by issuing requests such as add, sub, mul, and div. You can also retrieve the process state with the value request.

Here's how you use the server:

```
iex(1)> calculator_pid = Calculator.start()     ⟵——— Starts the process

iex(2)> Calculator.value(calculator_pid)         │ Verifies the
0                                                │ initial value

iex(3)> Calculator.add(calculator_pid, 10)
iex(4)> Calculator.sub(calculator_pid, 5)          Issues
iex(5)> Calculator.mul(calculator_pid, 3)          requests
iex(6)> Calculator.div(calculator_pid, 5)

iex(7)> Calculator.value(calculator_pid)         ⟵——— Verifies the value
3.0
```

In this code, you start the process and check its initial state. Then, you issue some modifier requests and verify the result of the operations (((0 + 10) - 5) * 3) / 5, which is 3.0.

Now, it's time to implement this. First, let's look at the server's inner loop.

> **Listing 5.7 Concurrent stateful calculator (calculator.ex)**

```
defmodule Calculator do
  ...

  defp loop(current_value) do
```

```
    new_value =
      receive do
        {:value, caller} ->
          send(caller, {:response, current_value})        Getter request
          current_value

        {:add, value} -> current_value + value       Arithmetic
        {:sub, value} -> current_value - value       operations
        {:mul, value} -> current_value * value       requests
        {:div, value} -> current_value / value

        invalid_request ->                                          Unsupported
          IO.puts("invalid request #{inspect invalid_request}")      request
          current_value
      end

    loop(new_value)
  end

  ...
end
```

The loop handles various messages. The :value message is used to retrieve the server's state. Because you need to send the response back, the caller must include its PID in the message. Notice that the last expression of this block returns current_value. This is needed because the result of receive is stored in new_value, which is then used as the server's new state. By returning current_value, you specify that the :value request doesn't change the process state.

The arithmetic operations compute the new state based on the current value and the argument received in the message. Unlike a :value message handler, arithmetic operation handlers don't send responses back to the caller. This makes it possible to run these operations asynchronously, as you'll see soon when you implement interface functions.

The final receive clause matches all the other messages. These are the ones you're not supporting, so you log them to the screen and return current_value, leaving the state unchanged.

Next, you need to implement the interface functions that will be used by clients. This is done in the next listing.

Listing 5.8 Calculator interface functions (calculator.ex)

```
defmodule Calculator do
  def start do
    spawn(fn -> loop(0) end)        Starts the server and
  end                               initializes the state

  def value(server_pid) do
    send(server_pid, {:value, self()})        The value
                                              request
```

```
      receive do
        {:response, value} ->
          value
        end
      end
```

The value
request

```
    def add(server_pid, value), do: send(server_pid, {:add, value})
    def sub(server_pid, value), do: send(server_pid, {:sub, value})
    def mul(server_pid, value), do: send(server_pid, {:mul, value})
    def div(server_pid, value), do: send(server_pid, {:div, value})
```

Arithmetic operations

```
    ...
end
```

The interface functions follow the protocol specified in the `loop/1` function. The `:value` request is an example of the synchronous message passing mentioned in section 5.2.2. The caller sends a message, and then it awaits the response. The caller is blocked until the response comes back, which makes the request handling synchronous.

The arithmetic operations run asynchronously. There's no response message, so the caller doesn't need to wait for anything. Therefore, a caller can issue several of these requests and continue doing its own work while the operations run concurrently in the server process. Keep in mind that the server handles messages in the order received, so requests are handled in the proper order.

Why make the arithmetic operations asynchronous? Because you don't care when they're executed. Until you request the server's state (via the `value/1` function), you don't want the client to block. This makes the client more efficient because it doesn't block while the server is doing a computation.

REFACTORING THE LOOP

As you introduce multiple requests to your server, the `loop` function becomes more complex. If you have to handle many requests, it will become bloated, turning into a huge `switch/case`-like expression.

You can refactor this by relying on pattern matching and moving the message handling to a separate multiclause function. This keeps the code of the `loop` function very simple:

```
defp loop(current_value) do
  new_value =
    receive do
      message -> process_message(current_value, message)
    end

  loop(new_value)
end
```

Looking at this code, you can see the general workflow of the server. A message is first received and then processed. Message processing generally amounts to computing the new state based on the current state and the message received. Finally, you loop with this new state, effectively setting it in place of the old one.

`process_message/2` is a simple multiclause function that receives the current state and the message. Its task is to perform message-specific code and return the new state:

```
defp process_message(current_value, {:value, caller}) do
  send(caller, {:response, current_value})
  current_value
end

defp process_message(current_value, {:add, value}) do
  current_value + value
end

...
```

This code is a simple reorganization of the server process loop. It allows you to keep the loop code compact and move the message-handling details to a separate multi-clause function, with each clause handling a specific message.

5.3.4   *Complex states*

State is usually much more complex than a simple number. However, the technique always remains the same: you keep the mutable state using the private `loop` function. As the state becomes more complex, the code of the server process can become increasingly complicated. It's worth extracting the state manipulation to a separate module and keeping the server process focused only on passing messages and keeping the state.

Let's look at this technique using the `TodoList` abstraction developed in chapter 4. First, let's recall the basic usage of the structure:

```
iex(1)> todo_list =
          TodoList.new() |>
          TodoList.add_entry(%{date: ~D[2023-12-19], title: "Dentist"}) |>
          TodoList.add_entry(%{date: ~D[2023-12-20], title: "Shopping"}) |>
          TodoList.add_entry(%{date: ~D[2023-12-19], title: "Movies"})

iex(2)> TodoList.entries(todo_list, ~D[2023-12-19])
[
  %{date: ~D[2023-12-19], id: 1, title: "Dentist"},
  %{date: ~D[2023-12-19], id: 3, title: "Movies"}
]
```

As you may recall, a `TodoList` is a pure functional abstraction. To keep the structure alive, you must constantly hold on to the result of the last operation performed on the structure.

In this example, you'll build a `TodoServer` module that keeps this abstraction in the private state. Let's see how the server is used:

```
iex(1)> todo_server = TodoServer.start()

iex(2)> TodoServer.add_entry(
          todo_server,
```

```
        %{date: ~D[2023-12-19], title: "Dentist"}
      )

iex(3)> TodoServer.add_entry(
        todo_server,
        %{date: ~D[2023-12-20], title: "Shopping"}
      )

iex(4)> TodoServer.add_entry(
        todo_server,
        %{date: ~D[2023-12-19], title: "Movies"}
      )

iex(5)> TodoServer.entries(todo_server, ~D[2023-12-19])
[
  %{date: ~D[2023-12-19], id: 3, title: "Movies"},
  %{date: ~D[2023-12-19], id: 1, title: "Dentist"}
]
```

You start the server and then interact with it via the `TodoServer` API. In contrast to the pure functional approach, you don't need to take the result of a modification and feed it as an argument to the next operation. Instead, you constantly use the same `todo_server` variable to work with the to-do list.

Let's start implementing this server. First, you need to place all the modules in a single file.

Listing 5.9 `TodoServer` modules (todo_server.ex)

```
defmodule TodoServer do
  ...
end

defmodule TodoList do
  ...
end
```

Putting both modules in the same file ensures that you have everything available when you load the file while starting the `iex` shell. In more complicated systems, you'd use a proper Mix project, as will be explained in chapter 7, but for now, this is sufficient.

The `TodoList` implementation is the same as in chapter 4. It has all the features you need to use it in a server process.

Now, set up the basic structure of the to-do server process.

Listing 5.10 `TodoServer` basic structure (todo_server.ex)

```
defmodule TodoServer do
  def start do
    spawn(fn -> loop(TodoList.new()) end)      ⟵┐ Uses a to-do list as
  end                                             the initial state
```

```
defp loop(todo_list) do
  new_todo_list =
    receive do
      message -> process_message(todo_list, message)
    end

  loop(new_todo_list)
end

...
end
```

There's nothing new here. You start the loop using a new instance of the `TodoList` abstraction as the initial state. In the loop, you receive messages and apply them to the state by calling the `process_message/2` function, which returns the new state. Finally, you loop with the new state.

For each request you want to support, you must add a dedicated clause in the `process_message/2` function. Additionally, a corresponding interface function must be introduced. You'll begin by supporting the `add_entry` request.

Listing 5.11 The `add_entry` request (todo_server.ex)

```
defmodule TodoServer do
  ...

  def add_entry(todo_server, new_entry) do        ◀── Interface
    send(todo_server, {:add_entry, new_entry})          function
  end

  ...

  defp process_message(todo_list, {:add_entry, new_entry}) do   ◀── Message-handler
    TodoList.add_entry(todo_list, new_entry)                         clause
  end

  ...
end
```

The interface function sends the new entry data to the server. This message will be handled in the corresponding clause of `process_message/2`. Here, you delegate to the `TodoList.add_entry/2` function and return the modified `TodoList` instance. This returned instance is used as the new server's state.

Using a similar approach, you can implement the `entries` request, keeping in mind that you need to wait for the response message. The code is shown in the next listing.

Listing 5.12 The `entries` request (todo_server.ex)

```
defmodule TodoServer do
  ...

  def entries(todo_server, date) do
    send(todo_server, {:entries, self(), date})

    receive do
      {:todo_entries, entries} -> entries
    after
      5000 -> {:error, :timeout}
    end
  end

  ...

  defp process_message(todo_list, {:entries, caller, date}) do
    send(caller, {:todo_entries, TodoList.entries(todo_list, date)})
    todo_list
  end

  ...
end
```

> **Sends the response to the caller**

> **The state remains unchanged.**

This is a synthesis of techniques you've seen previously. You send a message and wait for the response. In the corresponding `process_message/2` clause, you delegate to `TodoList`, and then you send the response and return the unchanged to-do list. This is needed because `loop/2` takes the result of `process_message/2` as the new state.

In a similar way, you can add support for other to-do list requests, such as `update_entry` and `delete_entry`. The implementation of these requests is left for you as an exercise.

CONCURRENT VS. FUNCTIONAL APPROACH

A process that maintains mutable state can be regarded as a kind of mutable data structure. But you shouldn't abuse processes to avoid using the functional approach of transforming immutable data.

The data should be modeled using pure functional abstractions, just as you did with `TodoList`. A pure functional data structure provides many benefits, such as integrity, atomicity, reusability, and testability.

A stateful process serves as a container of such a data structure. The process keeps the state alive and allows other processes in the system to interact with this data via the exposed API.

With such separation of responsibilities, building a highly concurrent system becomes straightforward. For example, if you're implementing a web server that manages multiple to-do lists, you could run one server process for each to-do list. While handling an HTTP request, you can find the corresponding to-do server and have it perform the requested operation. Each to-do list manipulation runs concurrently, thus making your server scalable and more performant. Moreover, there are no synchronization problems because each to-do list is managed in a dedicated process. Recall that a single process is always sequential, so multiple competing requests that manipulate the same to-do list are serialized and handled sequentially in the corresponding process. Don't worry if this seems vague—you'll see it in action in chapter 7.

5.3.5   *Registered processes*

For a process to cooperate with other processes, it must know their whereabouts. In BEAM, a process is identified by its corresponding PID. To make process A send messages to process B, you must bring the PID of process B to process A.

Sometimes, it can be cumbersome to keep and pass PIDs. If you know there will always be only one instance of some type of server, you can give the process a *local name* and use that name to send messages to the process. The name is called *local* because it has meaning only in the currently running BEAM instance. This distinction becomes important when you start connecting multiple BEAM instances to a distributed system, as you'll see in chapter 12.

Registering a process can be done with `Process.register(pid, name)`, where a name must be an atom. Here's a quick illustration:

```
iex(1)> Process.register(self(), :some_name)      ⟵——  Registers a process

iex(2)> send(:some_name, :msg)   ⟵——┤ Sends a message via
                                     │ a symbolic name
iex(3)> receive do                          ⟵——┐
          msg -> IO.puts("received #{msg}")     │ Verifies that the
        end                                     │ message is received

received msg
```

The following constraints apply to registered names:

- The name can only be an atom.
- A single process can have only one name.
- Two processes can't have the same name.

If these constraints aren't met, an error is raised.

For practice, try to change the to-do server to run as a registered process. The interface of the server will then be simplified because you don't need to keep and pass the server's PID.

Here's an example of how such a server can be used:

```
iex(1)> TodoServer.start()

iex(2)> TodoServer.add_entry(%{date: ~D[2023-12-19], title: "Dentist"})
iex(3)> TodoServer.add_entry(%{date: ~D[2023-12-20], title: "Shopping"})
iex(4)> TodoServer.add_entry(%{date: ~D[2023-12-19], title: "Movies"})
```

```
iex(5)> TodoServer.entries(~D[2023-12-19])
[%{date: ~D[2023-12-19], id: 3, title: "Movies"},
 %{date: ~D[2023-12-19], id: 1, title: "Dentist"}]
```

To make this work, you must register a server process under a name (e.g., :todo_ server). Then, you change all the interface functions to use the registered name when sending a message to the process. If you get stuck, the solution is provided in the registered_todo_server.ex file.

Using the registered server is much simpler because you don't have to store the server's PID and pass it to the interface functions. Instead, the interface functions internally use the registered name to send messages to the process.

Local registration plays an important role in process discovery. Registered names provide a way of communicating with a process without knowing its PID. This becomes increasingly important when you start dealing with restarting processes (as you'll see in chapters 8 and 9) and distributed systems (discussed in chapter 12).

This concludes our initial exploration of stateful processes. They play an important role in Elixir-based systems, and you'll continue using them throughout the book. Next, we'll look at some important runtime properties of BEAM processes.

5.4 Runtime considerations

You've learned a great deal about how to work with processes. Now, its time to discuss some important runtime properties of BEAM concurrency.

5.4.1 A process is sequential

It has already been mentioned, but it's very important, so I'll stress it again: a single process is a sequential program—it runs expressions in a sequence one by one. Multiple processes run concurrently, so they may run in parallel with each other. But if many processes send messages to a single process, that single process may become a bottleneck, which significantly affects overall throughput of the system.

Let's look at an example. The code in the following listing implements a slow echo server.

Listing 5.13 Demonstration of a process bottleneck (process_bottleneck.ex)

```
defmodule Server do
  def start do
    spawn(fn -> loop() end)
  end

  def send_msg(server, message) do
    send(server, {self(), message})

    receive do
      {:response, response} -> response
    end
  end
```

```
defp loop do
  receive do
    {caller, msg} ->                      ┐  Simulates long processing
      Process.sleep(1000)    ◁────────────┘
      send(caller, {:response, msg}) ◁─┐
  end                                  └── Echoes the message back

  loop()
end
end
```

Upon receiving a message, the server sends the message back to the caller. Before that, it sleeps for a second to simulate a long-running request.

To test its behavior in a concurrent setting, start the server and fire up five concurrent clients:

```
iex(1)> server = Server.start()

iex(2)> Enum.each(
          1..5,
          fn i ->                            ┐  Spawns a concurrent client
            spawn(fn ->        ◁─────────────┘
              IO.puts("Sending msg ##{i}")
              response = Server.send_msg(server, i)  ◁─┐ Synchronous request
              IO.puts("Response: #{response}")          │ to the server
            end)
          end
        )
```

As soon as you start this, you'll see the following lines printed:

```
Sending msg #1
Sending msg #2
Sending msg #3
Sending msg #4
Sending msg #5
```

So far, so good. Five processes have been started and are running concurrently. But now, the problems begin—the responses come back slowly, one by one, a second apart:

```
                   ┐  One second later
Response: 1  ◁─────┘   ┐  Two seconds later
Response: 2  ◁─────────┘
Response: 3  ◁─────────  Three seconds later
Response: 4  ◁─────────┐
Response: 5  ◁─────────┘  Four seconds later
                       ┘
                   Five seconds later
```

What happened? The echo server can handle only one message per second. Because all other processes depend on the echo server, they're constrained by its throughput.

What can you do about this? Once you identify the bottleneck, you should try to optimize the process internally. Generally, a server process has a simple flow. It receives and handles messages one by one. So the goal is to make the server handle messages at least as fast as they arrive. In this example, server optimization amounts to removing the `Process.sleep/1` call.

If you can't make message handling fast enough, you can try to split the server into multiple processes, effectively parallelizing the original work and hoping that doing so will boost performance on a multicore system. This should be your last resort, though. Parallelization isn't a remedy for a poorly structured algorithm.

5.4.2 *Unlimited process mailboxes*

Theoretically, a process mailbox has unlimited size. In practice, though, the mailbox size is limited by available memory. Thus, if a process constantly falls behind, meaning messages arrive faster than the process can handle them, the mailbox will constantly grow and increasingly consume memory. Ultimately, a single slow process may cause an entire system to crash by consuming all the available memory.

A more subtle version of the same problem occurs if a process doesn't handle some messages at all. Consider the following server loop:

```
defp loop
  receive do
    {:message, msg} -> do_something(msg)
  end

  loop()
end
```

A server powered by this loop only handles messages in the following form: {`:message`, `something`}. All other messages remain in the process mailbox forever, taking up memory space for no reason.

Overgrown mailbox contents can significantly affect performance. It puts extra pressure on the garbage collector and can lead to slow pattern matches in `receive`.

To avoid this, you should introduce a *match-all* receive clause that deals with unexpected kinds of messages. Typically, you'll emit a warning that a process has received the unknown message and do nothing else about it:

```
defp loop
  receive
    {:message, msg} -> do_something(msg)
    other -> warn_about_unknown_message(other)    ⟵——— Match-all clause
  end

  loop()
end
```

Since the process handles every kind of message, the uncontrolled growth of its mailbox is less likely to happen.

It's also worth noting that BEAM gives you tools for analyzing processes at run time. In particular, you can query each process for its mailbox size and, thus, detect those for which the mailbox-queue buildup occurs. We'll discuss this feature in chapter 13.

5.4.3   *Shared-nothing concurrency*

As already mentioned, processes share no memory. Thus, sending a message to another process results in a deep copy of the message contents:

```
send(target_pid, data)      ⊲────  The contents of data are deep copied.
```

Less obviously, a variable closure in a spawned element also results in deep copying the closed variable:

```
data = ...

spawn(fn ->
  ...
  some_fun(data)      ⊲────  Results in a deep copy of the data variable
  ...
end)
```

This is something you should be aware of when moving code into a separate process. Deep copying is an in-memory operation, so it should be reasonably fast, and occasionally sending a big message shouldn't present a problem. But having many processes frequently send big messages may affect system performance. The notion of "small" versus "big" is subjective. Simple data, such as a number, an atom, or a tuple with few elements, is obviously small. On the other hand, a list of a million complex structures is big. The border lies somewhere in between and depends on your specific case.

There are a couple of special cases in which the data is copied by reference. This happens with binaries (including strings) larger than 64 bytes, hardcoded constants (also known as *literals*), and terms created via the `:persistent_term` API (https://www.erlang .org/doc/man/persistent_term.html).

Shared-nothing concurrency ensures complete isolation between processes: one process can't compromise the internal state of another. This promotes the integrity and fault tolerance of the system.

In addition, because processes share no memory, garbage collection can take place on a process level. Each process gets an initial small chunk of heap memory (~2 KB on 64-bit BEAM). When more memory is needed, garbage collection for that process takes place. As a result, garbage collection is concurrent and distributed. Instead of one large "stop-the-entire-system" collection, you end up running many smaller, typically faster, collections. This prevents unwanted long, complete blockages and keeps the entire system more responsive.

5.4.4   *Scheduler inner workings*

Generally, you can assume there are *n* schedulers that run *m* processes, with *m* most often being significantly larger than *n*. This is called *m:n* threading, and it reflects the fact that you run a large number of logical microthreads using a smaller number of OS threads, as illustrated in figure 5.3.

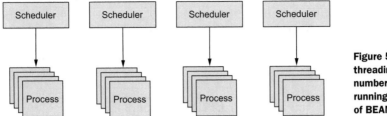

Figure 5.3 *m:n* threading: A small number of schedulers running a large number of BEAM processes

Each BEAM scheduler is an OS thread that manages the execution of BEAM processes. By default, BEAM uses only as many schedulers as there are logical processors available. You can change these settings via various Erlang emulator flags.

To provide Erlang flags, you can use the following syntax:

```
$ iex --erl "put Erlang emulator flags here"
```

A list of all Erlang flags can be found at https://erlang.org/doc/man/erl.html.

For example, to use only one scheduler thread, you can provide the +S 1 Erlang flag:

```
$ iex --erl "+S 1"
Erlang/OTP 26 [erts-14.0] [source] [64-bit] [smp:1:1] [ds:1:1:10]
```

Notice the smp:1:1 part in the output. This informs us that only one scheduler thread is used. You can also check the number of schedulers programmatically:

```
iex(1)> System.schedulers()
1
```

If you're running other external services on the system, you could consider reducing the number of BEAM scheduler threads. Doing this will leave more computational resources for non-BEAM services.

Internally, each scheduler picks one process, runs it for a while, and then picks another process. While in the scheduler, the process gets a small execution window of approximately 2,000 function calls, after which it's preempted. It's also worth mentioning that in some cases, long-running CPU-bound work or a larger garbage collection might be performed on another thread (called a *dirty scheduler*).

If a process is doing a network IO or waiting for a message, it yields the execution to the scheduler. The same thing happens when Process.sleep is invoked. As a result, you don't have to care about the nature of the work performed in a process. If you want to separate the execution of one function from the rest of the code, you just need to run that function in a separate process, regardless of whether the work is CPU or IO bound.

As a consequence of all of this, context switching is performed frequently. Typically, a single process is in the scheduler for less than one millisecond. This promotes the responsiveness of BEAM-powered systems. If one process performs a long CPU-bound operation, such as computing the value of pi to a billion decimals, it won't block the entire scheduler, and other processes shouldn't be affected.

This can easily be proven. Start an `iex` session with just one scheduler thread:

```
$ iex --erl "+S 1"
```

Spawn a process that runs an infinite CPU-bound loop:

```
iex(1)> spawn(fn ->
         Stream.repeatedly(fn -> :rand.uniform() end)
         |> Stream.run()
       end)
```

This code uses `Stream.repeatedly/1` to create a lazy infinite stream of random numbers. The stream is executed using `Stream.run/1` function, which will effectively run an infinite CPU-bound loop. To avoid blocking the `iex` shell session, the work is done in a separate process.

As soon as you start this computation, you should notice the CPU usage going to 100%, which proves you're now running an intensive, long-running CPU-bound work.

Still, even though BEAM is using only one scheduler thread, the `iex` session is responsive, and you can evaluate other expressions. For example, let's sum the first 1,000,000,000 integers:

```
iex(2)> Enum.sum(1..1_000_000_000)
500000000500000000
```

We were able to run another job on an already busy scheduler thread, and that job finished almost immediately. This is the consequence of frequent context switching, which ensures that an occasional long-running job won't significantly affect the responsiveness of the entire system.

Summary

- A BEAM process is a lightweight concurrent unit of execution. Processes are completely isolated and share no memory.
- Processes can communicate with asynchronous messages. Synchronous sends and responses are manually built on top of this basic mechanism.
- A server process is a process that runs for a long time (possibly forever) and handles various messages. Server processes are powered by endless recursion.
- Server processes can maintain their own private state, using the arguments of endless recursion.

Generic server processes

6

This chapter covers

- Building a generic server process
- Using `GenServer`

In chapter 5, you became familiar with basic concurrency techniques: you learned how to create processes and communicate with them. I also explained the idea behind stateful server processes—long-running processes that react to messages and maintain state.

Server processes play an important role and are used frequently when building highly concurrent systems in Elixir and Erlang, so we'll spend some time exploring them in detail. In this chapter, you'll learn how to reduce some of the boilerplate associated with server processes, such as infinite recursion, state management, and message passing.

Erlang provides a helper module for implementing server processes—it's part of the Open Telecom Platform (OTP) framework. Despite its misleading name, the framework has nothing to do with telecoms; rather, it provides patterns and abstractions for tasks such as creating components, building releases, developing server processes, handling and recovering from runtime errors, logging, event handling, and upgrading code.

You'll learn about various parts of OTP throughout this book, but in this chapter, we'll focus on one of its most important parts: GenServer, the module that simplifies the implementation of server processes. Before we look at GenServer, though, you'll implement a simplified version of it, based on the message-passing primitives you saw in chapter 5.

6.1 Building a generic server process

You saw a few examples of server processes in chapter 5. Although those processes serve different purposes, there are some commonalities in their implementations. In particular, all code that implements a server process needs to do the following:

- Spawn a separate process
- Run an infinite loop in the process
- Maintain the process state
- React to messages
- Send a response back to the caller

No matter what kind of server process you run, you'll always need to do these tasks, so it's worth moving this code to a single place. Concrete implementations can then reuse this code and focus on their specific needs. Let's look at how you can implement such generic code.

6.1.1 Plugging in with modules

The generic code will perform various tasks common to server processes, leaving the specific decisions to concrete implementations. For example, the generic code will spawn a process, but the concrete implementation must determine the initial state. Similarly, the generic code will run the loop; receive messages; and, optionally, send the responses, but the concrete implementation must decide how each message is handled and what the response is.

In other words, the generic code drives the entire process, and the specific implementation must fill in the missing pieces. Therefore, you need a plug-in mechanism that lets the generic code call into the concrete implementation when a specific decision needs to be made.

The simplest way to do this is to use modules. Remember that a module name is an atom. You can store that atom in a variable and use the variable later to invoke functions on the module:

```
iex(1)> some_module = IO     ◁──┐  Stores a module
                                 │  atom in a variable

iex(2)> some_module.puts("Hello")   ◁────── Dynamic invocation
Hello
```

You can use this feature to provide callback hooks from the generic code. In particular, you can take the following approach:

1 Make the generic code accept a plug-in module as the argument. That module is called a *callback module*.

2 Maintain the module atom as part of the process state.

3 Invoke callback-module functions when needed.

Obviously, for this to work, a callback module must implement and export a well-defined set of functions, which I'll gradually introduce as we implement the generic code.

6.1.2 Implementing the generic code

Let's start building a generic server process. First, you need to start the process and initialize its state.

Listing 6.1 Starting the server process (server_process.ex)

```
defmodule ServerProcess do
  def start(callback_module) do
    spawn(fn ->
      initial_state = callback_module.init()      <──┐ Invokes the callback
      loop(callback_module, initial_state)            to initialize the state
    end)
  end

  ...
end
```

`ServerProcess.start/1` takes a module atom as the argument and then spawns the process. In the spawned process, the callback function `init/0` is invoked to create the initial state. Obviously, for this to work, the callback module must export the `init/0` function.

Finally, you enter the loop that will power the server process and maintain this state. The return value of `ServerProcess.start/1` is a `pid`, which can be used to send messages to the request process.

Next, you need to implement the loop code that powers the process, waits for messages, and handles them. In this example, you'll implement a synchronous send-and-respond communication pattern. The server process must receive a message, handle it, send the response message back to the caller, and change the process state.

The generic code is responsible for receiving and sending messages, whereas the specific implementation must handle the message and return the response and the new state. The idea is illustrated in the following listing.

Listing 6.2 Handling messages in the server process (server_process.ex)

```
defmodule ServerProcess do
  ...

  defp loop(callback_module, current_state) do
```

```
      receive do
        {request, caller} ->
          {response, new_state} =
            callback_module.handle_call(
              request,                      Invokes the callback to
              current_state                 handle the message
            )

          send(caller, {:response, response})   ◁──── Sends the response back

          loop(callback_module, new_state)   ◁──── Loops with the new state
      end
    end

    ...
end
```

Here, you expect a message in the form of a {request, caller} tuple. The request is data that identifies the request and is meaningful to the specific implementation. The callback function handle_call/2 takes the request payload and the current state, and it must return a {response, new_state} tuple. The generic code can then send the response back to the caller and continue looping with the new state. There's only one thing left to do: provide a function to issue requests to the server process.

Listing 6.3   Helper for issuing requests (server_process.ex)

```
defmodule ServerProcess do
  ...

  def call(server_pid, request) do
    send(server_pid, {request, self()})   ◁──── Sends the message

    receive do
      {:response, response} ->      ◁──── Waits for the response
        response          ◁────┐
    end                         │ Returns the response
  end
end
```

At this point, you have the abstraction for the generic server process in place. Let's see how it can be used.

6.1.3 *Using the generic abstraction*

To test the server process, you'll implement a simple key–value store. It will be a process that can be used to store mappings between arbitrary terms.

Remember that the callback module must implement two functions: init/0, which creates the initial state, and handle_call/2, which handles specific requests.

Listing 6.4 Key–value store implementation (server_process.ex)

```
defmodule KeyValueStore do
  def init do
    %{}        ⟵─── Initial process state
  end

  def handle_call({:put, key, value}, state) do    Handles the
    {:ok, Map.put(state, key, value)}              put request
  end

  def handle_call({:get, key}, state) do    Handles the
    {Map.get(state, key), state}            get request
  end
end
```

That's all it takes to create a specific server process. Because the infinite loop and
message-passing boilerplate are pushed to the generic code, the specific implementation is more concise and focused on its main task.

Take particular note of how you use a multiclause in `handle_call/2` to handle different types of requests. This is the place where the specific implementation decides
how to handle each request. The `ServerProcess` module is generic code that blindly
forward requests from client processes to the callback module.

Let's test the process:

```
iex(1)> pid = ServerProcess.start(KeyValueStore)

iex(2)> ServerProcess.call(pid, {:put, :some_key, :some_value})
:ok

iex(3)> ServerProcess.call(pid, {:get, :some_key})
:some_value
```

Notice how you start the process with `ServerProcess.start(KeyValueStore)`. This is
where you plug the specific `KeyValueStore` into the generic code of `ServerProcess`. All
subsequent invocations of `ServerProcess.call/2` will send messages to that process,
which will, in turn, call `KeyValueStore.handle_call/2` to perform the handling.

It's beneficial to make clients completely oblivious to the fact that the `ServerProcess`
abstraction is used. This can be achieved by introducing helper functions.

Listing 6.5 Wrapping `ServerProcess` function calls (server_process.ex)

```
defmodule KeyValueStore do
  def start do
    ServerProcess.start(KeyValueStore)
  end

  def put(pid, key, value) do
    ServerProcess.call(pid, {:put, key, value})
```

```
    end

    def get(pid, key) do
      ServerProcess.call(pid, {:get, key})
    end

    ...
end
```

Clients can now use start/0, put/3, and get/2 to manipulate the key–value store. These functions are informally called *interface functions*. Clients use the interface functions of KeyValueStore to start and interact with the process.

In contrast, init/0 and handle_call/2 are callback functions used internally by the generic code. Note that interface functions run in client processes, whereas callback functions are always invoked in the server process.

6.1.4 *Supporting asynchronous requests*

The current implementation of ServerProcess supports only synchronous requests. Let's expand on this and introduce support for asynchronous fire-and-forget requests, in which a client sends a message and doesn't wait for a response.

In the current code, we use the term *call* for synchronous requests. For asynchronous requests, we'll use the term *cast*. This is the naming convention used in OTP, so it's good to adopt it.

Because you're introducing the second request type, you need to change the format of messages passed between client processes and the server. This will allow you to determine the request type in the server process and handle different types of requests in different ways.

This can be as simple as including the request-type information in the tuple being passed from the client process to the server.

> **Listing 6.6   Including the request type in the message (server_process_cast.ex)**

```
defmodule ServerProcess do
  ...

  def call(server_pid, request) do
    send(server_pid, {:call, request, self()})    <──┐ Tags the request
    ...                                                │ message as a call
  end

  defp loop(callback_module, current_state) do
    receive do
      {:call, request, caller} ->     <──── Handles a call request
        ...
    end
  end

  ...
end
```

Now, you can introduce support for `cast` requests. In this scenario, when the message arrives, the specific implementation handles it and returns the new state. No response is sent back to the caller, so the callback function must return only the new state.

Listing 6.7 Supporting casts in the server process (server_process_cast.ex)

```elixir
defmodule ServerProcess do
  ...

  def cast(server_pid, request) do          Issues a cast
    send(server_pid, {:cast, request})       message
  end

  defp loop(callback_module, current_state) do
    receive do
      {:call, request, caller} ->
        ...

      {:cast, request} ->       <──── Handles a cast message
        new_state =
          callback_module.handle_cast(
            request,
            current_state
          )

        loop(callback_module, new_state)
    end
  end

  ...
end
```

To handle a cast request, you need the callback function `handle_cast/2`. This function must handle the message and return the new state. In the server loop, you then invoke this function and loop with the new state. That's all it takes to support cast requests.

Finally, you'll change the implementation of the key–value store to use casts. Keep in mind that a cast is a fire-and-forget type of request, so it's not suitable for all requests. In this example, the `get` request must be a call because the server process needs to respond with the value associated with a given key. In contrast, the `put` request can be implemented as a cast because the client doesn't need to wait for the response.

Listing 6.8 Implementing `put` as a cast (server_process_cast.ex)

```elixir
defmodule KeyValueStore do
  ...

  def put(pid, key, value) do               Issues the put
    ServerProcess.cast(pid, {:put, key, value})   <──┘ request as a cast
```

```
      end

      ...

      def handle_cast({:put, key, value}, state) do      ◁—— Handles the put request
        Map.put(state, key, value)
      end

      ...
    end
```

Now, you can try the server process:

```
iex(1)> pid = KeyValueStore.start()

iex(2)> KeyValueStore.put(pid, :some_key, :some_value)

iex(3)> KeyValueStore.get(pid, :some_key)
:some_value
```

With a simple change in the generic implementation, you added another feature to the service process. Specific implementations can now decide whether each concrete request should be implemented as a call or a cast.

6.1.5   *Exercise: Refactoring the to-do server*

An important benefit of the generic `ServerProcess` abstraction is that it lets you easily create various kinds of processes that rely on this common code. For example, in chapter 5, you developed a simple to-do server that maintains a to-do list abstraction in its internal state. This server can also be powered by the generic `ServerProcess`.

   This is the perfect opportunity for you to practice a bit. Take the complete code from todo_server.ex from the chapter 5 source, and save it to a different file. Then, add the last version of the `ServerProcess` module to the same file. Finally, adapt the code of the `TodoServer` module to work with `ServerProcess`.

   Once you have everything working, compare the code between the two versions. The new version of `TodoServer` should be smaller and simpler, even for such a simple server process that supports only two different requests. If you get stuck, you can find the solution in the server_process_todo.ex file.

> **NOTE**   It's clumsy to place multiple modules in a single file and maintain multiple copies of the `ServerProcess` code in different files. In chapter 7, you'll start using a better approach to code organization powered by the `mix` tool. But for the moment, let's stick with our current, overly simple approach.

You're now finished implementing a basic abstraction for generic server processes. The current implementation is simple and leaves a lot of room for improvement, but it demonstrates the basic technique of generic server processes. Now, it's time to use the full-blown OTP abstraction for generic server processes: `GenServer`.

6.2   *Using GenServer*

When it comes to production-ready code, it doesn't make much sense to build and use the manually baked `ServerProcess` abstraction. That's because Elixir ships with a much better support for generic server processes, called `GenServer`. In addition to being much more feature rich than `ServerProcess`, `GenServer` also handles several edge cases and is battle tested in production in complex concurrent systems.

Some of the compelling features provided by `GenServer` include the following:

- Support for calls and casts
- Customizable timeouts for call requests
- Propagation of server process crashes to client processes waiting for a response
- Support for distributed systems

Note that there's no special magic behind `GenServer`. Its code relies on concurrency primitives explained in chapter 5 and fault-tolerance features explained in chapter 9. After all, `GenServer` is implemented in plain Erlang and Elixir. The heavy lifting is done in the `:gen_server` module, which is included in the Erlang standard library. Some additional wrapping is performed in the Elixir standard library, in the `GenServer` module.

In this section, you'll learn how to build your server processes with `GenServer`. But first, let's examine the concept of OTP *behaviours*.

> **NOTE**   Note the British spelling of the word *behaviour*: this is the preferred spelling both in OTP code and official documentation. This book uses the British spelling to specifically denote an OTP behaviour but retains the American spelling (*behavior*) for all other purposes.

6.2.1   *OTP behaviours*

In Erlang terminology, a *behaviour* is generic code that implements a common pattern. The generic logic is exposed through the behaviour module, and you can plug into it by implementing a corresponding callback module. The callback module must satisfy a contract defined by the behaviour, meaning it must implement and export a set of functions. The behaviour module then calls into these functions, allowing you to provide your own specialization of the generic code.

This is exactly what `ServerProcess` does. It powers a generic server process, requiring specific implementations to provide the callback module that implements the `init/0`, `handle_call/2`, and `handle_cast/2` functions. `ServerProcess` is a simple example of a behaviour.

It's even possible to specify the behaviour contract and verify that the callback module implements required functions during compilation. For details, see the official documentation (https://hexdocs.pm/elixir/Module.html#module-behaviour).

The Erlang standard library includes the following OTP behaviours:

- `gen_server`—Generic implementation of a stateful server process
- `supervisor`—Provides error handling and recovery in concurrent systems
- `application`—Generic implementation of components and libraries

- gen_event—Provides event-handling support
- gen_statem—Runs a finite state machine in a stateful server process

Elixir provides its own wrappers for the most frequently used behaviours via the modules GenServer, Supervisor, and Application. This book focuses on these behaviours. The GenServer behaviour receives detailed treatment in this chapter and chapter 7, Supervisor is discussed in chapters 8 and 9, and Application is presented in chapter 11.

The remaining behaviours, although useful, are used less often and won't be discussed in this book. Once you get a grip on GenServer and Supervisor, you should be able to research other behaviours on your own and use them when the need arises. You can find more about gen_event and gen_statem in the Erlang documentation (https://erlang.org/doc/design_principles/des_princ.html).

6.2.2   *Plugging into GenServer*

Using GenServer is roughly similar to using ServerProcess. There are some differences in the format of the returned values, but the basic idea is the same.

The GenServer behaviour defines eight callback functions, but frequently, you'll need only a subset of those. You can get some sensible default implementations of all required callback functions if you use the GenServer module:

```
iex(1)> defmodule KeyValueStore do
          use GenServer
        end
```

The use macro is a language feature we haven't previously discussed. During compilation, when this instruction is encountered, the specific macro from the GenServer module is invoked. That macro then injects several functions into the calling module (KeyValueStore, in this case). You can verify this in the shell:

```
iex(2)> KeyValueStore.__info__(:functions)
[child_spec: 1, code_change: 3, handle_call: 3, handle_cast: 2,
 handle_info: 2, init: 1, terminate: 2]
```

Here you use the __info__/1 function that's automatically added to each Elixir module during compilation. It lists all exported functions of a module (except __info__/1).

As you can see in the output, many functions are automatically included in the module due to use GenServer. These are all callback functions that need to be implemented for you to plug into the GenServer behaviour.

Of course, you can then override the default implementation of each function, as required. If you define a function of the same name and arity in your module, it will overwrite the default implementation you get through use.

At this point, you can plug your callback module into the behaviour. To start the process, use the GenServer.start/2 function:

```
iex(3)> GenServer.start(KeyValueStore, nil)
{:ok, #PID<0.51.0>}
```

This works roughly like `ServerProcess`. The server process is started, and the behaviour uses `KeyValueStore` as the callback module. The second argument of `GenServer.start/2` is a custom parameter that's passed to the process during its initialization. For the moment, you don't need this, so you send the `nil` value. Finally, notice that the result of `GenServer.start/2` is a tuple of the form {`:ok`, `pid`}.

6.2.3   Handling requests

Now you can convert the `KeyValueStore` to work with `GenServer`. To do this, you need to implement three callbacks: `init/1`, `handle_cast/2`, and `handle_call/3`.

Listing 6.9   Implementing `GenServer` callbacks (key_value_gen_server.ex)

```
defmodule KeyValueStore do
  use GenServer

  def init(_) do
    {:ok, %{}}
  end

  def handle_cast({:put, key, value}, state) do
    {:noreply, Map.put(state, key, value)}
  end

  def handle_call({:get, key}, _, state) do
    {:reply, Map.get(state, key), state}
  end
end
```

These callbacks work similarly to the ones in `ServerProcess`, with a couple of differences:

- `init/1` accepts one argument. This is the second argument provided to `GenServer.start/2`, and you can use it to pass data to the server process while starting it.
- The result of `init/1` must be in the format {`:ok`, `initial_state`}.
- `handle_cast/2` accepts the request and the state and should return the result in the format {`:noreply`, `new_state`}.
- `handle_call/3` takes the request, caller information, and state. It should return the result in the following format {`:reply`, `response`, `new_state`}.

The second argument to `handle_call/3` is a tuple that contains the request ID (used internally by the `GenServer` behaviour) and the PID of the caller. This information is, in most cases, not needed, so in this example, you ignore it.

   With these callbacks in place, the only things missing are interface functions. To interact with a `GenServer` process, you can use functions from the `GenServer` module. In particular, you can use `GenServer.start/2` to start the process and `GenServer.cast/2` and `GenServer.call/2` to issue requests. The code is shown in the next listing.

Listing 6.10   Adding interface functions (key_value_gen_server.ex)

```
defmodule KeyValueStore do
  use GenServer

  def start do
    GenServer.start(KeyValueStore, nil)
  end

  def put(pid, key, value) do
    GenServer.cast(pid, {:put, key, value})
  end

  def get(pid, key) do
    GenServer.call(pid, {:get, key})
  end

  ...
end
```

That's it! With only a few changes, you've moved from a basic `ServerProcess` to a full-blown `GenServer`. Let's test the server:

```
iex(1)> {:ok, pid} = KeyValueStore.start()

iex(2)> KeyValueStore.put(pid, :some_key, :some_value)

iex(3)> KeyValueStore.get(pid, :some_key)
:some_value
```

It works as expected.

There are many differences between `ServerProcess` and `GenServer`, but a couple of points deserve special mention.

First, `GenServer.start/2` returns only after the `init/1` callback has finished in the server process. Consequently, the client process that starts the server is blocked until the server process is initialized.

Second, `GenServer.call/2` doesn't wait indefinitely for a response. By default, if the response message doesn't arrive in 5 seconds, an error is raised in the client process. You can alter this by using `GenServer.call(pid, request, timeout)`, where the timeout is given in milliseconds. In addition, if the receiver process happens to terminate while you're waiting for the response, `GenServer` detects it and raises a corresponding error in the caller process.

6.2.4   *Handling plain messages*

Messages sent to the server process via `GenServer.call` and `GenServer.cast` contain more than just a request payload. Those functions include additional data in the message sent to the server process. This is something you did in the `ServerProcess` example in section 6.1:

```
defmodule ServerProcess do
  ...

  def call(server_pid, request) do
    send(server_pid, {:call, request, self()})    ◁────── Calls a message
    ...
  end

  def cast(server_pid, request) do
    send(server_pid, {:cast, request})    ◁────── Casts a message
  end

  ...

  defp loop(callback_module, current_state) do
    receive do
      {:call, request, caller} ->    ◁────── Special handling of a call message
        ...

      {:cast, request} ->    ◁────── Special handling of a cast message
        ...
    end
  end
  ...
end
```

Notice that you don't send the plain `request` payload to the server process; you include additional data, such as the request type and the caller, for call requests.

`GenServer` uses a similar approach, using `:"$gen_cast"` and `:"$gen_call"` atoms to decorate cast and call messages. You don't need to worry about the exact format of those messages, but it's important to understand that `GenServer` internally uses particular message formats and handles those messages in a specific way.

Occasionally, you may need to handle messages that aren't specific to `GenServer`. For example, imagine you need to do a periodic cleanup of the server process state. You can use the Erlang function `:timer.send_interval/2`, which periodically sends a message to the caller process. Because this message isn't a `GenServer`-specific message, it's not treated as a cast or call. Instead, for such plain messages, `GenServer` calls the `handle_info/2` callback, giving you a chance to do something with the message.

Here's a sketch of this technique:

```
iex(1)> defmodule KeyValueStore do
          use GenServer

          def init(_) do
            :timer.send_interval(5000, :cleanup)    ◁─┐ Sets up periodic
            {:ok, %{}}                                 │ message sending
          end

          def handle_info(:cleanup, state) do    ◁─┐ Handles the plain
            IO.puts "performing cleanup..."         │ :cleanup message
            {:noreply, state}
```

```
            end
          end

iex(2)> GenServer.start(KeyValueStore, nil)

performing cleanup...    ←—— Printed every 5 seconds
performing cleanup...
performing cleanup...
```

During process initialization, you ensure a `:cleanup message` is sent to the process every 5 seconds. This message is handled in the `handle_info/2` callback, which essentially works like `handle_cast/2`, returning the result as `{:noreply, new_state}`.

6.2.5   *Other GenServer features*

There are several other features and subtleties I haven't mentioned in this basic introduction to `GenServer`. You'll learn about some of them elsewhere in this book, but you should definitely take the time to look over the documentation for the `GenServer` module (https://hexdocs.pm/elixir/GenServer.html) and its Erlang foundation (https://erlang .org/doc/man/gen_server.html). A couple of points still deserve special mention.

COMPILE-TIME CHECKING

One problem with the callback mechanism is that it's easy to make a subtle mistake when defining a callback function. Consider the following example:

```
iex(1)> defmodule EchoServer do
          use GenServer

          def handle_call(some_request, server_state) do
            {:reply, some_request, server_state}
          end
        end
```

Here, you have a simple echo server, which handles every call request by sending the request back to the client. Try it out:

```
iex(2)> {:ok, pid} = GenServer.start(EchoServer, nil)
{:ok, #PID<0.96.0>}

iex(3)> GenServer.call(pid, :some_call)
** (exit) exited in: GenServer.call(#PID<0.96.0>, :some_call, 5000)
    ** (EXIT) an exception was raised:
        ** (RuntimeError) attempted to call GenServer #PID<0.96.0> but
                          no handle_call/3 clause was provided
```

Issuing a call caused the server to crash with an error that no `handle_call/3` clause is provided, although the clause is listed in the module. What happened? If you look closely at the definition of `EchoServer`, you'll see that you defined `handle_call/2`, while `GenServer` requires `handle_call/3`.

You can get a compile-time warning here if you tell the compiler that the function being defined is supposed to satisfy a contract by some behaviour. To do this, you need to provide the @impl module attribute immediately before the first clause of the call-back function:

```
iex(1)> defmodule EchoServer do
      use GenServer
                                    Indicates an upcoming definition
                                    of a callback function
      @impl GenServer    ◁─────┘
      def handle_call(some_request, server_state) do
        {:reply, some_request, server_state}
      end
    end
```

The @impl GenServer tells the compiler that the function about to be defined is a call-back function for the GenServer behaviour. As soon as you execute this expression in the shell, you'll get a warning:

```
warning: got "@impl GenServer" for function handle_call/2 but this
behaviour does not specify such callback.
```

The compiler tells you that GenServer doesn't deal with handle_call/2, so you already get a hint that something is wrong during compilation. It's a good practice to always specify the @impl attribute for every callback function you define in your modules.

NAME REGISTRATION

Recall from chapter 5 that a process can be registered under a local name (an atom), where *local* means the name is registered only in the currently running BEAM instance. This allows you to create a singleton process you can access by name without needing to know its PID.

Local registration is an important feature because it supports patterns of fault tolerance and distributed systems. You'll see exactly how this works in later chapters, but it's worth mentioning that you can provide the process name as an option to GenServer.start:

```
GenServer.start(
  CallbackModule,
  init_param,
  name: :some_name    ◁─────── Registers the process under a name
)
```

You can then issue calls and casts using the name:

```
GenServer.call(:some_name, ...)
GenServer.cast(:some_name, ...)
```

The most frequent approach is to use the same name as the module name. As explained in section 2.4.2, module names are atoms, so you can safely pass them as the :name option. Here's a sketch of this approach:

```
defmodule KeyValueStore do
  def start() do
    GenServer.start(KeyValueStore, nil, name: KeyValueStore)    ◁─┐  Registers the
  end                                                              │  server process

  def put(key, value) do                                          │  Sends a request to the
    GenServer.cast(KeyValueStore, {:put, key, value})    ◁─┐      │  registered process
  end

  ...
end
```

Notice how KeyValueStore.put now doesn't need to take the PID. It will simply issue a request to the registered process.

You can also replace KeyValueStore with the special form __MODULE__. During compilation, __MODULE__ is replaced with the name of the module where the code resides:

```
defmodule KeyValueStore do
  def start() do
    GenServer.start(__MODULE__, nil, name: __MODULE__)    ◁─┐  Registers the
  end                                                         │  server process

  def put(key, value) do                                      Sends a request to the
    GenServer.cast(__MODULE__, {:put, key, value})    ◁─┐     registered process
  end

  ...
end
```

After compilation, this code is equivalent to the previous version, but some future refactoring is made easier. If, for example, you rename KeyValueStore as KeyValue.Store, you only need to do it in one place in the module.

STOPPING THE SERVER

Different callbacks can return various types of responses. So far, you've seen the most common cases:

- {:ok, initial_state} from init/1
- {:reply, response, new_state} from handle_call/3
- {:noreply, new_state} from handle_cast/2 and handle_info/2

There are additional possibilities, with the most important being the option to stop the server process.

In init/1, you can decide against starting the server. In this case, you can either return {:stop, reason} or :ignore. In both cases, the server won't proceed with the loop and will instead terminate.

If init/1 returns {:stop, reason}, the result of start/2 will be {:error, reason}. In contrast, if init/1 returns :ignore, the result of start/2 will also be :ignore. The difference between these two return values is their intention. You should opt for {:stop, reason} when you can't proceed further due to some error. In contrast, :ignore should be used when stopping the server is the normal course of action.

Returning {:stop, reason, new_state} from handle_* callbacks causes GenServer to stop the server process. If the termination is part of the standard workflow, you should use the atom :normal as the stoppage reason. If you're in handle_call/3 and also need to respond to the caller before terminating, you can return {:stop, reason, response, new_state}.

You may wonder why you need to return a new state if you're terminating the process. This is because just before the termination, GenServer calls the callback function terminate/2, sending it the termination reason and the final state of the process. This can be useful if you need to perform cleanup.

Finally, you can also stop the server process by invoking GenServer.stop/3 from the client process. This invocation will issue a synchronous request to the server. The behaviour will handle the stop request itself by stopping the server process.

6.2.6   *Process life cycle*

It's important to always be aware of how GenServer-powered processes tick and where (in which process) various functions are executed. Let's do a quick recap by looking at figure 6.1, which shows the life cycle of a typical server process.

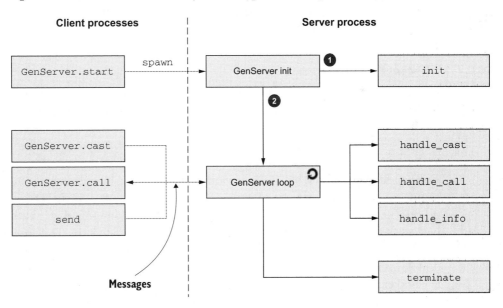

Figure 6.1   **Life cycle of a** GenServer**-powered process**

A client process starts the server by calling GenServer.start and providing the callback module (**1**). This creates the new server process, which is powered by the GenServer behaviour.

Requests can be issued by client processes using various `GenServer` functions or plain `send`. When a message is received, `GenServer` invokes callback functions to handle it. Therefore, callback functions are always executed in the server process.

The process state is maintained in the `GenServer` loop but is defined and manipulated by the callback functions. It starts with `init/1`, which defines the initial state that's then passed to subsequent `handle_*` callbacks (**2**). Each of these callbacks receives the current state and must return its new version, which is used by the `GenServer` loop in place of the old one.

The actor model

Erlang is an accidental implementation of the *actor model*, originally described by Carl Hewitt. An actor is a concurrent computational entity that encapsulates state and can communicate with other actors. When processing a single message, an actor can designate the new state that will be used when processing the next message. This is roughly similar to how `GenServer`-based processes work in Erlang. Note, though, that as Robert Virding (one of Erlang's co-inventors) has repeatedly stated, Erlang developers arrived at this idea on their own and learned about the existence of the actor model much later.

There are some disagreements about whether Erlang is a proper implementation of the actor model, and the term *actor* isn't used much in the Erlang community. This book doesn't use this terminology either. Still, it's worth keeping in mind that in the context of Erlang, an actor corresponds to a server process—most frequently, a `GenServer`.

6.2.7 *OTP-compliant processes*

For various reasons, once you start building production systems, you should avoid using plain processes started with `spawn`. Instead, all of your processes should be so-called *OTP-compliant processes*. Such processes adhere to OTP conventions; they can be used in supervision trees (described in chapter 9); and errors in those processes are logged with more details.

All processes powered by OTP behaviours, such as `GenServer` and `Supervisor`, are OTP-compliant. Elixir also includes other modules that can be used to run OTP-compliant processes. For example, the `Task` module (https://hexdocs.pm/elixir/Task.html) is perfect to run one-off jobs that process some input and then stop. The `Agent` module (https://hexdocs.pm/elixir/Agent.html) is a simpler (but less powerful) alternative to `GenServer`-based processes and is appropriate if the sole purpose of the process is to manage and expose state. Both `Task` and `Agent` are discussed in chapter 10.

In addition, there are various other OTP-compliant abstractions available via third-party libraries. For example, `GenStage` (https://hexdocs.pm/gen_stage) can be used for back pressure and load control. The `Phoenix.Channel` module (https://hexdocs.pm/phoenix/Phoenix.Channel.html), which is part of the Phoenix web framework (https://phoenixframework.org), is used to facilitate bidirectional communication between a client and a web server over protocols such as WebSocket or HTTP.

There isn't enough space in this book to treat every possible OTP-compliant abstraction, so you'll need to do some research on your own. But it's worth pointing out that most such abstractions follow the ideas of GenServer. Except for the Task module, all of the OTP abstractions mentioned in this section are internally implemented on top of GenServer. Therefore, in my personal opinion, GenServer is likely the most important part of OTP. If you properly understand the principles of GenServer, most other abstractions should be much easier to grasp.

6.2.8 *Exercise: GenServer-powered to-do server*

Let's wrap up this chapter with a simple, but important, exercise. For practice, try to change the to-do server implemented earlier in this chapter to work with the GenServer behaviour. This should be a straightforward task, but if you get stuck, the solution is in the todo_server.ex file.

Be sure to either finish this exercise or analyze and understand the solution, because in future chapters, you'll gradually expand on this simple server process and build a highly concurrent distributed system.

Summary

- A generic server process is an abstraction that implements tasks common to any kind of server process, such as recursion-powered looping and message passing.
- A generic server process can be implemented as a behaviour. A behaviour drives the process, whereas specific implementations can plug into the behaviour via callback modules.
- The behaviour invokes callback functions when the specific implementation needs to make a decision.
- GenServer is a behaviour that implements a generic server process.
- A callback module for GenServer must implement various functions. The most frequently used of these are init/1, handle_cast/2, handle_call/3, and handle_info/2.
- You can interact with a GenServer process with the GenServer module.
- Two types of requests can be issued to a server process: calls and casts.
- A cast is a fire-and-forget type of request—a caller sends a message and immediately moves on to do something else.
- A call is a synchronous send-and-respond request—a caller sends a message and waits until the response arrives, the timeout occurs, or the server crashes.

Building
a concurrent system

7

This chapter covers

- Working with the Mix project
- Managing multiple to-do lists
- Persisting data
- Reasoning with processes

The concurrent examples you've seen so far have relied on a single server process instance. But typical Elixir and Erlang systems are powered by a multitude of processes—many of which are stateful server processes. It's not uncommon for a moderately complex system to run a few thousand processes, whereas larger systems may be powered by hundreds of thousands, or even millions, of processes. Remember that processes are cheap, so you can create them in abundance. And owing to message-passing concurrency, it's still fairly easy to reason about highly concurrent systems. Therefore, it's useful to run different tasks in separate processes. Such a highly concurrent approach can often improve the scalability and reliability of your systems.

In this chapter, you'll see an example of a more involved system powered by many processes that cooperate to provide the full service. Your ultimate goal is to build a distributed HTTP server that can handle many end users who are simultaneously manipulating many to-do lists. You'll do this throughout the remaining chapters and reach the final goal in chapter 12. In this chapter, you'll develop an infrastructure for handling multiple to-do lists and persisting them to disk.

But first, let's look at how you can manage more complex projects with the `mix` tool.

7.1 Working with the Mix project

As code becomes more involved, placing all the modules in a single file becomes increasingly clumsy. This is the right time to start working with multifile projects.

Chapter 2 briefly mentioned that Elixir ships with the `mix` tool, which you can use to create, build, and run projects as well as manage their dependencies, run tests, and create custom project-based tasks. Here, you'll learn just enough about `mix` to create and run a project. Additional `mix` features will be introduced as the need arises.

You'll use `mix` to create a project for the to-do list. Type the following at the command line:

```
$ mix new todo
```

This creates the todo folder and a project structure under it. The result is a folder that contains only a handful of files, including a readme file, unit test support files, and the .gitignore file. Mix projects are extremely simple and don't introduce too many auto-generated files.

> **TIP** This book doesn't provide a detailed treatment of the `mix` tool. Instead, essential features are introduced when needed. To find out more about `mix`, see the Introduction to Mix guide (https://mng.bz/A8do). Additionally, from the command line, you can run `mix help` to get a list of available commands and the `mix help command` to get detailed help for a particular command. Finally, the online reference for `mix` is available at https://hexdocs.pm/mix.

Once the project is in place, you can go to its folder and run `mix` tasks from there. For example, you can compile the project with the `mix compile` command, or you can run tests with `mix test`.

You can also use a special way of starting `iex`, which is useful when you want to play with Mix projects in the Elixir shell. When you run `iex -S mix`, two things happen. First, the project is compiled (just as with `mix compile`). If this is successful, the shell is started, and all modules from the project can be referenced and used.

Using `mix`, it's possible to organize your code into multiple files and folders. You can place .ex files under the lib folder, and they'll automatically be included in the next build. You can also use arbitrarily nested subfolders under the lib folder.

There are no hard rules regarding how files should be named and organized, but there are some preferred conventions:

- You should place your modules under a common top-level alias. For example, modules might be called Todo.List, Todo.Server, or similar. This reduces the chance of module names conflicting when you combine multiple projects into a single system.
- In general, one file should contain one module. Occasionally, if a helper module is small and used only internally, it can be placed in the same file as the module using it. If you want to implement protocols for the module, you can do this in the same file as well.
- A filename should be an underscore-case (aka *snake-case*) version of the main module name it implements. For example, a TodoServer module would reside in a todo_server.ex file in the lib folder.
- The folder structure should correspond to multipart module names. A module called Todo.Server should reside in the lib/todo/server.ex file.

These aren't strict rules, but they're the ones used by the Elixir project as well as many third-party libraries.

With this out of the way, you can start adding code to the project. In chapter 4 you developed the module TodoList. In chapter 6, as a part of the exercises, you developed the TodoServer module, which implements a server process that maintains the state of a single to-do list. The final version of both modules resides in the todo_server.ex file from chapter 6.

Now, you'll add the code of those modules to the newly generated todo project. Here's what you need to do:

1 Remove the file todo/lib/todo.ex.
2 Remove the file todo/test/todo_test.exs.
3 Place the TodoList code in the todo/lib/todo/list.ex file. Rename the module as Todo.List.
4 Place the TodoServer code in the todo/lib/todo/server.ex file. Rename the module to Todo.Server.
5 Replace all references to TodoServer with Todo.Server and all references to TodoList with Todo.List.

The final version is available in the todo folder. Now, you can start the system with iex -S mix and verify that it works:

```
$ iex -S mix

iex(1)> {:ok, todo_server} = Todo.Server.start()

iex(2)> Todo.Server.add_entry(
          todo_server,
          %{date: ~D[2023-12-19], title: "Dentist"}
        )

iex(3)> Todo.Server.entries(todo_server, ~D[2023-12-19])
[%{date: ~D[2023-12-19], id: 1, title: "Dentist"}]
```

At this point, the to-do code is in the Mix project, and you can continue to extend it with additional features.

7.2 *Managing multiple to-do lists*

This section introduces support for managing multiple to-do lists. Before starting, let's recap what you've built so far:

- A pure functional Todo.List abstraction
- A to-do server process that can be used to manage one to-do list for a long time

There are two approaches to extending this code to work with multiple lists:

- Implement a pure functional abstraction to work with multiple to-do lists. Modify Todo.Server to use the new abstraction as its internal state.
- Run one instance of the existing to-do server for each to-do list.

The problem with the first approach is that you'll end up having only one process to serve all users. This approach isn't very scalable. If the system is used by many different users, they'll frequently block each other, competing for the same resource—a single-server process that performs all tasks.

The alternative is to use as many processes as there are to-do lists. With this approach, each list is managed concurrently, and the system should be more responsive and scalable.

To run multiple to-do server processes, you need another entity—something you'll use to create Todo.Server instances or fetch the existing ones. That "something" must manage a state—essentially a key–value structure that maps to-do list names with to-do server PIDs. This state will, of course, be mutable (the number of lists changes over time) and must be available during the system's lifetime.

Therefore, you'll introduce another server process: a to-do cache. You'll run only one instance of this process, and it will be used to create and return a pid of a to-do server process that corresponds to the given name. The module will export only two functions: start/0, which starts the process, and server_process/2, which retrieves a to-do server process (its pid) for a given name, optionally starting the process, if it isn't already running.

7.2.1 *Implementing a cache*

Let's begin implementing the cache process. First, copy the entire Mix project (the todo folder) to the todo_cache folder. Then, add the new todo_cache/lib/todo/cache.ex file, which is where the code for Todo.Cache will reside.

Now, you need to decide what the process state will be. Remember that the process will provide to-do server processes. You give it a name, and it returns the pid of the corresponding process. In this case, it seems reasonable to use a map that associates to-do list names with to-do server PIDs. This is implemented in the following listing.

Listing 7.1 Cache initialization (todo_cache/lib/todo/cache.ex)

```
defmodule Todo.Cache do
  use GenServer

  def init(_) do
    {:ok, %{}}
  end

  ...
end
```

With this in place, you can begin introducing the `server_process` request. You need to decide whether this request will be a call or cast. Because this request must return a result to the caller (a to-do server `pid`), there are no options—it needs to be a call.

Listing 7.2 Handling the `server_process` request (todo_cache/lib/todo/cache.ex)

```
defmodule Todo.Cache do
  ...

  def handle_call({:server_process, todo_list_name}, _, todo_servers) do
    case Map.fetch(todo_servers, todo_list_name) do
      {:ok, todo_server} ->                                  # The server exists in the map.
        {:reply, todo_server, todo_servers}

      :error ->                                              # The server doesn't exist.
        {:ok, new_server} = Todo.Server.start()              # Starts the new server

        {
          :reply,
          new_server,
          Map.put(todo_servers, todo_list_name, new_server)
        }
    end
  end

  ...
end
```

In this example, you use `Map.fetch/2` to query the map. If there's something for the given key, you return the value to the caller, leaving the state unchanged. Otherwise, you must start a server, return its `pid`, and insert an appropriate name–value pair in the process state. Finally, you shouldn't forget to include interface functions.

Listing 7.3 Interface functions (todo_cache/lib/todo/cache.ex)

```
defmodule Todo.Cache do
  ...

  def start do
```

```
    GenServer.start(__MODULE__, nil)
  end

  def server_process(cache_pid, todo_list_name) do
    GenServer.call(cache_pid, {:server_process, todo_list_name})
  end

  ...
end
```

Notice how __MODULE__ is passed as the first argument to GenServer.start/2. During compilation, this expression is replaced with the name of the current module. This is a simple convenience—you could write Todo.Cache instead—but this approach removes this minor duplication and guards the code against a possible change of the module name.

At this point, the to-do cache is complete, and you can try it. Start the shell with iex -S mix, and do the following:

```
iex(1)> {:ok, cache} = Todo.Cache.start()
```

```
iex(2)> Todo.Cache.server_process(cache, "Bob's list")       The first retrieval
#PID<0.69.0>                                                  starts a new process.
```

```
iex(3)> Todo.Cache.server_process(cache, "Bob's list")       The second retrieval
#PID<0.69.0>                                                  returns the same process.
```

```
iex(4)> Todo.Cache.server_process(cache, "Alice's list")     A different name returns
#PID<0.72.0>                                                  a different process.
```

The returned pid represents a to-do server process that manages a single to-do list. You can use it in the familiar way to manipulate the list:

```
iex(5)> bobs_list = Todo.Cache.server_process(cache, "Bob's list")
```

```
iex(6)> Todo.Server.add_entry(
          bobs_list,
          %{date: ~D[2023-12-19], title: "Dentist"}
        )
```

```
iex(7)> Todo.Server.entries(bobs_list, ~D[2023-12-19])
[%{date: ~D[2023-12-19], id: 1, title: "Dentist"}]
```

Of course, Alice's list isn't affected by these manipulations:

```
iex(8)> Todo.Cache.server_process(cache, "Alice's list") |>
          Todo.Server.entries(~D[2023-12-19])
[]
```

Having the cache in place makes it possible for you to manage many to-do lists independently. The following session creates 100,000 to-do list servers and verifies that you have that many processes running:

```
iex(1)> {:ok, cache} = Todo.Cache.start()

iex(2)> length(Process.list())
65

iex(3)> Enum.each(
          1..100_000,
          fn index ->
            Todo.Cache.server_process(cache, "to-do list #{index}")
          end
        )

iex(4)> length(Process.list())
100065
```

Here, you use the `Process.list/0` function to get the list of currently running processes.

You might be puzzled about why you initially have 65 processes running, even though you started just 1. The remaining processes are those started and used internally by Elixir and Erlang.

7.2.2 *Writing tests*

Now that the code is organized in the Mix project, you can write automated tests. The testing framework for Elixir is called `ex_unit`, and it's included in the Elixir distribution. Running tests is as easy as invoking `mix test`. All you need to do is write the test code.

Let's look at a quick example by testing the behavior of `Todo.Cache.server_process/2`. First, you need to create the test file. The sketch is provided in the following listing.

Listing 7.4   Test file skeleton (todo_cache/test/todo/cache_test.exs)

```
defmodule Todo.CacheTest do
  use ExUnit.Case          ◁──── Prepares the module for testing

  ...
end
```

Take note of the file location and the name. A test file must reside in the test folder, and its name must end with _test.exs to be included in the test execution. As explained in chapter 2, the .exs extension stands for *Elixir script*, and it's used to indicate that a file isn't compiled to disk. Instead, `mix` will interpret this file every time the tests are executed.

The script file must define the test module that contains the tests. The expression `use ExUnit.Case` prepares the test module for testing. This expression injects some boilerplate that makes the module compliant with `ex_unit` and imports some helper test macros to the module.

One such macro is `test`, which can be used to define tests. You'll use it to test the behavior of `Todo.Cache.server_process/2`.

Listing 7.5 Testing `server_process` (todo_cache/test/todo/cache_test.exs)

```
defmodule Todo.CacheTest do
  use ExUnit.Case

  test "server_process" do           ←—— Defines a test
    {:ok, cache} = Todo.Cache.start()
    bob_pid = Todo.Cache.server_process(cache, "bob")

    assert bob_pid != Todo.Cache.server_process(cache, "alice")   │ Test
    assert bob_pid == Todo.Cache.server_process(cache, "bob")     │ assertions
  end

  ...
end
```

To define a test, you need to write `test test_description do … end`. The test description is a string that's included in the output if the test fails. The code of the test itself is included in the `do` block.

The `test` macro is an example of metaprogramming capabilities in Elixir. This macro will generate a function that contains some boilerplate and the code provided in the `do` block. This function will then be invoked by `ex_unit` when you execute tests.

In this particular test, you first start the cache process and then fetch one server process. Then, you verify the expected behavior. This is done with the help of the `assert` macro, which takes an expression and verifies its outcome. If the expression fails, `assert` will raise an error with a descriptive output. This error will be caught by `ex_unit` and displayed.

For example, take a look at the first assertion:

```
assert bob_pid != Todo.Cache.server_process(cache, "alice")
```

In this assertion, you're verifying that Alice and Bob's to-do lists are powered by different processes.

Just like `test`, `assert` is a macro and, therefore, is invoked during compilation. The macro introspects the expression and transforms it into different code. An approximation of the generated code could be something like this:

```
left_value = bob_pid
right_value = Todo.Cache.server_process(cache, "alice")

if left_value == right_value do
  # raise an error
end
```

In other words, the `assert` macro generates the code that will fail if the expression `bob_pid != Todo.Cache.server_process(cache, "alice")` returns `false`.

A great benefit of the way `assert` works is that you don't need to learn a completely new set of functions, such as `assert_equal`, `assert_not_equal`, or `assert_gt`, to write your assertions. Instead, you use the same expressions as in the regular code to verify the desired behavior. You can assert on standard comparisons, such as `==`, `!=`, `>`, `<`, and so on.

You can even assert that a pattern-matching expression succeeded. Let's look at a quick example. You'll add another test that verifies the behavior of to-do server operations. To keep things simple, you'll include the test in the same file.

Listing 7.6 Testing to-do server operations (todo_cache/test/todo/cache_test.exs)

```
defmodule Todo.CacheTest do
  use ExUnit.Case

  ...

  test "to-do operations" do
    {:ok, cache} = Todo.Cache.start()

    alice = Todo.Cache.server_process(cache, "alice")
    Todo.Server.add_entry(alice, %{date: ~D[2023-12-19], title: "Dentist"})

    entries = Todo.Server.entries(alice, ~D[2023-12-19])
    assert [%{date: ~D[2023-12-19], title: "Dentist"}] = entries   ⟵──┐
  end                                               **Asserts a matching expression**
end
```

Here, you create one to-do server, add a single entry, and then fetch the entries for the given date. Finally, using pattern matching, you assert that the list of entries has exactly one element, with date and title fields having proper values. Relying on pattern matching allowed you to check only the relevant fields and to verify the size of the result in a single expression.

At this point, you've created a single test file with a couple of tests. The test project in the todo_cache folder also includes another test file called test/todo/list_test.exs, which verifies the behavior of the `Todo.List` module. For the sake of brevity, that code isn't presented here.

> **NOTE** The example projects in this book aren't test driven or particularly well tested. In this book, the focus is on extremely simple code that illustrates a point. Such code is often not very testable, and some improvisations have been used to ensure basic correctness.

Now, you can run all the tests with `mix test`:

```
$ mix test
.......

Finished in 0.05 seconds
7 tests, 0 failures
```

There are many other features available in ex_unit, but we'll stop here. To learn more about unit testing in Elixir, check out the official ExUnit reference at https://hexdocs.pm/ ex_unit and the mix test documentation at https://hexdocs.pm/mix/Mix.Tasks.Test.html.

7.2.3 Analyzing process dependencies

Let's reflect a bit on the current system. You've developed support for managing many to-do list instances, and the end goal is to use this infrastructure in an HTTP server. In the Elixir and Erlang world, HTTP servers typically use a separate process for each request. Thus, if you have many simultaneous end users, you can expect many BEAM processes to access your to-do cache and to-do servers. The dependency between processes is illustrated in figure 7.1.

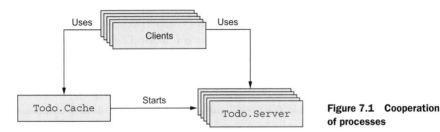

Figure 7.1 Cooperation of processes

Here, each box represents a single process. The client boxes are arbitrary clients, such as HTTP request-handler processes. Looking at this diagram, you can immediately spot some characteristics of your system's concurrent behavior:

- Several clients (possibly a large number of them) issue requests to the single to-do cache process.
- Several clients communicate with multiple to-do server processes.

The first point identifies the possible source of a bottleneck. Because you have only one to-do cache process, you can handle only one server_process request at a time, regardless of how many CPU resources you have.

This problem may not be significant in practice. If your server_process takes, for example, one microsecond, the to-do cache could handle a load of up to 1,000,000 requests per second, which should be sufficient for most needs. But if request handling takes 100 milliseconds, you could process only 10 requests per second, and your system wouldn't be able to handle higher loads.

It's easy to reason about an individual process. Regardless of how many concurrent requests are coming in, a single process can handle only one request at a time. Thus, a process is good enough if its request-handling rate is at least equal to the incoming rate. Otherwise, you have to either optimize the process or do other interventions.

In this case, the to-do cache performs a very simple operation: a map lookup followed by an optional process creation and map update. According to a quick test on my machine, for 1 million to-do lists, it takes about 5 microseconds to start a new to-do server and put it in the map or 1.5 microseconds to fetch the existing one. This should be sufficient for a load of at least 200,000 requests per second, which seems like reasonable performance for this initial attempt. If you want to repeat the test on your machine, take a look at the instructions in todo_cache/lib/load_test.ex.

I'll briefly cover a few topics related to client interactions with to-do servers. Once a client gets a to-do server PID, the list manipulation runs concurrently to all other activities in the system. Because you can expect list manipulations to be fairly involved, it's beneficial to run those operations concurrently. This is where your system is concurrent and scalable—it can manipulate several lists, using as many resources as possible.

Also recall from chapter 5 that a process waiting for a message is suspended and doesn't waste CPU resources. Thus, regardless of the number of processes, only those processes that are actually doing computations consume CPU. In this case, that means a client process doesn't use CPU while it waits for a to-do server to finish.

Finally, you can be sure that a single list can't be modified by two simultaneous clients. Recall that the list is managed by a single process. Even if a million clients try to modify the same list, their requests will be serialized in the corresponding to-do server and handled one by one. Because a process runs only one request at a time, its internal state is consistent. You know there can't be multiple simultaneous updates of the process state, which makes race conditions in a single process impossible.

> **TIP** If you need to make sure part of the code is synchronized—that is, that there are no multiple simultaneous executions of critical code—it's best to run that code in a dedicated process. When multiple clients want this code to run, they issue a request to that process. The process then serves as a synchronization point, making sure the critical code is run in a single process.

Now, you have a basic system you can use to manipulate many to-do lists. It's time to include basic persistence so that your data can outlive server restarts.

7.3   *Persisting data*

In this section, you'll extend the to-do cache and introduce basic data persistence. The focus here isn't so much on the persistence itself but on exploring the process model—how you can organize your system into various server processes, analyze dependencies, and identify and address bottlenecks. You'll start with the code from the todo_cache folder and extend it gradually. For data persistence, you'll use simple disk-based persistence, encoding the data into the Erlang external term format. The complete solution is in the persistable_todo_cache folder.

7.3.1 Encoding and persisting

To encode an arbitrary Elixir or Erlang term, you use the `:erlang.term_to_binary/1` function, which accepts an Erlang term and returns an encoded byte sequence as a binary value. The input term can be of arbitrary complexity, including deep hierarchies of nested lists and tuples. The result can be stored to disk, retrieved at a later point, and decoded to an Erlang term with the inverse function `:erlang.binary_to_term/1`.

Equipped with this knowledge, you'll introduce another process: a database powered by the `Todo.Database` module. This will be a server process that supports two requests: `store` and `get`. When storing data, clients will provide a key and the corresponding data. The data will be stored in the file that bears the same name as the key. This approach is far from perfect and is error prone, but it's simple enough to let us focus on the concurrency aspect of the problem. The full implementation of the database process is given in the following listing.

Listing 7.7 Database process (persistable_todo_cache/lib/todo/database.ex)

```elixir
defmodule Todo.Database do
  use GenServer

  @db_folder "./persist"

  def start do
    GenServer.start(__MODULE__, nil,
      name: __MODULE__            ⟵── Locally registers the process
    )
  end

  def store(key, data) do
    GenServer.cast(__MODULE__, {:store, key, data})
  end

  def get(key) do
    GenServer.call(__MODULE__, {:get, key})
  end

  def init(_) do
    File.mkdir_p!(@db_folder)      ⟵── Confirms the folder exists
    {:ok, nil}
  end

  def handle_cast({:store, key, data}, state) do
    key
    |> file_name()                                  ⎫ Stores
    |> File.write!(:erlang.term_to_binary(data))    ⎬ the data

    {:noreply, state}
  end

  def handle_call({:get, key}, _, state) do         ⎫ Reads
    data = case File.read(file_name(key)) do         ⎭ the data
```

```
      {:ok, contents} -> :erlang.binary_to_term(contents)
        _ -> nil
    end

    {:reply, data, state}
  end

  defp file_name(key) do
    Path.join(@db_folder, to_string(key))
  end
end
```

**Reads
the data**

This is mostly a synthesis of techniques mentioned earlier. First, you set the module attribute `@db_folder` to the hardcoded value of the database folder. As explained in section 2.3.6, this works as a compile-time constant, allowing you to encode the knowledge about the database folder in a single place in code.

The database server is locally registered under a name; this keeps things simple and relieves you from passing around the `Todo.Database` PID. Of course, a downside is that you can run only one instance of the database process.

It's worth noting that the `store` request is a cast, whereas `get` is a call. In this implementation, I decided to turn `store` into a cast because the client isn't interested in a response. Using casts promotes scalability of the system because the caller issues a request and goes about its business.

A huge downside of a cast is that the caller can't know whether the request was successfully handled. In fact, the caller can't even be sure the request reached the target process. This is a property of casts. Casts promote overall availability by allowing client processes to move on immediately after a request is issued. But this comes at the cost of consistency because you can't be confident about whether a request has succeeded.

In this example, you'll start with the `store` request being a cast. This makes the entire system more scalable and responsive, with the downside being that you can't guarantee that all changes have been persisted.

During initialization, you use `File.mkdir_p!/1` to create the specified folder if it doesn't exist. The exclamation mark at the end of the name indicates a function that raises an error if the folder can't be created for some reason. The data is stored by encoding the given term to the binary and then persisting it to the disk. Data fetching is the inverse of storing. If the given file doesn't exist on the disk, you return `nil`.

7.3.2   *Using the database*

With the database process in place, it's time to use it from your existing system. You have to do three things:

1 Ensure that a database process is started.
2 Persist the list on every modification.
3 Try to fetch the list from disk during the first retrieval.

To start the server, you'll plug into the `Todo.Cache.init/1` function. This is a quick hack, but it's sufficient for the moment.

Listing 7.8 Starting the database (persistable_todo_cache/lib/todo/cache.ex)

```
defmodule Todo.Cache do
  ...

  def init(_) do
    Todo.Database.start()
    {:ok, %{}}
  end

  ...
end
```

Here, you use the persist subfolder of the current folder as the place to store data.

STORING THE DATASTORE REQUEST

Next, you need to persist the list after it's modified. Obviously, this must be done from the to-do server. But remember that the database's `store` request requires a key. For this purpose, you'll use the to-do list name. As you may recall, this name is currently maintained only in the to-do cache, so you must propagate it to the to-do server as well. This means extending the to-do server state to be in the format {`list_name`, `todo_list`}. The code isn't shown here, but these are the corresponding changes:

- `Todo.Server.start` now accepts the to-do list name and passes it to `GenServer.start/2`.
- `Todo.Server.init/1` uses this parameter and keeps the list name in the process state.
- `Todo.Server.handle` callbacks are updated to work with the new state format.

When starting the new to-do server, the cache process passes the list name. After these modifications, the to-do server knows its own name. Now, it's trivial to persist the data.

Listing 7.9 Persisting the data (persistable_todo_cache/lib/todo/server.ex)

```
defmodule Todo.Server do
  ...

  def handle_cast({:add_entry, new_entry}, {name, todo_list}) do
    new_list = Todo.List.add_entry(todo_list, new_entry)
    Todo.Database.store(name, new_list)      ◁─────┐  Persists the data
    {:noreply, {name, new_list}}
  end

  ...
end
```

You can immediately test whether this works. Run `iex -S mix`, and try the following:

```
iex(1)> {:ok, cache} = Todo.Cache.start()

iex(2)> bobs_list = Todo.Cache.server_process(cache, "bobs_list")

iex(3)> Todo.Server.add_entry(
          bobs_list,
          %{date: ~D[2023-12-19], title: "Dentist"}
        )
```

If all goes well, there should be a file named persist/bobs_list on the disk.

READING THE DATA

All that's left to do is to read the data from the disk when the server is started. The first idea that comes to mind is to perform this in the `init/1` callback:

```
def init(name) do
  todo_list = Todo.Database.get(name) || Todo.List.new()
  {:ok, {name, todo_list}}
end
```

Here, you try to fetch the data from the database, and you resort to the empty list if there's nothing on disk.

While this approach would work, in general, you should be careful about possibly long-running `init/1` callbacks. Recall that `GenServer.start` returns only after the process has been initialized. Consequently, a long-running `init/1` function will cause the client (starter) process to block. In this case, a long initialization of a to-do server will block the cache process. And since the cache process is used by many clients, this can, in turn, block a larger part of the system.

Thankfully, `GenServer` comes with a solution to this problem, by allowing you to split the initialization into two phases: one that blocks the client process and another one that can be performed after the `GenServer.start` invocation in the client has finished.

To do this, `init/1` must return the result in the shape of `{:ok, initial_state, {:continue, some_arg}}`. In this case, the following things happen:

- The initial state of the server process is set.
- The `GenServer.start` invocation in the caller process is unblocked.
- The `handle_continue` callback is invoked in the server process. The callback receives the provided argument (from the `{:continue, some_arg}` tuple) and the server state.

The `handle_continue/2` function is the first callback invoked immediately after `init/1`. Therefore, it can be used as the second phase of the process initialization.

At the time `handle_continue/2` is invoked, the `GenServer.start` invocation in the client process has already finished. Therefore, this phase of the initialization doesn't block the client anymore, so it's a fitting place for performing potentially longer-running initialization work, such as reading from the database. The idea can be seen in the following listing.

Listing 7.10 Two-phase initialization (persistable_todo_cache/lib/todo/server.ex)

```
defmodule Todo.Server do
  ...

  def init(name) do
    {:ok, {name, nil}, {:continue, :init}}        ⟵─ Schedules the post-
  end                                                init continuation

  def handle_continue(:init, {name, nil}) do                    Potentially
    todo_list = Todo.Database.get(name) || Todo.List.new()  ⟵─ long-running
    {:noreply, {name, todo_list}}                              initialization
  end

  ...
end
```

The execution of `init/1` is kept as short as possible, and the to-do list is set to `nil`. There's no point in setting it to anything else because it's going to be overwritten in `handle_continue/2`, which is the first callback invoked immediately after `init/2`.

In any case, the to-do server now reads data from the database on creation. You can immediately test this. If you have the previous shell session open, close it, and start a new one. Then try the following:

```
iex(1)> {:ok, cache} = Todo.Cache.start()

iex(2)> bobs_list = Todo.Cache.server_process(cache, "bobs_list")

iex(3)> Todo.Server.entries(bobs_list, ~D[2023-12-19])
[%{date: ~D[2023-12-19], id: 1, title: "Dentist"}]
```

As you can see, your to-do list contains data proving that deserialization works.

7.3.3 Analyzing the system

Let's analyze how the new version of the system works. The process interaction is presented in figure 7.2.

You introduced just one process, but it can have a negative effect on the entire system. Recall that the database performs term encoding/decoding and, even worse, disk I/O operations.

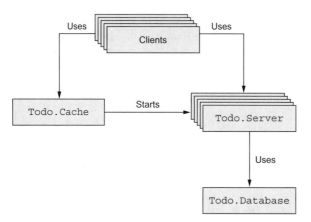

Figure 7.2 Process dependencies

Depending on the load and list sizes, this can negatively affect performance. Let's recall all the places database requests are issued:

```
defmodule Todo.Server do
  ...

  def handle_continue(:init, {name, nil}) do                    Synchronous
    todo_list = Todo.Database.get(name) || Todo.List.new()  ⟵   request
    ...
  end

  ...

  def handle_cast({:add_entry, new_entry}, {name, todo_list}) do
    ...
    Todo.Database.store(name, todo_list)   ⟵── Asynchronous request
    ...
  end

  ...
end
```

The store request may not seem problematic from the client perspective because it's an asynchronous cast. A client issues a store request and then goes about its business. But if requests to the database come in faster than they can be handled, the process mailbox will grow and increasingly consume memory. Ultimately, the entire system may experience significant problems, resulting in the possible termination of the BEAM OS process.

The get request can cause additional problems. It's a synchronous call, so the to-do server waits while the database returns the response. While it's waiting for the response, this to-do server can't handle new messages.

It's worth repeating that the synchronous call won't block indefinitely. Recall that GenServer.call has a default timeout of 5 seconds, and you can configure it to be less for better responsiveness. Still, when a request times out, it isn't removed from the receiver's mailbox. A request is a message placed in the receiver's mailbox. A timeout means you give up waiting on the response, but the message remains in the receiver's mailbox and will be processed at some point.

7.3.4   *Addressing the process bottleneck*

There are many approaches to addressing the bottleneck introduced by the singleton database process. Here, we'll discuss a few of them.

BYPASSING THE PROCESS

The simplest possible way to eliminate the process bottleneck is to bypass the process. You should ask yourself—does this need to be a process, or can it be a plain module?

There are various reasons for running a piece of code in a dedicated server process:

- The code must manage a long-living state.
- The code handles a kind of resource that can and should be reused between multiple invocations, such as a TCP connection, database connection, file handle, and so on.
- A critical section of the code must be synchronized. Only one instance of this code may be running in any moment.

If none of these conditions are met, you probably don't need a process and can run the code in client processes, which will completely eliminate the bottleneck and promote parallelism and scalability.

In the current code, you could, indeed, store to the file directly from the to-do server process. All operations on the same list are serialized in the same process, so there are no race conditions. But the problem with this approach is that concurrency is unbound. If you have 100,000 simultaneous clients, then you'll issue that many concurrent I/O operations, which may negatively affect the entire system.

HANDLING REQUESTS CONCURRENTLY

Another option is to keep the database process and make it handle database operations concurrently. This is useful when requests depend on a common state but can be handled independently. The idea is illustrated in figure 7.3.

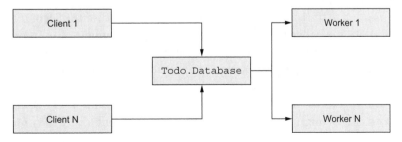

Figure 7.3   Handling requests concurrently

As you can see, each request is still serialized through the central server process, but this server process spawns one-off worker processes that perform the actual request handling. If you keep the code in the database process short and fast, you'll get to keep a high degree of scalability with many workers running concurrently.

To implement this, you must run each database operation in a spawned, one-off process. For casts, this means transforming the body of the handler:

```elixir
def handle_cast({:store, key, data}, state) do
  spawn(fn ->
    key                                                    Handled in a
    |> file_name()                                         spawned process
    |> File.write!(:erlang.term_to_binary(data))
  end)

  {:noreply, state}
end
```

The handler function spawns the new worker process and immediately returns. While the worker is running, the database process can accept new requests.

For synchronous calls, this approach is slightly more complicated because you must return the response from the spawned worker process:

```elixir
def handle_call({:get, key}, caller, state) do
  spawn(fn ->                                   ⟵──── Spawns the reader
    data = case File.read(file_name(key)) do
      {:ok, contents} -> :erlang.binary_to_term(contents)
      _ -> nil
    end

    GenServer.reply(caller, data)    ⟵──── Responds from the spawned process
  end)

  {:noreply, state}    ⟵──── No reply from the database process
end
```

The server process spawns another worker process and then returns `{:noreply, state}`, indicating to GenServer that you won't reply at this point. In the meantime, the spawned process handles the request and reports back to the caller with GenServer.reply/2. This is one situation where you need to use the second argument of handle_call/3: the caller PID and the unique ID of the request. This information is used in the spawned process to send the response message to the caller.

This technique keeps the processing in the database process short, while still allowing concurrent execution of database operations. This approach has the same drawbacks as the previous idea. The concurrency is still unbound, so too many simultaneous clients might overload the disk I/O to the point where the entire system becomes unresponsive.

LIMITING CONCURRENCY WITH POOLING

A typical remedy for this problem is to introduce pooling. For example, your database process might create three worker processes and keep their PIDs in their internal state. When a request arrives, it's delegated to one of the worker processes, perhaps in a round-robin fashion or with some other load-distribution strategy. The idea is presented in figure 7.4.

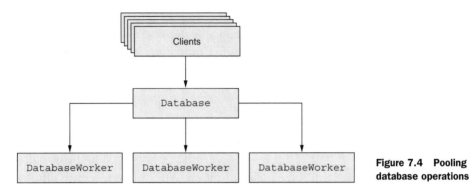

Figure 7.4 Pooling database operations

All requests still arrive at the database process first, but they're quickly forwarded to one of the workers. Essentially, this technique keeps the concurrency level under control, and it works best when dealing with resources that can't handle unbound concurrency.

This approach will work correctly in this example, so it's the one you'll use. In a different situation, some other approach might work better. The point of this analysis is to illustrate how you can think in terms of processes. Always keep in mind that multiple processes run concurrently, whereas a single process handles requests sequentially. If computations can safely run in parallel, you should consider running them in separate processes. In contrast, if an operation must be synchronized, you'll want to run it in a single process.

Database connection pool

In this example, increasing the number of concurrent disk-based operations doesn't yield significant improvements. In this sense, the optimizations serve more as a didactic example than an efficient solution. But in real life, you'd probably talk to a database that can handle multiple concurrent requests efficiently. In such a case, you'd typically need to constrain the number of simultaneous database operations. And this is the purpose of a pool of processes.

There's no need to implement such a pool yourself. A couple of generic pool libraries are available for the Elixir and Erlang ecosystem, with one of the most popular being Poolboy (https://github.com/devinus/poolboy). Depending on which database library you're using, you'll either need to combine it with Poolboy (or another pooling solution), or this will be done by the library (as is the case, for example, with the Ecto library: https://github.com/elixir-lang/ecto). In chapter 11, when you learn how to manage application dependencies, you'll replace the custom implementation with Poolboy.

7.3.5 *Exercise: Pooling and synchronizing*

Now, it's time for you to practice a bit. This exercise introduces pooling and makes the database internally delegate to three workers that perform the actual database operations. Moreover, there should be per-key (to-do list name) synchronization on the database level. Data with the same key should always be treated by the same worker.

Here are some pointers for doing this:

- Start with the existing solution, and migrate it gradually. Of the existing code, the only thing that needs to change is the `Todo.Database` implementation. You don't have to touch any of the other modules.

- Introduce a `Todo.DatabaseWorker` module. It will be almost a copy of the current `Todo.Database`, but the process must not be registered under a name because you need to run multiple instances.

- `Todo.DatabaseWorker.start` should receive the database folder as its argument and pass it as the second argument to `GenServer.start/2`. This argument is received in the `init/1` callback, and it should be stored in the worker state.

- `Todo.Database` will receive a significant rewrite, but its interface must remain the same. This means it still implements a locally registered process that's used via the functions `start/0`, `get/1`, and `store/2`.

- During the `Todo.Database` initialization, start three workers and store their PIDs in a map, using zero-based indexes as keys.

- In `Todo.Database`, implement a single request, `choose_worker`, that will return a worker's PID for a given key.

- `choose_worker` should always return the same worker for the same key. The easiest way to do this is to compute the key's numerical hash and normalize it to fall in the range [0, 2]. This can be done by calling `:erlang.phash2(key, 3)`.

- The interface functions `get` and `store` of `Todo.Database` internally call `choose_worker` to obtain the worker's PID and then forward to interface functions of `DatabaseWorker`, using the obtained PID as the first argument.

Always try to work in small steps, and test as often as possible. For example, once you implement `Todo.DatabaseWorker`, you can immediately start `iex -S mix` and try it in isolation.

The same goes for `Todo.Database`. First, you can initialize the state without implementing a request handler. Call `IO.inspect` from `init/1` to verify that the state is correct. Then, implement `choose_worker`, and test that it works in the shell. Finally, add interface functions and test the entire system.

How can you be sure that requests for different keys are running in different processes? You can use `IO.inspect` and, from within the worker, print the PID and the key using something like `IO.inspect "#{inspect(self())}: storing #{inspect(key)}"`. Use `IO.inspect` extensively. It's your friend and can help you significantly during development.

If you get stuck, the complete solution is in the todo_cache_pooling folder. Make sure you understand the solution because you'll continue extending this version in subsequent chapters.

7.4 *Reasoning with processes*

You've now seen various examples of server processes in action. The point of these examples has been to demonstrate how to reason about an involved concurrent system.

From within, a server process is a sequential program that accepts and handles requests, optionally managing internal state. From the outside, it's a concurrent agent that exposes a well-defined communication interface.

Another way to look at server processes is to think of them as services. Each process is like a small service that's responsible for a single task. In the to-do example, there's a to-do server that handles a distinct to-do list. Different lists are handled by different to-do servers, which makes the system more efficient. But a single list is always handled by the same process, which eliminates race conditions and keeps consistency. The to-do cache is a service that maps to-do names to corresponding to-do servers. Finally, the database process is a service that handles database requests. Internally, it distributes the work over a limited pool of workers, making sure the same item is always handled by the same worker.

Those services (processes) are mostly independent, but in some cases, they need to cooperate. For this purpose, you can use calls and casts. Obviously, when a client needs a response, you should use calls. But even when a response isn't needed, calls can sometimes be the better fit. The main problem with a cast is that it's a fire-and-forget kind of request, so the caller doesn't get any guarantees. You can't be sure that the request has reached the target, and you most certainly don't know about its outcome.

Essentially, both types have benefits and downsides. Casts promote system responsiveness (because a caller isn't blocked) at the cost of reduced consistency (because a caller doesn't know about the outcome of the request). On the other hand, calls promote consistency (i.e., a caller gets a response) but reduce system responsiveness (i.e., a caller is blocked while waiting for a response).

Finally, calls can also be used to apply back pressure to client processes. Because a call blocks a client, it prevents the client from generating too much work. The client becomes synchronized with the server and can never produce more work than the server can handle. In contrast, if you use casts, clients may overload the server, and requests may pile up in the message box and consume memory. Ultimately, you may run out of memory, and the entire system may be terminated.

Which approach is a better fit depends on the specific situation and circumstances. If you're unsure, it's probably better to start with a call because it's more consistent. You can then consider switching to casts in places where you establish that calls hurt performance and system responsiveness.

Summary

- When a system needs to perform various tasks, it's often beneficial to run different tasks in separate processes. Doing so promotes the scalability and fault tolerance of the system.

- A process is internally sequential and handles requests one by one. A single process can, thus, keep its state consistent, but it can also cause a performance bottleneck if it serves many clients.

- Carefully consider calls versus casts. Calls are synchronous and, therefore, block the caller. If a response isn't needed, casts may improve performance at the expense of reduced guarantees because a client process doesn't know the outcome.

- You can use Mix projects to manage projects that consist of multiple modules.

Fault tolerance basics

Fault tolerance is a first-class concept in BEAM. The ability to develop reliable systems that can operate even when faced with run-time errors is what brought us Erlang in the first place.

The aim of fault tolerance is to acknowledge the existence of failures, minimize their impact, and, ultimately, recover without human intervention. In a sufficiently complex system, many things can go wrong. Occasional bugs will happen, components you're depending on may fail, and you may experience hardware failures. A system may also become overloaded and fail to cope with an increased incoming request rate. Finally, if a system is distributed, you can experience additional issues, such as a remote machine becoming unavailable, perhaps due to a crash or a broken network link.

It's hard to predict everything that can go wrong, so it's better to face the harsh reality that anything can fail. Regardless of which part of the system happens to fail, it shouldn't take down the entire system; you want to be able to provide at least some service. For example, if the database server becomes unreachable, you can still serve data from the cache. You might even queue incoming store requests and try to resolve them later, when the connection to the database is reestablished.

You also must detect failures and try to recover from them. In the previous example, the system may try to reconnect to the database until it succeeds and then resume providing full service.

These are the properties of a resilient, self-healing system. Whatever goes wrong (and remember, anything can go wrong), the system should keep providing as much service as possible and fully recover as soon as possible.

Such thinking significantly changes the approach to error handling. Instead of obsessively trying to reduce the number of errors, your priority should be to minimize their effects and recover from them automatically. In a system that must run continuously, it's better to experience many isolated errors than encounter a single error that takes down the entire system.

It's somewhat surprising that the core tool for error handling is concurrency. In the BEAM world, two concurrent processes are completely separated; they share no memory, and a crash in one process can't, by default, compromise the execution flow of another. Process isolation allows you to confine the negative effects of an error to a single process or a small group of related processes, which keeps most of the system functioning normally.

Of course, when a process crashes, you'll usually want to detect this state and do something about it. In this chapter, you'll learn the basic techniques of detecting and handling errors in a concurrent system. Then, in chapter 9, you'll expand on this knowledge and implement fine-grained error isolation. Let's start with a bit of theory about run-time errors.

8.1 Run-time errors

In previous chapters, I loosely mentioned that in various situations, an error is raised. One of the most common examples is a failed pattern match. If a match fails, an error is raised. Another example is a synchronous `GenServer.call`. If the response message doesn't arrive in a given time interval (5 seconds by default), a run-time error happens. There are many other examples, such as invalid arithmetic operations (e.g., division by zero), invocation of a nonexistent function, and explicit error signaling.

When a run-time error happens, execution control is transferred up the call stack to the error-handling code. If you didn't specify such code, the process where the error happened is terminated. All other processes run unaffected by default.

8.1.1 Error types

BEAM distinguishes three types of run-time errors: *errors*, *exits*, and *throws*. Here are some typical examples of errors:

```
                              | Invalid arithmetic expression
iex(1)> 1/0               ⟵──────┘
** (ArithmeticError) bad argument in arithmetic expression

iex(1)> Module.nonexistent_function()   ⟵────── Calls a nonexistent function
```

```
** (UndefinedFunctionError) function Module.nonexistent_function/0 is
   undefined or private
```

                                              Pattern-matching error

```
iex(1)> List.first({1,2,3})        ⟵─────┘
** (FunctionClauseError) no function clause matching in List.first/2
```

You can also raise your own error by using the `raise/1` macro, passing an error string:

```
iex(1)> raise("Something went wrong")
** (RuntimeError) Something went wrong
```

If your function explicitly raises an error, you should append the `!` character to its name. This is a convention used in Elixir standard libraries. For example, `File.open!` raises an error if a file can't be opened:

```
iex(1)> File.open!("nonexistent_file")
** (File.Error) could not open non_existing_file: no such file or directory
```

In contrast, `File.open` (notice the lack of a `!`) just returns the information that the file couldn't be opened:

```
iex(1)> File.open("nonexistent_file")
{:error, :enoent}
```

Notice that in this snippet, there's no run-time error. `File.open` returns a result, which the caller can handle in some way.

Another type of a run-time error is the *exit*, which is used to deliberately terminate a process. To exit the current process, you can call `exit/1`, providing an exit reason:

```
iex(2)> spawn(fn ->
          exit("I'm done")              ⟵─── Exits the current process
          IO.puts("This doesn't happen")
        end)
```

The exit reason is an arbitrary term that describes why you're terminating the process. As you'll see later, it's possible for some other process to detect a process crash and obtain this exit reason.

The final run-time error type is a *throw*. To issue a throw, you can call `throw/1`:

```
iex(3)> throw(:thrown_value)
** (throw) :thrown_value
```

The purpose of throws is to allow nonlocal returns. As you saw in chapters 3 and 4, Elixir programs are organized in many nested function calls. In particular, loops are implemented as recursions. The consequence is that there are no constructs such as `break`, `continue`, and `return`, which you've probably seen in other languages. When you're deep in a loop, it's not trivial to stop the loop and return a value; throws can help with this. You can throw a value and catch it up the call stack. But using throws for control flow is hacky and somewhat reminiscent of `goto`, and you should avoid this technique as much as possible.

8.1.2   *Handling errors*

It is, of course, possible to intercept any kind of run-time error (error, exit, or throw) and do something about it. The main tool for this is the `try` expression. Here's how to run some code and catch errors:

```
try do
  ...
catch error_type, error_value ->
  ...
end
```

This works much like what you've probably seen in other languages. The code in the `do` block is executed, and if an error happens, execution is transferred to the `catch` block.

Notice that two things are specified in the `catch`. The `error_type` will contain an atom `:error`, `:exit`, or `:throw`, indicating the type of error that has occurred. The `error_value` will contain error-specific information, such as a value that was thrown or an error that was raised.

Let's play with this a bit by writing a helper lambda to make it easier to experiment with errors:

```
iex(1)> try_helper = fn fun ->
          try do
            fun.()
            IO.puts("No error.")

          catch type, value ->
            IO.puts("""
              Error
                #{inspect(type)}
                #{inspect(value)}
              """)
          end
        end
```

This helper lambda takes a function as its argument, calls this function in a `try`, and reports the type of error and the corresponding value. Since the output spans multiple lines, the heredoc syntax (`"""`) is used, which has briefly mentioned in chapter 2.

Let's try it out:

```
iex(2)> try_helper.(fn -> raise("Something went wrong") end)
Error                                    | Error type
  :error                          ⊲────────┘
  %RuntimeError{message: "Something went wrong"}    ⊲──────  Error value
```

Notice how the string message is wrapped in a `RuntimeError` struct. This is an Elixir-specific decoration done from within the `raise/1` macro. If you want to raise a plain, undecorated error, you can use Erlang's `:erlang.error/1` and provide an arbitrary term. The resulting error value will be the term you've raised.

If you attempt to throw a value, you'll get a different error type:

```
iex(3)> try_helper.(fn -> throw("Thrown value") end)
Error
  :throw
  "Thrown value"
```

Calling `exit/1` produces a different type:

```
iex(4)> try_helper.(fn -> exit("I'm done") end)
Error
  :exit
  "I'm done"
```

Remember that in Elixir, everything is an expression that has a return value. With `try`, the return value is the result of the last executed expression—either from the `do` block or, if an error was raised, the `catch` block:

```
iex(5)> result =
          try do
            throw("Thrown value")
          catch type, value -> {type, value}
          end

iex(6)> result
{:throw, "Thrown value"}
```

It's also worth noting that the `type` and `value` specified in the `catch` block are patterns. If you want to handle a specific type of error, you can do this by providing corresponding patterns.

For example, let's say you want to immediately return a value from inside a deep nested loop. You could invoke the following:

```
throw({:result, some_result})
```

Then, somewhere up the call stack, you would handle this throw:

```
try do
  ...
catch
  :throw, {:result, x} -> x
end
```

In this example, you only match for a specific run-time error: a throw in the form `{:result, x}`. If anything else is raised, you won't catch it, and an error will be propagated further up the call stack. If the error isn't handled, the process terminates.

Because `catch` is a pattern match, multiple clauses can be specified, just as you've seen with `case` and `receive` expressions:

```
try do
  ...

catch
  type_pattern_1, error_value_1 ->
    ...

  type_pattern_2, error_value_2 ->
    ...

  ...
end
```

The block under the first pattern that matches a raised error is invoked, and the result of the last expression is returned.

If you want to catch anything, you can use the `type, value` pattern or `_, _` if you're not interested in values. These patterns will handle any error that can occur.

It's also possible to specify code that should always be executed after the `try` block, regardless of whether an error was raised:

```
iex(7)> try do
          raise("Something went wrong")
        catch
          _,_ -> IO.puts("Error caught")
        after
          IO.puts("Cleanup code")     ◁——— Always executed
        end

Error caught
Cleanup code
```

Because it's always executed, the `after` block is useful for cleaning up resources—for example, to close an open file.

It's worth noting that the `after` clause doesn't affect the result of the entire `try` expression. The result of `try` is the result of the last expression, either from the `do` block or from the corresponding `catch` block if something was caught.

> **try and tail calls**
>
> You may recall the tail-call optimization from chapter 3. If the last thing a function does is call another function (or itself), then a simple jump will occur without a stack push. This optimization isn't possible if the function call resides in a `try` expression. This is fairly obvious because the last thing a function does is a `try` block, and it won't finish until its `do` or `catch` block is done. Consequently, whatever is called in `try` isn't the last thing a function does and is, therefore, not available for tail-call optimization.

There's much more to signaling and handling run-time errors. Elixir provides some abstractions on top of this basic mechanism. You can define custom errors via a `defexception` macro (see https://hexdocs.pm/elixir/Kernel.html#defexception/1) and handle them in a slightly more elegant fashion. The `try` special form also has a couple other features we haven't discussed. You should definitely research the official `try` documentation (https://hexdocs.pm/elixir/Kernel.SpecialForms.html#try/1) as well as the corresponding "Getting Started" section (https://elixir-lang.org/getting-started/try-catch-and-rescue.html).

What I've presented here are the core concepts of run-time errors. All other extensions supported by Elixir eventually boil down to these concepts and have the same properties:

- A run-time error has a type, which can be `:error`, `:exit`, or `:throw`.
- A run-time error also has a value, which can be any arbitrary term.
- If a run-time error isn't handled, the corresponding process will terminate.

Compared to languages such as C++, C#, Java, and JavaScript, there's much less need to catch run-time errors. A more common idiom is to let the process crash and then do something about it (usually, restart the process). This approach may seem hacky, but there's reasoning behind it. In a complex system, most bugs are flushed out in the testing phase. The remaining bugs mostly fall into a so-called *Heisenbug category*—unpredictable errors that occur irregularly in special circumstances and are difficult to reproduce. The cause of such errors usually lies in corruptness of the state. Therefore, a reasonable remedy for such errors is to let the process crash and start another one.

This may help because you're getting rid of the process state (which may be corrupt) and starting with a clean state. In many cases, doing so resolves the immediate problem. Of course, the error should be logged so that you can analyze it later and detect the root cause. But in the meantime, you can recover from an unexpected failure and continue providing service.

Don't worry if this discussion seems vague. This approach to error handling, also known as *letting it crash*, will be explained in detail throughout this chapter and the next. In the following section, we'll look at the basics of error handling in concurrent systems.

8.2 Errors in concurrent systems

Concurrency plays a central role in building fault-tolerant, BEAM-based systems. This is due to the total isolation and independence of individual processes. A crash in one process won't affect the others (unless you explicitly want it to).

Here's a quick demonstration:

```
iex(1)> spawn(fn ->          ◁─────────  Starts process 1
          spawn(fn ->        ◁────────  Starts process 2
            Process.sleep(1000)
            IO.puts("Process 2 finished")
```

```
    end)
                                                    Raises an error from
    raise("Something went wrong")    ⊲──    within process 1
end)
```

Running this yields the following output:

```
                                                    Error logger
17:36:20.546 [error] Process #PID<0.116.0> raised an exception    ⊲──  output
...
Process 2 finished    ⊲──── Output of process 2
```

As you can see, the execution of process 2 goes on, despite the fact that process 1 crashes. Information about the crash of process 1 is printed to the screen, but the rest of the system—including process 2 and the `iex` shell prompt—runs normally.

Furthermore, because processes share no memory, a crash in one process won't leave memory garbage that might corrupt another process. Therefore, by running independent actions in separate processes, you automatically ensure isolation and protection.

You already benefit from process isolation in this book's example to-do system. Recall the current architecture, shown in figure 8.1.

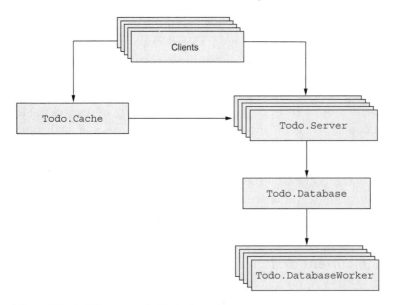

Figure 8.1   Isolating errors in the to-do system

All the boxes in the figure are BEAM processes. A crash in a single to-do server doesn't affect operations on other to-do lists. A crash in `Todo.Database` doesn't block cached reads that take place in to-do server processes.

Of course, this isolation isn't enough by itself. As you can see in figure 8.1, processes often communicate with each other. If a process isn't running, its clients can't use its services. For example, if the database process goes down, the to-do servers can't query it. What's worse, modifications to the to-do list won't be persisted. Obviously this isn't desirable behavior, and you must have a way of detecting a process crash and somehow recovering from it.

8.2.1 Linking processes

A basic primitive for detecting a process crash is the concept of *links*. If two processes are linked, and one of them terminates, the other process receives an *exit signal*—a notification that a process has crashed.

An exit signal contains the PID of the crashed process and the *exit reason*—an arbitrary Elixir term that provides a description of why the process has terminated. In the case of a normal termination (when the spawned function has finished), the exit reason is the atom `:normal`. By default, when a process receives an exit signal from another process and that signal is anything other than `:normal`, the linked process terminates as well. In other words, when a process terminates abnormally, the linked process is also taken down.

One link connects exactly two processes and is always bidirectional. To create a link, you can use `Process.link/1`, which connects the current process with another process. More often, a link is created when you start a process. You can do this by using `spawn_link/1`, which spawns a process and links it to the current one.

Let's verify this. In the following example, you again spawn two processes, this time linking them together. Then you take down one process:

```
iex(1)> spawn(fn ->
          spawn_link(fn ->    <──── Starts process 2 and links it to process 1
            Process.sleep(1000)
            IO.puts("Process 2 finished")
          end)

          raise("Something went wrong")
        end)
```

Unsurprisingly, this example gives the following output:

```
17:36:20.546 [error] Process #PID<0.116.0> raised an exception
```

Notice that you don't see the output from process 2. This is because process 1 terminated abnormally, which caused an exit signal to be emitted to process 2. One process can be linked to an arbitrary number of other processes, and you can create as many links in the system as you want, as shown in figure 8.2.

This illustrates the transitive nature of process links. In this structure, the crash of a single process will emit exit signals to all of its linked processes. If the default behavior isn't overridden, those processes will crash as well. Ultimately, the entire tree of linked processes will be taken down.

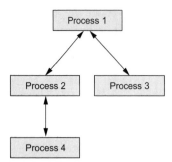

Figure 8.2   Example of links with multiple processes

TRAPPING EXITS

You may be puzzled by the consequences of links. Earlier, I explained how process isolation makes it possible to isolate the effect of a run-time error. Links break this isolation and propagate errors over process boundaries. You can think of a link as a communication channel for providing notifications about process terminations.

Usually, you don't want a linked process to crash. Instead, you want to detect the process crash and do something about it. This can be done by *trapping exits*. When a process is trapping exits, it isn't taken down when a linked process crashes. Instead, an exit signal is placed in the current process's message queue, in the form of a standard message. A trapping process can receive this message and do something about the crash.

To set up an exit trap, you call `Process.flag(:trap_exit, true)`, which makes the current process trap exit signals. Let's look at how this works:

```
iex(1)> spawn(fn ->
          Process.flag(:trap_exit, true)        ⟵┘  Traps exits in the
                                                     current process
          spawn_link(fn -> raise("Something went wrong") end)    ⟵┘  Spawns a
                                                                     linked process

          receive do                          Receives and prints
            msg -> IO.inspect(msg)            the message
          end
        end)
```

Here, you make the parent process trap exits and then spawn a linked process that will crash. Then you receive a message and print it to the screen. The shell session produces the following output:

```
{:EXIT, #PID<0.118.0>,
 {%RuntimeError{message: "Something went wrong"},
  [{:elixir_eval, :__FILE__, 1 [file: ~c"iex", line: 4]}]}}
```

The general format of the exit signal message is `{:EXIT, from_pid, exit_reason}`, where `from_pid` is the `pid` of the crashed process, and `exit_reason` is an arbitrary term that describes the reason for process termination. If a process is terminated due to a throw or an error, the exit reason is a tuple in the form {reason, where}, with where containing the stack trace. Otherwise, if a process is terminated due to an exit, the reason is a term provided to exit/1.

8.2.2 *Monitors*

As mentioned earlier, links are always bidirectional. Most of the time, this is exactly what you need, but in some cases, unidirectional propagation of a process crash works better. Sometimes, you need to connect two processes, A and B, in such a way that process A is notified when B terminates but not the other way around. In such cases, you can use a *monitor*, which is something like a unidirectional link.

To monitor a process, you use Process.monitor:

```
monitor_ref = Process.monitor(target_pid)
```

This makes the current process monitor the target process. The result is a unique reference that identifies the monitor. A single process can create multiple monitors.

If the monitored process dies, your process receives a message in the {:DOWN, monitor_ref, :process, from_pid, exit_reason} format. If you want to, you can also stop the monitor by calling Process.demonitor(monitor_ref).

Here's a quick example:

```
iex(1)> target_pid = spawn(fn ->          Spawns a process that
          Process.sleep(1000)              terminates after one second
        end)

iex(2)> Process.monitor(target_pid)   ◁——— Monitors the spawned process

iex(3)> receive do                        Waits for a
          msg -> IO.inspect(msg)          monitor message
        end

{:DOWN, #Reference<0.1398266903.3291480065.256365>, :process,    Monitor
  #PID<0.111.0>, :noproc}                                        message
```

There are two main differences between monitors and links. First, monitors are unidirectional—only the process that creates a monitor receives notifications. Additionally, unlike a link, the observer process won't crash when the monitored process terminates. Instead, a message is sent, which you can handle or ignore.

> ### Exits are propagated through GenServer calls
>
> When you issue a synchronous request via GenServer.call, if a server process crashes, an exit signal will occur in your client process. This is a simple but very important example of cross-process error propagation. Internally, GenServer sets up a temporary monitor that targets the server process. While waiting for a response from the server, if a :DOWN message is received, GenServer can detect that a process has crashed and raise a corresponding exit signal in the client process.

Links, exit traps, and monitors make it possible to detect errors in a concurrent system. You can introduce a process with the responsibility of receiving links and monitoring notifications as well as doing something when other processes in the system crash. Such processes, called *supervisors*, are the primary tools of error recovery in concurrent systems.

8.3   Supervisors

A *supervisor* is a generic process that manages the life cycle of other processes in a system. A supervisor process can start other processes, which are then considered to be its children. Using links, monitors, and exit traps, a supervisor detects possible terminations of any child, and can restart it if needed.

Processes that aren't supervisors are called *workers*. These are the processes that provide the actual services of the system. Your current version of the to-do system consists of only worker processes, such as the to-do cache and to-do server processes.

If any of the worker processes crashes, perhaps due to a bug, some part of your system will be gone forever. This is where supervisors can help. By running workers under a supervisor, you can ensure a failing process is restarted and the service of your system is restored.

To do that, you need at least one supervisor process in the system. In Elixir, this can be done using the `Supervisor` module (https://hexdocs.pm/elixir/Supervisor.html). By invoking `Supervisor.start_link/2`, you can start the supervisor process, which then works as follows:

1 The supervisor process traps exits and then starts the child processes.
2 If, at any point in time, a child terminates, the supervisor process receives a corresponding exit message and performs corrective actions, such as restarting the crashed process.
3 If the supervisor process terminates, its children are also taken down.

There are two different ways of starting a supervisor. In a basic approach, you invoke the function `Supervisor.start_link`, passing it a list that describes each child to be started under the supervisor, together with some additional supervisor options. Alternatively, you can pass a module defining a callback function that returns this information. We'll start with the basic approach and explain the second version a bit later.

Let's introduce one supervisor to the to-do system. Figure 8.3 recaps these processes in the system:

- `Todo.Server`—Allows multiple clients to work on a single to-do list
- `Todo.Cache`—Maintains a collection of to-do servers and is responsible for their creation and discovery
- `Todo.DatabaseWorker`—Performs read–write operations on the database
- `Todo.Database`—Manages a pool of database workers and forwards database requests to them

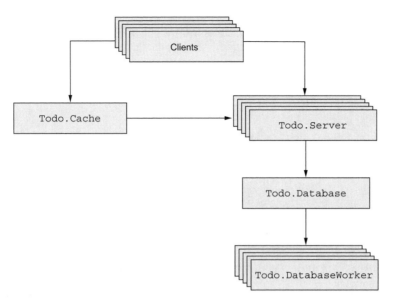

Figure 8.3 Processes in the to-do system

The to-do cache process is the system entry point. When you start the cache, all the needed processes are started, so the cache can be considered the root of the system. Now, we'll introduce a new supervisor process that will supervise the to-do cache process.

8.3.1 Preparing the existing code

Before you start working with the supervisor, you'll need to make a couple of changes to the cache. First, you'll register the cache process. This will allow you to interact with the process without needing to know its PID.

You'll also need to create a link while starting the to-do cache process. This is required if you want to run the process under a supervisor. Why is the supervisor using links rather than monitors? Because links work in both directions, so the termination of a supervisor means all its children will be automatically taken down. This, in turn, allows you to properly terminate any part of the system without leaving behind dangling processes. You'll see how this works in this chapter and the next, when you work with finer-grained supervision.

Creating a link to the caller process is as simple as using `GenServer.start_link` in place of `GenServer.start`. While you're at it, you can also rename the corresponding `Todo.Cache` interface function as `start_link`.

Finally, you'll make the `start_link` function take one argument and ignore it. This seems confusing, but it makes starting a supervised process a bit easier. The reasons will be explained later, when we discuss child specifications. The changes are shown in the following listing.

Listing 8.1 Changes in the to-do cache (supervised_todo_cache/lib/todo/cache.ex)

```
defmodule Todo.Cache do
  use GenServer

  def start_link(_) do          ←——— Renamed interface function          Registers under a
    GenServer.start_link(__MODULE__, nil, name: __MODULE__)  ←———  name and links to
  end                                                               the caller process

  def server_process(todo_list_name) do
    GenServer.call(__MODULE__, {:server_process, todo_list_name})   ←——
  end                                              Interface function that uses
                                                        the registered name
  def init(_) do
    IO.puts("Starting to-do cache.")   ←——
    ...                                    Debug message
  end

  ...
end
```

Notice that you also call `IO.puts/1` from the `init/1` callback for debugging purposes. This debug expression is included in all other `GenServer` callback modules (`Todo.Database`, `Todo.DatabaseWorker`, and `Todo.Server`).

8.3.2 *Starting the supervisor process*

With these changes in place, you can immediately try to start the supervisor process with to-do cache as its only child. Change the current folder to supervised_todo_cache, and start the shell (`iex -S mix`). Now, you can start the supervisor:

```
iex(1)> Supervisor.start_link([Todo.Cache], strategy: :one_for_one)   ←——

Starting to-do cache.                          Starts a supervisor and
Starting database server.                      to-do cache as its child
Starting database worker.
Starting database worker.
Starting database worker.
```

As you can see from the console output, invoking `Supervisor.start_link/2` caused the to-do cache to start. The cache process then started the database processes.

Let's take a closer look at the invocation of `Supervisor.start_link/2`:

```
Supervisor.start_link(         List of child specifications
  [Todo.Cache],      ←——
  strategy: :one_for_one   ←——
)                             Supervisor strategy
```

As the function name hints, `Supervisor.start_link/2` starts a supervisor process and links it to the caller.

The first argument is the list of desired children. More precisely, each element of this list is a child specification that describes how the child should be started and managed. We'll discuss child specifications in detail a bit later. In this simple form, the provided child specification is a module name. In this case, the child is described by some callback function in the `Todo.Cache` module.

When the supervisor process is started, it will go through this list and start each child according to the specification. In this example, the supervisor will invoke `Todo.Cache.start_link/1`. Once all the children are started, `Supervisor.start_link/2` returns `{:ok, supervisor_pid}`.

The second argument to `Supervisor.start_link/2` is the list of supervisor-specific options. The `:strategy` option, also known as the *restart strategy*, is mandatory. This option specifies how a supervisor should handle termination of its children. The `one_for_one` strategy states that if a child terminates, another child should be started in its place. There are a couple of other strategies (e.g., "Restart all children if a single child crashes"), and we'll discuss them in chapter 9.

> **NOTE** The term *restart* is used casually here. Technically, a process can't be restarted. It can only be terminated; then, another process, powered by the same module, can be started in its place. The new process has a different PID and doesn't share any state with the old one.

In any case, after `Supervisor.start_link/2` returns, all the required processes in the system are running, and you can interact with the system. For example, you can start one to-do server:

```
iex(2)> bobs_list = Todo.Cache.server_process("Bob's list")
Starting to-do server for Bob's list.
#PID<0.161.0>
```

The cache process is started as the child of the supervisor process, so we say that it's supervised. This means that if the cache process crashes, its supervisor will restart it.

You can quickly verify this by provoking a crash of the cache process. First, you need to get the PID of the cache. As mentioned, the cache is now registered under a name (its own module name), so getting its PID is easily done with the help of `Process.whereis/1`:

```
iex(3)> cache_pid = Process.whereis(Todo.Cache)
#PID<0.155.0>
```

Now, you can kill the process using the `Process.exit/2` function, which accepts a PID and the exit reason and then sends the corresponding exit signal to the given process. The exit reason can be an arbitrary term. Here, you'll use the atom `:kill`, which is treated in a special way. The exit reason `:kill` ensures that the target process is unconditionally taken down, even if the process is trapping exits. Let's see it in action:

```
iex(4)> Process.exit(cache_pid, :kill)
Starting to-do cache.
```

As you can see from the output, the process is immediately restarted. You can also prove that the to-do cache is now a process with a different PID:

```
iex(5)> Process.whereis(Todo.Cache)
#PID<0.164.0>
```

And you can use the new process, just as you did the old one:

```
iex(6)> bobs_list = Todo.Cache.server_process("Bob's list")
Starting to-do server for Bob's list.
#PID<0.167.0>
```

This brief experiment proves some basic fault-tolerance capabilities. After the crash, the system healed itself and resumed the full service.

> **Names allow process discovery**
>
> It's important to explain why you register the to-do cache under a local name. You should always keep in mind that to talk to a process, you need to have its PID. In chapter 7, you used a naive approach in which you created a process and then passed around its PID. This works fine until you enter the supervisor realm.
>
> The problem is that supervised processes can be restarted. Remember that restarting boils down to starting another process in place of the old one—the new process has a different PID. This means any reference to the PID of the crashed process becomes invalid, identifying a nonexistent process.
>
> That's why registered names are important. They provide a reliable way of finding a process and talking to it, regardless of possible process restarts.

8.3.3   *Child specification*

To manage a child process, a supervisor needs some information, such as answers to the following questions:

- How should the child be started?
- What should be done if the child terminates?
- What term should be used to uniquely identify each child?

These pieces of information are collectively called the *child specification*. Recall that when invoking `Supervisor.start_link/2`, you sent a list of child specifications. In its basic shape, a specification is a map with a couple of fields configuring the properties of the child.

For example, here's what the specification for the to-do cache could look like:

```
%{
  id: Todo.Cache,          ⟵───┤ The id of the child
  start: {Todo.Cache, :start_link, [nil]},  ⟵─── The start specification
}
```

The :id field is an arbitrary term that's used to distinguish this child from any other child of the same supervisor.

The :start field is a triplet in the shape of {module, start_function, list_of_arguments}. When starting the child, the generic supervisor code will use apply(module, start_function, list_of_arguments) to invoke the function described by this tuple. The invoked function must start and link the process.

There are some other fields you can omit from the specification—in which case, some sensible defaults are chosen. We'll discuss some of them later, in chapter 9. You can also refer to the official documentation at https://hexdocs.pm/elixir/Supervisor .html#module-child-specification for more details.

In any case, you can pass the specification map directly to Supervisor.start_link. Here's an example:

```
Supervisor.start_link(
  [
    %{
      id: Todo.Cache,
      start: {Todo.Cache, :start_link, [nil]}
    }
  ],
  strategy: :one_for_one
)
```

This will instruct the supervisor to invoke Todo.Cache.start_link(nil) to start the child. Recall that you changed Todo.Cache.start_link to take one argument (which is ignored), so you need to pass some value (nil, in this example).

One problem with this approach is that it's error prone. If something changes in the implementation of the cache, such as the signature of the start function, you need to remember to adapt the specification in the code starting the supervisor.

To address this issue, Supervisor allows you to pass a tuple {module_name, arg} in the child specification list. In this case, Supervisor will first invoke module_name .child_spec(arg) to get the actual specification. This function must return the specification map. The supervisor then proceeds to start the child according to the returned specification.

The Todo.Cache module already has child_spec/1 defined, even though you didn't write it yourself. The default implementation is injected by use GenServer. Therefore, you can also start the supervisor in the following way:

```
Supervisor.start_link(
  [{Todo.Cache, nil}],
  strategy: :one_for_one
)
```

As a consequence, Supervisor will invoke Todo.Cache.child_spec(nil) and start the child according to the returned specification. It's easy to verify what the injected implementation of child_spec/1 returns:

```
iex(1)> Todo.Cache.child_spec(nil)
%{id: Todo.Cache, start: {Todo.Cache, :start_link, [nil]}}
```

In other words, the generated `child_spec/1` returns a specification that invokes the module's `start_link/1` function with the argument passed to `child_spec/1`. This is precisely why you made `Todo.Cache.start_link` take one argument, even though the argument is ignored:

```
defmodule Todo.Cache do        │ Generates the
  use GenServer    ⟵──────────┘  default child_spec/1

  def start_link(_) do   ⟵───┐
    ...                       │ Conforms to the
  end                         └ default child_spec/1

  ...
end
```

By doing this, you made `Todo.Cache` compatible with the generated `child_spec/1`, which means you can include `Todo.Cache` in the list of children without needing to do any extra work.

If you don't like that approach, you can provide some options to `use GenServer` to tweak the output of the generated `child_spec/1`. Refer to the official documentation (https://hexdocs.pm/elixir/GenServer.html#module-how-to-supervise) for more details. If you need even more control, you can simply define `child_spec/1` yourself, which will override the default implementation.

Finally, if you don't care about the argument passed to `child_spec/1`, you can include just the module name in the child specification list. In this case, `Supervisor` will pass the empty list `[]` to `child_spec/1`. Therefore, you can also start `Todo.Cache` like this:

```
Supervisor.start_link(
  [Todo.Cache],
  strategy: :one_for_one
)
```

Before going further, let's recap how supervisor starting works. When you invoke `Supervisor.start_link(child_specs, options)`, the following happens:

1   The new process is started, powered by the `Supervisor` module.
2   The supervisor process goes through the list of child specifications and starts each child, one by one.
3   Each specification is resolved, if needed, by invoking `child_spec/1` from the corresponding module.
4   The supervisor starts the child process according to the `:start` field of the child specification.

8.3.4 Wrapping the supervisor

So far, you've played with the supervisor in the shell. But in real life, you'll want to work with supervisor in the code. Just like with `GenServer`, it's advised to wrap the `Supervisor` in a module.

The following listing implements the module for your first supervisor.

Listing 8.2 To-do system supervisor (supervised_todo_cache/lib/todo/system.ex)

```
defmodule Todo.System do
  def start_link do
    Supervisor.start_link(
      [Todo.Cache],
      strategy: :one_for_one
    )
  end
end
```

With this simple addition, starting the whole system becomes easy:

```
$ iex -S mix

iex(1)> Todo.System.start_link()

Starting to-do cache.
Starting database server.
Starting database worker.
Starting database worker.
Starting database worker.
```

The name `Todo.System` is chosen to describe the purpose of the module. By invoking `Todo.System.start_link()`, you start the entire to-do system with all the required services, such as the cache and database.

8.3.5 Using a callback module

Another way of starting a supervisor is by providing a callback module. This works similarly to `GenServer`. You develop the module that must implement the `init/1` function. This function must return the list of child specifications and additional supervisor options, such as its strategy.

Here's how you could rewrite `Todo.System` to use this approach:

```
defmodule Todo.System do        Includes some
  use Supervisor        ◄───    common boilerplate

  def start_link do
    Supervisor.start_link(__MODULE__, nil)      ◄──┐  Starts the supervisor with
  end                                               Todo.System as the callback module
```

```
def init(_) do
  Supervisor.init([Todo.Cache], strategy: :one_for_one)
end
end
```

**Implements the required
callback function**

As with GenServer, you start with use Supervisor to get some common boilerplate in
your module.

The crucial part happens when you invoke Supervisor.start_link/2. Instead of the
list of child specifications, you're now passing the callback module. In this case, the
supervisor process will invoke the init/1 function to provide the supervisor specification. The argument passed to init/1 is the second argument you pass to Supervisor
.start_link/2. Finally, in init/1, you describe the supervisor with the help of the
Supervisor .init/2 function, passing it the list of children and the supervisor options.

The preceding code is a more elaborate equivalent of Supervisor.start_
link([Todo.Cache], strategy: :one_for_one). Clearly, you need more lines of code to
get the same effect. On the upside, this approach gives you more control. For example, if you need to perform some extra initialization before starting the children, you
can do it in init/1. Moreover, the callback module is more flexible with respect to hot-
code reloading, allowing you to modify the list of children without needing to restart
the entire supervisor.

In most cases, the simple approach of passing the list of child specifications
directly will be sufficient. Moreover, as you've seen in the preceding examples, if you
wrap the use of Supervisor in a dedicated module, it's easy to switch from one
approach to the other. Therefore, in this book, you'll exclusively use the simple
approach without a callback module.

8.3.6   *Linking all processes*

At this point, you're supervising the to-do cache process, so you get some basic fault
tolerance. If the cache process crashes, a new process is started, and the system can
resume providing the service.

However, there's a problem in your current implementation. When the supervisor
restarts the to-do cache, you'll get a completely separate process hierarchy, and there
will be a new set of to-do server processes that are in no way related to the previous
ones. The previous to-do servers will be unused garbage that's still running and consuming both memory and CPU resources.

Let's demonstrate this issue. First, start the system and request one to-do server:

```
iex(1)> Todo.System.start_link()

iex(2)> Todo.Cache.server_process("Bob's list")
Starting to-do server for Bob's list.
#PID<0.159.0>
```

A cached to-do server isn't started on subsequent requests:

```
iex(3)> Todo.Cache.server_process("Bob's list")
#PID<0.159.0>
```

Check the number of running processes:

```
iex(4)> length(Process.list())
71
```

Now, terminate the to-do cache:

```
iex(5)> Process.exit(Process.whereis(Todo.Cache), :kill)
Starting to-do cache.
```

Finally, request a to-do server for Bob's list:

```
iex(6)> Todo.Cache.server_process("Bob's list")
Starting to-do server for Bob's list.
#PID<0.165.0>
```

As you can see, after you restart the to-do cache, retrieving a previously fetched server creates a new process. This isn't surprising because you killed the previous cache process, which also destroyed the process state.

When a process terminates, its state is released, and the new process starts with the fresh state. If you want to preserve the state, you must handle it yourself; we'll discuss this in chapter 9.

After the cache process is restarted, you have a completely new process that has no notion of what was previously cached. At the same time, your old cache structure (to-do servers) isn't cleaned up. You can see this by rechecking the number of running processes:

```
iex(7)> length(Process.list())
72
```

You have one additional process, which is the previously started to-do server for Bob's list. This obviously isn't good. Terminating a to-do cache destroys its state, so you should also take down all existing to-do servers. This way, you ensure proper process termination.

To do this, you must establish links between processes. Each to-do server must be linked to the cache. Going further, you'll also link the database server to the to-do cache and the database workers to the database server. This will effectively ensure the entire structure is linked, as illustrated in figure 8.4.

By linking a group of interdependent processes, you can ensure that the crash of one process takes down its dependencies as well. Regardless of which process crashes, links ensure the entire structure is terminated. Because this will lead to the termination of the cache process, it will be noticed by the supervisor, which will start a new system.

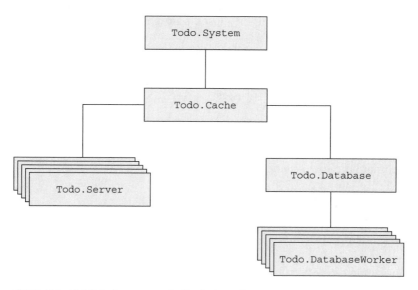

Figure 8.4 Linking all processes in the to-do system

With this approach, you can detect an error in any part of the system and recover from it without leaving dangling processes behind. On the downside, you're allowing errors to have a wide impact. An error in a single database worker or to-do server will take down the entire structure. This is far from perfect, and you'll make improvements in chapter 9.

For now, let's stick with this simple approach and implement the required code. In your present system, you have a to-do supervisor that starts and supervises the cache. You must ensure that the cache is directly or indirectly linked to all other worker processes.

The change is simple. All you need to do is switch from `start` to `start_link` for all the processes in the project. In the corresponding modules, you currently have something like this:

```
def start(...) do
  GenServer.start(...)
end
```

This snippet must be transformed into the following:

```
def start_link(...) do
  GenServer.start_link(...)
end
```

And, of course, every `module.start` invocation must be replaced with `module .start_link`. These changes are mechanical, and the code isn't presented here. The complete solution resides in the todo_links folder.

Let's see how the new system works:

```
iex(1)> Todo.System.start_link()

iex(2)> Todo.Cache.server_process("Bob's list")
Starting to-do server for Bob's list.

iex(3)> length(Process.list())
71                                                              ┌─ Terminates the entire
                                                                │  process structure
iex(4)> Process.exit(Process.whereis(Todo.Cache), :kill)  ◁────┘

iex(5)> bobs_list = Todo.Cache.server_process("Bob's list")
Starting to-do server for Bob's list.

iex(6)> length(Process.list())
71                        ◁──────── The process count remains the same.
```

When you crash a process, the entire structure is terminated, and a new process starts in its place. Links ensure that dependent processes are terminated as well, which keeps the system consistent.

8.3.7   Restart frequency

It's important to keep in mind that a supervisor won't restart a child process forever. The supervisor relies on the *maximum* restart frequency, which defines how many restarts are allowed in a given time period. By default, the maximum restart frequency is three restarts in 5 seconds. You can change these parameters by passing :max_restarts and :max_seconds options to Supervisor.start_link/2. If this frequency is exceeded, the supervisor gives up and terminates itself together with all of its children.

Let's verify this in the shell. First, start the supervisor:

```
iex(1)> Todo.System.start_link()
Starting the to-do cache.
```

Now, you need to perform frequent restarts of the to-do cache process:

```
iex(1)> for _ <- 1..4 do
          Process.exit(Process.whereis(Todo.Cache), :kill)
          Process.sleep(200)
        end
```

Here, you terminate the cache process and sleep for a short while, allowing the supervisor to restart the process. This is done four times, meaning that in the last iteration, you'll exceed the default maximum restart frequency (three restarts in 5 seconds).

Here's the output:

```
Starting the to-do cache.    │ Repeated
Starting database server.    │ three times
...

** (EXIT from #PID<0.149.0>) :shutdown    ◁──────── The supervisor terminates.
```

After the maximum restart frequency was exceeded, the supervisor gave up and terminated, taking down the child processes as well.

You may wonder about the reason for this mechanism. When a critical process in the system crashes, its supervisor tries to bring it back online by starting a new process. If this doesn't help, there's no point in infinite restarting. If too many restarts occur in a given time interval, it's clear that the problem can't be fixed. In this case, the only sensible thing a supervisor can do is give up and terminate itself, which also terminates all of its children.

This mechanism plays an important role in so-called *supervision trees*, where supervisors and workers are organized in a deeper hierarchy that allows you to control how the system recovers from errors. This will be thoroughly explained in the next chapter, where you'll build a fine-grained supervision tree.

Summary

- There are three types of run-time errors: throws, errors, and exits.
- When a run-time error occurs, execution moves up the stack to the corresponding `try` block. If an error isn't handled, a process will crash.
- Process termination can be detected in another process. To do this, you can use links or monitors.
- Links are bidirectional—a crash of either process is propagated to the other process.
- By default, when a process terminates abnormally, all processes linked to it terminate as well. By trapping exits, you can react to the crash of a linked process and do something about it.
- A supervisor is a process that manages the life cycle of other processes. It can start, supervise, and restart crashed processes.
- The `Supervisor` module is used to start supervisors and work with them.
- A supervisor is defined by the list of child specifications and the supervision strategy. You can provide these as the arguments to `Supervisor.start_link/2`, or you can implement a callback module.

Isolating error effects

This chapter covers

- Understanding supervision trees
- Starting workers dynamically
- "Let it crash"

In chapter 8, you learned about the basic theory behind error handling in concurrent systems based on the concept of supervisors. The idea is to have a process whose only job is to supervise other processes and to restart them if they crash. This gives you a way to deal with all sorts of unexpected errors in your system. Regardless of what goes wrong in a worker process, you can be sure that the supervisor will detect an error and restart the worker.

In addition to providing basic error detection and recovery, supervisors play an important role in isolating error effects. By placing individual workers directly under a supervisor, you can confine an error's impact to a single worker. This has an important benefit: it makes your system more available to its clients. Unexpected errors will occur no matter how hard you try to avoid them. Isolating the effects of such errors allows other parts of the system to run and provide service while you're recovering from the error.

For example, a database error in this book's example to-do system shouldn't stop the cache from working. While you're trying to recover from whatever went wrong in the database part, you should continue to serve existing cached data, thus providing at least partial service. Going even further, an error in an individual database worker shouldn't affect other database operations. Ultimately, if you can confine an error's impact to a small part of the system, your system can provide most of its services all the time.

Isolating errors and minimizing their negative effects is the topic of this chapter. The main idea is to run each worker under a supervisor, which makes it possible to restart each worker individually. You'll see how this works in the next section, in which you start to build a fine-grained supervision tree.

9.1 Supervision trees

In this section, we'll discuss how to reduce the effect of an error on the entire system. The basic tools are processes, links, and supervisors, and the general approach is fairly simple. You must always consider what will happen to the rest of the system if a process crashes due to an error, and you should take corrective measures when an error's impact is too wide (when the error affects too many processes).

9.1.1 Separating loosely dependent parts

Let's look at how errors are propagated in the to-do system. Links between processes are depicted in figure 9.1.

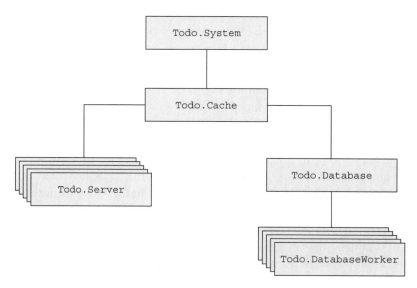

Figure 9.1 Process links in the to-do system

As you can see in the diagram, the entire structure is connected. Regardless of which process crashes, the exit signal will be propagated to its linked processes. Ultimately, the to-do cache process will crash as well, and this will be noticed by the Todo.System, which will, in turn, restart the cache process.

This is a correct error-handling approach because you restart the system and don't leave behind any dangling processes. But such a recovery approach is too coarse. Wherever an error happens, the entire system is restarted. In the case of a database error, the entire to-do cache will terminate. Similarly, an error in one to-do server process will take down all the database workers.

This coarse-grained error recovery is due to the fact that you're starting worker processes from within other workers. For example, a database server is started from the to-do cache. To reduce error effects, you need to start individual workers from the supervisor. Such a scheme makes it possible for the supervisor to supervise and restart each worker separately.

Let's see how to do this. First, you'll move the database server so that it's started directly from the supervisor. This will allow you to isolate database errors from those that happen in the cache.

Placing the database server under supervision is simple enough. You must remove the call to Todo.Database.start_link from Todo.Cache.init/1. Then, you must add another child specification when invoking Supervisor.start_link/2.

Listing 9.1 Supervising database server (supervise_database/lib/todo/system.ex)

```
defmodule Todo.System do
  def start_link do
    Supervisor.start_link(
      [
        Todo.Database,    <──── Includes database in the specification list
        Todo.Cache
      ],
      strategy: :one_for_one
    )
  end
end
```

There's one more small change that needs to be made. Just like you did with Todo.Cache, you need to adapt Todo.Database.start_link to take exactly one argument and ignore it. This will make it possible to rely on the autogenerated Todo.Database.child_spec/1, obtained by use GenServer.

Listing 9.2 Adapting start_link (supervise_database/lib/todo/database.ex)

```
defmodule Todo.Database do
  ...

  def start_link(_) do
    ...
```

```
    end

    ...
end
```

These changes ensure that the cache and the database are separated, as shown in figure 9.2. Running both the database and cache processes under the supervisor makes it possible to restart each worker individually. An error in the database worker will crash the entire database structure, but the cache will remain undisturbed. This means all clients reading from the cache will be able to get their results while the database part is restarting.

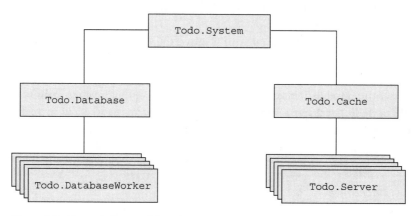

Figure 9.2 Separated supervision of database and cache

Let's verify this. Go to the supervise_database folder, and start the shell (iex -S mix). Then, start the system:

```
iex(1)> Todo.System.start_link()

Starting database server.
Starting database worker.
Starting database worker.
Starting database worker.
Starting to-do cache.
```

Now, kill the database server:

```
iex(2)> Process.exit(Process.whereis(Todo.Database), :kill)

Starting database server.
Starting database worker.
Starting database worker.
Starting database worker.
```

As you can see from the output, only database-related processes are restarted. The same is true if you terminate the to-do cache. By placing both processes under a supervisor, you localize the negative impact of an error. A cache error will have no effect on the database part, and vice versa.

Recall chapter 8's discussion of process isolation. Because each part is implemented in a separate process, the database server and the to-do cache are isolated and don't affect each other. Of course, these processes are indirectly linked via the supervisor, but the supervisor is trapping exit signals, thus preventing further propagation. This is a property of `one_for_one` supervisors in particular: they confine an error's impact to a single worker and take the corrective measure (restart) only on that process.

In this example, the supervisor starts two child processes. It's important to be aware that children are started synchronously, in the order specified. The supervisor starts a child, waits for it to finish, and then moves on to start the next child. When the worker is a `GenServer`, the next child is started only after the `init/1` callback function for the current child is finished.

You may recall from chapter 7 that `init/1` shouldn't run for a long time. This is precisely why. If `Todo.Database` was taking, say, 5 minutes to start, you wouldn't have the to-do cache available all that time. Always make sure your `init/1` functions run quickly, and use the technique mentioned in chapter 7 (post-initialization continuation via the `handle_continue/2` callback) when you need more complex initialization.

9.1.2 *Rich process discovery*

Although you now have some basic error isolation, there's still a lot to be desired. An error in one database worker will crash the entire database structure and terminate all running database operations. Ideally, you want to confine a database error to a single worker. This means each database worker must be directly supervised.

There's one problem with this approach. Recall that in the current version, the database server starts the workers and keeps their PIDs in its internal list. But if a process is started from a supervisor, you don't have access to the PID of the worker process. This is a property of supervisors. You can't keep a worker's PID for a long time because that process might be restarted, and its successor will have a different PID.

Therefore, you need a way to give symbolic names to supervised processes and access each process via this name. When a process is restarted, the successor will register itself under the same name, which will allow you to reach the right process even after multiple restarts.

You could use registered names for this purpose. The problem is that names can only be atoms, and in this case, you need something more elaborate that will allow you to use arbitrary terms, such as {:database_worker, 1}, {:database_worker, 2}, and so on. What you need is a process registry that maintains a key–value map, where the keys are names and the values are PIDs. A process registry differs from standard local registration in that names can be arbitrarily complex.

Every time a process is created, it can register itself to the registry under a name. If a process is terminated and restarted, the new process will reregister itself. Having a registry will give you a fixed point where you can discover processes (their PIDs). The idea is illustrated in figure 9.3.

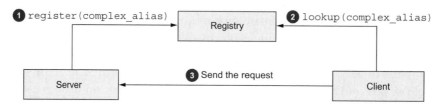

Figure 9.3   Discovering processes through a registry

First, the worker process registers itself, usually during initialization. Sometime later, the client process will query the registry for the PID of the desired worker. The client can then issue a request to the server process.

Elixir's standard library includes the implementation of a process registry in the `Registry` module. This module allows you to associate a process with one or more arbitrary complex keys and then find the process (its PID) by performing a key-based lookup.

Let's look at a couple of examples. The process registry is, itself, a process. You can start it by invoking `Registry.start_link/1`:

```
iex(1)> Registry.start_link(name: :my_registry, keys: :unique)
```

The single argument is a keyword list of registry options. The mandatory options are `:name` and `:keys`.

The `:name` option is an atom, and it specifies the name of the registry process. You'll use this name to interact with the registry.

The `:keys` option can either be `:unique` or `:duplicate`. In a unique registry, names are unique—only one process can be registered under any key. This is useful when you want to assign a unique role to processes. For example, in your system, only one process could be associated with `{:database_worker, 1}`. In contrast, in a duplicate registry, several processes can have the same name. Duplicate registry is useful in scenarios where a single publisher process needs to send notifications to a dynamic number of subscriber processes that tend to come and go over time.

Once you have the registry started, you can register a process under some key. Let's try it out. You'll spawn a mock `{:database_worker, 1}` process that waits for a message and then prints it to the console:

```
iex(2)> spawn(fn ->                              Registers the process at the registry
          Registry.register(:my_registry, {:database_worker, 1}, nil)   ←┐

        receive do
```

```
      msg -> IO.puts("got message #{inspect(msg)}")
    end
  end)
```

The crucial bit happens when invoking `Registry.register/3`. Here, you're passing the name of the registry (`:my_registry`), the desired name of the spawned process (`{:database_worker, 1}`), and an arbitrary value. The `Registry` will then store a mapping of the name to the provided value and the PID of the caller process.

At this point, the registered process can be discovered by other processes. Notice how in the preceding snippet, you didn't take the PID of the database worker. That's because you don't need it. You can look it up in the registry by invoking `Registry.lookup/2`:

```
iex(3)> [{db_worker_pid, _value}] =
          Registry.lookup(
            :my_registry,
            {:database_worker, 1}
          )
```

`Registry.lookup/2` takes the name of the registry and the key (process name) and returns a list of {pid, value} tuples. When the registry is unique, this list can be either empty (no process is registered under the given key), or it can have one element. For a duplicate registry, this list can have any number of entries. The `pid` element in each tuple is the PID of the registered process, whereas the `value` is the value provided to `Registry.register/3`.

Now that you've discovered the mock database worker, you can send it a message:

```
iex(4)> send(db_worker_pid, :some_message)
got message :some_message
```

A very useful property of `Registry` is that it links to all the registered processes. This allows the registry to notice the termination of these processes and remove the corresponding entry from its internal structure.

You can immediately verify this. The database worker mock was a one-off process. It received a message, printed it, and then stopped. Try to discover it again:

```
iex(5)> Registry.lookup(:my_registry, {:database_worker, 1})
[]
```

As you can see, no entry is found under the given key because the database worker terminated.

> **NOTE** It's worth mentioning that `Registry` is implemented in plain Elixir. You can think of `Registry` as something like a `GenServer` that holds the map of names to PIDs in its state. In reality, the implementation is more sophisticated and relies on the ETS table feature, which you'll learn about in chapter 10. ETS tables allow `Registry` to be very efficient and scalable. Lookups and writes are very fast, and in many cases, they won't block each other, meaning multiple operations on the same registry may run in parallel.

`Registry` has more features and properties, which we won't discuss here. You can take a look at the official documentation at https://hexdocs.pm/elixir/Registry.html for more details. But there's one very important feature of OTP processes that you need to learn about: *via tuples*.

9.1.3   Via tuples

A *via tuple* is a mechanism that allows you to use an arbitrary third-party registry to register OTP-compliant processes, such as `GenServer` and supervisors. Recall that you can provide a `:name` option when starting a `GenServer`:

```
GenServer.start_link(callback_module, some_arg, name: some_name)
```

So far, you've only passed atoms as the `:name` option, which caused the started process to be registered locally. But the `:name` option can also be provided in the shape of `{:via, some_module, some_arg}`. Such a tuple is also called a *via tuple*.

If you provide a via tuple as the name option, `GenServer` will invoke a well-defined function from `some_module` to register the process. Likewise, you can pass a via tuple as the first argument to `GenServer.cast` and `GenServer.call`, and `GenServer` will discover the PID using `some_module`. In this sense, `some_module` acts like a custom third-party process registry, and the via tuple is the way of connecting such a registry with `GenServer` and similar OTP abstractions.

The third element of the via tuple, `some_arg`, is a piece of data that's passed to functions of `some_module`. The exact shape of this data is defined by the registry module. At the very least, this piece of data must contain the name under which the process should be registered and looked up.

In the case of `Registry`, the third argument should be a pair, `{registry_name, process_key}`, so the entire via tuple then has the shape of `{:via, Registry, {registry_name, process_key}}`.

Let's look at an example. We'll revisit our old friend from chapter 6: the `EchoServer`. This is a simple `GenServer` that handles a call request by returning the request payload. Now, you'll add registration to the echo server. When you start the server, you'll provide the server ID—an arbitrary term that uniquely identifies the server. When you want to send a request to the server, you'll pass this ID, instead of the PID.

Here's the full implementation:

```
defmodule EchoServer do
  use GenServer

  def start_link(id) do
    GenServer.start_link(__MODULE__, nil, name: via_tuple(id))    ⟵── Registers the server using a via tuple
  end

  def init(_), do: {:ok, nil}

  def call(id, some_request) do
```

```
        GenServer.call(via_tuple(id), some_request)        ⟵┐  Discovers the server
    end                                                      │  using a via tuple

    defp via_tuple(id) do
        {:via, Registry, {:my_registry, {__MODULE__, id}}}  ⟵┐  Registry-compliant
    end                                                      │  via tuple

    def handle_call(some_request, _, state) do
        {:reply, some_request, state}
    end
end
```

Here, you consolidate the shaping of the via tuple in the `via_tuple/1` helper function. The registered name of the process will be `{__MODULE__, id}` or, in this case, `{EchoServer, id}`.

Try it out. Start the `iex` session, copy and paste the module definition, and then start `:my_registry`:

```
iex(1)> defmodule EchoServer do ... end

iex(2)> Registry.start_link(name: :my_registry, keys: :unique)
```

Now, you can start and interact with multiple echo servers without needing to keep track of their PIDs:

```
iex(3)> EchoServer.start_link("server one")
iex(4)> EchoServer.start_link("server two")

iex(5)> EchoServer.call("server one", :some_request)
:some_request

iex(6)> EchoServer.call("server two", :another_request)
:another_request
```

Notice that the IDs here are strings, and also recall that the whole registered key is, in fact, `{EchoServer, some_id}`, which proves that you're using arbitrary complex terms to register processes and discover them.

9.1.4 Registering database workers

Now that you've learned the basics of `Registry`, you can implement registration and discovery of your database workers. First, you need to create the `Todo.ProcessRegistry` module.

Listing 9.3 To-do process registry (pool_supervision/lib/todo/process_registry.ex)

```
defmodule Todo.ProcessRegistry do
  def start_link do
    Registry.start_link(keys: :unique, name: __MODULE__)
  end
```

```
    def via_tuple(key) do
      {:via, Registry, {__MODULE__, key}}
    end

    def child_spec(_) do
      Supervisor.child_spec(
        Registry,                            Child
        id: __MODULE__,                      specification
        start: {__MODULE__, :start_link, []}
      )
    end
end
```

The interface functions are straightforward. The start_link function simply forwards to the Registry module to start a unique registry. The via_tuple/1 function can be used by other modules, such as Todo.DatabaseWorker, to create the appropriate via tuple that registers a process with this registry.

Because the registry is a process, it should be supervised. Therefore, you include child_spec/1 in the module. Here, you're using Supervisor.child_spec/2 to adjust the default specification from the Registry module. This invocation essentially states that you'll use whatever child specification is provided by Registry, with :id and :start fields changed. By doing this, you don't need to know about the internals of the Registry implementation, such as whether the registry process is a worker or a supervisor.

With this in place, you can immediately put the registry under the Todo.System supervisor.

Listing 9.4   Supervising registry (pool_supervision/lib/todo/system.ex)

```
defmodule Todo.System do
  def start_link do
    Supervisor.start_link(
      [
        Todo.ProcessRegistry,      ◁─── Starts the process registry
        Todo.Database,
        Todo.Cache
      ],
      strategy: :one_for_one
    )
  end
end
```

Keep in mind that processes are started synchronously, in the order you specify. Thus, the order in the child specification list matters and isn't chosen arbitrarily. A child must always be specified after its dependencies. In this case, you must start the registry first because database workers will depend on it.

With Todo.ProcessRegistry in place, you can start adapting the database workers. The relevant changes are presented in the following listing.

Listing 9.5   Registering workers (pool_supervision/lib/todo/database_worker.ex)

```elixir
defmodule Todo.DatabaseWorker do
  use GenServer

  def start_link({db_folder, worker_id}) do
    GenServer.start_link(
      __MODULE__,
      db_folder,
      name: via_tuple(worker_id)      ◁──── Registration
    )
  end

  def store(worker_id, key, data) do
    GenServer.cast(via_tuple(worker_id), {:store, key, data}) ◁──┐
  end                                                            │
                                                                 │  Discovery
  def get(worker_id, key) do                                     │
    GenServer.call(via_tuple(worker_id), {:get, key})    ◁───────┘
  end

  defp via_tuple(worker_id) do
    Todo.ProcessRegistry.via_tuple({__MODULE__, worker_id})
  end

  ...
end
```

This code introduces the notion of a `worker_id`, which is an integer in the range `1..pool_size`. The `start_link` function now takes this parameter together with `db_folder`. However, notice that the function takes both parameters as a single `{db_folder, worker_id}` tuple. The reason is again in conformance with the autogenerated `child_spec/1`, which forwards to `start_link/1`. To manage a worker under a supervisor, you can now use the `{Todo.DatabaseWorker, {db_folder, worker_id}}` child specification.

When invoking `GenServer.start_link`, you provide the via tuple as the name option. The exact shape of the tuple is wrapped in the internal `via_tuple/1` function, which takes the worker ID and returns the corresponding via tuple. This function just delegates to `Todo.ProcessRegistry`, passing it the desired name in the form `{__MODULE__, worker_id}`. Therefore, a worker is registered with the key `{Todo.DatabaseWorker, worker_id}`. Such a name eliminates possible clashes with other types of processes that might be registered with the same registry.

Similarly, you use the `via_tuple/1` helper to discover the processes when invoking `GenServer.call` and `GenServer.cast`. Notice that `store/3` and `get/2` functions now receive a worker ID as the first argument. This means their clients don't need to keep track of the PIDs anymore.

9.1.5   Supervising database workers

Now, you can create a new supervisor that will manage the pool of workers. Why introduce a separate supervisor? Theoretically, placing workers under `Todo.System` would work fine. But remember from the previous chapter that if restarts happen too often, the supervisor gives up at some point and terminates all of its children. If you keep too many children under the same supervisor, you might reach the maximum restart intensity sooner—in which case, all processes are restarted. In other words, problems in a single process could easily ripple out to the majority of the system.

In this case, I made an arbitrary decision to place a distinct part of the system (the database) under a separate supervisor. This approach may limit the impact of a failed restart to database operations. If restarting one database worker fails, the supervisor will terminate, which means the parent supervisor will try to restart the entire database service without touching other processes in the system.

Either way, the consequence of these changes is that you don't need the database GenServer anymore. The purpose of this server was to start a pool of worker processes and manage the mapping of a worker ID to PID. With these new changes, the workers are started by the supervisor; the mapping is already handled by the registry. Therefore, the database GenServer is redundant.

You can keep the Todo.Database module. It will now implement a supervisor of database worker processes and retain the same interface functions as before. As a result, you don't need to change the code of the client Todo.Server module at all, and you can keep Todo.Database in the list of Todo.System children.

Next, you'll convert the database into a supervisor.

Listing 9.6   Supervising workers (pool_supervision/lib/todo/database.ex)

```
defmodule Todo.Database do
  @pool_size 3
  @db_folder "./persist"

  def start_link do
    File.mkdir_p!(@db_folder)

    children = Enum.map(1..@pool_size, &worker_spec/1)
    Supervisor.start_link(children, strategy: :one_for_one)
  end

  defp worker_spec(worker_id) do
    default_worker_spec = {Todo.DatabaseWorker, {@db_folder, worker_id}}
    Supervisor.child_spec(default_worker_spec, id: worker_id)
  end

  ...
end
```

You start off by creating a list of three child specifications, each of them describing one database worker. Then, you pass this list to Supervisor.start_link/2.

The specification for each worker is created in worker_spec/1. You start off with the default specification for the database worker, {Todo.DatabaseWorker, {@db_folder, worker_id}}. Then, you use `Supervisor.child_spec/2` to set the unique ID for the worker.

Without that, you'd end up having multiple children with the same ID. Recall from chapter 8 that a default `child_spec/1`, generated via `use GenServer`, provides the name of the module in the `:id` field. Consequently, if you use that default specification and try to start two database workers, they'll both get the same ID of `Todo.DatabaseWorker`. Then, the `Supervisor` module will complain about it and raise an error.

You also need to implement `Todo.Database.child_spec/1`. You just converted the database into a supervisor, so the module doesn't contain `use GenServer` anymore, meaning `child_spec/1` isn't autogenerated. The code is shown in the following listing.

Listing 9.7 Database operations (pool_supervision/lib/todo/database.ex)

```
defmodule Todo.Database do
  ...

  def child_spec(_) do
    %{
      id: __MODULE__,
      start: {__MODULE__, :start_link, []},
      type: :supervisor
    }
  end

  ...
end
```

The specification contains the field `:type`, which hasn't been mentioned before. This field can be used to indicate the type of the started process. The valid values are `:supervisor` (if the child is a supervisor process) or `:worker` (for any other kind of process). If you omit this field, the default value of `:worker` is used.

The `child_spec/1` in listing 9.7, therefore, specifies that `Todo.Database` is a supervisor and that it can be started by invoking `Todo.Database.start_link/0`.

This is a nice example of how `child_spec/1` helps you keep implementation details in the module that powers a process. You just turned the database into a supervisor, and you changed the arity of its `start_link` function (it now takes zero arguments), but nothing needs to be changed in the `Todo.System` module.

Next, you need to adapt the `store/2` and `get/1` functions.

Listing 9.8 Database operations (pool_supervision/lib/todo/database.ex)

```
defmodule Todo.Database do
  ...

  def store(key, data) do
    key
    |> choose_worker()
```

```
      |> Todo.DatabaseWorker.store(key, data)
  end

  def get(key) do
    key
    |> choose_worker()
    |> Todo.DatabaseWorker.get(key)
  end

  defp choose_worker(key) do
    :erlang.phash2(key, @pool_size) + 1
  end

  ...
end
```

The only difference from the previous version is in the choose_worker/1 function. Previously, this function issued a call to the database server. Now, it just selects the worker ID in the range 1..@pool_size. This ID is then passed to Todo.DatabaseWorker functions, which will perform a registry lookup and forward the request to the corresponding database worker.

At this point, you can test how the system works. Start everything:

```
iex(1)> Todo.System.start_link()

Starting database server.
Starting database worker.
Starting database worker.
Starting database worker.
Starting to-do cache.
```

Now, verify that you can restart individual workers correctly. To do that, you need to get the PID of a worker. Because you know the internals of the system, this can easily be done by looking it up in the registry. Once you have the PID, you can terminate the worker:

```
iex(2)> [{worker_pid, _}] =
          Registry.lookup(
            Todo.ProcessRegistry,
            {Todo.DatabaseWorker, 2}
          )

iex(3)> Process.exit(worker_pid, :kill)
Starting database worker.
```

The worker is restarted, as expected, and the rest of the system is undisturbed.

It's worth repeating how the registry supports proper behavior in the system regarding restarted processes. When a worker is restarted, the new process has a different PID. But owing to the registry, the client code doesn't care about that. You resolve the PID at the latest possible moment, doing a registry lookup prior to issuing a request to the database worker. Therefore, in most cases, the lookup will succeed, and you'll talk to the proper process.

In some cases, the discovery of the database worker might return an invalid value, such as if the database worker crashes after the client process found its PID but before the request is sent. In this case, the client process has a stale PID, so the request will fail. A similar problem can occur if a client wants to find a database worker that has just crashed. Restarting and registration run concurrently with the client, so the client might not find the worker PID in the registry.

Both scenarios lead to the same result: the client process—in this case, a to-do server—will crash, and the error will be propagated to the end user. This is a consequence of the highly concurrent nature of the system. A failure recovery is performed concurrently in the supervisor process, so some part of the system might not be in a consistent state for a brief period.

9.1.6 *Organizing the supervision tree*

Let's stop for a moment and reflect on what you've done so far. The relationship between processes is presented in figure 9.4.

This is an example of a simple *supervision tree*—a nested structure of supervisors and workers. The tree describes how the system is organized into a hierarchy of services. In this example, the system consists of three services: the process registry, the database, and the cache.

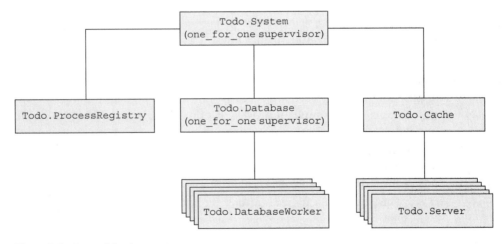

Figure 9.4 Supervision tree

Each service can be further subdivided into subservices. For example, the database is composed of several workers, and the cache is composed of multiple to-do servers. Even the registry is further subdivided into multiple processes, but that's an implementation detail of the `Registry` module, so it's not shown on the diagram.

Although supervisors are frequently mentioned in the context of fault tolerance and error recovery, defining the proper starting order is their most essential role. The supervision tree describes how the system is started and how it's taken down.

A more granular tree allows you to take down an arbitrary part of the system, without touching anything else. In the current version, stopping the database service is as easy as asking its parent (`Todo.System`) to stop the `Todo.Database` child, using the `Supervisor.terminate_child/2` function. This will take down the database process together with its descendants.

If worker processes are small services in a system, you can think of supervisors as being service managers—a built-in equivalent of systemd, Windows Service Manager, and the like. They're responsible for the life cycles of services they directly manage. If any critical service stops, its parent will try to restart it.

Looking at the supervision tree, you can reason about how errors are handled and propagated throughout the system. If a database worker crashes, the database supervisor will restart it, leaving the rest of the system alone. If that doesn't help, you'll exceed the maximum restart frequency, and the database supervisor will terminate all database workers and then itself.

This will be noticed by the system supervisor, which will then start a fresh database pool in hopes of solving the problem. What does all this restarting get you? By restarting an entire group of workers, you effectively terminate all pending database operations and begin clean. If that doesn't help, there's nothing more you can do, so you propagate the error up the tree (in this case, killing everything). This is how error recovery works in supervision trees—you try to recover from an error locally, affecting as few processes as possible. If that doesn't work, you move up and try to restart the wider part of the system.

OTP-COMPLIANT PROCESSES

All processes that are started directly from a supervisor should be *OTP compliant*. To implement an OTP-compliant process, it's not enough to spawn or link a process; you also must handle some OTP-specific messages in a particular way. The details of what exactly must be done are provided in the Erlang documentation at https://www.erlang.org/doc/design_principles/spec_proc.html#special-processes.

Luckily, you usually won't need to implement an OTP-compliant process from scratch. Instead, you can use various higher-level abstractions, such as `GenServer`, `Supervisor`, and `Registry`. The processes started with these modules will be OTP-compliant. Elixir also ships with `Task` and `Agent` modules that can be used to run OTP-compliant processes. You'll learn about tasks and agents in the next chapter.

Plain processes started by `spawn_link` aren't OTP-compliant, so such processes shouldn't be started directly from a supervisor. You can freely start plain processes from workers, such as `GenServer`, but it's generally better to use OTP-compliant processes wherever possible.

SHUTTING DOWN PROCESSES

An important benefit of supervision trees is the ability to stop the entire system without leaving dangling processes. When you terminate a supervisor, all of its immediate children are also terminated. If all other processes are directly or indirectly linked to those children, they will eventually be terminated as well. Consequently, you can stop the entire system by terminating the top-level supervisor process.

Most often, a supervisor subtree is terminated in a controlled manner. A supervisor process will instruct its children to terminate gracefully, thus giving them the chance to do final cleanup. If some of those children are, themselves, supervisors, they will take down their own trees in the same way. Graceful termination of a GenServer worker involves invoking the terminate/2 callback but only if the worker process is trapping exits. Therefore, if you want to do some cleanup from a GenServer process, make sure you set up an exit trap from an init/1 callback.

Because graceful termination involves the possible execution of cleanup code, it may take longer than desired. The :shutdown option in a child specification lets you control how long the supervisor will wait for the child to terminate gracefully. If the child doesn't terminate in this time, it will be forcefully terminated. You can choose the shutdown time by specifying shutdown: shutdown_strategy in child_spec/1 and passing an integer representing a time in milliseconds. Alternatively, you can pass the atom :infinity, which instructs the supervisor to wait indefinitely for the child to terminate. Finally, you can pass the atom :brutal_kill, telling the supervisor to immediately terminate the child in a forceful way. The forceful termination is done by sending a :kill exit signal to the process, like you did with Process.exit(pid, :kill). The default value of the :shutdown option is 5_000 for a worker process or :infinity for a supervisor process.

AVOIDING PROCESS RESTARTING

By default, a supervisor restarts a terminated process regardless of the exit reason. Even if the process terminates with the reason :normal, it will be restarted. Sometimes, you may want to alter this behavior.

For example, consider a process that handles an HTTP request or a TCP connection. If such a process fails, the socket will be closed, and there's no point in restarting the process (the remote party will be disconnected anyway). You still want to have such processes under a supervision tree because this makes it possible to terminate the entire supervisor subtree without leaving dangling processes. In this situation, you can set up a *temporary* worker by providing restart: :temporary in child_spec/1. A temporary worker isn't restarted on termination.

Another option is a *transient* worker, which is restarted only if it terminates abnormally. Transient workers can be used for processes that may terminate normally as part of the standard system workflow. A typical example for this is a one-off job you want to execute when the system is started. You could start the corresponding process (usually powered by the Task module) in the supervision tree, and then configure it as transient. A transient worker can be specified by providing `restart: :transient` in `child_spec/1`.

RESTART STRATEGIES

So far, you've been using only the `:one_for_one` restart strategy. In this mode, a supervisor handles a process termination by starting a new process in its place, leaving other children alone. There are two additional restart strategies:

- `:one_for_all`—When a child crashes, the supervisor terminates all other children and then starts all children.
- `:rest_for_one`—When a child crashes, the supervisor terminates all younger siblings of the crashed child. Then, the supervisor starts new child processes in place of the terminated ones.

These strategies are useful if there's tight coupling between siblings, where the service of some child doesn't make any sense without its siblings. One example is when a process keeps the PID of some sibling in its own state. In this case, the process is tightly coupled to an instance of the sibling. If the sibling terminates, so should the dependent process.

By opting for `:one_for_all` or `:rest_for_one`, you can make that happen. The former is useful when there's tight dependency in all directions (every sibling depends on other siblings). The latter is appropriate if younger siblings depend on the older ones.

For example, in the to-do system, you could use `:rest_for_one` to take down database workers if the registry process terminates. Without the registry, these processes can't serve any purpose, so taking them down would be the proper thing to do. In this case, however, you don't need to do that because `Registry` links each registered process to the registry process. As a result, a termination of the registry process is properly propagated to the registered processes. Any such process that doesn't trap exits will be taken down automatically; processes that trap exits will receive a notification message.

This concludes our initial look at fine-grained supervision. You've made several changes that minimize the effects of errors, but there's still a lot of room for improvement. You'll continue extending the system in the next section, where you'll learn how to start workers dynamically.

9.2   *Starting processes dynamically*

With the changes you made in the previous section, the impact of a database-worker error is now confined to a single worker. It's time to do the same thing for to-do servers. You'll use roughly the same approach as you did with database workers: running each to-do server under a supervisor and registering the servers in the process registry.

9.2.1   *Registering to-do servers*

You'll start off by adding registration to to-do servers. The change is simple, as shown in the following listing.

Listing 9.9 Registering to-do servers (dynamic_workers/lib/todo/server.ex)

```
defmodule Todo.Server do
  use GenServer, restart: :temporary
                                                    Registers the server
  def start_link(name) do
    GenServer.start_link(__MODULE__, name, name: via_tuple(name))
  end

  defp via_tuple(name) do
    Todo.ProcessRegistry.via_tuple({__MODULE__, name})
  end

  ...
end
```

This is the same technique you used with database workers. You pass the via tuple as the name option. The via tuple will state that the server should be registered with the {__MODULE__, name} key to the process registry. Using this form of the key avoids possible collisions between to-do server keys and database worker keys.

The functions add_entry/2 and entries/2 are unchanged, and they still take the PID as the first argument, so the usage remains the same. A client process first obtains the PID of the to-do server by invoking Todo.Cache.server_process/1, and then it invokes Todo.Server functions.

9.2.2 Dynamic supervision

Next, you need to supervise to-do servers. There's a twist, though. Unlike database workers, to-do servers are created dynamically when needed. Initially, no to-do server is running; each is created on demand when you call Todo.Cache.server_process/1. This effectively means you can't specify supervisor children up front because you don't know how many children you'll need.

For such cases, you need a dynamic supervisor that can start children on demand. In Elixir, this feature is available via the DynamicSupervisor module.

DynamicSupervisor is similar to Supervisor, but where Supervisor is used to start a predefined list of children, DynamicSupervisor is used to start children on demand. When you start a dynamic supervisor, you don't provide a list of child specifications, so only the supervisor process is started. Then, whenever you want to, you can start a supervised child using DynamicSupervisor.start_child/2.

Let's see this in action. You'll convert Todo.Cache into a dynamic supervisor, much like what you did with the database. The relevant code is presented in the following listing.

Listing 9.10 To-do cache as a supervisor (dynamic_workers/lib/todo/cache.ex)

```
defmodule Todo.Cache do
  def start_link() do
    IO.puts("Starting to-do cache.")
```

```
    DynamicSupervisor.start_link(     ←——— Starts a dynamic supervisor
      name: __MODULE__,
      strategy: :one_for_one
    )
  end

  ...
end
```

You start the supervisor using `DynamicSupervisor.start_link/1`. This will start the supervisor process, but no children are specified at this point. Notice that when starting the supervisor, you're also passing the `:name` option. This will cause the supervisor to be registered under a local name.

By making the supervisor locally registered, it's easier for you to interact with the supervisor and ask it to start a child. You can immediately use this by adding the `start_child/1` function, which starts the to-do server for the given to-do list:

```
defmodule Todo.Cache do
  ...

  defp start_child(todo_list_name) do
    DynamicSupervisor.start_child(
      __MODULE__,
      {Todo.Server, todo_list_name}
    )
  end

  ...
end
```

Here, you're invoking `DynamicSupervisor.start_child/2`, passing it the name of your supervisor and the child specification of the child you want to start. The `{Todo.Server, todo_list_name}` specification will lead to the invocation of `Todo.Server.start_link(todo_list_name)`. The to-do server will be started as the child of the `Todo.Cache` supervisor.

It's worth noting that `DynamicSupervisor.start_child/2` is a cross-process synchronous call. A request is sent to the supervisor process, which then starts the child. If several client processes simultaneously try to start a child under the same supervisor, the requests will be serialized.

For more details on dynamic supervisors, refer to the official documentation at https://hexdocs.pm/elixir/DynamicSupervisor.html.

One small thing left to do is implement `child_spec/1`:

```
defmodule Todo.Cache do
  ...

  def child_spec(_arg) do
    %{
      id: __MODULE__,
```

```
        start: {__MODULE__, :start_link, []},
        type: :supervisor
      }
    end

    ...
end
```

At this point, the to-do cache is converted into a dynamic supervisor.

9.2.3 Finding to-do servers

The final thing left to do is to change the discovery Todo.Cache.server_process/1 function. This function takes a name and returns the pid of the to-do server, starting it if it's not running. The implementation is provided in the following listing.

Listing 9.11 Finding a to-do server (dynamic_workers/lib/todo/cache.ex)

```
defmodule Todo.Cache do
  ...

  def server_process(todo_list_name) do
    case start_child(todo_list_name) do
      {:ok, pid} -> pid                                    ◁──── A new server is started.
      {:error, {:already_started, pid}} -> pid             ◁──┐ The server was
    end                                                       │ already running.
  end

  defp start_child(todo_list_name) do
    DynamicSupervisor.start_child(
      __MODULE__,
      {Todo.Server, todo_list_name}
    )
  end
end
```

The function first invokes the local start_child/1 function, which you prepared in the previous section and which is a simple wrapper around DynamicSupervisor.start_child/2.

This invocation can have two successful outcomes. In the most obvious case, the function returns {:ok, pid} with the pid of the newly started to-do server.

The second outcome is more interesting. If the result is {:error, {:already_started, pid}}, the to-do process failed to register because another process is already registered with the same name—a to-do server for the list with the given name is already running. For the to-do example, this outcome is also a success. You tried to start the server, but it was already running. That's fine. You have the pid of the server, and you can interact with it.

The result {:error, {:already_started, pid}} is returned, due to the inner workings of GenServer registration. When the :name option is provided to GenServer.start_link, the registration is performed in the started process before init/1 is invoked. This registration can fail if some other process is already registered under the same key. In this case, GenServer.start_link doesn't resume to run the server loop. Instead, it returns {:error, {:already_started, pid}}, where the pid points to the process that's registered under the same key. This result is then returned by DynamicSupervisor.start_child.

It's worth briefly discussing how server_process/1 behaves in a concurrent scenario. Consider the case of two processes invoking this function at the same time. The execution moves to DynamicSupervisor.start_child/2, so you might end up with two simultaneous executions of start_child on the same supervisor. Recall that a child is started in the supervisor process. Therefore, the invocations of start_child are serialized and server_process/1 doesn't suffer from race conditions.

On the flip side, the way start_child is used here is not very efficient. Every time you want to work with a to-do list, you issue a request to the supervisor, so the supervisor process can become a bottleneck. Even if the to-do server is already running, the supervisor will briefly start a new child, which will immediately stop. This process can easily be improved, but we'll leave it for now because the current implementation is behaving properly. We'll revisit this issue in chapter 12 when we move to a distributed registration.

9.2.4   *Using the temporary restart strategy*

There's one thing left to do. You'll configure the to-do server to be a :temporary child. As a result, if a to-do server stops—say, due to a crash—it won't be restarted.

Why choose this approach? Servers are started on demand, so when a user tries to interact with a to-do list, if the server process isn't running, it will be started. If a to-do list server crashes, it will be started on the next use, so there's no need to restart it automatically.

Opting for the :temporary strategy also means the parent supervisor won't be restarted, due to too many failures in its children. Even if there are frequent crashes in one to-do server—say, due to corrupt state—you'll never take down the entire cache, which should improve the availability of the entire system.

Changing the restart strategy is easily done by providing the :restart option to use GenServer.

> **Listing 9.12   Changing to-do server restart strategy (dynamic_workers/lib/todo/server.ex)**

```
defmodule Todo.Server do
  use GenServer, restart: :temporary

  ...
end
```

The :temporary value will be included under the :restart key in the result of child_spec/1, so the parent supervisor will treat the child as temporary. If the child terminates, it won't be restarted.

You might wonder why to-do servers are supervised if they're not restarted. There are two important benefits of this. First, this structure ensures that the failure of a single to-do server doesn't affect any other process in the system. In addition, as explained in section 9.1.6, this allows you to properly take down the system, or some service in the system, without leaving any dangling processes behind. To stop all to-do servers, you need to stop the Todo.Cache supervisor. In other words, supervision isn't just about restarting crashed processes but also about isolating individual crashes and enabling proper termination.

9.2.5 Testing the system

At this point, the to-do servers are supervised, and you can test the code. Notice that you didn't have to make any change in the Todo.System supervisor. The Todo.Cache was already listed as a child, and you only changed its internals. Let's see if this works.

Start the shell and the entire system:

```
iex(1)> Todo.System.start_link()

Starting database server.
Starting database worker.
Starting database worker.
Starting database worker.
Starting to-do cache.
```

Now, you can get one to-do server:

```
iex(2)> bobs_list = Todo.Cache.server_process("Bob's list")
Starting to-do server for Bob's list
#PID<0.118.0>
```

Repeating the request doesn't start another server:

```
iex(3)> bobs_list = Todo.Cache.server_process("Bob's list")
#PID<0.118.0>
```

In contrast, using a different to-do list name creates another process:

```
iex(4)> alices_list = Todo.Cache.server_process("Alice's list")
Starting to-do server for Alice's list
#PID<0.121.0>
```

Crash one to-do server:

```
iex(5)> Process.exit(bobs_list, :kill)
```

The subsequent call to Todo.Cache.server_process/1 will return a different PID:

```
iex(6)> Todo.Cache.server_process("Bob's list")
Starting to-do server for Bob's list
#PID<0.124.0>
```

Of course, Alice's server remains undisturbed:

```
iex(7)> Todo.Cache.server_process("Alice's list")
#PID<0.121.0>
```

The supervision tree of the new code is presented in figure 9.5. The diagram depicts how you supervise each process, limiting the effect of unexpected errors.

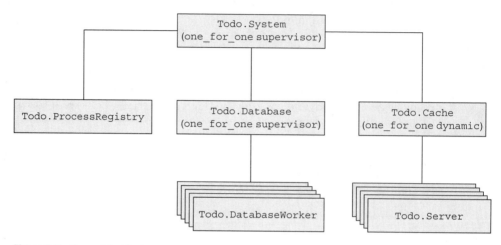

Figure 9.5 Supervising to-do servers

With this, you're finished making your to-do system fault tolerant. You've introduced additional supervisor processes to the system, and you've also managed to simplify some other parts (removing the to-do cache and database server processes). You'll make many more changes to this system, but for now, let's leave it and look at some important, practical considerations.

9.3   *"Let it crash"*

In general, when you develop complex systems, you should employ supervisors to do your error handling and recovery. With properly designed supervision trees, you can limit the impact of unexpected errors, and the system will, hopefully, recover. I can personally testify that supervisors have helped me in occasional weird situations in production, keeping the running system stable and saving me from unwanted phone calls in the middle of the night. It's also worth noting that OTP provides logging facilities, so process crashes are logged and you can see that something went wrong. It's even possible to set up an event handler that will be triggered on every process crash, thus allowing you to perform custom actions, such as sending an email or reporting to an external system.

An important consequence of this style of error handling is that the worker code is liberated from paranoid, defensive `try/catch` constructs. Usually, these aren't needed because you use supervisors to handle error recovery. Joe Armstrong, one of the inventors of Erlang, described such a style in his PhD thesis ("Making reliable distributed systems in the presence of software errors," https://erlang.org/download/armstrong_thesis_2003.pdf) as *intentional programming*. Using this approach, the code states the programmer's intention, rather than being cluttered with all sorts of defensive constructs.

This style is also known as *let it crash*. In addition to making the code shorter and more focused, "let it crash" promotes clean-slate recovery. Remember, when a new process starts, it starts with new state, which should be consistent. Furthermore, the message queue (mailbox) of the old process is thrown away. This will cause some requests in the system to fail. However, the new process starts fresh, which gives it a better chance to resume normal operation.

Initially, "let it crash" may seem confusing, and people may mistake it for the "let *everything* crash" approach. There are two important situations in which you should explicitly handle an error:

- In critical processes that shouldn't crash
- When you expect an error that can be dealt with in a meaningful way

Let's look at each of these.

9.3.1 Processes that shouldn't crash

Processes that shouldn't crash are informally called a system's *error kernel*—processes that are critical for the entire system to work and whose state can't be restored in a simple and consistent way. Such processes are the heart of your system, and you generally don't want them to crash because, without them, the system can't provide any service.

You should keep the code of such important processes as simple as possible. The less logic that happens in the process, the smaller the chance of a process crash. If the code of your error-kernel process is complex, consider splitting it into two processes: one that holds state and another that does the actual work. The former process then becomes extremely simple and is unlikely to crash, whereas the worker process can be removed from the error kernel (because it no longer maintains critical state).

Additionally, you could consider including defensive try/catch expressions in each handle_* callback of a critical process, to prevent a process from crashing. Here's a simple sketch of the idea:

```
def handle_call(message, _, state) do
  try
    new_state =
      state
      |> transformation_1()
      |> transformation_2()
      ...

    {:reply, response, new_state}

  catch _, _ ->                          Catches all errors and
    {:reply, {:error, reason}, state}    uses the original state
  end
end
```

This snippet illustrates how immutable data structures allow you to implement a fault-tolerant server. While processing a request, you make a series of transformations on the state. If anything bad happens, you use the initial state, effectively performing a rollback of all changes. This preserves state consistency while keeping the process constantly alive.

Keep in mind that this technique doesn't completely guard against a process crash. For example, you can always kill a process by invoking `Process.exit(pid, :kill)` because a `:kill` exit reason can't be intercepted, even if you're trapping exits. Therefore, you should always have a recovery plan for the crash of a critical process. Set up a proper supervision hierarchy to ensure the termination of all dependent processes in the case of an error-kernel process crash.

9.3.2 *Handling expected errors*

The whole point of the "let it crash" approach is to leave recovery of unexpected errors to supervisors. But if you can predict an error and you have a way to deal with it, there's no reason to let the process crash.

Here's a simple example. Look at the `:get` request in the database worker:

```
def handle_call({:get, key}, _, db_folder) do
  data =
    case File.read(file_name(db_folder, key)) do
      {:ok, contents} -> :erlang.binary_to_term(contents)
      _ -> nil                    ⟵──────┐
    end                                  │ Handles a file-read error

  {:reply, data, db_folder}
end
```

When handling a `get` request, you try to read from a file, covering the case when this read fails. If it doesn't succeed, you return `nil`, treating this case as if an entry for the given key isn't in the database.

But you can do better. Consider using an error only when the file isn't available. This error is identified with `{:error, :enoent}`, so the corresponding code would look like this:

```
case File.read(...) do
  {:ok, contents} -> do_something_with(contents)
  {:error, :enoent} -> nil
end
```

Notice how you rely on pattern matching here. If neither of these two expected situations happens, a pattern match will fail, and so will your process. This is the idea of "let it crash." You deal with expected situations (the file is either available or doesn't exist), crashing if anything else goes wrong (e.g., you don't have permissions).

In contrast, when storing data, you use `File.write!/2` (notice the exclamation mark), which may throw an exception and crash the process. If you don't succeed in saving the data, your database worker has failed, and there's no point in hiding this fact. It's better to fail fast, which will cause an error that will be logged and (hopefully) noticed and fixed.

Of course, restarting may not help. In this case, the supervisor will give up and crash itself, and the system will quickly come to a halt, which is probably a good thing. There is no point in working if you can't persist the data.

As a general rule, if you know what to do with an error, you should definitely handle it. Otherwise, for anything unexpected, let the process crash and ensure proper error isolation and recovery via supervisors.

9.3.3 *Preserving the state*

Keep in mind that state isn't preserved when a process is restarted. Remember from chapter 5 that a process's state is its own private affair. When a process crashes, the memory it occupied is reclaimed, and the new process starts with new state. This has the important advantage of starting clean. Perhaps the process crashed due to inconsistent state, and starting fresh may fix the error.

That said, in some cases, you'll want the process's state to survive the crash. This isn't provided out of the box; you need to implement it yourself. The general approach is to save the state outside of the process (e.g., in another process or to a database) and then restore the state when the successor process is started.

You already have this functionality in the to-do server. Recall that you have a simple database system that persists to-do lists to disk. When the to-do server is started, the first thing it tries to do is to restore the data from the database. This makes it possible for the new process to inherit the state of the old one.

In general, be careful when preserving state. As you learned in chapter 4, a typical change in a functional data abstraction goes through chained transformations:

```
new_state =
  state
  |> transformation_1(...)
  ...
  |> transformation_n(...)
```

As a rule, the state should be persisted after all transformations are completed. Only then can you be certain that your state is consistent, so this is a good opportunity to save it. For example, you do this in the to-do server after you modify the internal data abstraction:

```
def handle_cast({:add_entry, new_entry}, {name, todo_list}) do
  new_list = Todo.List.add_entry(todo_list, new_entry)
  Todo.Database.store(name, new_list)          ⟵──┐
  {:noreply, {name, new_list}}                     │ Persists the state
end
```

TIP Persistent state can have a negative effect on restarts. Let's say an error is caused by state that's somehow invalid (perhaps due to a bug). If this state is persisted, your process can never restart successfully because the process will restore the invalid state and then crash again (either on starting or when handling a request). You should be careful when persisting state. If you can afford to, it's better to start clean and terminate all other dependent processes.

Summary

- Supervisors allow you to localize the impact of an error, keeping unrelated parts of the system undisturbed.

- The registry helps you find processes without needing to track their PIDs. This is very helpful if a process is restarted.

- Each process should reside somewhere in a supervision tree. This makes it possible to terminate the entire system (or an arbitrary subpart of it) by terminating the supervisor.

- `DynamicSupervisor` is used for on-demand starting.

- When a process crashes, its state is lost. You can deal with this by storing state outside the process, but more often than not, it's best to start with a clean state.

- In general, you should handle unexpected errors through a proper supervision hierarchy. Explicit handling through a `try` construct should be used only when you have a meaningful way to deal with an error.

Beyond GenServer

10

This chapter covers

- Tasks
- Agents
- ETS tables

Chapters 8 and 9 introduced the distinction between worker and supervisor processes. Workers are the processes that provide some part of your service, whereas supervisors organize the worker processes into a tree. This allows you to start and stop processes in the desired order as well as to restart critical processes if they fail.

As was mentioned in section 9.1.6, all processes started directly from a supervisor should be OTP-compliant processes. Processes started with plain `spawn` and `spawn_link` are not OTP compliant, so you should refrain from running such processes in production. Modules such as `Supervisor`, `GenServer`, and `Registry` allow you to start OTP-compliant processes that can be placed into a supervision tree.

In this chapter, you'll learn about two additional modules that also allow you to run OTP-compliant workers: `Task` and `Agent`. Tasks can be very useful when you need to run one-off jobs, whereas agents can be used to manage state and provide concurrent access to it. Finally, we'll discuss a related feature called *ETS tables*, which, under some conditions, can serve as more efficient alternatives to `GenServer` and `Agent`. There's a lot of new ground to cover, so let's start by discussing tasks.

10.1 *Tasks*

The `Task` module can be used to concurrently run a job—a process that takes some input, performs some computation, and then stops. In this sense, task-powered processes have a different flow than server processes. Whereas a `GenServer` process acts as a long-running server, a `Task`-powered process starts its work immediately, doesn't serve requests, and stops when the work is done.

The `Task` module can be used in two different ways, depending on whether the task process needs to send a result back to the process that started it or not. The former case is also called an *awaited task* because the starter process waits for the task to send the result back. Let's discuss this option first.

10.1.1 *Awaited tasks*

An *awaited task* is a process that executes some function, sends the function result back to the starter process, and then terminates. Let's look at a basic example.

Suppose you want to start a concurrent, possibly long-running, job and get its result back. You can simulate a long-running job with the following function:

```
iex(1)> long_job =
         fn ->
           Process.sleep(2000)
           :some_result
         end
```

This lambda, when invoked, sleeps for 2 seconds and then returns `:some_result`.

To run this lambda concurrently, you can use `Task.async/1`:

```
iex(2)> task = Task.async(long_job)
```

The `Task.async/1` function takes a zero-arity lambda, spawns a separate process, and invokes the lambda in the spawned process. The return value of the lambda will be sent as a message back to the starter process.

Because the computation runs in a separate process, `Task.async/1` returns immediately, even if the lambda itself takes a long time to finish. This means the starter process isn't blocked and can perform some additional work concurrently with the task process.

The return value of `Task.async/1` is a struct that describes the running tasks. This struct can be passed to `Task.await/1` to await the result of the task:

```
iex(3)> Task.await(task)
:some_result
```

The function `Task.await/1` waits for the response message from the task process. This message will contain the result of the lambda. When the message arrives, `Task.await/1` returns the lambda's result. If the message doesn't arrive within 5 seconds, `Task.await/1` will raise an exception. You can provide a different timeout as the second parameter to `Task.await/2`.

Awaited tasks can be very useful when you need to run a couple of mutually independent, one-off computations and wait for all the results. To illustrate this, we'll reuse the example from section 5.2.2. In that example, you needed to execute multiple independent queries and collect all the results. Because queries are mutually independent, you can improve the total execution time by running each query in a separate process and sending the result as a message to the starter process. The starter process then needs to await all the results.

Back in chapter 5, you implemented this from scratch, using `spawn`, `send`, and `receive`. Here, you'll rely on `Task.async/1` and `Task.await/1`.

First, define a helper lambda that simulates a long-running query execution:

```
iex(1)> run_query =
          fn query_def ->
            Process.sleep(2000)
            "#{query_def} result"
          end
```

Now, you can start five queries, each in a separate task:

```
iex(2)> queries = 1..5

iex(3)> tasks =
          Enum.map(
            queries,
            &Task.async(fn -> run_query.("query #{&1}") end)
          )
```

Here, you create five queries, and then start each query execution in a separate task. The result in the `tasks` variable is a list of five `%Task{}` structs, each describing one task executing a query.

To wait for all the results, you pass each task from the `tasks` variable to the `Task.await/1` function:

```
iex(4)> Enum.map(tasks, &Task.await/1)
["query 1 result", "query 2 result", "query 3 result", "query 4 result",
 "query 5 result"]
```

Using the pipe operator, you can write this code in a slightly shorter way:

```
iex(5)> 1..5
        |> Enum.map(&Task.async(fn -> run_query.("query #{&1}") end))
        |> Enum.map(&Task.await/1)

["query 1 result", "query 2 result", "query 3 result", "query 4 result",
 "query 5 result"]    ⟵——————— Returns after 2 seconds
```

The fact that all the results are collected in 2 seconds proves each task is running in a separate process.

This code waits for the tasks using the order in which the tasks were started. Therefore, the result ordering is deterministic. The first element of the result list is the result of query 1, the second element is the result of query 2, and so on.

It should be noted that `Task.async/1` links the new task to the starter process. Therefore, if any task process crashes, the starter process will crash too (unless it's trapping exits). The crash of the starter process will, in turn, cause all the other tasks started by the same process to crash. In other words, starting multiple tasks with `Task.async/1` has all-or-nothing semantics. The crash of a single task takes down all other tasks as well as the starter process.

If you want to explicitly handle failures of individual tasks, you'll need to trap exits and handle corresponding exit messages in the starter process. There are some functions available in the `Task` module that can help you here, most notably `Task.async_stream/3`. You can refer to the official documentation at https://hexdocs.pm/elixir/Task.html for more details. In the meantime, let's take a look at how you can work with tasks when the starter process doesn't need to wait for their results.

10.1.2 *Non-awaited tasks*

If you don't want to send a result message back to the starter process, you can use `Task.start_link/1`. This function can be thought of as an OTP-compliant wrapper around plain `spawn_link`. The function starts a separate process and links it to the caller. Then, the provided lambda is executed in the started process. Once the lambda finishes, the process terminates with the reason `:normal`. Unlike `Task.async/1`, `Task.start_link/1` won't send any message to the starter process. Here's a basic example:

```
iex(1)> Task.start_link(fn ->
          Process.sleep(1000)
          IO.puts("Hello from task")
        end)

{:ok, #PID<0.89.0>}     ◁——— Result of Task.start_link/1

Hello from task!     ◁——— Printed 1 second later
```

Let's look at a more concrete example. Suppose you want to gather some metrics about your system and report them at regular intervals. This is an example of a non-responsive job. You don't really need a `GenServer` here because you don't need to serve requests from other client processes. Instead, you want a process that sleeps for a while and then gathers relevant metrics and reports them.

Let's start implementing this in your to-do system. First, you'll implement a sequential loop that periodically gathers metrics and prints them to the screen.

Listing 10.1   Reporting system metrics (todo_metrics/lib/todo/metrics.ex)

```
defmodule Todo.Metrics do
  ...
```

```
  defp loop() do
    Process.sleep(:timer.seconds(10))
    IO.inspect(collect_metrics())
    loop()
  end

  defp collect_metrics() do
    [
      memory_usage: :erlang.memory(:total),
      process_count: :erlang.system_info(:process_count)
    ]
  end
end
```

In real life, you'd likely want to collect much more data and send it to an external service, but this example keeps things simple.

You want to run this loop as a part of your system. To do this, you need to start a task.

Listing 10.2 Metrics reporter as task (todo_metrics/lib/todo/metrics.ex)

```
defmodule Todo.Metrics do
  use Task

  def start_link(_arg), do: Task.start_link(&loop/0)

  ...
end
```

First, you specify use Task, which will inject the child_spec/1 function into the Todo.Metrics module. As with GenServer, the injected specification will invoke start_link/1, so you need to define start_link/1, even if you don't use the argument. The implementation of start_link/1 simply invokes Task.start_link/1 to start a task process where the loop is running.

With these two simple lines of code, the Todo.Metrics module is ready to be injected into the supervision tree.

Listing 10.3 Starting a supervised metrics task (todo_metrics/lib/todo/system.ex)

```
defmodule Todo.System do
  def start_link do
    Supervisor.start_link(
      [
        Todo.Metrics,
        ...
      ],
      strategy: :one_for_one
    )
  end
end
```

This is the main purpose of `Task.start_link/1`—it allows you to start an OTP-compliant process that you can safely run as a child of some supervisor.

Try it out:

```
$ iex -S mix

iex(1)> Todo.System.start_link()

[memory_usage: 48110864, process_count: 74]   ⟵     Printed after 10 seconds
[memory_usage: 48505592, process_count: 74]   ⟵     Printed after 20 seconds
```

This was a simple way of implementing a periodic job in your system, without needing to run multiple OS processes and use external schedulers such as `cron`.

In more complex scenarios, it's worth separating scheduling from the job logic. The idea is to use one process for periodic scheduling and then start each job instance in a separate one-off process. Such an approach improves fault-tolerance because the crash of a job process won't disturb the scheduling process. You can try to implement this approach as an exercise, but when it comes to production, it's better to rely on battle-tested, third-party libraries, such as Quantum (https://github.com/quantum-elixir/quantum-core).

10.1.3 *Supervising dynamic tasks*

In many situations, you'll want to start non-awaited tasks dynamically. A common example is when you need to communicate with a remote service, such as a payment gateway, while handling a web request.

A naive approach would be to perform this communication synchronously, while the request is being handled. However, this approach can lead to poor user experience. If there are some intermittent networking issues, communicating with a remote service might be slow, or it might completely fail.

A better approach is to perform this communication asynchronously, from a separate task process. You accept the incoming request, start a task that communicates with the remote service, and immediately respond that the request has been accepted. Once the task is done, you issue a notification about the outcome, perhaps via Web-Socket or an email. This improves system responsiveness and enhances system resilience to various networking issues. You could retry the failed communication over a longer period of time, without needing to block the request handler—or even keep the user connected.

This is an example of a dynamically started independent task. The task is started on demand, and its life cycle must be decoupled from the life cycle of the process that started it (the process that handles the incoming request).

In such situations, it's best to run the task under a dedicated supervisor. You could use `DynamicSupervisor` for this purpose, but Elixir includes a task-specific wrapper around it called `Task.Supervisor` (https://hexdocs.pm/elixir/Task.Supervisor.html).

To run dynamically supervised tasks, start the task supervisor:

```
iex(1)> Task.Supervisor.start_link(name: MyTaskSupervisor)
```

Now, you can use `Task.Supervisor.start_child/2` to start a task under that supervisor:

```
iex(2)> Task.Supervisor.start_child(
          MyTaskSupervisor,
          fn ->
            IO.puts("Task started")
            Process.sleep(2000)
            IO.puts("Task stopping")
          end
        )
{:ok, #PID<0.118.0>}       <─────┐   **Result of start_child**

Task started       <──────┐   **Printed immediately**
Task stopping      <───────   **Printed after 2 seconds**
```

It's important to understand the distinction between the logical and the actual starter process. The shell process is the process that initiated task creation. However, the task is actually started as a child of the task supervisor. As a result of this process structure, the life cycles of the logical starter (the `iex` shell process) and the task are separated. A crash of one process won't affect the other.

This concludes our brief tour of tasks. We haven't covered all the nuances, so I advise you to study the official module documentation in more detail at https://hexdocs .pm/elixir/Task.html. Next, we'll take a look at agents.

10.2   Agents

The `Agent` module provides an abstraction that's similar to `GenServer`. Agents require a bit less ceremony and can, therefore, eliminate some boilerplate associated with `GenServer`. On the flip side, `Agent` doesn't support all the scenarios that `GenServer` does. If a `GenServer` implements only `init/1`, `handle_cast/2`, and   `handle_call/3`, it can be replaced with an `Agent`. But if you need to use `handle_info/2` or `terminate/1`, `Agent` won't suffice, and you'll need to use `GenServer`. Let's explore this further, starting with the basic use of agents.

10.2.1   Basic use

To start an agent, you can use `Agent.start_link/1`:

```
iex(1)> {:ok, pid} = Agent.start_link(fn -> %{name: "Bob", age: 30} end)
{:ok, #PID<0.86.0>}
```

`Agent.start_link/1` will start a new process and execute the provided lambda in that process. Unlike a task, an agent process doesn't terminate when the lambda is finished. Instead, an agent uses the return value of the lambda as its state. Other processes can access and manipulate an agent's state using various functions from the `Agent` module.

To fetch the agent's state, or some part of it, you can use `Agent.get/2`:

```
iex(2)> Agent.get(pid, fn state -> state.name end)
"Bob"
```

`Agent.get/2` takes the PID of the agent and a lambda. The lambda is invoked in the agent's process, and it receives the agent's state as the argument. The return value of the lambda is sent back to the caller process as a message. This message is received in `Agent.get/2`, which then returns the result to its caller.

To modify the agent's state, you can use `Agent.update/2`:

```
iex(3)> Agent.update(pid, fn state -> %{state | age: state.age + 1} end)
:ok
```

This will cause the internal state of the agent process to change. You can verify the change with `Agent.get/2`:

```
iex(2)> Agent.get(pid, fn state -> state end)
%{age: 31, name: "Bob"}
```

It's worth mentioning that `Agent.update/2` is synchronous. The function only returns after the update has succeeded. An asynchronous update can be performed with `Agent.cast/2`.

There are some other functions available in the `Agent` module, so you're advised to study the official documentation at https://hexdocs.pm/elixir/Agent.html. In the meantime, let's discuss how agents work in a concurrent setting.

10.2.2 *Agents and concurrency*

A single agent, being a process, can be used by multiple client processes. A change made by one process can be observed by other processes in subsequent agent operations. Let's demonstrate this.

You'll start an agent that's used as a counter:

```
iex(1)> {:ok, counter} = Agent.start_link(fn -> 0 end)
```

The initial state of the agent is 0. Now, manipulate the agent's state from another process:

```
iex(2)> spawn(fn -> Agent.update(counter, fn count -> count + 1 end) end)
```

Finally, let's check the agent's state from the shell process:

```
iex(3)> Agent.get(counter, fn count -> count end)
1
```

This example demonstrates that the state is associated with the agent process. When one client process changes the state of the agent, subsequent operations issued by other processes will see the new state.

An agent process works exactly like a `GenServer`. If multiple clients try to work with the same agent at the same time, the operations will be serialized and executed one by one. In fact, the `Agent` module is implemented in plain Elixir on top of `GenServer`. To demystify this, let's sketch a naive implementation of an `Agent`-like module.

Here's how you can implement the agent-like state initialization:

```
defmodule MyAgent do        │ Agent is implemented
  use GenServer      ◁───┘ with GenServer.

  def start_link(init_fun) do                      │ Passes the lambda as the
    GenServer.start_link(__MODULE__, init_fun)  ◁─┘ argument to the server
  end

  def init(init_fun) do        │ Invokes the lambda and uses
    {:ok, init_fun.()}   ◁───┘ its result as the server's state
  end

  ...
end
```

Recall from chapter 5 that any term can be sent as a message. This includes anonymous functions, and the agent implementation takes advantage of that fact. Agent interface functions take an anonymous function as an argument and pass the function to the server process, which, in turn, invokes the function and does something with its result.

The same approach is used to provide `get` and `update` operations:

```
defmodule MyAgent do
  ...

  def get(pid, fun) do
    GenServer.call(pid, {:get, fun})
  end

  def update(pid, fun) do
    GenServer.call(pid, {:update, fun})
  end

  def handle_call({:get, fun}, _from, state) do
    response = fun.(state)
    {:reply, response, state}
  end

  def handle_call({:update, fun}, _from, state) do
    new_state = fun.(state)
    {:reply, :ok, new_state}
  end

  ...
end
```

The real implementation of the Agent module is more sophisticated and feature rich, but the basic idea is the same as in the preceding example. The Agent module is a plain GenServer that can be controlled by sending lambdas to the process. Therefore, concurrent reasoning about agents is exactly the same as with GenServer.

10.2.3 *Agent-powered to-do server*

Because Agent can be used to manage concurrent state, it's a perfect candidate to power your to-do list server. Converting a GenServer into an agent is a fairly straightforward job. You need to replace a pair of interface functions and the corresponding GenServer callback clause with a single function that uses the Agent API.

The full code of the Todo.Server as an agent is provided in the following listing.

Listing 10.4 **Agent-powered to-do server (todo_agent/lib/todo/server.ex)**

```elixir
defmodule Todo.Server do
  use Agent, restart: :temporary

  def start_link(name) do
    Agent.start_link(
      fn ->
        IO.puts("Starting to-do server for #{name}")
        {name, Todo.Database.get(name) || Todo.List.new()}
      end,
      name: via_tuple(name)
    )
  end

  def add_entry(todo_server, new_entry) do
    Agent.cast(todo_server, fn {name, todo_list} ->
      new_list = Todo.List.add_entry(todo_list, new_entry)
      Todo.Database.store(name, new_list)
      {name, new_list}
    end)
  end

  def entries(todo_server, date) do
    Agent.get(
      todo_server,
      fn {_name, todo_list} -> Todo.List.entries(todo_list, date) end
    )
  end

  defp via_tuple(name) do
    Todo.ProcessRegistry.via_tuple({__MODULE__, name})
  end
end
```

It's worth noting that the interface of the module remains unchanged, so there's no need to modify the code of any other module.

There are two things worth discussing in this code. The first is the expression `use Agent` at the start of the module. Just like with `GenServer` and `Task`, this expression will inject the default implementation of `child_spec/1`, allowing you to list the module in a child specification list.

In addition, the implementation of `add_entry/2` uses `Agent.cast/2`. This function is the asynchronous version of `Agent.update/2`, which means the function returns immediately and the update is performed concurrently. `Agent.cast/2` is used here to keep the same behavior as in the previous version, where `GenServer.cast/2` was used.

> **Always wrap agent code in a module**
>
> One problem with agents is that they completely open the process's state. Recall that with `GenServer`, the state is private to the server and can only be manipulated via well-defined messages. With an `Agent`, though, the state can be manipulated in an arbitrary way through lambdas passed to `Agent` functions, which means the state is prone to accidental corruption. To guard against this problem, you're advised to always wrap an agent in a dedicated module and to only manipulate the agent process through functions of that module. This is precisely what you did when you converted `Todo.Server` into an agent.

The new version of `Todo.Server` requires only 29 lines of code, which is somewhat shorter than the previous 41 lines of code in the `GenServer`. An agent definitely seems like an appealing alternative to `GenServer`.

But agents can't handle all the scenarios `GenServer` can, so they're not always appropriate. In the next section, we'll take a look at those limitations.

10.2.4 Limitations of agents

The `Agent` module can't be used if you need to handle plain messages or if you want to run some logic on termination. In such cases, you need to use `GenServer`. Let's look at an example.

In the current version of your system, you never expire items from the to-do cache. This means that when a user manipulates a single to-do list, the list will remain in memory until the system is terminated. This is clearly not good because as users work with different to-do lists, you'll consume more and more memory until the whole system runs out of memory and blows up.

Let's introduce a simple expiry of to-do servers. You'll stop to-do servers that have been idle for a while.

One way to implement this is to create a single cleaning process that would terminate an idle to-do server. In this approach, each to-do server would need to notify the cleaning process every time it's been used, and that would cause the cleaning process to become a possible bottleneck. You'd end up with one process that needs to handle the possibility of a high load of messages from many other processes, and it might not be able to keep up.

A better approach is to make each to-do server decide on its own when it wants to terminate. This will simplify the logic and avoid any performance bottlenecks. This is an example of something that can be done with GenServer but can't be implemented with Agent.

An idle period in a GenServer can be detected in a few ways, and here you'll use a simple approach. In values returned from GenServer callbacks, you can include one extra element at the end of the return tuple. This element, if it's an integer, represents an idle time after which the timeout message is sent to the GenServer process.

For example, in init/1, instead of returning {:ok, initial_state}, you can return {:ok, initial_state, 1000}. The value of 1000 states that if no call, cast, or plain message arrives to the server process in 1,000 milliseconds, the handle_info/2 callback will be invoked, and the first argument will have the value of :timeout.

The same thing holds true for other callbacks such as handle_cast/2 and handle_call/3, where you can return {:noreply, new_state, timeout} and {:reply, response, new_state, timeout}, respectively.

Therefore, to make the to-do server stop itself after a period of inactivity, you need to do the following:

1 Convert the implementation of the to-do server back to GenServer.
2 Include the idle timeout integer in all result tuples of all callback functions.
3 Add handle_info/2 and stop the server if the :timeout message arrives.

Starting with the last GenServer-powered version of the Todo.Server, you'll include the idle timeout integer in the callback functions' results.

Listing 10.5 Specifying idle timeout (todo_cache_expiry/lib/todo/server.ex)

```elixir
defmodule Todo.Server do
  ...

  @expiry_idle_timeout :timer.seconds(10)    ⟵—— Declares the idle timeout

  def init(name) do
    IO.puts("Starting to-do server for #{name}.")
    {:ok, {name, nil}, {:continue, :init}}
  end

  def handle_continue(:init, {name, nil}) do
    todo_list = Todo.Database.get(name) || Todo.List.new()

    {
      :noreply,
      {name, todo_list},          │ Includes the idle
      @expiry_idle_timeout    ⟵——┤ timeout in response
    }
  end
end
```

```
def handle_cast({:add_entry, new_entry}, {name, todo_list}) do
  new_list = Todo.List.add_entry(todo_list, new_entry)
  Todo.Database.store(name, new_list)
  {:noreply, {name, new_list}, @expiry_idle_timeout}    ◁─┐  Includes the idle
end                                                         │  timeout in response

def handle_call({:entries, date}, _, {name, todo_list}) do
  {
    :reply,
    Todo.List.entries(todo_list, date),
    {name, todo_list},
    @expiry_idle_timeout    ◁─┐  Includes the idle
  }                            │  timeout in response
end

  ...
end
```

First, you declare a module attribute, `@expiry_idle_timeout`, which will contain the value of 10,000 (obtained by invoking `:timer.seconds(10)`). This attribute serves as a module-level constant, which you include as the last element of each return tuple of almost every callback function.

The only exception is `init/1`, where the continuation tuple (`{:continue, …}`) is provided. As explained in chapter 7, this is used to perform a potentially long-running server initialization without blocking the caller. `GenServer` doesn't support returning both the continue info and the timeout. Therefore, in `init/1` you only include the continuation, while the timeout is provided in `handle_continue`. This is perfectly fine because `handle_continue` is unconditionally invoked immediately after `init/1`. These changes ensure that `handle_info(:timeout, state)` will be invoked when there's no activity in the server process for 10 seconds.

Finally, you need to handle the `:timeout` message and stop the server.

Listing 10.6 Stopping an idle to-do server (todo_cache_expiry/lib/todo/server.ex)

```
defmodule Todo.Server do
  ...

  def handle_info(:timeout, {name, todo_list}) do
    IO.puts("Stopping to-do server for #{name}")
    {:stop, :normal, {name, todo_list}}    ◁──── Stops the process
  end
end
```

Now, quickly verify if expiration works properly. Go to the todo_cache_expiry folder, start the system, and start one to-do server:

```
$ iex -S mix

iex(1)> Todo.System.start_link()
iex(2)> pid = Todo.Cache.server_process("bobs_list")
```

Now, wait for a while, and you should see the debug message:

```
Stopping to-do server for bobs_list
```

Finally, verify whether the process is still alive:

```
iex(3)> Process.alive?(pid)
false
```

This is an example of a scenario in which agents just won't suffice and you need to use `GenServer`. But until you wanted to implement expiry, agents were just as appropriate a solution as `GenServer`. As long as you don't need to handle plain messages or you don't need to run some termination code in `terminate/1`, you can use `Agent`.

Personally, most often, I don't use `Agent` and start immediately with `GenServer`. Because converting an `Agent` into a `GenServer` requires some work, I'd much rather start with `GenServer` immediately. As an added bonus, this keeps the code more uniform, because all the server processes are implemented using the same abstraction. If you feel confused and aren't sure whether to use `Agent` or `GenServer`, my advice is to always go for `GenServer` because it covers more scenarios and is not much more complicated than `Agent`.

This concludes the story about agents. Next, we'll take a look at a feature called ETS tables.

10.3   *ETS tables*

ETS (Erlang Term Storage) tables are a mechanism that allows you to share some state between multiple processes in a more efficient way. ETS tables can be thought of as an optimization tool. Whatever you can do with an ETS table can also be done with `GenServer` or `Agent`, but the ETS version can often perform much better. However, ETS tables can only handle limited scenarios, so, often, they can't replace server processes.

Typical situations where ETS tables can be useful are shared key–value structures and counters. Although these scenarios can also be implemented with `GenServer` (or `Agent`), such solutions might lead to performance and scalability issues.

Let's look at a simple demonstration of those issues by implementing a concurrent key–value store with `GenServer`. First, let's look at the example use of such a store:

```
iex(1)> KeyValue.start_link()
{:ok, #PID<0.118.0>}

iex(2)> KeyValue.put(:some_key, :some_value)
:ok

iex(3)> KeyValue.get(:some_key)
:some_value
```

The full implementation of the `KeyValue` module is provided in the following listing.

Listing 10.7 GenServer-powered key–value store (key_value/lib/key_value.ex)

```elixir
defmodule KeyValue do
  use GenServer

  def start_link do
    GenServer.start_link(__MODULE__, nil, name: __MODULE__)
  end

  def put(key, value) do
    GenServer.cast(__MODULE__, {:put, key, value})
  end

  def get(key) do
    GenServer.call(__MODULE__, {:get, key})
  end

  def init(_) do
    {:ok, %{}}
  end

  def handle_cast({:put, key, value}, store) do
    {:noreply, Map.put(store, key, value)}
  end

  def handle_call({:get, key}, _, store) do
    {:reply, Map.get(store, key), store}
  end
end
```

Nothing new happens here. The `KeyValue` module is a simple `GenServer` that holds a map in its state. The `put` and `get` requests boil down to invoking `Map.put/3` and `Map.get/2` in the server process.

Next, you'll do some quick and inconclusive performance measurements of this key–value store. Go to the key_value folder, and run the following command:

```
mix run -e "Bench.run(KeyValue)"
```

The `mix run` command compiles the project, starts a BEAM instance, and then executes the expression provided via the `-e` argument, which means `Bench.run/1` is invoked. Once the function is done, the BEAM instance stops.

The `Bench` module, available in key_value/lib/bench.ex, conducts a simple load test. It starts the `KeyValue` server and then performs operations on one million keys. For each key, the bench program executes 10 `put` operations. Each `put` is followed by a `get`, so, in total, the program performs 20,000,000 operations.

Once the test is done, the function prints the observed throughput:

```
mix run -e "Bench.run(KeyValue)"
953182 operations/sec
```

The throughput of about 950,000 operations/sec seems decent enough. But let's see how the key–value server performs when it must serve multiple client processes. You can verify this by providing the `:concurrency` option to `Bench.run`:

```
mix run -e "Bench.run(KeyValue, concurrency: 10000)"
735369 operations/sec
```

Somewhat unexpectedly, with 10,000 client processes, you got worse throughput. What happened? The main problem is that despite having so many processes, there's just one key–value server process, so all of the key–value operations are synchronized, as shown in figure 10.1.

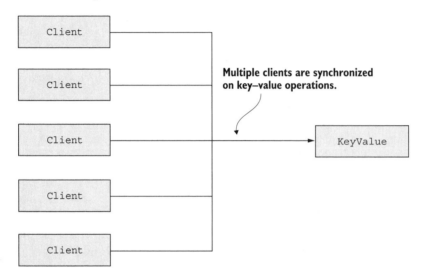

Figure 10.1   Single-process bottleneck

The key–value server, therefore, becomes a performance bottleneck and a scalability killer. The system can't efficiently utilize all the hardware resources. Even though there are 10,000 client processes running, all the key–value operations are serialized.

Moreover, keep in mind that even in moderately concurrent systems, you usually run many more processes than there are CPU cores. In this case, you have 10,000 clients, which is many more than the number of CPU cores available. Consequently, not all processes can run at the same time—some must wait their turn.

As explained in chapter 5, the VM goes to great lengths to use CPUs as well as possible, but the fact remains that you have many processes competing for limited resources. As a result, the key–value server doesn't get a single CPU core all to itself. The process must sometimes wait for its turn if BEAM schedulers run other processes in the system. Because the key–value server has fewer CPU resources for doing its job, it will take more time to compute the results.

This isn't to say that processes are bad. In general, you should strive to run independent tasks concurrently to improve scalability and fault tolerance. Processes should also be your first choice for maintaining state that changes over time. The problem isn't the many processes running in the system, but the single process on which many other processes depend. In this scenario, you can do much better with ETS tables, so let's see what they are and how you can work with them.

10.3.1 Basic operations

ETS tables are special in-memory structures where you can store Erlang terms. This makes it possible to share some state between multiple processes without introducing a dedicated server process.

Compared to other data structures, ETS tables have some unusual characteristics:

- There's no specific ETS data type. A table is identified by its ID (a reference type) or a global name (an atom).
- ETS tables are mutable. A write to a table will affect subsequent read operations.
- Multiple processes can write to or read from a single ETS table. Writes and reads might be performed simultaneously.
- Minimum concurrency safety is ensured. Multiple processes can safely write to the same row of the same table. The last write wins.
- An ETS table resides in a separate memory space. Any data coming in or out is deep copied.
- ETS doesn't put pressure on the garbage collector. Overwritten or deleted data is immediately released.
- An ETS table is deeply connected to its owner process (by default, the process that created the table). If the owner process terminates, the ETS table is reclaimed.
- Other than on owner-process termination, there's no automatic garbage collection of an ETS table. Even if you don't hold a reference to the table, it still occupies memory.

These characteristics mean ETS tables somewhat resemble processes. In fact, it's often said that ETS tables have process semantics. You could implement ETS tables with processes, but such an implementation would be much less efficient. In BEAM, ETS tables are powered by C code, which ensures better speed and efficiency.

The fifth point in the previous list is especially interesting. Because data is deep copied to and from an ETS table, there's no classical mutability problem. Once you read data from an ETS table, you have a snapshot no one can change. Regardless of other processes possibly modifying the contents of those rows in the ETS table, the data you read remains unaffected.

Let's look at some examples. All functions related to ETS tables are contained in the Erlang `:ets` module (https://erlang.org/doc/man/ets.html). To create a table, you can call `:ets.new/2`:

```
iex(1)> table = :ets.new(:my_table, [])
#Reference<0.970221231.4117102596.53103>
```

The first argument is a table name, which is important only if you want to register the table (we'll discuss this in a minute). Additionally, you can pass various options—some of which are discussed shortly. You should definitely spend some time researching the official documentation about `:ets.new/2` to see which options are possible. The result of `:ets.new/2` is a reference, a unique opaque term that represents the ETS table in the running system.

Because the structure is a table, you can store multiple rows into it. Each row is an arbitrarily sized tuple (with at least one element), and each tuple element can contain any Erlang term, including a deep hierarchy of nested lists, tuples, maps, or anything else you can store in a variable.

To store data, you can use `:ets.insert/2`:

```
iex(2)> :ets.insert(table, {:key_1, 1})      ◁──┐
true                                             │  Inserts the
                                                 │  new row
iex(3)> :ets.insert(table, {:key_2, 2})      ◁──┘
true

iex(4)> :ets.insert(table, {:key_1, 3})      ◁──── Overwrites the existing row
true
```

The first element of the tuple represents the *key*—something you can use for a fast lookup on the table. By default, ETS tables are of the `set` type, which means you can't store multiple tuples with the same key. Consequently, your last write overwrites the row from the first write.

To verify this, you can use `:ets.lookup/2`, which returns a list of rows for a given key:

```
iex(5)> :ets.lookup(table, :key_1)
[key_1: 3]

iex(6)> :ets.lookup(table, :key_2)
[key_2: 2]
```

You may wonder why the list is returned if you can have only one row per distinct key. The reason is that ETS tables support other table types—some of which allow duplicate rows. In particular, the following table types are possible:

- `:set`—This is the default. One row per distinct key is allowed.
- `:ordered_set`—This is just like `:set`, but rows are in term order (comparison via the < and > operators).

- :bag—Multiple rows with the same key are allowed, but two rows can't be completely identical.
- :duplicate_bag—This is just like :bag, but it allows duplicate rows.

Another important option is the table's access permissions. The following values are possible:

- :protected—This is the default. The owner process can read from and write to the table. All other processes can read from the table.
- :public—All processes can read from and write to the table.
- :private—Only the owner process can access the table.

To create a table of a different type or use a different access level, you can simply include the desired option in the list passed to :ets.new/2. For example, to create a public duplicate bag list, you can invoke this:

```
:ets.new(:some_table, [:public, :duplicate_bag])
```

Finally, it's worth discussing the table name. This argument must be an atom, and by default, it serves no purpose (although, strangely enough, you must still provide it). You can create multiple tables with the same name, and they're still different tables.

But if you provide a :named_table option, the table becomes accessible via its name:

```
iex(1)> :ets.new(:my_table, [:named_table])    ◁—— Creates a named table
:my_table

iex(2)> :ets.insert(:my_table, {:key_1, 3})        Manipulates the table
                                                   using the name
iex(3)> :ets.lookup(:my_table, :key_2)
[]
```

In this sense, a table name resembles a locally registered process name. It's a symbolic name of a table, and it relieves you of having to pass around the ETS reference.

Trying to create a duplicate named table will result in an error:

```
iex(4)> :ets.new(:my_table, [:named_table])
** (ArgumentError) errors were found at the given arguments:
  * 2nd argument: invalid options
```

10.3.2 *ETS-powered key–value store*

Equipped with this new knowledge, you'll implement key–value store with ETS tables. Since a table must be owned by some process, we'll still keep a GenServer around. Its sole purpose is to create the table in init/1 and keep it alive. All interactions with the table (reads and writes) will be done directly from the caller process, without needing to issue a request to the server process.

The relevant code is contained in the same project as the initial attempt. First, you need to start and initialize the table owner process, as shown in the next listing.

Listing 10.8   Creating the ETS table (key_value/lib/ets_key_value.ex)

```
defmodule EtsKeyValue do
  use GenServer

  def start_link do
    GenServer.start_link(__MODULE__, nil, name: __MODULE__)      Starts the table
  end                                                            owner process

  def init(_) do
    :ets.new(      Creates the table
      __MODULE__,
      [:named_table, :public, write_concurrency: true]
    )

    {:ok, nil}
  end

  ...
end
```

In start_link, you start a GenServer. Then, in the init/1 callback, the new ETS table is created. The table is configured as named, so the client processes can access it by its name (the name of the module). The access is set to public, which allows client processes to write to the table. The table type isn't provided, so it will default to set.

Notice the :write_concurrency option provided to :ets.new. This option allows you to issue concurrent writes to the table, which is exactly what you want in this case. There's also a :read_concurrency option, which can improve read performance in some cases. This option isn't set here because the Bench module performs a lot of interleaved reads and writes, and in such cases, :read_concurrency can lead to worse performance. Instead of randomly setting these options, it's always good to measure and observe their effects.

At this point, you can implement the operations:

```
defmodule EtsKeyValue do
  ...

  def put(key, value) do
    :ets.insert(__MODULE__, {key, value})      Inserts a key–value pair
  end

  def get(key) do
    case :ets.lookup(__MODULE__, key) do      Performs an ETS lookup
      [{^key, value}] -> value      Something is found.
      [] -> nil      Nothing is found.
    end
  end

  ...
end
```

The preceding code is a simple application of the presented `:ets` functions. To store an entry, you invoke `:ets.insert/2`. To perform a lookup, you invoke `:ets.lookup/2`. Because the ETS table is a `set`, the result list can contain at most one element: the key–value pair for the given key. If there's no row for the given key, the result is an empty list.

The crucial thing to notice here is that `get` and `put` operations now don't go through the server process. This means multiple clients can work with the key–value store simultaneously, without blocking each other, as shown in figure 10.2.

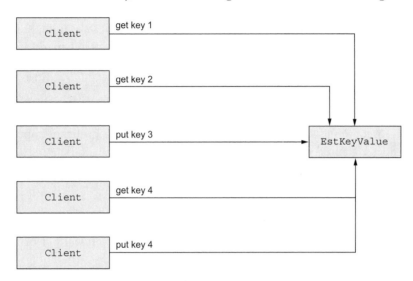

Figure 10.2   Concurrency in an ETS-powered key–value store

As you can see, operations working on different keys can be executed in parallel. Multiple operations working on the same key will be properly synchronized to prevent possible race conditions. When you have many keys, the chances for collisions are small, so you can expect better scheduler use, and therefore better scalability.

Now, verify that the new key–value store works correctly:

```
iex(1)> EtsKeyValue.start_link()
{:ok, #PID<0.109.0>}

iex(2)> EtsKeyValue.put(:some_key, :some_value)
true

iex(3)> EtsKeyValue.get(:some_key)
:some_value
```

The key–value store seems to be working. Now, let's see how it performs. You'll start with a sequential bench:

```
mix run -e "Bench.run(EtsKeyValue)"
5700062 operations/sec
```

On my machine, I obtained a projected throughput of about 5.7 million requests per second. Recalling that the pure `GenServer` version managed about 950,000 requests per second, this is an almost 6x increase in throughput!

There are a couple of reasons for this improvement. First, ETS operations are handled immediately in the client process. In contrast, a cross-process request involves putting a message in the mailbox of the receiver and then waiting for the receiver to be scheduled in and to handle the request. If the request is a synchronous call, the client process also must wait for the response message to arrive.

In addition, changes to ETS tables are destructive. If a value under some key is changed, the old value is immediately released. Therefore, data managed in ETS tables doesn't put any pressure on a garbage collector. In contrast, transforming standard immutable data generates garbage. In a `GenServer`-based key–value store, frequent writes will generate a lot of garbage, which means the server process is occasionally blocked while it's being garbage collected.

In this case, even in a plain sequential scenario, you get a significant improvement. But how does ETS hold up against multiple clients? Let's see:

```
mix run -e "Bench.run(EtsKeyValue, concurrency: 10000, num_updates: 100)"
52009220 operations/sec
```

Notice the `num_updates: 100` option. Because the ETS-based implementation is much faster, you're passing this option to run a longer test. This test will perform 100 `put` (and, therefore, also 100 `get`) operations on each key.

Using 10,000 client processes yields a 9x greater throughput. Compared to the plain `GenServer` solution, the improvement is 70x (52,000,000 versus 735,000 requests per second). The single-process key–value server starts to slow down with an increase in the total number of running processes in the system. In contrast, the ETS-based cache scales better.

The main reason for this scaling lies in the fact that cache operations are executed in the client process, so you don't need to perform `GenServer`-based serialization. The atomic operations provided by the `:ets` module are properly synchronized and can safely run simultaneously in multiple processes. Operations working on different keys can run in parallel. Even the reads of the same key can work in parallel. Only writes will block other operations on the same key.

On the flip side, the vocabulary of write operations is small. You can perform key–value writes with `:ets.insert/2`, delete a row with `:ets.delete/2`, modify a row with `:ets.update_element/3`, and atomically update an integer in a row with `:ets.update_counter/4`. For more complex scenarios, you'll likely need to channel writes through a `GenServer`. Therefore, you can think of ETS tables as being an optimization tool. They're extremely efficient in simple scenarios but not as powerful or flexible as server processes.

If you're unsure whether you should use a `GenServer` or an ETS table, it's best to start with a `GenServer`. This will be a simple solution, and in many cases, the performance will be sufficient. If you establish that a particular server is a bottleneck, you can see if an ETS table would be a good fit. In many cases, moving to an ETS table will only require changing the implementation. For example, if you compare the `KeyValue` module to `EtsKeyValue`, you'll notice that they have the same public interface. That makes it possible to have a generic `Bench` module that can work with both.

You might wonder why `GenServer` is still used in the ETS-based key–value store. The sole purpose of this process is to keep the table alive. Remember that an ETS table is released from memory when the owner process terminates. Therefore, you need to have a distinct, long-running process that creates and owns the table.

10.3.3 *Other ETS operations*

So far, we've covered only basic insertions and key-based lookups. These are arguably the most important operations you'll need, together with `:ets.delete/2`, which deletes all rows associated with a given key.

Key-based operations are extremely fast, and you should keep this in mind when structuring your tables. Your aim should be to maximize key-based operations, thus making ETS-related code as fast as possible.

Occasionally, you may need to perform non-key-based lookups or modifications, retrieving a list of rows based on value criteria. There are a couple of ways you can do this.

The simplest but least efficient approach is to convert the table to a list using `:ets.tab2list/1`. You can then iterate over the list and filter out your results, for example, by using functions from the `Enum` and `Stream` modules.

Another option is to use `:ets.first/1` and `:ets.next/2`, which make it possible to traverse the table iteratively. Keep in mind that this traversal isn't isolated. If you want to make sure no one modifies the table while you're traversing it, you should serialize all writes and traversals in the same process. Alternatively, you can call `:ets.safe_fixtable/2`, which provides some weak guarantees about traversal. If you're iterating a fixed table, you can be certain there won't be any errors, and each element will be visited only once. But an iteration through the fixed table may or may not pick up rows that are inserted during the iteration.

Traversals and `:ets.tab2list/1` aren't very performant. Given that data is always copied from the ETS memory space to the process, you end up copying the entire table. If you only need to fetch a couple of rows based on non-key criteria, this is overkill and a waste of resources. A better alternative is to rely on *match patterns*—features that allow you to describe the data you want to retrieve.

MATCH PATTERNS

Match patterns are a simple way to match individual rows. For example, let's say you're managing a to-do list in an ETS table:

```
iex(1)> todo_list = :ets.new(:todo_list, [:bag])
iex(2)> :ets.insert(todo_list, {~D[2023-05-24], "Dentist"})
iex(3)> :ets.insert(todo_list, {~D[2023-05-24], "Shopping"})
iex(4)> :ets.insert(todo_list, {~D[2023-05-30], "Dentist"})
```

Here, you use a `bag` ETS table because it allows you to store multiple rows with the same key (date).

Most often, you'll want to query a table by key, asking, "What appointments are on the given date?"

```
iex(5)> :ets.lookup(todo_list, ~D[2023-05-24])
[{~D[2023-05-24], "Dentist"}, {~D[2023-05-24], "Shopping"}]
```

Occasionally, you may be interested in obtaining all dates for an appointment type. Here's an example of how to do this using match patterns:

```
iex(6)> :ets.match_object(todo_list, {:_, "Dentist"})
[{~D[2023-05-24], "Dentist"}, {~D[2023-05-30], "Dentist"}]
```

The function `:ets.match_object/2` accepts a match pattern—a tuple that describes the shape of the row. The atom `:_` indicates that you accept any value, so the pattern `{:_, "Dentist"}` essentially matches all rows where the second element is `"Dentist"`.

Notice that this isn't classical pattern matching. Instead, this tuple is passed to `:ets.match_object/2`, which iterates through all rows and returns the matching ones. Therefore, when you don't care about a tuple element, you must pass an atom (`:_`) instead of a typical match-all anonymous variable (`_`). It's also worth mentioning the `:ets.match_delete/2` function, which can be used to delete multiple objects with a single statement.

In addition to being a bit shorter, match patterns have an important performance benefit over simple traversal. Recall that data is always copied from the ETS table to the selected process. If you used `:ets.tab2list/1` or plain traversal, you'd have to copy every single row into your own process. In contrast, `:ets.match_object/2` performs filtering in the ETS memory space, which is more efficient.

Going beyond match patterns, it's possible to perform even richer queries, specifying more complex filters and even choosing individual fields you want to return. This is done by writing a full-blown *match specification* that consists of the following parts:

- *Head*—A match pattern describing the rows you want to select
- *Guard*—Additional filters
- *Result*—The shape of the returned data

Such specifications can be passed to the `:ets.select/2` function, which produces the corresponding result.

Match specifications can become complicated quickly, as you can see by looking at the documentation for `:ets.select/2` (https://erlang.org/doc/man/ets.html#select-2). To make that task simpler, take a look at the third-party library called ex2ms (https://github.com/ericmj/ex2ms).

OTHER USE CASES FOR ETS

Managing server-wide shared state is arguably the most common use case for ETS tables. In addition, ETS tables can be used to allow processes to persist their data.

Remember from chapters 8 and 9 that processes lose their state on termination. If you want to preserve state across process restarts, the simplest way is to use a public ETS table as a means of providing in-memory state persistence. This should work reasonably quickly and allow you to recover from process crashes.

Be cautious when considering taking this road. As mentioned in chapters 8 and 9, it's generally better to recover from a crash with clean state. You should also consider whether you can restore state based on data from other processes. Persisting state in the ETS table (or anywhere else, for that matter) should be used mostly for critical processes that are part of your error kernel.

It's also possible to use ETS tables as a faster alternative to immutable data structures, such as maps. Because changes to ETS tables are destructive and data is immediately released, there won't be any garbage-collection penalty involved, so you can expect more predictable latency, with fewer deviations.

There is a caveat, though. Remember that data is copied between an ETS table and a client process. Consequently, if your row data is complex and large, ETS tables may yield worse performance than pure, immutable data structures. Another important downside of ETS tables is that, unlike plain data, they can't be sent over the network to another BEAM instance. That means that relying on ETS makes it harder to take advantage of distribution facilities (described in chapter 12).

In general, you should avoid using ETS and instead favor immutable structures as much as possible. Resort to ETS only in cases in which you can obtain significant performance gains.

BEYOND ETS

Erlang ships with two facilities that are closely related to ETS and that provide a simple way of implementing an embedded database that runs in the BEAM OS process. I won't discuss these features in detail in this book, but they deserve a brief mention so you can be aware that they exist and research them more deeply on your own.

The first feature, *disk-based* ETS (DETS, https://erlang.org/doc/man/dets.html), is disk-based term storage. Just like ETS, DETS relies on the concept of tables, and each table is managed in a single file. The interface of the corresponding :dets module is somewhat similar to ETS, but more limited in features. DETS provides a simple way of persisting data to disk. Basic isolation is supported—concurrent writes are allowed, even when you're storing to the same row.

Erlang also ships with a database called Mnesia (https://erlang.org/doc/apps/mnesia/users_guide.html), built on top of ETS and DETS, that has many interesting features:

- Mnesia is an embedded database—it runs in the same BEAM instance as the rest of your Elixir/Erlang code.
- Data consists of Erlang terms.
- Tables can be in memory (powered by ETS) or disk based (powered by DETS).

- Some typical database features are provided, such as complex transactions, dirty operations, and fast searches via secondary indexes.
- Sharding and replication are supported.

These features make Mnesia a compelling option for storing data. You initialize the database from your startup Elixir or Erlang code, and you're good to go. This has the huge benefit of allowing you to run the entire system in a single OS process.

On the downside, Mnesia is a somewhat esoteric database and isn't used much outside the Elixir and Erlang community. This means there's less community and tooling support compared to popular DBMS solutions. It also takes some trickery to make Mnesia work on a larger scale. For example, one problem is that disk-based tables can't exceed 2 GB (this is a limitation of the underlying DETS storage), which means you must fragment larger tables.

10.3.4 *Exercise: Process registry*

Now is a good time to practice a bit. A textbook example of ETS in practice is a process registry. The `Registry` module uses a smart combination of `GenServer` and ETS to obtain maximum efficiency. In this exercise, you'll implement a basic version of a `:unique` registry.

Here's an example of using such a registry:

```
iex(1)> SimpleRegistry.start_link()
{:ok, #PID<0.89.0>}

iex(2)> SimpleRegistry.register(:some_name)      Successful
:ok                                              registration

iex(3)> SimpleRegistry.register(:some_name)      Error on duplicate
:error                                           registration

iex(4)> SimpleRegistry.whereis(:some_name)       Successful
#PID<0.87.0>                                     lookup

iex(5)> SimpleRegistry.whereis(:unregistered_name)   ◁——— Failed lookup
nil
```

The interface of `SimpleRegistry` is very basic. The server process is started and registered locally. Then, any process can register itself by invoking `SimpleRegistry.register/1`, passing an arbitrary term for the process key. The function returns `:ok` on successful registration or `:error` if the name is occupied. Lookup is done by invoking `SimpleRegistry.whereis/1`, which returns the `pid` for the given key or `nil` if no process is registered under a given name. In addition, the registry process can detect a termination of each registered process and remove all the registration entries for that process.

`SimpleRegistry` has no other fancy features of the `Registry` module, such as support for via tuples, duplicate registrations, or multiple registry instances. Here's how you could build such a registry:

1 Implement the first version of `SimpleRegistry` as a `GenServer`. Both `register` and `whereis` will be implemented as calls.

2 The state of the `GenServer` should be a map, where keys are registered names and values are PIDs.

3 While handling the `:register` call, the registry process should link to the caller, so it can detect the process termination and deregister it. Therefore, the registry server also must trap exits (by invoking `Process.flag(:trap_exit, true)` in `init/1`). Links are chosen over monitors to ensure that registered processes are informed if the registry process goes down.

4 The registry process should handle `{:EXIT, pid, reason}` in its `handle_info` and remove all entries for the given process from the map.

Once you have this registry in place, you can consider moving some parts out of the server process. In particular, by using ETS tables, it's possible to perform both registration and lookup in client processes. Here's how:

1 During `init/1`, the registry process should create a named ETS table with public access. This table will map names to PIDs, so the registry process doesn't need to maintain any state.

2 Registration can be done via `:ets.insert_new/2` (https://erlang.org/doc/man/ets.html#insert_new-2). This function will only insert the new entry if there's no entry under the given key. Therefore, you can safely call this function simultaneously from separate processes. The function returns a Boolean to indicate whether the entry has been inserted or not.

3 Prior to invoking `:ets.insert_new/2`, the caller process should link to the server process by invoking `Process.flag(:trap_exit, true)`. You can wrap this linking in `SimpleRegistry.register/1`.

4 The implementation of `whereis/1` boils down to invoking `:ets.lookup/2` and matching the result.

5 Finally, the server process still needs to handle `:EXIT` messages and remove the entries for the terminated processes. This can easily be done with the help of `:ets.match_delete/2`.

This exercise is a bit more involved than previous ones, but it's a nice synthesis of some techniques you've seen in the past few chapters. If you get stuck, take a look at the solution in the process_registry folder. There, you'll find both versions—the basic one implemented completely in a `GenServer` and a more performant one that uses an ETS table to store registrations.

Summary

- Tasks can be used to run OTP-compliant concurrent job processes.
- Agents can be used to simplify the implementation of processes that manage some state but don't need to handle any plain messages.
- ETS tables can be used to improve performance in some cases, such as shared key–value memory structures.

Part 3

Production

This part of the book focuses on production aspects of BEAM-powered systems. Chapter 11 discusses OTP applications. You'll learn how to package components, reuse third-party libraries, and build a simple web server. Then, in chapter 12, we look at the basic building blocks of distributed systems. Chapter 13 finishes the book by explaining how to build a deployable standalone release and how to interact with the running system.

Working with components

This chapter covers

- Creating OTP applications
- Working with dependencies
- Building a web server
- Configuring applications

It's time to turn our attention toward producing releasable systems that can be deployed. To reach that goal, you need to learn about OTP *applications*, which let you organize your system into reusable components. Applications are a standard way of building Elixir or Erlang production systems and libraries. Relying on them brings various benefits, such as dependency management; simplified system starting; and the ability to build standalone, deployable releases.

In this chapter, you'll learn how to create applications and work with dependencies. In the process, you'll turn your to-do system into a proper OTP application and use some third-party libraries from the Erlang and Elixir ecosystem to expose an HTTP interface for your existing system. There's a lot of work ahead, so let's get started with OTP applications.

11.1 OTP applications

An *OTP application* is a component that consists of multiple modules and that can depend on other applications. This makes it possible to start the entire system with a single function call. As you're about to see, it's reasonably easy to turn code into an application. Your current version of the to-do system is already an OTP application, but there are some minor details you can improve. You'll see this in action shortly; first, let's look at what OTP applications consist of.

11.1.1 Creating applications with the mix tool

An application is an OTP-specific construct. The resource that defines an application is called an *application resource file*—a plain-text file written in Erlang terms that describes the application. (Don't worry; you won't need to write this directly. You'll instead rely on the mix tool to do this for you). This file contains several pieces of information, such as the following:

- The application name and version, and a description
- A list of application modules
- A list of application dependencies (which must be applications themselves)
- An optional application-callback module

Relying on the mix tool simplifies and automates some of the work of generating application resource files. For example, the application resource file must contain a list of all application modules. When you use mix, this list is generated for you automatically, based on the modules defined in the source code.

Some things, such as the application name, version, and description, must of course be provided by you. The mix tool can then use this data and your source code to generate the corresponding resource file while compiling the project.

Let's see this in practice. Go to a temporary folder, and run mix new hello_world --sup. This command creates the hello_world folder with the minimum Mix project skeleton. The parameter --sup makes the mix tool generate the application callback module and start the empty (childless) supervisor from it.

You can now change to the hello_world folder and start the system with the familiar iex -S mix. On the surface, nothing spectacular happens. But mix automatically starts your application, which you can verify by calling Application.started_applications/0:

```
iex(1)> Application.started_applications()
[
  {:iex, ~c"iex", ~c"1.15.0"},
  {:hello_world, ~c"hello_world", ~c"0.1.0"},      ⟵——— The application is running.
  {:logger, ~c"logger", ~c"1.15.0"},
  {:mix, ~c"mix", ~c"1.15.0"},
  {:elixir, ~c"elixir", ~c"1.15.0"},
  {:compiler, ~c"ERTS  CXC 138 10", ~c"8.3"},
  {:stdlib, ~c"ERTS  CXC 138 10", ~c"5.0"},
  {:kernel, ~c"ERTS  CXC 138 10", ~c"9.0"}
]
```

As you can see, the `hello_world` application is running, together with some additional applications, such as Elixir's `mix`, `iex`, and `elixir`, as well as Erlang's `stdlib` and `kernel`.

You'll see the benefits of this shortly, but first, let's look at how the application is described. The main place you specify an application is in the mix.exs file. Here are the full contents of the generated file (comments are stripped out):

```
defmodule HelloWorld.MixProject do
  use Mix.Project

  def project do
    [
      app: :hello_world,
      version: "0.1.0",
      elixir: "~> 1.15",
      start_permanent: Mix.env() == :prod,
      deps: deps()
    ]
  end

  def application do
    [
      extra_applications: [:logger],
      mod: {HelloWorld.Application, []}
    ]
  end

  defp deps do
    []
  end
end
```

Describes
the project

Describes the
application

Lists
dependencies

The first interesting thing happens in the `project/0` function, where you describe the Mix project. The `app: :hello_world` gives a name to your application. Only an atom is allowed as an application name, and you can use this atom to start and stop the application at run time.

The application is described in the `application/0` function. Here, you specify some options that will eventually make it to the application resource file. In this case, the description includes the list of other Erlang and Elixir applications you depend on, together with the module that will be used to start the application. By default, Elixir's `:logger` application is listed (https://hexdocs.pm/logger/Logger.html).

Finally, the `deps` function returns the list of third-party dependencies—other libraries you want to use in your project. By default, this list is empty. You'll see how dependencies are used a bit later in this chapter.

11.1.2   *The application behavior*

The critical part of the application description is `mod: {HelloWorld.Application, []}`, provided in mix.exs by `application/0`. This part specifies the module that will be used to start the application. When the application is started, the function `HelloWorld.Application.start/2` is called.

Obviously, you need to implement the `HelloWorld.Application` module. This is done for you by the `mix` tool, so let's see what it looks like:

```
defmodule HelloWorld.Application do
  use Application                    ◁────── Uses the Application module

  def start(_type, _args) do        ◁────── Callback function
    children = []                                                      Starts the
    opts = [strategy: :one_for_one, name: HelloWorld.Supervisor]       top-level
    Supervisor.start_link(children, opts)                              supervisor
  end
end
```

An application is an OTP behaviour, powered by the `Application` module (https://hexdocs.pm/elixir/Application.html), which is a wrapper around Erlang's `:application` module (https://www.erlang.org/doc/man/application.html). To be able to work with `Application`, you must implement your own callback module and define some callback functions.

At a minimum, your callback module must contain the `start/2` function. The arguments passed are the application start type (which you'll usually ignore) and an arbitrary argument (a term specified in mix.exs under the `mod` key). See the official documentation (https://hexdocs.pm/elixir/Application.html#c:start/2) for details.

The task of the `start/2` callback is to start the top-level process of your system, which should usually be a supervisor. The function returns its result in the form of `{:ok, pid}` or `{:error, reason}` if something went wrong.

11.1.3 *Starting the application*

To start the application in the running BEAM instance, you can call `Application.start/1`. This function first looks for the application resource file (which is generated by `mix`) and interprets its contents. Then, it verifies whether all the applications you're depending on are started. Finally, the application is started by calling the callback module's `start/2` function. The `Application.ensure_all_started/2` function is also available, which recursively starts all dependencies that aren't yet started.

Usually, you won't need to invoke these functions because `mix` automatically starts the application implemented by the project. Calling `iex -S mix` automatically starts the application together with its dependencies.

It should be noted that you can't start multiple instances of a single application. Trying to start an already running application will return an error:

```
$ iex -S mix

iex(1)> Application.start(:hello_world)
{:error, {:already_started, :hello_world}}
```

You can stop the application using `Application.stop/1`:

```
iex(2)> Application.stop(:hello_world)
[info] Application hello_world exited: :stopped
```

Stopping the application terminates its top-level process. If that process is a supervisor, it will stop its own children before it stops itself. This is why it's important to organize the processes in the supervision tree, as described in chapter 9. Doing so ensures the application is stopped in a controlled manner, leaving no dangling processes behind.

`Application.stop/1` stops only the specified application, leaving dependencies (other applications) running. To stop the entire system in a controlled way, you can invoke `System.stop/0`. This function will take down all the OTP applications and then the BEAM instance itself. Both `Application.stop/1` and `System.stop/0` work in a polite way. Every process in the supervision tree can perform some final cleanup in its `terminate/2` callback, as explained in section 9.1.6.

11.1.4 *Library applications*

You don't need to provide the `mod:` ... option from the `application/0` function in mix.exs:

```
defmodule HelloWorld.Application do
  ...

  def application do
    []
  end

  ...
end
```

In this case, there's no application callback module, which, in turn, means there's no top-level process to be started. This is still a proper OTP application. You can even start it and stop it.

What's the purpose of such applications? This technique is used for *library applications*—components that don't need to create their own supervision tree. As the name indicates, these are usually libraries, such as a JSON or a CSV parser. Erlang's own STDLIB application (https://erlang.org/doc/apps/stdlib/index.html) is a pure library application because it exposes various utility modules but doesn't need to manage its own supervision tree.

Library applications are useful because you can list them as runtime dependencies. This plays an important role when you start to assemble the deployable release, as you'll see in chapter 13.

11.1.5 *Implementing the application callback*

Equipped with this knowledge, you can turn your to-do system into a proper application. As mentioned earlier, it's already an OTP application, albeit a library one that doesn't implement a callback module for the application behavior. In fact, there is usually a 1:1 relationship between a Mix project and an OTP application. A Mix project implements exactly one OTP application. An exception is a so-called umbrella project, which can contain multiple OTP applications.

Given that the to-do system runs a set of its own processes under a supervision tree, it makes sense to implement the application callback module. Once you do that, the system can be automatically started as soon as you run `iex -S mix`.

The first thing you need to do is edit the mix.exs file. Recall that you created your initial project back in chapter 7, using the `mix` tool. Therefore, you already have this file in place and only need to add some information. The complete code for mix.exs is provided in the following listing.

> **Listing 11.1 Specifying application parameters (todo_app/mix.exs)**

```
defmodule Todo.MixProject do
  use Mix.Project

  def project do
    [
      app: :todo,
      version: "0.1.0",
      elixir: "~> 1.15",
      start_permanent: Mix.env() == :prod,
      deps: deps()
    ]
  end

  def application do
    [
      extra_applications: [:logger],      ┐ Specifying the application
      mod: {Todo.Application, []}       ◁──┘ callback module
    ]
  end

  defp deps do
    []
  end
end
```

The only change to mix.exs is in the `application/0` function, where the callback module is specified.

Next, you need to implement the callback module. The code is shown next.

Listing 11.2   Implementing the application module (todo_app/lib/todo/application.ex)

```elixir
defmodule Todo.Application do
  use Application

  def start(_, _) do
    Todo.System.start_link()
  end
end
```

As already mentioned, starting the application is as simple as starting the top-level supervisor. Given that you've already structured your system to reside under the `Todo.System` supervisor, this is all it takes to turn your system into a full-blown OTP application.

Let's see it in action:

```
$ iex -S mix
```

```
Starting database server
Starting database worker     │   The system is started
Starting database worker     │   automatically.
Starting database worker     │
Starting to-do cache
```

By implementing the OTP application callback, you've made it possible to start the system automatically.

It's worth noting that you get the same benefit when running tests. When you invoke `mix test`, all of the essential processes in your system are started. Back in chapter 7, when you added a couple of tests, you had to manually start the cache process:

```elixir
defmodule Todo.CacheTest do
  use ExUnit.Case

  test "server_process" do
    {:ok, cache} = Todo.Cache.start()                    ◁────── Manually started cache
    bob_pid = Todo.Cache.server_process(cache, "bob")

    assert bob_pid != Todo.Cache.server_process("alice")
    assert bob_pid == Todo.Cache.server_process("bob")
  end

  ...
end
```

The code has since seen a bunch of transformations, but in every incarnation, there was some version of the preceding pattern. Inside `Todo.CacheTest`, you needed to manually start the supporting processes, such as cache. With the system turned into a proper OTP application, this is not the case anymore, as you can see in the following listing.

Listing 11.3   Testing `server_process` (todo_app/test/todo_cache_test.exs)

```elixir
defmodule Todo.CacheTest do
  use ExUnit.Case

  test "server_process" do
    bob_pid = Todo.Cache.server_process("bob")        ⟵⎤  Works without manually
                                                         ⎦  starting the cache

    assert bob_pid != Todo.Cache.server_process("alice")
    assert bob_pid == Todo.Cache.server_process("bob")
  end

  ...
end
```

11.1.6 *The application folder structure*

Let's briefly discuss your compiled application's folder structure. Owing to the `mix` tool, you usually won't need to worry about this, but it can sometimes be useful to understand the folder structure of a compiled system.

MIX ENVIRONMENTS

Before you look at the application structure, you should know a bit about *Mix environments*. A Mix environment is a compile-time option that can be used to affect the shape of the compiled code.

Mix projects use three environments: dev, test, and prod. These three environments produce slight variations in the compiled code. For example, in a version compiled for development (the dev environment), you'll likely want to run some extra debug logging, whereas in a version compiled for production (the prod environment), you don't want to include such logging. In a version compiled for tests (the test environment), you want to further reduce the amount of logging and use a different database to prevent the tests from polluting your development database.

You can introduce your own Mix environment if you want to, but this is rarely needed, if ever. The three environments mentioned here should be sufficient to cover all possible scenarios.

For most `mix` tasks, the default environment is dev, indicating that you're dealing with development. One exception to that rule is the test task. When you invoke `mix test`, the Mix environment is automatically set to `test`.

You can specify a Mix environment by setting the `MIX_ENV` OS environment variable. By convention, when building for production, you should use the prod environment. To compile the code for prod, you can invoke `MIX_ENV=prod mix compile`. To compile and start a prod version, you can invoke `MIX_ENV=prod iex -S mix`.

The prod environment is a frequent source of confusion. Many teams conflate prod with the production machine. A prod version indeed runs on the production machine, but it will also run on other machines, such as staging. Most importantly, it should be possible and simple to start a version compiled for prod on a local developer machine. You won't need to do this frequently, but it's occasionally useful to analyze the behavior of the system which is as close to the deployed production version as possible. This is exactly what the prod-compiled version is. Therefore, you're advised to support running a prod-compiled version locally. Commit to this goal from the start of the project because doing this later, after the codebase grows significantly, is typically much more difficult.

THE COMPILED CODE STRUCTURE

Once you compile your project, compiled binaries reside in the _build/project_env folder, where project_env is the Mix environment that was in effect during compilation.

Because dev is the default environment, if you run `mix compile` or `iex -S mix`, you get binaries in the _build/dev folder. The OTP itself recommends the following folder convention:

```
lib/
  App1/
    ebin/
    priv/

  App2/
    ebin/
    priv/
  ...
```

Here, `App1` and `App2` represent application names (such as `todo`). The ebin folder contains compiled binaries (.beam files and application resource files), whereas the priv folder contains application-specific private files (images, compiled C binaries, and so on). This isn't a mandatory structure, but it's a convention used in most Elixir and Erlang projects. Some tools may rely on this structure, so it's best to follow this convention.

Luckily, you don't need to maintain this structure yourself because `mix` does so automatically. The final folder structure of a compiled Mix project has the following shape:

```
YourProjectFolder
_build
  dev
    lib
      App1
        ebin
        priv

      App2
      ...
```

In addition to your application, the lib folder also contains the application dependencies, except for the standard applications included in Elixir and Erlang, which reside in the folder where Elixir and Erlang are installed and which are accessible via the load path.

As mentioned, the application resource file resides in lib/YourApp/ebin and is named YourApp.app. For the to-do system, the file resides in _build/dev/lib/todo/ebin/ (relative to the root project folder). When you attempt to start the application, the generic application behavior looks for the resource file in the load paths (the same paths that are searched for compiled binaries).

This concludes our discussion of application basics. Now that you have a grasp of some theory, let's look at how to work with dependencies.

Deployable systems

Applications play an important role in building a deployable system. You'll learn about this in chapter 13, where we'll discuss OTP releases. In short, the general idea is to assemble a minimal self-contained system that includes only required applications and the Erlang runtime. For this to work, you must turn your code into an OTP application because only then can you specify dependencies to other applications. This is ultimately used to bundle all required applications into a single deployable release.

Therefore, anything reusable in Elixir and Erlang should reside in an application. This holds even for Elixir and Erlang: examples include the `elixir` application, which bundles the Elixir standard library as well as `iex` and `mix`, which are implemented as separate applications. The same thing happens in Erlang, which is divided into many applications (https://www.erlang.org/doc/applications.html), such as `kernel` and `stdlib`.

11.2 Working with dependencies

Depending on third-party libraries is an important feature. As soon as you start developing more complicated projects, you'll probably want to use various libraries, such as web frameworks, the JSON parser, and database drivers, to name a few examples. Such libraries can simplify various side concerns, prevent you from going down too many rabbit holes, and allow you to focus on the core challenges of your system.

For example, in the current implementation of the to-do system, you maintain a small pool of database workers, which allows you to have controlled parallelism of database operations. You implemented this pool completely from scratch back in chapter 7. But as it happens, managing a pool of processes is a frequent pattern in Elixir and Erlang, so a couple of third-party libraries offer a solution to this challenge. In this chapter, you'll replace your naive implementation of the process pool with a proven and battle-tested process pool library.

11.2.1 Adding a dependency

In this section, you'll add a dependency to the Poolboy library (https://github.com/devinus/poolboy). This library provides a mature implementation of a process pool.

The dependency to an external library must be specified in the mix.exs file, as illustrated in the next listing.

Listing 11.4 Adding an external dependency (todo_poolboy/mix.exs)

```
defmodule Todo.MixProject do
  ...

  defp deps do
    [
      {:poolboy, "~> 1.5"}    ⊲─── Specifies an external dependency
    ]
  end
end
```

An external dependency is specified as a tuple. The first element is always an atom, which should correspond to the application name of the dependency. The second element in the tuple, `"~> 1.5"`, is the version requirement. Here, you indicate that you want version 1.5 or any later 1.x version. For more information about the version syntax, take a look at the official documentation at https://hexdocs.pm/elixir/Version.html #module-requirements.

At this point, you've specified that your project depends on an external library, so you need to fetch your dependencies. This can be done by running `mix deps.get` from the command line. Dependencies are fetched from Elixir's external package manager, which is called Hex (https://hex.pm). Other possible dependency sources include the GitHub repository, a Git repository, or a local folder. For more information, take a look at the official documentation at https://hexdocs.pm/mix/ Mix.Tasks.Deps.html.

Running `mix deps.get` fetches all dependencies (recursively) and stores the reference to the exact version of each dependency in the mix.lock file, unless mix.lock already exists on the disk—in which case, this file is consulted to fetch the proper versions of dependencies. This ensures reproducible builds across different machines, so make sure you include mix.lock in the source control where your project resides.

Now that you've fetched all of your dependencies, you can build the entire system by running `mix compile`, which will compile all the dependencies and the project. It's worth mentioning that Poolboy is an Erlang library, but `mix` will still know how to compile it.

11.2.2 Adapting the pool

With these preparations in place, you can start adapting the pool implementation. Using Poolboy requires starting a process called the *pool manager* that manages a pool of workers. While starting the pool manager, you pass the desired pool size (the number of worker processes) and the module that powers each worker. During its startup, the pool manager starts the worker processes as its children.

Other processes can ask the pool manager to give them the PID of one worker. This operation is called *checkout*. Once a process gets the worker's PID, it can issue requests to that worker. When the client process doesn't need the worker process anymore, it notifies the pool manager. This operation is called *checkin*.

This workflow is a bit more sophisticated than your own simple pool. The checkout and checkin operations allow the pool manager to keep track of which worker processes are being used. If some workers are available, a client can immediately get a worker. Otherwise, if all the workers are checked out, the client will have to wait. As soon as the first worker is returned to the pool, a waiting client will check out that worker.

Poolboy also relies on monitors and links to detect the termination of a client. If a client checks out a worker and then crashes, the pool manager process will detect it and return the worker to the pool. Likewise, if a worker process crashes, a new one will be started.

Equipped with this knowledge, you're going to adapt the pool. First, you need to start the pool manager somewhere in your supervision tree. You could do that by invoking :poolboy.start_link, but there's a slightly more elegant way. You can invoke :poolboy.child_spec/3, which describes how Poolboy is supposed to be started. Therefore, to switch the database to the Poolboy-powered pool, you only need to change the implementation of Todo.Database.child_spec/1.

Listing 11.5 Starting a Poolboy-powered pool (todo_poolboy/lib/todo/database.ex)

```
defmodule Todo.Database do
  @db_folder "./persist"

  def child_spec(_) do
    File.mkdir_p!(@db_folder)

    :poolboy.child_spec(
      __MODULE__,          ⟵——— The child ID
      [
        name: {:local, __MODULE__},
        worker_module: Todo.DatabaseWorker,
        size: 3
      ],

      [@db_folder]         ⟵——— Worker arguments
    )
  end

  ...
end
```

Pool options (bracket annotation for the second argument)

The first argument passed to :poolboy.child_spec/3 is the ID of the child. This information is needed by the parent supervisor. Here, you use the module name (Todo.Database) as the ID.

The second argument is the pool options. The :name option states that the pool manager process should be locally registered, so you can interact with it without needing to know its PID. The :worker_module option specifies the module that will power each worker process, whereas :size specifies the pool size.

The final argument to `:poolboy.child_spec/3` is a list of arguments passed to the `start_link` of each worker when they're being started.

These arguments state that you want three worker processes, with each worker powered by the `Todo.DatabaseWorker` module. The pool manager will start each worker by invoking `Todo.DatabaseWorker.start_link(@db_folder)`.

It's worth noting that with this change, you don't need `Todo.Database.start_link` anymore because the new specification states that the database should be started by invoking `:poolboy.start_link`.

Next, you need to adapt the `store` and `get` functions of the `Todo.Database`. Previously, these functions selected a worker ID and then forwarded this ID to the corresponding function in the `Todo.DatabaseWorker` module. Now, these functions need to check out the worker from the pool, make a request to the worker, and return the worker to the pool. All of this can be easily done with the function `:poolboy .transaction/2`.

Listing 11.6   Adapted operation functions (todo_poolboy/lib/todo/database.ex)

```elixir
defmodule Todo.Database do
  ...

  def store(key, data) do          | Asks the pool for a single worker
    :poolboy.transaction(   <──┘
      __MODULE__,                    | Performs an operation on the worker
      fn worker_pid ->     <────────┘
        Todo.DatabaseWorker.store(worker_pid, key, data)
      end
    )
  end

  def get(key) do
    :poolboy.transaction(
      __MODULE__,
      fn worker_pid ->
        Todo.DatabaseWorker.get(worker_pid, key)
      end
    )
  end
end
```

Here, you invoke `:poolboy.transaction/2`, passing the registered name of the pool manager. This will issue a checkout request to fetch a single worker. Once a worker is available, the provided lambda is invoked. When the lambda is finished, `:poolboy .transaction/2` will return the worker to the pool.

In the provided lambda, you get the PID of the checked-out worker and issue a `Todo.DatabaseWorker` request. This means you need to slightly change the implementation of `Todo.DatabaseWorker`. Previously, the functions from this module accepted a worker ID and then did a registry lookup to find the worker process. In this version, the discovery of the PID is performed by the pool, so you don't need to register the workers anymore or perform any lookup to discover the process.

Listing 11.7   Adapted worker interface

```
defmodule Todo.DatabaseWorker do
  use GenServer

  def start_link(db_folder) do
    GenServer.start_link(__MODULE__, db_folder)
  end

  def store(pid, key, data) do
    GenServer.cast(pid, {:store, key, data})
  end

  def get(pid, key) do
    GenServer.call(pid, {:get, key})
  end

  ...
end
```

That's all it took to change the pool implementation. The code in the client modules, `Todo.System` and `Todo.Server`, as well as the testing code remain exactly the same. This is thanks to the fact that you hid the implementation details behind the interface functions.

11.2.3   *Visualizing the system*

Once you have a full-blown OTP application, you can visualize it with the help of a tool called `observer`, which is part of the standard Erlang/OTP distribution.

Let's see this in action. First, start the system, and then create two to-do servers:

```
$ iex -S mix

iex(1)> Todo.Cache.server_process("Alice")
iex(2)> Todo.Cache.server_process("Bob")
```

Now, you can start the `observer` tool:

```
iex(3)> :observer.start()
```

A GUI window should appear, which presents some basic information about the system. If you click the Applications tab, you can see the supervision tree of your application, as illustrated in figure 11.1.

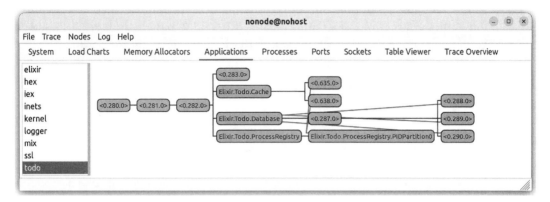

Figure 11.1   Observing the application

The two top processes, with the PIDs <0.280.0> and <0.281.0>, are the processes used by OTP to manage the application. The third process, with the PID <0.282.0>, is the top-level `Todo.System` supervisor. Then, you can see the four children: the process with the PID <0.283.0>, `Todo.Cache`, `Todo.Database`, and `Todo.ProcessRegistry`.

If available, the observer uses the registered name of a process. Otherwise, the process PID is used to display the process. In this example, the first process with the PID <0.283.0> is the metrics reporter powered by the `Todo.Metrics` module.

Under the cache, you can see two children, which are to-do servers that you just started from the shell. You can easily verify this by double-clicking on the process box and clicking the State button in the new window. In the last row, you'll see the process state, which will contain the name of the to-do list.

The `observer` tool can be useful for visualizing the behavior of the running system. For example, in the Processes tab you can see a list of all processes running in the system and easily figure out which processes are very busy or use a lot of memory. This tab is frequently used to find bottlenecks in the system. You can even use the `observer` to visualize the system running in production. This will be explained in chapter 13.

11.3   Building a web server

The time has finally come to introduce an HTTP interface into your to-do system. You'll implement a rudimentary server, wrapping only `entries` and `add_entry` requests.

Our focus won't be so much on the details and finesse of web servers. Instead, the aim is to demonstrate how you can work with OTP applications and show you how everything connects in a simple simulation of a real-world system.

11.3.1 Choosing dependencies

You could, of course, implement the entire server from scratch, but that would be too much work. Instead, you'll reach for a couple of existing libraries to make your life easier. Note that it's not the purpose of this section to provide detailed descriptions of those libraries; they're just a simple means to an end (a basic, working, HTTP server). You're encouraged to research those libraries in more detail on your own.

Several web server frameworks and libraries are available for both Elixir and Erlang. If you plan on doing any serious production development, you should definitely take a look at the Phoenix Framework (https://phoenixframework.org/). Phoenix is versatile and highly modular, so it's a great choice for powering all kinds of web servers. At first glance, Phoenix might seem a bit daunting, so we'll keep things simple here and reach for two lower-level libraries.

The first one is an Erlang library called Cowboy (https://github.com/extend/cowboy). It's a fairly lightweight and efficient HTTP server library that's a popular choice for HTTP servers in Erlang and Elixir ecosystems.

But you won't use Cowboy directly. Instead, you'll interface with it via the Plug library (https://github.com/elixir-lang/plug), which provides a unified API that hides the details of the actual HTTP server implementation.

You can add both libraries to your project with a single dependency.

Listing 11.8   External dependencies for the web server (todo_web/mix.exs)

```
defmodule Todo.Mixfile do
  ...

  defp deps do
    [
      {:poolboy, "~> 1.5"},
      {:plug_cowboy, "~> 2.6"}    ⟵—— New dependency
    ]
  end
end
```

We're adding a new dependency called `plug_cowboy`. This library provides the glue code between Plug and Cowboy. Internally, this library depends on the Plug and Cowboy libraries, which are therefore transitive dependencies of our project. We don't need to explicitly list them. The `mix` tool can resolve this automatically.

11.3.2 Starting the server

With the dependencies configured, you can now run `mix deps.get` and start implementing the HTTP interface. As mentioned, your primary interface for working with Cowboy is Plug. Plug is a reasonably complex library, and I won't provide an in-depth treatment here. Our focus is on getting a basic version running and understanding how all the pieces work together.

To start a server powered by Plug and Cowboy, you can reach for `Plug.Cowboy` `.child_spec/1`. This function returns a child specification describing how to start the processes responsible for the HTTP server part of the system. As usual, it's best to wrap this in a dedicated module.

Listing 11.9 HTTP server specification (todo_web/lib/todo/web.ex)

```
defmodule Todo.Web do
  ...

  def child_spec(_arg) do
    Plug.Cowboy.child_spec(
      scheme: :http,
      options: [port: 5454],
      plug: __MODULE__
    )
  end

  ...
end
```

The argument passed to `Plug.Cowboy.child_spec/1` provides the server options. Here, you specify that you want to serve HTTP traffic on port 5454. The final option, `:plug`, indicates that some function from this module will be invoked to handle the request.

When you include `Todo.Web` in a supervisor, several new processes will be started. There will be at least one process that listens on a given port and accepts requests. Then, each distinct TCP connection will be handled in a separate process, and your callbacks (which you must implement) will be invoked in those request-specific processes. But you don't need to worry about any of these details. Owing to `child_spec/1`, the Plug library keeps these internals to itself.

> **NOTE** Remember that applications are singletons—you can start only one instance of a distinct application in a running BEAM instance. But this doesn't mean you can run only one HTTP server in your system. The Plug and Cowboy applications can be considered factories of HTTP servers. When you start these applications, no HTTP server is started yet. You use `child_spec/1` to inject an HTTP server somewhere in your supervision tree. You can, of course, run multiple HTTP servers in your system. For example, you could add another HTTP server for administration purposes.

With `child_spec/1` in place, you can inject the HTTP server into the supervision tree. This is done in the `Todo.System` supervisor.

Listing 11.10 Starting the HTTP server (todo_web/lib/todo/system.ex)

```
defmodule Todo.System do
  def start_link do
    Supervisor.start_link(
```

```
    [
      Todo.Metrics,
      Todo.ProcessRegistry,
      Todo.Database,
      Todo.Cache,
      Todo.Web      ◁──── The new child
    ],
      strategy: :one_for_one
    )
  end
end
```

Thanks to wrapping and proper naming, the `Todo.System` module clearly describes what the system is made of: metrics, a process registry, a database, a cache, and a web server.

11.3.3 Handling requests

Now, you can start handling some requests. Let's introduce support for `add_entry`. This will be a POST request. To keep the implementation simple, you'll transfer all parameters via URL. The example request looks like this:

```
http://localhost:5454/add_entry?list=bob&date=2023-12-19&title=Dentist
```

Begin by setting up a route for this request. The skeleton is provided next.

> **Listing 11.11 Setting up a route for `add_entry` (todo_web/lib/todo/web.ex)**

```
defmodule Todo.Web do
  use Plug.Router      ◁──── Includes boilerplate

  plug :match          │ Sets up plugs
  plug :dispatch       │

  ...

  post "/add_entry" do    ◁──── Defines a handler
    ...
  end

  ...
end
```

There are some strange constructs here, which are part of how Plug is used. I'll provide a simple explanation, but you don't need to understand all this because it isn't the aim of this exercise.

Calling `use Plug.Router` adds some functions to your module. This is similar to how you used the Elixir behavior helper (by calling `use GenServer`). For the most part, the imported functions will be used internally by Plug.

Expressions such as plug :match and plug :dispatch deserve special mention. These calls will perform some additional compile-time work that will allow you to match different HTTP requests. These expressions are examples of Elixir macro invocations, and they'll be resolved at compilation time. As a result, you'll get some additional functions in your module (which are again used only by Plug).

Finally, you call a post macro to define request-handling code. The post macro works similarly to the test macro you saw in chapter 7. Under the hood, this macro will generate a function that's used by all the other generated boilerplate you got by calling the plug macro and use Plug.Router. The generated function will look roughly like the following:

```
defp do_match(conn, "POST", ["add_entry"], _) do
  ...
end
```

The code of the generated do_match function will contain the code passed to the plug macro. The generated do_match function is invoked by some other generated code that exists in your module courtesy of the use Plug.Router and plug :match expressions.

If you issue multiple calls to the post macro, you'll have multiple clauses for this do_match function, each clause corresponding to the single route you're handling. You'll end up with something like this:

```
defp do_match(conn, "POST", ["add_entry"], _), do: ...
defp do_match(conn, "POST", ["delete_entry"], _), do: ...
...
defp do_match(conn, _, _, _), do: ...    ◁——— Handles all other requests
```

You can check this yourself with the help of a tool called *decompile* (https://github .com/michalmuskala/decompile). Install the tool according to the README instructions, change to the to-do project root folder, compile the project, and then run mix decompile Todo.Web --to expanded. This will generate the file Elixir.Todo.Web.ex, which will contain the Elixir code after all the macros have been expanded.

Long story short, the code you provide to post "/add_entry" is invoked when an HTTP POST request with an /add_entry path arrives at your server.

Let's now look at the implementation of the request handler.

Listing 11.12 Implementing the add_entry request (todo_web/lib/todo/web.ex)

```
defmodule Todo.Web do
  ...

  post "/add_entry" do
    conn = Plug.Conn.fetch_query_params(conn)
    list_name = Map.fetch!(conn.params, "list")        Decodes input
    title = Map.fetch!(conn.params, "title")           parameters
    date = Date.from_iso8601!(Map.fetch!(conn.params, "date"))
```

```
    list_name
    |> Todo.Cache.server_process()
    |> Todo.Server.add_entry(%{title: title, date: date})

    conn
    |> Plug.Conn.put_resp_content_type("text/plain")
    |> Plug.Conn.send_resp(200, "OK")
  end

  ...
end
```

| Performs the operation
| Returns the response

Notice that in the request handler, you use the `conn` variable, which doesn't exist anywhere. This variable is brought to you by the `post` macro, which generates this variable and binds it to the proper value.

As the name implies, the `conn` variable holds your connection. This is an instance of a `Plug.Conn` struct that holds a TCP socket together with information about the state of the request you're processing. From your handler code, you must return the modified connection, which will hold response information, such as its status and body.

The implementation of the request handler consists of three parts. You first decode the input parameters. Then, you invoke the code that performs some action in your system—in this case, adding the new entry. Finally, you respond to the client.

To decode input parameters, you need to invoke `Plug.Conn.fetch_query_params/1`. This function returns a new version of the connection structure with the `params` field containing request parameters (in the form of a map). This is essentially a caching technique. Plug caches the result of `fetch_query_params` in the connection struct, so repeated calls to `fetch_query_params` won't result in excessive parsing.

Once you have the parameters ready, you can add the entry. Finally, you set the response content type, status, and body.

The same approach is used to handle the `entries` request.

Listing 11.13   Implementing the `entries` request (todo_web/lib/todo/web.ex)

```
defmodule Todo.Web do
  ...

  get "/entries" do
    conn = Plug.Conn.fetch_query_params(conn)
    list_name = Map.fetch!(conn.params, "list")
    date = Date.from_iso8601!(Map.fetch!(conn.params, "date"))

    entries =
      list_name
      |> Todo.Cache.server_process()
      |> Todo.Server.entries(date)

    formatted_entries =
```

```
      entries
      |> Enum.map(&"#{&1.date} #{&1.title}")
      |> Enum.join("\n")

    conn
    |> Plug.Conn.put_resp_content_type("text/plain")
    |> Plug.Conn.send_resp(200, formatted_entries)
  end

  ...
end
```

This code follows the same approach as in add_entry. Because entries is a GET request, you use the get macro instead of post.

In this implementation, you decode the parameters and then fetch the desired entries. You then produce the textual representation sent to the client and return the response.

> **NOTE** The presented code organization treats the HTTP server as merely an interface to the core of the system. Notice how in both requests, you convert the input into domain-specific types and then invoke HTTP-agnostic code, such as Todo.Server.add_entry, to perform the operation. The core of the system, which we implemented in the previous chapters, doesn't know or care that it's running in the context of an HTTP request. Such separation of concerns makes the code easier to work with, test, and expand.

At this point, you can start the system with iex -S mix and issue requests. For example, this is what you get using the command-line curl tool:

```
$ curl -d "" \
   "http://localhost:5454/add_entry?list=bob&date=2023-12-19&title=Dentist"
OK

$ curl "http://localhost:5454/entries?list=bob&date=2023-12-19"
2023-12-19 Dentist
```

This proves that your system is working, but let's see how everything combines.

11.3.4 *Reasoning about the system*

First, let's look at how the HTTP server works. The simplified idea is illustrated in figure 11.2.

The most important thing to notice is that each connection is managed in a distinct process. In practice, this means different requests are handled in different processes. There's no special magic here—this is how the underlying Cowboy web server is implemented. It uses one process to listen on a port, and then it spawns a separate process for each incoming request.

This architecture has all sorts of benefits due to the way BEAM treats processes. Because processes are concurrent, CPU resources are maximally used and the system is

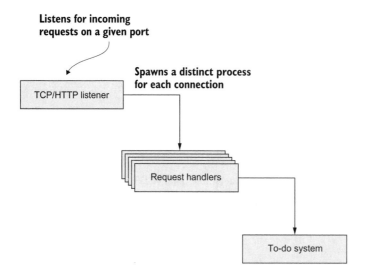

Figure 11.2 **Requests are handled in separate processes.**

scalable. Because processes are lightweight, you can easily manage many simultaneous connections. Moreover, thanks to the BEAM scheduler being preemptive, you can be certain that occasional long-running, CPU-intensive requests won't paralyze the entire system. Finally, due to process isolation, a crash in a single request won't affect the rest of the system.

Processes also make it easy to reason about the system. For example, you can be certain that independent requests won't block each other, whereas multiple requests on the same to-do list are synchronized, as illustrated in figure 11.3.

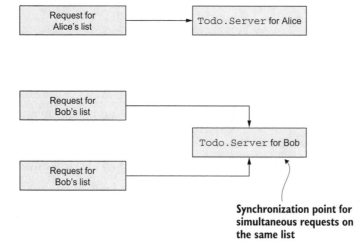

Figure 11.3 **Independent simultaneous requests are handled concurrently, whereas requests on the same to-do list are synchronized.**

This is due to the way the to-do cache works. Whenever you want to manipulate Bob's list, you first ask the to-do cache to return the PID of the process in charge. All requests for Bob's list go through that same process and are, therefore, handled one by one.

PERFORMANCE

After so much development, it's worth measuring the performance of the system. I quickly tested the system using a tool called wrk (https://github.com/wg/wrk). A brief 30-second load test on my machine gives a throughput of about 40,000 requests per second, with an average latency of 1 ms, and a 99 percentile latency of 7 ms. While the test was running, all the CPU cores were completely busy, which proves there are no bottlenecks in the system. The system is highly concurrent and able to use all of the cores at its disposal.

The observed results are quite decent, especially given that we made some naive decisions in the implementation. Here are a couple of possible issues in the implementation:

- On every list modification, you store the entire list.
- Date-based lookups in the to-do list abstraction iterate through the entire list.
- Every to-do server lookup goes through a to-do cache dynamic supervisor.

There's definitely some room for improvement here, but it's comforting to know that the system performs well out of the box, even though you didn't do any fine tuning.

CALLS VS. CASTS

Let's discuss some effects that calls and casts may have on your system. To refresh your memory, *casts* are fire-and-forget requests. A caller sends a message to the server and then immediately moves on to do something else. In contrast, a *call* is a blocking request, where a caller waits for the server to respond.

Remember that you've opted to use casts for all operations, except where you need to return a response. This was a somewhat arbitrary decision, made mostly for didactic purposes. In reality, casts have a drawback: you don't know what happened with your request. This, in turn, means you may be giving false responses to end users, as illustrated in figure 11.4.

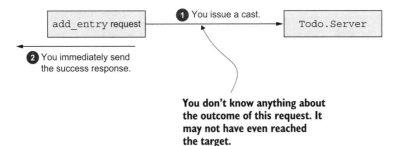

You don't know anything about the outcome of this request. It may not have even reached the target.

Figure 11.4 Using casts reduces the certainty of your responses.

Because you use a cast to add a to-do entry in your system, you have no way of knowing what happened with your request. When you're telling the end user that you succeeded, this is a guess, rather than a truthful statement.

Obviously, the simple way to resolve this is to use calls, which are synchronous, meaning the client must wait until the response arrives, as illustrated in figure 11.5.

This approach is more consistent: you return success only when you're certain that the entry has been stored. But the downside is that the entire system now depends on

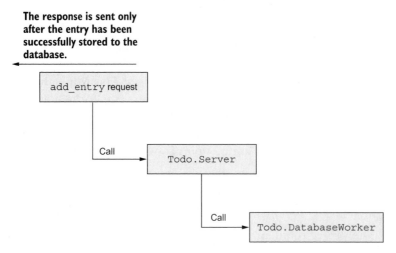

The response is sent only after the entry has been successfully stored to the database.

Figure 11.5   Using calls promotes consistency but reduces the responsiveness of the system.

the throughput of database workers, and as you may recall, you're running only three workers, and you're using a relatively inefficient database.

This can be resolved by introducing an intermediate process. The idea is to provide an immediate response stating that the request has been queued. Then, you do your best to process the request, and you send a subsequent notification about the request's status (see figure 11.6).

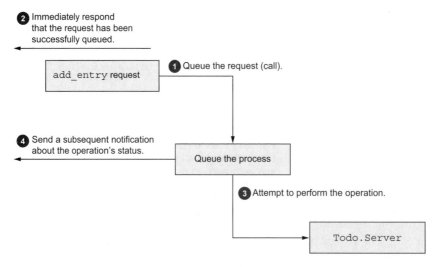

Figure 11.6   Queuing the request and sending a notification about the status

This scheme is more elaborate and involved, so it's not appropriate for simpler cases in which using plain calls is enough. But in cases when the load is very high and end-to-end operations can take longer, introducing an intermediate process may be beneficial. This process can increase the responsiveness of the system while retaining consistency. Moreover, this process can serve as a proactive agent in dealing with congestion and increased load. If the system becomes overloaded and the queue starts piling up, you can refuse to take more requests into the queue process until you regain some breathing space.

As always, no single approach works for all cases. Using calls can be a reasonable first attempt because it promotes consistency. Later, you can easily switch to casts or introduce an intermediate process, depending on the specific situation.

If you need to perform more complex load management, you can introduce an intermediate process. Instead of rolling your own solution, you can consider using the GenStage library (https://github.com/elixir-lang/gen_stage), which allows you to build various pipelines of producers and consumers.

At this point, you're finished implementing a basic HTTP server. Next, we'll talk about application configuration.

11.4   Configuring applications

An OTP application can be configured using a feature called an *application environment* —a key–value, in-memory store, where keys are atoms and values are Elixir terms. You can provide application environment values through config script files—Elixir scripts that reside in the config folder.

The `mix` tool makes sure the configuration is loaded into the application environment before the application is started. Finally, you can retrieve an environment value using functions from the `Application` module.

11.4.1   Application environment

Let's look at a simple example. The to-do HTTP server currently listens on a hard-coded port: 5454. In this example, you'll make the HTTP port configurable via an OS environment variable.

The most typical way of setting an application environment is to use the config/ runtime.exs file. This is a script evaluated at run time, just before the application is started. In here, you can set the environment configuration of your application as well as any of its dependencies.

To make the HTTP port configurable, you can read the configuration from the OS environment variable and store it into the application environment.

Listing 11.14   Configuring the HTTP port (todo_env/config/runtime.exs)

```
import Config      <─── Imports configuration helpers          Reads the OS
                                                               environment variable
http_port = System.get_env("TODO_HTTP_PORT", "5454")   <─┘
config :todo, http_port: String.to_integer(http_port)    <─┐

                     Sets the application's environment value │
```

Here, you use `System.get_env/2` to read the OS environment variable `TODO_HTTP_PORT`, using the default value of `5454` if the variable is not set. Then, you use the imported `Config.config/2` function to configure the `:http_port` setting of the `:todo` application.

As soon as you start the system, this setting is available in the application environment, and you can retrieve it—for example, with the `Application.fetch_env!/2` function:

```
$ iex -S mix

iex(1)> Application.fetch_env!(:todo, :http_port)
5454
```

Setting the OS environment variable before the system is started affects the application environment:

```
$ TODO_HTTP_PORT=1337 iex -S mix

iex(1)> Application.fetch_env!(:todo, :http_port)
1337
```

Now, you can adapt the code of `Todo.Web` to read the port from the application environment.

Listing 11.15   Fetching the `http_port` setting (todo_env/lib/todo/web.ex)

```
defmodule Todo.Web do
  ...

  def child_spec(_arg) do
    Plug.Cowboy.child_spec(
      scheme: :http,
      options: [port: Application.fetch_env!(:todo, :http_port)],    ⟵─┐
      plug: __MODULE__                             Retrieves the HTTP port from the
    )                                              :todo application environment
  end

  ...
end
```

In this case, you use `Application.fetch_env!/2`, which will raise an error if the HTTP port isn't configured. To provide a default value if none is set, you can use `Application.get_env/3` (https://hexdocs.pm/elixir/Application.html#get_env/3).

11.4.2 Varying configuration

In some cases, you might want to use different settings in different Mix environments. For example, you currently always use the same HTTP port for development and for tests. As a consequence, you can't run tests if the to-do system is started in development. The solution for this problem is to use a different HTTP port in the test Mix environment.

NOTE It's worth noting that the term *environment* is overloaded. An application environment is a key–value store that holds various settings for your OTP application. A Mix environment determines the compilation target, such as development, test, or production. Finally, the OS environment consists of the OS-level variables present at the current shell session.

To vary the settings in different Mix environments, you need to make some changes to config/runtime.exs.

Listing 11.16 Mix environment-specific settings (todo_env/config/runtime.exs)

```
import Config

http_port =
  if config_env() != :test,                                    Making the decision
    do: System.get_env("TODO_HTTP_PORT", "5454"),              based on the Mix
    else: System.get_env("TODO_TEST_HTTP_PORT", "5455")        environment

config :todo, http_port: String.to_integer(http_port)
```

Here, you rely on the imported `Config.config_env/0` to determine the Mix environment used to build the project. Then, in the test environment, you'll use a different OS environment variable and a different default HTTP port. The app environment name is always the same (`:http_port`), so the rest of the code doesn't need to be changed.

Let's quickly verify if this works. Start the application in the default dev environment:

```
$ iex -S mix

iex(1)> Application.fetch_env!(:todo, :http_port)
5454
```

Now, try the same in the test environment:

```
$ MIX_ENV=test iex -S mix

iex(1)> Application.fetch_env!(:todo, :http_port)
5455
```

At this point, you can run tests, even if the system is started in another OS process.

There is one additional inconvenience. The database folder is currently always the same, regardless of the Mix environment. As a result, running the tests will pollute your current dev data.

To avoid this, you can make the database folder configurable, using a different OS environment variable and a different default value in the test environment, just like you did with the HTTP port. For the sake of brevity, the code is not presented here, but you're advised to try it on your own or check the implementation in the todo_env folder.

11.4.3 *Config script considerations*

It's worth mentioning that Elixir also supports build-time config scripts. If you create the config/config.exs file, this script will be evaluated before the project is compiled. As a result, any setting you read from external sources, such as OS environment, is done on the build machine.

If you're building the system on a different machine than the one where you're running it (which is good practice), the system might end up being improperly configured. Because of this subtle confusion, and due to its special semantics (it's evaluated at compile time), try to use config.exs as little as possible. In most cases, runtime.exs should serve all your needs.

If you're developing a library, try to avoid taking your parameters through the application environment. If a library is accepting its parameters via application environment, its users are forced to provide the values through config scripts. A much more flexible approach is to design the API of your library to accept all the parameters as function arguments. With such an approach, library users have complete freedom in deciding how to provide the parameters. They can hardcode the parameters, configure them through the application environment, or fetch the parameters from external sources at run time. For more details, refer to the "Library Guidelines" page in the official documentation (https://hexdocs.pm/elixir/library-guidelines.html#avoid-application-configuration).

Summary

- An OTP application is a reusable component. The application can run the entire supervision tree or just provide utility modules (as in a library application).
- A non-library application is a callback module that must start the supervision tree.
- Applications allow you to specify runtime dependencies to other applications. This isn't the same as compile-time dependencies that allow you to fetch external code and compile it from your project.
- Application environments allow you to provide application settings. This can be useful if you want to expose some configuration to the system operators.

Building
a distributed system

Now that you have a to-do HTTP server in place, it's time to make it more reliable. To have a truly reliable system, you need to run it on multiple machines. A single machine represents a single point of failure because a machine crash leads to a system crash. In contrast, with a cluster of multiple machines, a system can continue providing service even when individual machines are taken down.

Moreover, by clustering multiple machines, you have a chance of scaling horizontally. When demand for the system increases, you can add more machines to the cluster to accommodate the extra load. This idea is illustrated in figure 12.1.

Here, you have multiple nodes sharing the load. If a node crashes, the remaining load will be spread across survivors, and you can continue to provide service. If the load increases, you can add more nodes to the cluster to take the extra load. Clients access a well-defined endpoint and are unaware of internal cluster details.

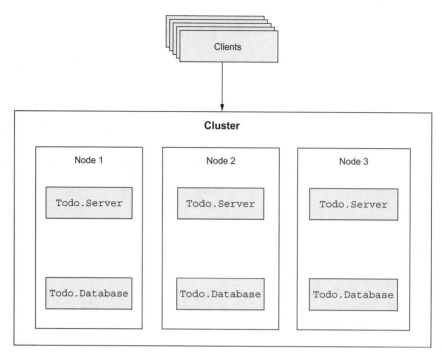

Figure 12.1   The to-do system as a cluster

Distributed systems obviously offer significant benefits, and Elixir and Erlang give you some simple and yet powerful distribution primitives. The central tools for distributed Erlang-based systems are processes and messages. You can send a message to another process, regardless of whether it's running in the same BEAM instance or on another instance on a remote machine.

Don't confuse this with a traditional RPC approach, wherein a remote call is wrapped to look like a local call. Erlang and, by extension, Elixir take the opposite route, and their distributed nature appears early in the game. If you think about it, a typical concurrent system that runs a multitude of processes can already be considered distributed.

Much like remote services, processes live their own lives and run in total isolation from each other. Issuing a request to another local process can be considered a remote call, and message passing has much in common with remote network communication. In the basic version, you send a message and don't know anything about its outcome. You can't even be sure whether the message will reach the target. If you want stronger guarantees, you can design the protocol to make the target send you a response (e.g., by using a synchronous call). Moreover, you must consider the cost of passing a message (the contents are copied), and this property sometimes affects the design of the communication protocol among multiple processes.

All these properties are common to the Erlang concurrency model and distributed systems, and you need to take them into consideration. The good news is that a properly designed concurrent system is, in many ways, ready to be distributed across multiple machines.

This transformation is by no means free. Distributed systems introduce an additional set of nontrivial challenges that need to be tackled. But thanks to the simple distribution building blocks that are available—many of which you're already familiar with—you can focus on the core challenges of distributed systems.

As you'll see in this chapter, it doesn't take much to turn your to-do system into a basic fault-tolerant cluster. To do this, you need to become familiar with basic distribution primitives.

12.1 Distribution primitives

Distributed BEAM systems are built by connecting multiple nodes in a cluster. A node is a BEAM instance that has a name associated with it.

You can start multiple nodes on the same host machine or on different machines, and you can connect those nodes. Once the nodes are connected, you can communicate between different processes on different nodes by relying on the familiar message-passing mechanism.

12.1.1 Starting a cluster

To set up a cluster, you need to start a couple of nodes. Starting a node can be as simple as using the `--sname` parameter while starting the shell:

```
$ iex --sname node1@localhost      ⟵───┘ Provides the node name
iex(node1@localhost)1>  ⟵─────
                              │ The shell reports the node name.
```

Using `--sname` turns your BEAM instance into a node with the name `node1@localhost`. The part before the `@` character is a prefix that uniquely identifies a node on a single machine. The second part (`localhost`) identifies the host machine. If you omit the host part, the host machine's name is automatically used.

The `--sname` parameter sets a *short name*, in which the host machine is identified only by its name. It's also possible to provide a *long name*, in which the host machine is identified by a fully qualified symbolic name or an IP address. This will be discussed in more detail in the final section of this chapter.

Once you've started a node, you can obtain its name by calling the `Kernel.node/0` function:

```
iex(node1@localhost)1> node()
:node1@localhost           ⟵──── The name of this node
```

As you can see from the output, a node name is represented internally as an atom.

Using a node usually makes sense when you want to connect it to another node. Let's try this. Keep `node1` running, and start another OS shell session. Now, start `node2` and connect it to `node1`:

```
$ iex --sname node2@localhost

iex(node2@localhost)1> Node.connect(:node1@localhost)      ⟵—— Connects to
true                                                            another node
```

The argument to `Node.connect/1` is an atom that represents the target node name. When `Node.connect/1` is invoked, BEAM tries to establish a TCP connection with the target BEAM instance. Once the connection is established, nodes are considered to be connected, and all communication between them takes place via this connection.

You can prove that nodes are connected by calling `Node.list/0`, which returns a list of all nodes connected to the current one (the current node isn't listed). Trying this on `node1` and `node2` gives the expected results:

```
iex(node1@localhost)2> Node.list()
[:node2@localhost]              ⟵—— Nodes connected to node1

iex(node2@localhost)2> Node.list()
[:node1@localhost]              ⟵—— Nodes connected to node2
```

It's possible to connect multiple nodes. In fact, by default, BEAM tries to establish a fully connected cluster. If you start a third node, `node3`, and connect it to `node2`, a connection is established to all other nodes that `node2` is connected to:

```
$ iex --sname node3@localhost

iex(node3@localhost)1> Node.connect(:node2@localhost)

iex(node3@localhost)2> Node.list()
[:node2@localhost, :node1@localhost]     ⟵—— node3 is connected to all nodes.
```

This is useful in scenarios in which you want to set up a fully connected cluster of multiple nodes. Adding a new node to such a cluster amounts to establishing a connection to a single node from the cluster. The new node will then automatically connect to all nodes in the cluster.

To get a list of all nodes in a cluster, including the current one, you can use `Node.list/1`:

```
iex(node1@localhost)3> Node.list([:this, :visible])
[:node1@localhost, :node2@localhost, :node3@localhost]
```

The `:this` option states that you want the current node to appear in the list. The `:visible` option indicates that you also want to get the list of all *visible* nodes. It's possible to start a node as *hidden*, as I'll explain in the last section of this chapter.

Detecting disconnected nodes

Node disconnection deserves a special mention. After the connection is established, each node periodically sends tick messages to all of its connected peers, to check whether they're still alive. All nodes that fail to respond to four consecutive tick messages are considered disconnected and are removed from the list of connected nodes.

There's no automatic attempt to reconnect those nodes, but it's possible to register and receive notifications when a node is disconnected, using the `Node.monitor/1` function (https://hexdocs.pm/elixir/Node.html#monitor/2). Moreover, you can monitor all node connections and disconnections with the help of `:net_kernel.monitor_nodes` (https://www.erlang.org/doc/man/net_kernel.html#monitor_nodes-1). I'll demonstrate how this works a bit later when I discuss network partitions.

12.1.2 Communicating between nodes

Once you have some nodes started and connected, you can make them cooperate. A simple way to try this is to use `Node.spawn/2`, which receives a node name (an atom) and a lambda. The function then spawns a new process on the target node and runs the lambda in that process.

For example, from `node1` you can spawn a process on `node2`.

Listing 12.1 Spawning a process on another node

```
iex(node1@localhost)4> Node.spawn(
                         :node2@localhost,    ◁──── Target node
                         fn -> IO.puts("Hello from #{node()}") end   ◁──── Runs on the target node
                       )
Hello from node2@localhost
```

The output proves that the lambda has been executed on another node.

Group leader process

Something unexpected is happening in listing 12.1. Even though the lambda has been executed on `node2`, the output is printed in the shell of `node1`. How is this possible? The reason lies in how Erlang does standard I/O operations.

All standard I/O calls (such as `IO.puts/1`) are forwarded to the *group leader*—a process that's in charge of performing the actual input or output. A spawned process inherits the group leader from the process that spawned it, even when you're spawning a process on another node. Therefore, your process may run on `node2`, but its group leader is still on `node1`. As a consequence, the string to be printed is created on `node2` (as the string contents prove), but the output is printed on `node1`.

Another important primitive is the ability to send messages to processes, regardless of their location. This property is also known as *location transparency*. The send operation always works the same way, regardless of the node on which the target process is running.

Let's look at a simple example. From `node1`, you'll start a computation that runs on `node2` and then sends the result back to `node1`:

```
iex(node1@localhost)5> caller = self()

iex(node1@localhost)6> Node.spawn(
                          :node2@localhost,
                          fn -> send(caller, {:response, 1+2}) end
                        )
```

Sends the response back to the caller

```
iex(node1@localhost)7> flush()
{:response, 3}
```

The response is received on the caller.

This example clearly resembles standard use of processes. You spawn a process on a remote node and then, from the spawned process, send the message back to the `caller`. Notice how the `caller` variable is used. Even though the lambda runs on another node, the closure mechanism still works.

Finally, you use the `iex` shell's `flush` helper, which takes all messages from the current process mailbox and prints them to the console. This proves that the messages have been received on the caller node.

There are no limits to what can be sent as a message. Whatever works in one BEAM instance will work across different instances (with a small caveat, described in the sidebar on lambdas). When the destination process is on another node, the message is encoded using `:erlang.term_to_binary/1` and decoded on the target node with `:erlang.binary_to_term/1`.

Avoid spawning lambdas or sending them to different nodes

You can spawn lambdas from your shell, which is a somewhat special case because shell-defined lambdas embed their own code and are interpreted dynamically on each invocation. In contrast, lambdas defined in module functions can be spawned remotely (or sent to a remote node via a message) only if both nodes are powered by exactly the same compiled code. These requirements are difficult to satisfy if you start running a multinode cluster and then need to update the code. You can't simultaneously upgrade all the nodes in the cluster, so at some point, the code on the nodes will differ.

Therefore, it's generally better to avoid passing lambdas to a remote node. Instead, you should use the `Node.spawn/4` function, which accepts a module, function, arguments (MFA) list that identifies a function to be invoked on the target node. This is safe to use as long as the module exists on the target node and exports the corresponding function.

In a multinode environment, the term "local registration" finally starts to make sense. When you register a process locally, the scope of registration is only the current node. This means you can use the same registered name on different nodes (but only once on each node). For example, register shell processes for both `node1` and `node2`:

```
iex(node1@localhost)8> Process.register(self(), :shell)
true

iex(node2@localhost)3> Process.register(self(), :shell)
true
```

Calling `send(:shell, some_message)` will send the message to either `node1` or `node2`, depending on the node where you invoke `send`.

It's possible to reference a locally registered process on another node by using `{some_alias, some_node}`. For example, to send a message from the `node1` to `node2` shell, you can do this:

```
iex(node1@localhost)9> send(                        Identifies a process
                         {:shell, :node2@localhost},   ⟵ registered on another node
                         "Hello from node1!"
                       )
```

Then, on `node2`, you can verify that a message is received:

```
iex(node2@localhost)4> flush()
"Hello from node1!"
```

You can also use the `{some_alias, some_node}` form when making `GenServer` requests (casts and calls). Finally, there are two special functions, `GenServer.abcast/3` and `GenServer.multi_call/4`, that let you issue a request to all locally registered processes on given nodes.

12.1.3 *Process discovery*

Process discovery is a very important operation in a cluster, but this same operation is used in clusterless mode as well. In fact, distributed system or not, the typical pattern of process communication is always the same:

1 A client process must obtain the server's PID.
2 A client sends a message to the server.

In step 1, you discover a process. You used a form of discovery with the `Registry` module in chapter 9.

Even in a single-node system, you must somehow find the target process's PID. This doesn't change in a distributed setting, but you must use another means of discovery because `Registry` isn't cluster aware and works only in the scope of a local node.

GLOBAL REGISTRATION

The simplest way to do cluster-wide discovery is to use the `:global` module (https://www.erlang.org/doc/man/global.html), which provides a global name registration facility. For example, if you run the to-do system as a multinode cluster, you may want to run exactly one process per to-do list (unless you aim for redundancy, of course). Global name registration allows you to achieve this.

As an example, you can register the `node1` shell process to act as the process responsible for handling Bob's to-do list:

```
iex(node1@localhost)10> :global.register_name({:todo_list, "bob"}, self())
:yes
```

The result (:yes) means global registration is successful. The global (cluster-wide) alias of the current process is now {:todo_list, "bob"}.

At this point, all processes on all nodes in the cluster can find the process registered under this alias. Attempting to globally register the node2 shell process under the same alias will fail:

```
iex(node2@localhost)5> :global.register_name({:todo_list, "bob"}, self())
:no
```

How global registration works

There's no special magic to global registration. It's implemented in pure Erlang, and you can reimplement it yourself in Elixir. It's just an elaborate, multinode-aware version of a process registry.

When you attempt to register a global alias, a cluster-wide lock is set, preventing any competing registration on other nodes. Then, a check is performed to see whether the alias is already registered. If not, all nodes are informed about the new registration. Finally, the lock is released. Obviously, this involves a lot of chatter, and several small messages are passed between nodes.

You can use :global.whereis_name/1 to find the process:

```
iex(node2@localhost)6> :global.whereis_name({:todo_list, "bob"})
#PID<7954.90.0>
```

Note that lookups are local. When a registration is being performed, all nodes are contacted, and they cache the registration information in their local ETS tables. Each subsequent lookup on any node is performed on that node, without any additional chatter. This means a lookup can be performed quickly, whereas registration requires chatting between nodes.

Take a look at the shape of this PID: #PID<7954.90.0>. The first number in the PID string representation isn't 0, which indicates you're dealing with a process from some other node.

Recognizing remote processes

It should be obvious by now that a PID identifies both a local and remote process. In almost all cases, you don't need to worry about the physical location of a process. But you should know some network-specific details about PIDs.

All the PIDs you've seen up to now have had a similar form: <0.X.0>, where X is a positive integer. Internally, each process has a node-wide unique identifier. This identifier can be seen in the last two numbers of the string representation. If you create enough processes on a single node, the third number will also be greater than zero.

> The first number represents the node number—an internal identifier of the node where the process is running. When this number is zero, the process is from the local node. Conversely, when the output includes a PID in the form `<X.Y.Z>` and `X` isn't zero, you can be sure it's a remote process. To programmatically determine the node where a process is running, you can use `Kernel.node/1` (https://hexdocs.pm/elixir/Kernel .html#node/1).

Global registration allows you to forward all requests that need to manipulate the same resource (in this case, a to-do list) to a single synchronization point (a process) in your cluster. This is exactly the same pattern you use in a single-node setting, now applied to a cluster of nodes. You'll see this in action a bit later when you start making the to-do system distributed.

Global registration can also be used with `GenServer`, as illustrated in the following snippet:

```
GenServer.start_link(
  __MODULE__,
  arg,
  name: {:global, some_global_alias}     ◁─── Registers the process
)                                              under a global alias

GenServer.call({:global, some_global_alias}, ...)  ◁─── A global alias can be used
                                                         to make a request.
```

Finally, if a registered process crashes or the owner node disconnects, the alias is automatically unregistered on all other machines.

GROUPS OF PROCESSES

Another frequent discovery pattern occurs when you want to register several processes under the same alias. This may sound strange, but it's useful in situations in which you want to categorize processes in a cluster and broadcast messages to all processes in a category.

For example, in redundant clusters, you want to keep multiple copies of the same data. Having multiple copies allows you to survive node crashes. If one node terminates, a copy should exist somewhere else in the cluster.

For this problem, you can use the `:pg` (process groups) module (https:// www.erlang.org/doc/man/pg.html). This module allows you to create arbitrarily named cluster-wide groups and add multiple processes to those groups. This addition is propagated across all nodes, and, later, you can query the group and get the list of all processes belonging to it.

Let's try this. You'll set up both shell processes of `node1` and `node2` to handle Bob's to-do list. To do this, you'll need to add both processes to this group.

Start the first node, and ensure `:pg` is running by invoking `:pg.start_link/0`:

```
iex(node1@localhost)1> :pg.start_link()
```

Start the second node, connect it to the first node, and start :pg:

```
iex(node2@localhost)1> Node.connect(:node1@localhost)

iex(node2@localhost)2> :pg.start_link()
```

You can add both shell processes to a group with the function :pg.join/2:

```
iex(node1@localhost)2> :pg.join({:todo_list, "bob"}, self())
:ok

iex(node2@localhost)3> :pg.join({:todo_list, "bob"}, self())
:ok
```

The first argument is an arbitrary term that uniquely identifies the group. The second argument is the PID of the process, which is added to the group.

At this point, both processes are in the process group, and both nodes can see this:

```
iex(node1@localhost)3> :pg.get_members({:todo_list, "bob"})
[#PID<8531.90.0>, #PID<0.90.0>]

iex(node2@localhost)4> :pg.get_members({:todo_list, "bob"})
[#PID<0.90.0>, #PID<7954.90.0>]
```

How can you use this technique? When you want to make an update to Bob's to-do list, you can query the corresponding process group and get a list of all processes responsible for Bob's list. Then, you can issue your request to all processes (e.g., by using `GenServer.multi_call/4`). This ensures all replicas in the cluster are updated.

But when you need to issue a query (e.g., to retrieve to-do list entries), you can do this on a single process from the group (no need to perform multiple queries on all replicas, unless you want better confidence). Therefore, you can choose a single PID from the process group.

Just like the :global module, :pg is implemented in pure Erlang and is also an elaborate version of a process registry. Group creations and joins are propagated across the cluster, but lookups are performed on a locally cached ETS table. Process crashes and node disconnects are automatically detected, and nonexistent processes are removed from the group.

12.1.4 *Links and monitors*

Links and monitors work even if processes reside on different nodes. A process receives an exit signal or a :DOWN notification message (in the case of a monitor) if any of the following events occur:

- Crash of a linked or monitored process
- Crash of a BEAM instance or the entire machine where the linked or monitored process is running
- Network connection loss

Let's quickly prove this. You'll start two nodes, connect them, and set up a monitor from the `node1` shell to the shell of `node2`:

```
$ iex --sname node1@localhost
$ iex --sname node2@localhost

iex(node2@localhost)1> Node.connect(:node1@localhost)
iex(node2@localhost)2> :global.register_name({:todo_list, "bob"}, self())

iex(node1@localhost)1> Process.monitor(
  :global.whereis_name({:todo_list, "bob"})
)
```

Monitors a process on another node

Now, you can terminate `node2` and flush messages in `node1`:

```
iex(node1@localhost)2> flush()
{:DOWN, #Reference<0.0.0.99>, :process, #PID<7954.90.0>, :noconnection}
```

As you can see, you have a notification that the monitored process isn't running anymore. This allows you to detect errors in distributed systems and recover from them. In fact, the error-detection mechanism works the same way as in concurrent systems, which isn't surprising, given that concurrency is also a distribution primitive.

12.1.5 *Other distribution services*

Other interesting services are provided as part of the Erlang standard library. I'll mention them briefly here, but once you start writing distributed systems, you should definitely spend time researching them.

I already mentioned that many basic primitives can be found in the `Node` module (https://hexdocs.pm/elixir/Node.html). On top of that, you may find some useful services in the `:net_kernel` (https://www.erlang.org/doc/man/net_kernel.html) and `:net_adm` (https://www.erlang.org/doc/man/net_adm.html) modules.

Occasionally, you'll need to issue function calls on other nodes. As you've seen, this can be done with `Node.spawn`, but this is a low-level approach and often isn't suitable. The problem with `Node.spawn` is that it's a fire-and-forget kind of operation, so you don't know anything about its outcome.

More often, you'll want to obtain the result of a remote function call or invoke a function on multiple nodes and collect all the results. In such cases, you can refer to the `:rpc` Erlang module (https://erlang.org/doc/man/rpc.html), which provides various useful helpers.

For example, to call a function on another node and get its result, you can use `:rpc.call/4`, which accepts a node and an MFA identifying the function to be called remotely. Here's an example that performs a remote call of `Kernel.abs(-1)` on `node2`:

```
iex(node1@localhost)1> :rpc.call(:node2@localhost, Kernel, :abs, [-1])
1
```

Other useful helpers included in the :rpc module allow you to issue a remote function call on multiple nodes in the cluster. You'll see this in action a bit later when you add replication features to your database.

Message passing is the core distribution primitive

Many services, such as :rpc, are implemented in pure Erlang. Just like :global and :pg, :rpc relies on transparent message passing and the ability to send messages to locally registered processes on remote nodes. For example, :rpc relies on the existence of a locally registered :rex process (which is started when Erlang's :kernel application is started). Making an RPC call on other nodes amounts to sending a message containing MFA to :rex processes on target nodes, calling apply/3 from those servers, and sending back the response.

If you want to dive deeper into distributed programming on Erlang systems, I recommend spending some time studying the code for rpc.erl, pg.erl, and global.erl to learn about various distributed idioms and patterns.

I also want to mention cluster-wide locks. These are implemented in the :global module, and they allow you to grab an arbitrarily named lock. Once you have a particular lock, no other process in the cluster can acquire it until you release it.

Let's see this in action. Start node1 and node2 and connect them. Then, on node1, try to acquire the lock using :global.set_lock/1:

```
iex(node1@localhost)1> :global.set_lock({:some_resource, self()})
true
```

The tuple you provide consists of the resource ID and the requester ID. The resource ID is an arbitrary term, whereas the requester ID identifies a unique requester. Two different requesters can't acquire the same lock in the cluster. Usually, you'll want to use the process ID as the requester ID, which means that at any point, at most one process can acquire the lock.

Acquiring the lock involves chatting with other nodes in the cluster. Once :set_lock returns, you know that you have the lock, and no one else in the cluster can acquire it. Attempt to acquire a lock on node2:

Blocks until the lock is released

```
iex(node2@localhost)1> :global.set_lock({:some_resource, self()})         ◄──┐
```

The shell process on node2 will wait indefinitely (this can be configured via an additional parameter) until the lock becomes available. As soon as you release the lock on node1, it's obtained on node2:

```
iex(node1@localhost)2> :global.del_lock({:some_resource, self()})
iex(node2@localhost)2>         ◄──┐
```
The lock is now held by the shell process on node2.

There's also a simple helper for the acquire–release pattern available in the form of :global.trans/2 (https://erlang.org/doc/man/global.html#trans-2), which takes the lock; runs the provided lambda; and, finally, releases the lock.

Locking is something you should usually avoid because it causes the same kinds of problems as classical synchronization approaches. Excessively relying on locks increases the possibility of deadlocks, livelocks, or starvation. Generally, you should synchronize through processes because it's easier to reason about the system this way.

But used judiciously, locks can sometimes improve performance. Remember that message passing has an associated cost; this is especially true in distributed systems, where a message must be serialized and transmitted over the network. If a message is very large, this can introduce significant delays and hurt system performance.

Locks can help here because they let you synchronize multiple processes on different nodes without needing to send large messages to another process. Here's a sketch of this idea. Let's say you need to ensure that the processing of a large amount of data is serialized in the entire cluster (at any point in time, at most one process may run in the entire cluster). Normally, this is done by passing the data to a process that acts as a synchronization point. But passing a large chunk of data may introduce a performance penalty because data must be copied and transmitted over the network. To avoid this, you can synchronize different processes with locks and then process the data in the caller context:

```
def process(large_data) do
  :global.trans(           <——— Acquires the cluster-wide lock
    {:some_resource, self},
    fn ->
      do_something_with(large_data)      <——— Runs in the caller process
    end
  )
end
```

Calling `:global.trans/2` ensures cluster-wide isolation. At most, one process in the cluster can be running `do_something_with/1` on `:some_resource` at any point in time. Because `do_something_with/1` is running in the caller process, you avoid sending a huge message to another synchronization process. Invoking `:global.trans/2` introduces additional chatter between nodes, but messages used to acquire the lock are much smaller than passing the contents of `large_data` to another process on another node, so you save bandwidth.

This concludes our discussion of the basics of distribution. I didn't mention some important aspects that arise once you start using a network as a communication channel for message passing. We'll revisit this topic in the last section of this chapter. For now, let's focus on making the to-do system more distributed.

12.2 Building a fault-tolerant cluster

With some distribution primitives in your arsenal, you can begin building a cluster of to-do web servers. The aim is to make the system more resilient to all sorts of outages, including crashes of entire nodes. The solution presented here will be simplistic. Making a proper distributed system requires much more attention to various details, and the topic could easily fill an entire book.

On the plus side, making a basic BEAM-powered distributed system isn't complicated. In this section, you'll get a feel for how distribution primitives fit nicely into the existing BEAM concurrency model.

Most of your work here will be based on the `GenServer` abstraction. This shouldn't come as a surprise, given that message passing is the main distribution tool in BEAM. Before continuing, make sure you remember how `GenServer` works; if needed, revisit the explanation in chapter 6.

12.2.1 Cluster design

The goals of this cluster are deceptively simple:

- The cluster will consist of multiple nodes, all of which are powered by the same code and provide the same service (a web interface for managing multiple to-do lists).
- Changes should be propagated across the cluster. A modification made on a single to-do list on one node should be visible on all other nodes. From the outside, clients shouldn't care which node they access.
- The crash of a single node shouldn't disturb the cluster. Service should be provided continuously, and data from the crashed node shouldn't be lost.

These goals describe a fault-tolerant system. You always provide service, and individual crashes don't cause a disturbance. Thus, the system becomes more resilient and highly available.

> **Network partitions**
>
> Note that you won't tackle the most difficult challenge of distributed systems: network partitions. A *partition* is a situation in which a communication channel between two nodes is broken and the nodes are disconnected. In this case, you may end up with a "split-brain" situation: when the cluster gets broken into two (or more) disconnected smaller clusters—all of which work and provide service. This situation can cause problems because you have multiple isolated systems, each accepting input from users. Ultimately, you may end up with conflicting data that's impossible to reconcile. For most of this section, we'll ignore this issue, but we'll discuss some consequences before parting.

Let's begin work on making the system distributed. First, we'll look at the to-do cache.

12.2.2 The distributed to-do cache

In a sense, the to-do cache is the centerpiece of the system. This is the primary element that maintains the consistency of the data, so let's recall how it works. The main idea is illustrated in figure 12.2.

When you want to modify a to-do list, you ask the to-do cache to provide the corresponding to-do server process for you. This to-do server then acts as a synchronization point for a single to-do list. All requests for Bob's list go through that process, which ensures consistency and prevents race conditions.

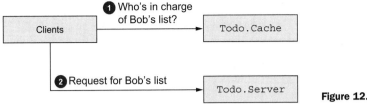

Figure 12.2 Using a to-do cache

When clustering your system, you'll aim to keep this property. The difference is that your cache must somehow be made to work across all nodes in the cluster. No matter where in the cluster you ask the question "Who's in charge of Bob's list?" the answer will always point to the same process in the cluster (until that process crashes, of course). This is the single thing you need to change to make your to-do cache distributed. As you'll see, the changes are reasonably straightforward.

DISCOVERING TO-DO SERVERS

There are various ways to complete cluster-wide discovery. Probably the simplest (although not necessarily the most efficient) relies on services from the :global module that allow you to register a process under a global alias—an arbitrary term that identifies a process in the cluster. Here's what you need to do:

1 Adapt the Todo.Server module to use global registration.
2 Adapt Todo.Cache to work with the new registration.

Let's start implementing this. The first thing you need to do is modify the Todo.Server module to rely on global registration. So far, you've been using Registry, which is suitable only for single-node registrations. For distributed process registration and discovery, you can use the :global module.

> **Process registrations**
>
> You may be puzzled by all these different registration facilities, so let's recall the key differences:
>
> - The basic registration facility is a local registration that allows you to use a simple atom as an alias to the single process on a node.
> - Registry extends this by letting you use rich aliases—any term can be used as an alias.
> - :global allows you to register a cluster-wide alias.
> - :pg is useful for registering multiple processes behind a cluster-wide alias (process group), which is usually suitable for distributed pub–sub scenarios.

Replacing Registry with :global requires a single change in the Todo.Server module. The current version of the relevant code, introduced in chapter 9, looks like this:

```
defmodule Todo.Server do
  def start_link(name) do
    GenServer.start_link(Todo.Server, name, name: via_tuple(name))
```

```
  end

  defp via_tuple(name) do
    Todo.ProcessRegistry.via_tuple({__MODULE__, name})
  end

  ...
end
```

To make the registration use the `:global` module, you need to return `{:global, registered_name}` from `via_tuple/1`. While you're at it, you can also rename the function.

```
defmodule Todo.Server do
  ...

  def start_link(name) do
    GenServer.start_link(Todo.Server, name, name: global_name(name))
  end

  defp global_name(name) do
    {:global, {__MODULE__, name}}        <──── Global registration
  end

  ...
end
```

With this single simple change, you've switched to distributed registration and discovery. There's no need to change anything else; the system will work properly.

But there's one possible performance issue with the current implementation. When you register a process under a global alias, the `:global` module performs a synchronized chat across the entire cluster. This means a global registration is much more expensive than a local one, which is particularly problematic with the current implementation of the cache, introduced in chapter 9. Let's recall the relevant parts:

```
defmodule Todo.Cache do
  ...

  def server_process(todo_list_name) do
    case start_child(todo_list_name) do        <──── A new process is always started.
      {:ok, pid} -> pid
      {:error, {:already_started, pid}} -> pid
    end
  end

  defp start_child(todo_list_name) do
    DynamicSupervisor.start_child(
      __MODULE__,
      {Todo.Server, todo_list_name}
```

```
      )
    end

    ...
end
```

Way back in section 9.2.3, you opted for this simplistic approach. Whenever a child lookup is done, you start the new process and attempt to register it. If the registration fails, `DynamicSupervisor.start_child/2` will return `{:error, {:already_started, pid}}`. This was a simple solution that served you well. But now, with the system being distributed, this unconditional registration attempt can become a serious bottleneck. Every time you want to work with a to-do list, even if the server process is already running, you attempt a `:global` registration, which will in turn grab a cluster-wide lock and will then chat with all other nodes in the system.

This can be improved by performing an explicit lookup first. You'll check whether the to-do server is registered and attempt to start the server only if the lookup returns nothing. To do this, you need to first expand the `Todo.Server` module with the `whereis/1` function, which takes a name and returns a PID of the registered process or `nil` if no process is registered under the given name.

Listing 12.3 Discovering to-do servers (todo_distributed/lib/todo/server.ex)

```
defmodule Todo.Server do
  ...

  def whereis(name) do
    case :global.whereis_name({__MODULE__, name}) do
      :undefined -> nil
      pid -> pid
    end
  end

  ...
end
```

It's worth repeating that `:global.whereis_name/1` doesn't lead to any cross-node chatting. This function only makes a single lookup to a local ETS table. Therefore, you can expect pretty good and stable performance from the `Todo.Server.whereis/1` function.

Now, you can adapt the code in `Todo.Cache`..

Listing 12.4 Optimized process discovery (todo_distributed/lib/todo/cache.ex)

```
defmodule Todo.Cache do
  ...

  def server_process(todo_list_name) do
```

```
      existing_process(todo_list_name) || new_process(todo_list_name)
    end

    defp existing_process(todo_list_name) do
      Todo.Server.whereis(todo_list_name)
    end

    defp new_process(todo_list_name) do
      case DynamicSupervisor.start_child(
        __MODULE__,
        {Todo.Server, todo_list_name}
      ) do
        {:ok, pid} -> pid
        {:error, {:already_started, pid}} -> pid
      end

    end
end
```

Relying on a bit of wrapping and the || operator, the server_process/1 function highlights the approach of finding the to-do server. You either return the PID of the existing process, or you attempt to start the new process. As explained in section 9.2.3, the code in new_process/1 properly handles the situation in which two different client processes attempt to start the server for the same to-do list at the same time. The code will also work properly in a distributed setting, and it will handle race conditions between two clients on two different nodes.

With these changes in place, the Todo.ProcessRegistry module isn't used anymore, and it can, therefore, be removed from the project. The process registry entry can also be removed from the child specification list in the Todo.System module.

ALTERNATIVE DISCOVERY

Keep in mind that global registration is chatty and serialized (only one process at a time may perform global registration). This means the preceding approach isn't very scalable with respect to the number of different to-do lists or the number of nodes in the cluster. The solution will also perform poorly if the network is slow.

There are alternatives. The main challenge here is to reliably discover the process responsible for a to-do list while reducing network communication. This can be done by introducing a rule that always maps the same to-do list name to the same node in the network. Here's a simple sketch of the idea:

```
def node_for_list(todo_list_name) do
  all_sorted_nodes = Enum.sort(Node.list([:this, :visible]))

  node_index = :erlang.phash2(
    todo_list_name,
    length(all_sorted_nodes)
  )

  Enum.at(all_sorted_nodes, node_index)
end
```

You get the list of all nodes and sort it to ensure that it's always in the same order. Then, you hash the input name, making sure the result falls in the range `0..length(all_sorted_nodes)`. Finally, you return the node at the given position. This ensures that as long as the cluster is stable (the list of nodes doesn't change), the same to-do list will always be mapped to the same node.

Now, you can make a discovery in a single hop to the target node. Assuming the previous version of `Todo.Cache` (not the one you just implemented), retrieving the target process can be as simple as this:

```
:rpc.call(
  node_for_list(todo_list_name),
  Todo.Cache,
  :server_process,
  [todo_list_name]
)
```

You forward to the target node and retrieve the desired process there. You don't need to use global registration, and `Todo.Cache` can continue working as it was before this chapter. The result of the preceding invocation is a PID, which you can then use to make your call. The benefit is that you can discover the PID with less chatting.

The main downside of this approach is that it doesn't work properly when the cluster configuration changes. If you add another node or a node disconnects, the mapping rules will change. Dealing with this situation is complex. You need to detect the change in the cluster (which is possible, as will be explained a bit later) and migrate all data to different nodes according to new mapping rules. While this data is being migrated, you'll probably want to keep the service running, which will introduce another layer of complexity. The amount of data that needs to be migrated can be greatly reduced if you use some form of consistent hashing—a smarter mapping of keys to nodes that's more resilient to changes in the cluster.

It's obvious that the implementation can quickly become more involved, which is why you started simple and chose the global registration approach. Although it's not particularly scalable, it's a simple solution that works. But if you need better performance and scalability, you'll have to resort to a more complex approach. Instead of reinventing the wheel, consider looking at third-party solutions, such as Syn (https://github.com/ostinelli/syn) or Swarm (https://github.com/bitwalker/swarm).

12.2.3   Implementing a replicated database

After the changes you just made, you'll have the following behavior:

1. When the first request for Bob's list arrives, a to-do list is created on the node that handles that request.
2. All subsequent requests on Bob's to-do list are forwarded to the process created in step 1.
3. If the node (or the process) created in step 1 crashes, a new request for Bob's list will cause the new to-do server to be registered.

Everything seems fine at first glance, and the system looks properly distributed. You won't test it now because there's one important issue we haven't addressed yet: the database doesn't survive crashes. Let's say you performed several updates to Bob's list on node A. If this node crashes, some other node, such as node B, will take over the work for Bob's list. But previously stored data won't be on that node, and you'll lose all your changes.

Obviously, the database needs to be replicated so that data can survive node crashes. The simplest (although not the most efficient) way of preserving data is to replicate it in the entire cluster. This idea is illustrated in figure 12.3.

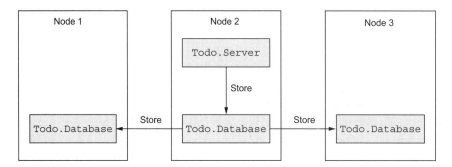

Figure 12.3   Replicating the database

This is pretty straightforward. When you store data to the database, you'll propagate the change to all nodes in the cluster. The corresponding implementation can be simple if you rely on services from the `:rpc` module. I mentioned that `:rpc`, among other things, allows you to issue a function call on all nodes in the cluster. You'll rely on this feature and make some changes to the `Database` module:

1 Rename the existing `Database.store` function to `Database.store_local`. The code remains the same.
2 Provide the new implementation to `Database.store`. This new implementation will call `Database.store_local` on all nodes in the cluster.

Another change you'll make (the code isn't presented here) will turn `Todo.Database-Worker.store/2` into a call. This request should have been implemented as a call in the first place. Back in chapter 7, I opted for a cast somewhat arbitrarily, mostly for didactic purposes. In reality, if you're asking another process to store data, you should request a confirmation message, so you know whether the data has been stored or something went wrong. This becomes increasingly important as you move to a less reliable communication medium (a network) in which all sorts of things can go wrong. When you expect a request to be used across nodes, you should usually implement it as a call.

No other changes are required. In particular, `Todo.Database.get/1` remains unchanged. When you want to read the data, you can do so from the local node, optimistically assuming all nodes have the same copy of the data. The changes are straightforward, as shown in the following listing.

```
defmodule Todo.Database do
  ...

  def store(key, data) do
    {_results, bad_nodes} =
      :rpc.multicall(
        __MODULE__,              Calls store_local
        :store_local,            on all nodes
        [key, data],
        :timer.seconds(5)
      )

    Enum.each(bad_nodes, &IO.puts("Store failed on node #{&1}"))   ←
    :ok                          Logs the failed results
  end

  ...
end
```

Here, you rely on `:rpc.multicall/4` to make a function call on all nodes in the cluster. `multicall` accepts MFA and a timeout. The target function is then invoked on all nodes in the cluster, all results are collected, and you get a tuple in the form `{results, bad_nodes}`: a list of results and a list of nodes that didn't respond in the given time.

> ## Always provide timeouts
>
> The timeout provided to `multicall` is important. Without it, `multicall` and, in turn, the `store` operation would be blocked forever.
>
> When doing distributed calls, you should usually specify a timeout. Note that this is no different from cross-process calls—when making a call to another process, you usually want to have a timeout as well, and `GenServer` recognizes this by providing a default 5-second timeout. Again, cross-node operations aren't all that different from cross-process operations, and in many cases, you'll have to consider a similar set of problems when developing a single-node system.

Finally, you print all nodes on which the request timed out. Note that, in practice, this isn't sufficient. You should also verify that each received response returns `:ok`. Moreover, you should do something meaningful in the case of a partial success. Otherwise, you'll end up with an inconsistent cluster, with different nodes containing different data. For the sake of brevity, I've refrained from doing this here, but in a real project, this is an issue that needs to be considered and addressed.

I made another small change in the database workers, which isn't presented here. Up to now, you've used the persist folder to store your data. This is changed to accommodate the node name. If your node is called `node1@localhost`, you'll store data in the persist/node1 folder. This is done mostly to simplify testing and allow you to start multiple nodes locally from the same root folder.

In any case, this simple change makes it possible to replicate your data across the cluster. With this, our basic take on a clustered to-do system is finished, and you can try it out.

12.2.4 *Testing the system*

Finally, it's time to test the system. You need to start a few nodes, connect them, and see how the cluster works. But recall that, in chapter 11, you made the web server listen on port 5454. You can't have two nodes listening on the same port, so you need to change this. Luckily, in section 11.4, you made the web port configurable via the application environment, so it's possible to change the default port from the command line.

Start two instances, `node1` and `node2`, that listen on ports 5454 and 5555, respectively:

```
$ TODO_SERVER_EXPIRY=600 iex --sname node1@localhost -S mix

$ TODO_SERVER_EXPIRY=600 TODO_HTTP_PORT=5555 \
    iex --sname node2@localhost -S mix
```

Starts node1, which listens on the default port

Starts node2, and sets the alternative port

Here, we're changing the system configuration via the OS environment variables. The to-do server auto-expiry timeout is increased to 600 seconds, so it doesn't interfere with our local experiments. The second node is also configured to use the nondefault port.

Next, you need to connect the two nodes:

```
iex(node1@localhost)1> Node.connect(:node2@localhost)
```

Now, the cluster is established, and you can use your servers. Add an entry for Bob on the first node:

```
$ curl -d "" \
    "http://localhost:5454/add_entry?list=bob&date=2023-12-19&title=Dentist"
OK
```

Then, verify that this entry is visible on another node:

```
$ curl "http://localhost:5555/entries?list=bob&date=2023-12-19"
2023-12-19 Dentist
```

This proves that your data is propagated across the cluster. Furthermore, looking at individual `iex` shells, you'll see the "Starting to-do server for bob" message in the `node1` shell but not in `node2`. This is clear proof that even when you try to access Bob's list on another node, you're forwarded to the corresponding process on `node1`.

You can, thus, safely modify Bob's list on `node2` without compromising the data:

```
$ curl -d "" \
    "http://localhost:5555/add_entry?list=bob&date=2023-12-19&title=Movies"

$ curl "http://localhost:5454/entries?list=bob&date=2023-12-19"
2023-12-19 Dentist
2023-12-19 Movies
```

Finally, crashing a single node won't disturb the system. Stop `node1`, where Bob's to-do server is running, and try to query `node2`:

```
$ curl "http://localhost:5555/entries?list=bob&date=2023-12-19"
2023-12-19 Dentist
2023-12-19 Movies
```

Sure enough, the cluster is still providing its service, and data is preserved. The new to-do server has been created on `node2`, and it restored the state from the replicated database.

At this point, your basic cluster is complete. There are some remaining issues, which I won't address here but will mention:

- You should set up a load balancer to serve as a single access point for all clients.
- You need a scheme for introducing new nodes to the running cluster. When a new node is introduced, it should first synchronize the database with one of the already connected nodes; then, it can begin serving requests.
- Database replication is fragile. You need some kind of two-phase commit strategy.
- You need to handle network partitions.

Some of these challenges aren't easy to tackle, but they're inherent to distributed systems, and you'll have to deal with them regardless of the underlying technology. It's important to understand that Erlang isn't a "magic wand" for distributed problems. In a distributed system, many things can go wrong, and it's up to you to decide how you want to recover from various failures. There's no one-size-fits-all solution: your job is to combine basic distribution primitives in a way that suits the problem at hand.

Of course, offloading the work to proven third-party components can often help. For example, by using the built-in Mnesia database, you could achieve better write guarantees and be able to easily migrate new nodes to the cluster. But even then, it's important to understand how a third-party library works in a distributed setting. In this example, Mnesia doesn't deal explicitly with network partitions and split-brain scenarios and, instead, leaves it to the developer to resolve this situation. Some other component might exhibit different drawbacks, so you need to understand how it works in a distributed setting.

Erlang distribution primitives can take you a long way. Only a few changes were needed to make your system distributed, even if you didn't prepare for the distributed system up front.

12.2.5 Detecting partitions

The work so far has been easy, but we've conveniently ignored the issue of network partitions. This is one of the biggest challenges when building a distributed system. Fully discussing this topic could easily turn into a substantial-sized book, so I'll just explain the basic mechanisms of detecting partitions.

When you decide to go distributed, partitions are a problem you'll have to deal with, one way or another. Network partitions shouldn't be ignored in a distributed system, so even if you reach for a third-party product (e.g., an external database) to handle clustering and replication, you should understand how that product behaves when partitions occur. It's best to be aware of the challenges you'll face so that you can make conscious and informed decisions about how to proceed.

A network partition, or *netsplit*, is a situation in which two nodes can no longer communicate with each other. There can be all sorts of underlying causes, and it's impossible to tell them apart:

- A network connection is lost.
- A network connection is extremely slow.
- A remote node has crashed.
- A remote node is overloaded and busy to the point that it can't respond in a timely manner.

From the standpoint of one node, all those situations look the same. The remote node doesn't respond, and you don't know why. It's, therefore, virtually impossible to guarantee that a netsplit will never take place. Even on an ultra-fast and reliable network, a bug or overload may cause one host to become so busy that it can't respond to another in a timely manner. The other node has no choice but to interpret this situation as a netsplit and conclude that the connection is lost. This means that when you're implementing a distributed system, you need to consider network partitions and devise a strategy to deal with such situations.

When a partition occurs, you may end up with multiple independent clusters that are mutually disconnected. The problem is that although those clusters can't talk to each other, a cluster's clients may be able to reach all nodes. This situation is also known as *split-brain*. If different clusters continue to serve users independently, you may end up with undesired behavior. A request issued on one cluster won't be visible on another, and users may face lost updates, or phantom entries may appear. Ultimately, once you reconnect those clusters, you may end up with conflicting data.

To deal with partitions, you need to be able to detect them. Remember that a partition always manifests as a loss of connection to the remote node, and it's possible to detect this situation. As mentioned earlier, a node periodically pings its peers via tick messages, and if a peer fails to respond to these messages, it will be considered disconnected. Each process can subscribe to notifications about changes in connected nodes via :net_kernel .monitor_nodes/1 (https://erlang.org/doc/man/net_kernel.html#monitor_nodes-1).

The argument you provide is a Boolean that indicates whether you're adding a new subscription (`true`) or installing a single subscriber that overwrites all previous ones on this node (`false`). Either way, a process that calls `monitor_nodes` will receive notifications whenever a remote node connects or disconnects.

Let's try this. First, start `node1` and subscribe to notifications:

```
$ iex --sname node1@localhost
iex(node1@localhost)1> :net_kernel.monitor_nodes(true)
```

This makes the caller process (in this case, the shell) receive notifications.

Now, start two additional nodes and connect them to `node1`:

```
$ iex --sname node2@localhost
iex(node2@localhost)1> Node.connect(:node1@localhost)

$ iex --sname node3@localhost
iex(node3@localhost)1> Node.connect(:node1@localhost)
```

In the `node1` shell, you can see the corresponding messages:

```
iex(node1@localhost)2> flush()
{:nodeup, :node2@localhost}
{:nodeup, :node3@localhost}
```

The same thing happens on disconnect. You can stop `node2` and `node3` and check the messages in `node1`:

```
iex(node1@localhost)3> flush()
{:nodedown, :node3@localhost}
{:nodedown, :node2@localhost}
```

Alternatively, you can also use `Node.monitor/2` if you want to monitor a particular node (https://hexdocs.pm/elixir/Node.html#monitor/2).

Finally, as I already mentioned, you can set up a monitor or a link to a remote process. This works just as it does with local processes. If a remote process crashes (or the node disconnects), you'll receive a message (when using monitors) or an exit signal (when using links).

12.2.6 Highly available systems

Way back in chapter 1, I described some properties of a highly available system. It may not be obvious, but you've gradually reached this goal in the to-do system, which now has some nice properties:

- *Responsiveness*—Because you have a highly concurrent system, you can use your hardware more efficiently and serve multiple requests concurrently. Owing to how BEAM processes work, you won't experience unexpected pauses, such as system-wide garbage collection (because processes are garbage collected individually and concurrently). Occasional long-running tasks won't block the entire system due to frequent preemption of processes. Ultimately, you should have a predictable running system with fairly constant latency that degrades gracefully if your system becomes overloaded.

- *Scalability*—Your system is both concurrent and distributed, so you can address increased popularity and load by using a more powerful machine or by adding more nodes to the system. The system can automatically take advantage of the new hardware.

- *Fault tolerance*—Due to process isolation, you can limit the effect of individual errors. Due to process links, you can propagate such errors across the system and deal with them. Supervisors can help the system self-heal and recover from errors. At the same time, the main code will follow the happy path, focusing on the work that needs to be done, liberated from error-detection constructs. Finally, due to distribution, you can survive crashes of entire machines in the system.

At this point, it should be clear that the main tool for high availability is the BEAM concurrency model. Relying on processes provided many nice properties and made it possible to come close to having a highly available system.

Of course, this system is extremely simplified: you haven't provided proper implementations for aspects such as the database, and you haven't dealt with netsplits, which makes these claims overconfident. Regardless, when you set out to implement a highly available system that must serve a multitude of users continuously, these are the properties you'll need to achieve, and processes are the main tool that can take you there.

At this point, you're finished making the system distributed. Before departing, though, there are some important network-related considerations to discuss.

12.3 Network considerations

So far, you've been running nodes locally. This is fine for making local experiments and doing development-time testing. But in production, you'll usually want to run different nodes on different machines. When running a cross-host cluster, you need to consider some additional details. Let's start with node names.

12.3.1 Node names

The names you've been using so far are *short names* that consist of an arbitrary name prefix (node1 and node2, in this case) and the host name (localhost, in these examples). You can also provide a fully qualified node name, also known as a *long name*, which consists of a name prefix and a fully qualified host name. A long name can be provided with the --name command-line option:

```
$ iex --name node1@127.0.0.1
iex(node1@127.0.0.1)1>    <———— Long node name
```

It's also possible to use symbolic names:

```
$ iex --name node1@some_host.some_domain
iex(node1@some_host.some_domain)1>
```

A node name plays an important role when establishing a connection. Recall that a name uses the form `arbitrary_prefix@host` (short name) or `arbitrary_prefix@host .domain` (long name). This name obviously identifies a BEAM instance on a machine. The second part of the name (`host` or `host.domain`) must be resolvable to the IP address of the machine where the instance is running. When you attempt to connect to `node2@some_host.some_domain` from `node1`, the `node1` host must be able to resolve `some_host.some_domain` to the IP address of the host machine.

It's also worth noting that a node can connect only to a node that has the same type of name. In other words, a connection between a long-named node and a short-named node isn't possible.

12.3.2 Cookies

To connect two nodes, they must agree on a magical *cookie*—a kind of passphrase that's verified while the nodes are connecting. The first time you start a BEAM instance, a random cookie is generated for you and persisted in your home folder in the .erlang.cookie file. By default, all nodes you start on that machine will have this cookie.

To see your cookie, you can use `Node.get_cookie/0`:

```
iex(node1@localhost)1> Node.get_cookie()
:JHSKSHDYEJHDKEDKDIEN
```

Notice that the cookie is internally represented as an atom. A node running on another machine will have a different cookie, so connecting two nodes on different machines won't work by default; you need to, somehow, make all nodes use the same cookie. This can be as simple as calling `Node.set_cookie/1` on all nodes you want to connect:

```
iex(node1@localhost)1> Node.set_cookie(:some_cookie)

iex(node1@localhost)2> Node.get_cookie()
:some_cookie
```

Another approach is to provide the `--cookie` option when you start the system:

```
$ iex --sname node1@localhost --cookie another_cookie

iex(node1@localhost)1> Node.get_cookie()
:another_cookie
```

Cookies provide a bare minimum of security and also help prevent a fully connected cluster in which all nodes can directly talk to each other. For example, let's say you want to connect node A to B and B to C, but you don't want to connect A and C. This can be done by assigning different cookies to all the nodes and then, in A and C, using the `Node.set_cookie/2` function, which allows you to explicitly set different cookies that need to be used when connecting to different nodes.

12.3.3 Hidden nodes

It should be clear by now that most node operations revolve around the cluster. Most often, you'll treat all connected nodes as part of your cluster. But in some cases, this isn't what you need. For example, various tools let you connect to a remote running node and interact with it. A simple example is starting a local node that acts as a remote shell to another node. Another example is an instrumentation tool—a node that connects to another node, collects all sorts of metrics from it, and presents the results in a GUI.

Such nodes are helpers that shouldn't be part of the cluster, and you usually don't want them to be seen as such. For this purpose, you can make a *hidden* connection. When you start your BEAM instance with the `--hidden` argument, the node isn't seen in other nodes' connected lists (and vice versa).

Keep in mind, though, that a hidden node is still maintained in the node's connection list, albeit under a different `hidden` tag. You can explicitly retrieve hidden nodes by calling `Node.list([:hidden])`. Calling `Node.list([:connected])` returns all connected nodes, both hidden and visible, whereas calling `Node.list([:visible])` returns only visible nodes. When you want to perform a cluster-wide operation, you should generally use the `:visible` option.

Services provided by `:global`, `:rpc`, and `:pg` ignore hidden nodes. Registering a global alias on one node won't affect any hidden peer, and vice versa.

12.3.4 Firewalls

Given that nodes communicate via TCP connection, it's obvious that you need to have some ports that are open to other machines. When one node wants to connect to another node on a different machine, it needs to communicate with two different components, as illustrated in figure 12.4.

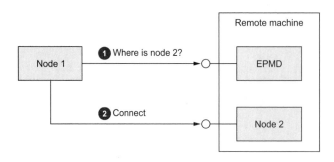

Figure 12.4   Connecting to a remote node

The first component, the Erlang Port Mapper Daemon (EPMD), is an OS process that's started automatically when you start the first Erlang node on the host machine. This component acts as a node name resolver on the host machine. EPMD knows the names of all currently running BEAM nodes on the machine. When a node wants to connect to a node on this machine, it first queries EPMD to determine which port the target node is listening on, and then it contacts the target node. EPMD listens on port 4369, and this port must be accessible from remote machines.

In addition, each node listens on a random port that needs to be accessible as well because it's used to establish the connection between two nodes. Obviously, it's not particularly helpful that the node's listening port is random because it's not possible to define firewall rules.

Luckily, you can provide a fixed range of ports on which a node will listen. This can be done by setting the `inet_dist_listen_min` and `inet_dist_listen_max` environment variables of the `kernel` app at the command line:

```
$ iex \
    --erl '-kernel inet_dist_listen_min 10000' \    Sets the range
    --erl '-kernel inet_dist_listen_max 10100' \    of ports
    --sname node1@localhost
```

The node will listen on the first port available in the given range. If you're sure there won't be a port clash, you can use the same value for both parameters, thus effectively designating a single port to be used.

You can manually inspect the ports of all nodes on the host machine via `:net_adm.names/0`:

```
iex(node1@localhost)1> :net_adm.names()
{:ok, [{~c"node1", 10000}]}
```

Alternatively, you can also invoke `epmd -names` from the OS command line.

To summarize, if you're behind a firewall, you need to open port 4369 (EPMD) and the range of ports on which your node will listen.

> **Security**
>
> Other than the magical cookie, no particular security model is provided. When you connect to a remote node, you can do anything on that node, including running system commands. If the remote node has root privileges, you have full access to the entire remote host.
>
> Erlang's distributed model was designed to run in a trusted environment, which is something you should be aware of. In particular, this means that in production your BEAM instances should run under minimal privileges. Moreover, you shouldn't expose your BEAM instances over the internet. If you need to connect nodes from different networks, you should consider switching to SSL as the communication protocol. Some pointers for doing this are provided in the Erlang documentation at https://erlang.org/doc/apps/ssl/ssl_distribution.html.

Summary

- Distributed systems can improve fault tolerance, eliminating the risk of a single point of failure.
- Clustering lets you scale out and spread the total load over multiple machines.
- BEAM-powered clusters are composed of nodes, which are named BEAM instances that can be connected and can communicate.
- Two nodes communicate via a single TCP connection. If this connection is broken, the nodes are considered disconnected.
- The main distribution primitive is a process. Sending a message works the same way, regardless of the process location. A remotely registered process can be accessed via {alias, node_name}.
- Many useful higher-level services built on top of those primitives are available in the :global, :rpc, and GenServer modules.
- When communicating between nodes, use calls rather than casts.
- Always consider and prepare for netsplit scenarios.

Running the system

You've spent a lot of time building a to-do system, and now it's time to prepare it for production. There are several ways to start a system, but the basic idea is always the same. You have to compile your code as well as your dependencies. Then, you start the BEAM instance and ensure all compiled artifacts are in the load path. Finally, from within the BEAM instance, you need to start your OTP application together with its dependencies. Once the OTP application is started, you can consider your system to be running.

There are various approaches to achieving this, and in this chapter, we'll focus on two of them. First, we'll look at how you can use Elixir tools, most notably `mix`, to start the system. Then, we'll discuss OTP releases. Finally, I'll end the chapter and the book by providing some pointers on how to interact with a running system, so you can detect and analyze faults and errors that inevitably happen at run time.

13.1   *Running a system with Elixir tools*

Regardless of the method you use to start the system, some common principles always hold. Running the system amounts to doing the following:

1   Compile all modules. Corresponding .beam files must exist somewhere on the disk (as explained in section 2.7). The same holds for the application resource (.app) files of all OTP applications needed to run the system.

2   Start the BEAM instance, and set up load paths to include all locations from step 1.

3   Start all required OTP applications.

Probably the simplest way to do this is to rely on standard Elixir tools. Doing so is straightforward, and you're already familiar with some aspects of `mix`, `iex`, and `elixir` command-line tools. So far, you've been using `iex`, which lets you start the system and interact with it. When you invoke `iex -S mix`, all the steps just mentioned are taken to start the system.

When running in production, you may want to start the system as a background process without the `iex` shell started. To do this, you need to start the system via the `mix` and `elixir` commands.

13.1.1   *Using the mix and elixir commands*

So far, we've been using the `iex -S mix` command to start the system. It's also possible to start the system with `mix run --no-halt`. This command starts the BEAM instance and then starts your OTP application together with its dependencies. The `--no-halt` option instructs `mix` to keep the BEAM instance running forever:

```
$ mix run --no-halt    ◁────┐  Starts the system
                            │  without the iex shell
Starting database worker.
Starting database worker.
Starting database worker.
Starting to-do cache.
```

Compared to `iex -S mix`, the important difference is that `mix run` doesn't start the interactive shell.

A slightly more elaborate option is to use the `elixir` command:

```
$ elixir -S mix run --no-halt

Starting database worker.
Starting database worker.
Starting database worker.
Starting to-do cache.
```

This approach requires a bit more typing, but it allows you to run the system in the background.

By using the `-detached` Erlang flag, you can start the system in *detached mode*. The OS process will be detached from the terminal, and there will be no console output. When starting a detached system, it's also useful to turn the BEAM instance into a node, so you can later interact with it and terminate it when needed:

```
$ elixir --erl "-detached" --sname todo_system@localhost \
    -S mix run --no-halt
```

This starts the BEAM instance in the background.

You can check that it's running by looking at which BEAM nodes exist on your system:

```
$ epmd -names
```

```
epmd: up and running on port 4369 with data:
name todo_system at port 51028          ⟵——— The node is running.
```

At this point, your system is running, and you can use it—for example, by issuing an HTTP request to manipulate to-do lists.

You can connect to a running BEAM instance and interact with it. It's possible to establish a *remote shell*—something like a terminal shell session to the running BEAM instance. In particular, with the the `--remsh` option, you can start another node and use it as a shell to the `todo_system` node:

```
$ iex --sname debugger@localhost --remsh todo_system@localhost --hidden
iex(todo_system@localhost)1>   ⟵——┐
                                    │  Shell is running on the todo_system node.
```

In this example, you start the `debugger` node, but the shell is running in the context of `todo_system`. Whatever function you call will be invoked on `todo_system`. This is extremely useful because you can now interact with the running system. BEAM provides all kinds of nice services that allow you to query the system and individual processes, as we'll discuss a bit later.

Notice that you start the `debugger` node as hidden. As mentioned in chapter 12, this means the `debugger` node won't appear in the results of `Node.list` (or `Node.list([:this, :visible])`) on `todo_system`, so it won't be considered part of the cluster.

To stop the running system, you can use the `System.stop` function (https://hexdocs .pm/elixir/System.html#stop/1), which takes down the system in a graceful manner. It shuts down all running applications and then terminates the BEAM instance:

```
iex(todo_system@localhost)1> System.stop()
```

The remote shell session is left hanging, and an attempt to run any other command will result in an error:

```
iex(todo_system@localhost)2>
*** ERROR: Shell process terminated! (^G to start new job) ***
```

At this point, you can close the shell and verify the running BEAM nodes:

```
$ epmd -names
epmd: up and running on port 4369 with data:
```

If you want to stop a node programmatically, you can rely on the distributed features described in chapter 12. Here's a quick example:

```
if Node.connect(:todo_system@localhost) == true do
  :rpc.call(:todo_system@localhost, System, :stop, [])      ◁——  Invokes System.stop
  IO.puts "Node terminated."                                      on a remote node
else
  IO.puts "Can't connect to a remote node."
end
```

Here, you connect to a remote node and then rely on `:rpc.call/4` to invoke `System`
`.stop` there.

  You can store the code in the stop_node.exs file (the .exs extension is frequently used for Elixir-based scripts). Then, you can run the script from the command line:

```
$ elixir --sname terminator@localhost stop_node.exs
```

Running a script starts a separate BEAM instance and *interprets* the code in that instance. After the script code is executed, the host instance is terminated. Because the script instance needs to connect to a remote node (the one you want to terminate), you need to give it a name to turn the BEAM instance into a proper node.

13.1.2 Running scripts

I haven't discussed scripts and tools so far, but they're worth a quick mention. Sometimes, you may want to build a command-line tool that does some processing, produces the results, and then stops. The simplest way to go about that is to write a script.

  You can create a plain Elixir file, give it an .exs extension to indicate it's a script, implement one or more modules, and invoke a function:

```
defmodule MyTool do
  def run do
    ...
  end

  ...
end

MyTool.run()     ◁——— Starts the tool
```

You can then invoke the script with the `elixir my_script.exs` command. All modules you define will be compiled in memory, and all expressions outside of any module will be interpreted. After everything finishes, the script will terminate. Of course, an Elixir script can run only on a system with correct versions of Erlang and Elixir installed.

External libraries can be added with `Mix.install` (https://hexdocs.pm/mix/Mix.html#install/2). For example, the following script uses the Jason library to parse the JSON content provided as the command line argument:

```
Mix.install([{:jason, "~> 1.4"}])      ◁─── Installs the Jason dependency

input = hd(System.argv())
decoded = Jason.decode!(input)   ◁─── Uses the Jason library

IO.inspect(decoded)
```

The list passed to `Mix.install` follows the same format as the dependency list used in mix.exs.

Let's try this out. Save the code above to the file named json_decode.exs. Then, execute the script:

```
$ elixir json_decode.exs '{"some_key": 42}'

Resolving Hex dependencies...        ┐
Resolution completed in 0.011s       │  Dependency
New:                                 │  installation and
  jason 1.4.0                        │  compilation
* Getting jason (Hex package)        │
==> jason                            │
Compiling 10 files (.ex)             │
Generated jason app                  ┘

%{"some_key" => 42}    ◁─── Script output
```

When the script is executed for the first time, Mix installs the dependency, compiles it, and caches the result to the disk. Subsequent executions will use the cached version, so the script will run much more quickly than on the first run.

An .exs script is fine for simpler tools, but it's not efficient when the code becomes more complex. In this case, it's best to use a proper Mix project and build a full OTP application.

But because you're not building a system that runs continuously, you also need to include a runner module in the project—something that does processing and produces output:

```
defmodule MyTool.Runner do
  def run do
    ...
  end
end
```

Then, you can start the tool with `mix run -e MyTool.Runner.run`. This starts the OTP application, invokes the `MyTool.Runner.run/0` function, and terminates as soon as the function is finished.

You can also package the entire tool in an *escript*—a single binary file that embeds all your .beam files, Elixir .beam files, and the start-up code. An escript file is, thus, a fully compiled, cross-platform script that requires only the presence of Erlang on the running machine. For more details, refer to the `mix escript.build` documentation (https://hexdocs.pm/mix/Mix.Tasks.Escript.Build.html).

A somewhat similar but more limited option is an Erlang *archive*, a zip file containing the compiled binaries. Compared to escripts, the main benefit of archives is that they can be installed globally with the `mix archive.install` task (https://hexdocs.pm/mix/Mix.Tasks.Archive.Install.html). This makes them perfect to distribute system-wide Mix tasks. A popular example is the `phx.new` task, which is used to generate a new project powered by the Phoenix web framework. You can read more about building archives at https://hexdocs.pm/mix/Mix.Tasks.Archive.Build.html.

13.1.3 *Compiling for production*

As mentioned in chapter 11, there's a construct called the *Mix environment*—a compile-time identifier that allows you to conditionally define code. The default Mix environment is dev, indicating you're dealing with development. In contrast, when you run tests with `mix test`, the code is compiled in the test environment.

You can use the Mix environment to conditionally include code for development- or test-time convenience. For example, you can rely on the `Mix.env/0` function to define different versions of a function. Here's a simple sketch:

```
defmodule Todo.Database do
  case Mix.env() do
    :dev ->
      def store(key, data) do ... end

    :test ->
      def store(key, data) do ... end

    _ ->
      def store(key, data) do ... end
  end
end
```

Notice how you branch on the result of `Mix.env/0` at the module level, outside of any functions. This is a compile-time construct, and this code runs during compilation. The final definition of `store/2` will depend on the Mix environment you're using to compile the code. In the dev environment, you might run additional logging and benchmarking, whereas in the test environment, you might use an in-memory storage, such as ETS.

It's important to understand that `Mix.env/0` has meaning only during compilation. You should never rely on it at run time. In any case, your code may contain such conditional definitions, so you should assume your project isn't completely optimized when compiled in the dev environment.

To start your system in production, you can set the `MIX_ENV` OS environment variable to the corresponding value:

```
$ MIX_ENV=prod elixir -S mix run --no-halt
```

This causes the recompilation of the code and all dependencies. All .beam files are stored in the _build/prod folder, and Mix ensures the BEAM instance loads files from this folder.

> **TIP** It should be obvious from the discussion that the default compiled code (in the dev environment) isn't optimized. The dev environment allows for better development convenience, but it makes the code perform less efficiently. When you decide to measure how your system behaves under a heavier load, you should always compile everything in the prod environment. Measuring with the dev environment may give you false indications about bottlenecks, and you may spend energy and time optimizing code that isn't problematic at all in production.

You've now seen the basics of starting the system with `mix` and `elixir`. This process is straightforward, and it fits nicely into your development flow.

There are some serious downsides, though. First, to start the project with Mix, you need to compile it, which means the system source code must reside on the host machine. You need to fetch all dependencies and compile them as well. Consequently, you'll need to install all the tools required for compilation on the target host machine. This includes Erlang and Elixir, Hex, and Mix, as well as any other third-party tools that you integrate in your Mix workflow.

Moreover, if you're running multiple systems on the same machine, it can become increasingly difficult to reconcile the different versions of support tools necessary for different systems. Luckily, there's a way out, in the form of OTP releases.

13.2 OTP releases

An *OTP release* is a standalone, compiled, runnable system that consists of the minimum set of OTP applications needed by the system. An OTP release can, optionally, include the minimum set of Erlang runtime binaries, which makes the release completely self-sufficient. A release doesn't contain artifacts, such as source code, documentation files, or tests.

This approach provides all sorts of benefits. First, you can build the system on your development machine or the build server and ship only binary artifacts. The host machine doesn't need to have any tools installed. If you embed the minimum Erlang runtime into the release, you don't even need Elixir and Erlang installed on the production server. Whatever is required to run the system will be part of your release package. In addition, releases simplify some operational tasks, such as connecting to the running system and executing custom Elixir code in the system context. Finally, releases pave the way for systematic online system upgrades (and downgrades), known in Erlang as *release handling*.

13.2.1 *Building a release*

To build a release, you need to compile your main OTP application and all of its dependencies. Then, you need to include all the binaries in the release, together with the Erlang runtime. This can be done with the `mix release` command (https://hexdocs.pm/mix/Mix.Tasks.Release.html).

Let's see it in action. Go to the to-do folder, and run the release command:

```
$ mix release

* assembling todo-0.1.0 on MIX_ENV=dev
* using config/runtime.exs to configure the release at runtime

Release created at _build/dev/rel/todo

...
```

This builds the release in the dev Mix environment. Since `release` is meant to be running in production, you typically want to build it in the prod environment. You can do this by prefixing the command with `MIX_ENV=prod`. Alternatively, you can enforce the default environment for the `release` task in mix.exs.

Listing 13.1   Enforcing the prod environment for the `release` task (todo_release/mix.exs)

```
defmodule Todo.MixProject do
  ...

  def cli do
    [
      preferred_envs: [release: :prod]
    ]
  end

  ...
end
```

The `cli` function can be used to configure the default Mix environments for different Mix tasks. The function must return a keyword list with supported options. The `:preferred_envs` option is a keyword list, where each key is the task name (provided as an atom), and the value is the desired default environment for that task.

With this change in place, you can invoke `mix release`, which will compile your project in the prod environment and then generate the release:

```
$ mix release

* assembling todo-0.1.0 on MIX_ENV=prod
...
```

After `mix release` is done, the release will reside in the _build/prod/rel/todo/ subfolder. We'll discuss the release's contents a bit later, but first, let's see how you can use it.

13.2.2 *Using a release*

The main tool used to interact with a release is the shell script that resides in _build/prod/rel/todo/bin/todo. You can use it to perform all kinds of tasks, such as these:

- Start the system and `iex` shell in the foreground.
- Start the system as a background process.
- Stop the running system.
- Attach a remote shell to the running system.

The simplest way to verify that the release works is to start the system in the foreground together with the `iex` shell:

```
$ RELEASE_NODE="todo@localhost" _build/prod/rel/todo/bin/todo start_iex

Starting database worker.
Starting database worker.
Starting database worker.
Starting to-do cache.

iex(todo@localhost)1>
```

Here, the `RELEASE_NODE` OS environment variable is set to the desired node name. Without it, Elixir would choose a default value based on the host name. To make the example work on different machines, the hardcoded value using localhost as the host part is chosen. Note that this is a short node name. If you want to use long names, you'll also need to set the `RELEASE_DISTRIBUTION` OS environment variable to the value `name`. Refer to the `mix release` documentation for more details on how to configure the release.

The release is no longer dependent on your system's Erlang and Elixir. It's fully standalone; you can copy the contents of the _build/prod/rel/todo subfolder to another machine where Elixir and Erlang aren't installed, and it will still work. Of course, because the release contains Erlang runtime binaries, the target machine must be powered by the same OS and architecture.

To start the system as a background process, you can use the `daemon` command:

```
$ RELEASE_NODE="todo@localhost" _build/prod/rel/todo/bin/todo daemon
```

This isn't the same as a detached process, mentioned earlier. Instead, the system is started via the `run_erl` tool (https://erlang.org/doc/man/run_erl.html). This tool redirects standard output to a log file residing in the _build/prod/rel/todo/tmp/log folder, which allows you to analyze your system's console output.

Once the system is running in the background, you can start a remote shell to the node:

```
$ RELEASE_NODE="todo@localhost" _build/prod/rel/todo/bin/todo remote

iex(todo@localhost)1>
```

At this point, you have an `iex` shell session running in the context of the production node. Pressing Ctrl-C twice to exit the shell stops the remote shell, but the `todo` node will still be running.

If the system is running as a background process, and you want to stop it, you can use the `stop` command:

```
$ RELEASE_NODE="todo@localhost" _build/prod/rel/todo/bin/todo stop
```

It's also possible to *attach* directly to the shell of the running process. Attaching offers an important benefit: it captures the standard output of the running node. Whatever the running node prints—for example, via `IO.puts`—is seen in the attached process (which isn't the case for the remote shell).

Let's see it in action. First, we'll start the release in background with `iex` running. This can be done with the `daemon_iex` command:

```
$ RELEASE_NODE="todo@localhost" _build/prod/rel/todo/bin/todo daemon_iex
```

Now, we can attach to the shell with the `to_erl` tool:

```
$ _build/prod/rel/todo/erts-13.0/bin/to_erl _build/prod/rel/todo/tmp/pipe/

iex(todo@localhost)1>

[memory_usage: 70117728, process_count: 230]    ◁─┐  Captured standard
                                                     │  output of the console
```

Back in chapter 10, you added a job that periodically prints memory usage and process count to the standard output. The output of this job is present when you attach to the shell. Conversely, when running a remote shell, this output won't be seen.

Be careful when attaching to the shell. Unlike a remote shell, an attached shell runs in the context of the running node. You're merely attached to the running node via an OS pipe. Consequently, you can only have one attached session at a time. In addition, you might accidentally stop the running node by hitting Ctrl-\. You should press Ctrl-D to detach from the running node, without stopping it.

The `todo` script can perform various other commands. To get the help, simply invoke `_build/prod/rel/todo/bin/todo` without any argument. This will print the help to the standard output. Finally, for more details on building a release, take a look at the official Mix documentation at https://hexdocs.pm/mix/Mix.Tasks.Release.html.

13.2.3 *Release contents*

Let's spend some time discussing the structure of your release. A fully standalone release consists of the following:

- Compiled OTP applications needed to run your system
- A file containing arguments that will be passed to the virtual machine
- A boot script describing which OTP applications need to be started
- A configuration file containing environment variables for OTP applications

- A helper shell script to start, stop, and interact with the system
- Erlang runtime binaries

In this case, all these reside somewhere in the _build/prod/rel/todo folder. Let's take a closer look at some important parts of the release.

COMPILED BINARIES

Compiled versions of all required applications reside in the _build/prod/rel/todo/lib folder:

```
$ ls -1 _build/prod/rel/todo/lib

asn1-5.1
compiler-8.3
cowboy-2.10.0
cowboy_telemetry-0.4.0
cowlib-2.12.1
crypto-5.2
eex-1.15.0
elixir-1.15.0
iex-1.15.0
kernel-9.0
logger-1.15.0
mime-2.0.3
plug-1.14.2
plug_cowboy-2.6.1
plug_crypto-1.2.5
poolboy-1.5.2
public_key-1.14
ranch-1.8.0
runtime_tools-2.0
sasl-4.2.1
ssl-11.0
stdlib-5.0
telemetry-1.2.1
todo-0.1.0
```

This list includes all of your runtime dependencies, both direct (specified in mix.exs) and indirect (dependencies of dependencies). In addition, some OTP applications, such as `kernel`, `stdlib`, and `elixir`, are automatically included in the release. These are core OTP applications needed by any Elixir-based system. Finally, the `iex` application is also included, which makes it possible to run the remote `iex` shell.

In each of these folders, there is an ebin subfolder, where the compiled binaries reside together with the .app file. Each OTP application folder may also contain the priv folder with additional application-specific files.

> **TIP** If you need to include additional files in the release, the best way to do it is to create a priv folder under your project root. This folder, if it exists, automatically appears in the release under the application folder. When you need to access a file from the priv folder, you can invoke `Application.app_dir(:an_app_name, "priv")` to find the folder's absolute path.

Bundling all required OTP applications makes the release standalone. Because the system includes all required binaries (including the Elixir and Erlang standard libraries), nothing else is required on the target host machine.

You can prove this by looking at the load paths:

```
$ RELEASE_NODE="todo@localhost" _build/prod/rel/todo/bin/todo start_iex

iex(todo@localhost)1> :code.get_path()     ◁——— Retrieves a list of load paths

[~c"ch13/todo_release/_build/prod/rel/todo/lib/../releases/0.1.0/consolidated",
 ~c"ch13/todo_release/_build/prod/rel/todo/lib/kernel-9.0/ebin",
 ~c"ch13/todo_release/_build/prod/rel/todo/lib/stdlib-5.0/ebin",
 ~c"ch13/todo_release/_build/prod/rel/todo/lib/compiler-8.3/ebin",
 ~c"ch13/todo_release/_build/prod/rel/todo/lib/elixir-1.15.0/ebin",
 ~c"ch13/todo_release/_build/prod/rel/todo/lib/sasl-4.2.1/ebin",
 ~c"ch13/todo_release/_build/prod/rel/todo/lib/logger-1.15.0/ebin",
 ~c"ch13/todo_release/_build/prod/rel/todo/lib/crypto-5.2/ebin",
 ~c"ch13/todo_release/_build/prod/rel/todo/lib/cowlib-2.12.1/ebin",
 ~c"ch13/todo_release/_build/prod/rel/todo/lib/asn1-5.1/ebin",
 ~c"ch13/todo_release/_build/prod/rel/todo/lib/public_key-1.14/ebin",
 ~c"ch13/todo_release/_build/prod/rel/todo/lib/ssl-11.0/ebin",
 ~c"ch13/todo_release/_build/prod/rel/todo/lib/ranch-1.8.0/ebin",
 ~c"ch13/todo_release/_build/prod/rel/todo/lib/cowboy-2.10.0/ebin",
 ~c"ch13/todo_release/_build/prod/rel/todo/lib/telemetry-1.2.1/ebin",
 ~c"ch13/todo_release/_build/prod/rel/todo/lib/cowboy_telemetry-0.4.0/ebin",
 ~c"ch13/todo_release/_build/prod/rel/todo/lib/eex-1.15.0/ebin",
 ~c"ch13/todo_release/_build/prod/rel/todo/lib/mime-2.0.3/ebin",
 ~c"ch13/todo_release/_build/prod/rel/todo/lib/plug_crypto-1.2.5/ebin",
 ~c"ch13/todo_release/_build/prod/rel/todo/lib/plug-1.14.2/ebin",
 ~c"ch13/todo_release/_build/prod/rel/todo/lib/plug_cowboy-2.6.1/ebin",
 ~c"ch13/todo_release/_build/prod/rel/todo/lib/poolboy-1.5.2/ebin",
 ~c"ch13/todo_release/_build/prod/rel/todo/lib/runtime_tools-2.0/ebin",
 ~c"ch13/todo_release/_build/prod/rel/todo/lib/todo-0.1.0/ebin",
 ~c"ch13/todo_release/_build/prod/rel/todo/lib/iex-1.15.0/ebin"]
```

Notice how all the load paths point to the release folder. In contrast, when you start a plain iex -s mix shell and run :code.get_path/0, you'll see a much longer list of load paths, with some pointing to the build folder and others pointing to the system Elixir and Erlang installation paths. This should convince you that your release is self-contained. The runtime will only look for modules in the release folder.

In addition, the minimum Erlang binaries are included in the release. They reside in _build/prod/rel/todo/erts-*X.Y*, where *X.Y* corresponds to the runtime version number (which isn't related to the Erlang version number). The fact that the Erlang runtime is included makes the release completely standalone. Moreover, it allows you to run multiple systems powered by different Elixir or Erlang versions on the same machine.

CONFIGURATIONS

Configuration files reside in the _build/prod/rel/todo/releases/0.1.0 folder, with 0.1.0 corresponding to the version of your todo application (as provided in mix.exs). The two most relevant files in this folder are vm.args and env.sh.

The vm.args file can be used to provide flags to the Erlang runtime, such as the +P flag, which sets the maximum number of running processes. The env.sh file can be used to set environment variables, such as RELEASE_NODE and RELEASE_DISTRIBUTION, mentioned earlier. For more details on how to provide your own versions of these files, see https://hexdocs.pm/mix/Mix.Tasks.Release.html#module-vm-args-and-env-sh-env-bat.

13.2.4 *Packaging in a Docker container*

There are many ways of running the system in production. You could deploy it to a platform as a service (PaaS), such as Heroku, Fly.io, or Gigalixir, or you could run it in a Kubernetes cluster. Yet another option is to run the system as a service under a service manager, such as systemd.

No matter which deployment strategy you choose, you should strive to run the system as an OTP release. In most cases, this means starting the release in the foreground. Therefore, the valid start commands are either start_iex or start.

The former command also starts the iex session. This allows you to attach to the iex shell of the running BEAM node and interact with the production system while capturing the node's standard output. On the flip side, this approach is risky because you might end up accidentally stopping the node (by pressing Ctrl-C twice).

In contrast, the start command will start the system in foreground but without the iex session. Consequently, you won't be able to attach to the main iex shell. You can still interact with the running system by establishing a remote iex shell session, but in this case, the node's standard output isn't captured.

Specific deployment steps depend on the chosen strategy. There are too many options to cover them all. A good basic introduction to some of the popular choices is given in the deployment guide of the Phoenix web framework (https://hexdocs.pm/phoenix/deployment.html).

As a small example, let's see how to run the to-do system inside a Docker container. Docker is a popular option chosen by many teams because it helps automate deployments, supports running a production-like version locally, and paves the way for various deployment options, especially in the cloud space. This part assumes you're somewhat familiar with Docker. If that's not the case, you can take a look at the official get started guide at https://docs.docker.com/get-started/.

The Docker image for an Elixir project is typically built in two stages. In the first stage, often called *build*, you need to compile the code and assemble the OTP release. Then, in the second stage, you copy the release over to the final image, which is going to be deployed to the target hosts. The final image doesn't contain build tools, such as Erlang and Elixir. Such tools are not needed because the OTP release itself contains the minimum set of the required Erlang and Elixir binaries.

To build the Docker image, we need to create the file named Dockerfile in the project root. The following listing presents the first build stage, which produces the OTP release.

Listing 13.2   The build stage (todo_release/Dockerfile)

```
ARG ELIXIR="1.15.4"
ARG ERLANG="26.0.2"                                      Base
ARG DEBIAN="bookworm-20230612-slim"                      image
ARG OS="debian-${DEBIAN}"
FROM "hexpm/elixir:${ELIXIR}-erlang-${ERLANG}-${OS}" as builder

WORKDIR /todo

ENV MIX_ENV="prod"   ◁───── Uses prod mix env by default

RUN mix local.hex --force && mix local.rebar --force   ◁───── Installs build tools

COPY mix.exs mix.lock ./      Copies the required
COPY config config            source files
COPY lib lib

RUN mix deps.get --only prod   ◁───── Fetches prod deps

RUN mix release   ◁───── Builds the release

...
```

The base Docker image used in this example is maintained by the Hex package manager team (https://hub.docker.com/r/hexpm/elixir).

It's worth noting that for the sake of brevity, this Docker file is too naive because it doesn't take advantage of the Docker layer caching. As a result, a change in any source file will require the full project recompilation, including all the dependencies. For a more refined way of building the image, take a look at the Dockerfile generated by the Phoenix web framework (https://hexdocs.pm/phoenix/releases.html#containers).

Next, let's move on to build the final image.

Listing 13.3   Building the final image (todo_release/Dockerfile)

```
ARG DEBIAN="bookworm-20230612-slim"

...

FROM debian:${DEBIAN}   ◁───── Base image

WORKDIR "/todo"

RUN apt-get update -y && apt-get install -y openssl locales

COPY \
  --from=builder \            Copies the
  --chown=nobody:root \       built release
  /todo/_build/prod/rel/todo ./

RUN sed -i '/en_US.UTF-8/s/^# //g' /etc/locale.gen && locale-gen
```

```
ENV LANG="en_US.UTF-8"
ENV LANGUAGE="en_US:en"
ENV LC_ALL="en_US.UTF-8"

CMD ["/todo/bin/todo", "start_iex"]     ◁─────  Defines the start command
```

The first thing to notice is that the base image is Debian, not Elixir or Erlang. It's important to use the same base OS as the one used in the builder image. Otherwise, you might experience crashes due to incompatibilities.

To build the final image, you need to copy the OTP release from the build stage, configure the locale, and define the default start command. In this example, the start_iex command is chosen, which makes it possible to attach to the running shell.

At this point, you can build the image:

```
$ docker build . -t elixir-in-action/todo
```

Next, you can start the container:

```
$ docker run               \
    --rm -it               \
    --name todo_system     \
    -p "5454:5454"         \     ◁─────  Publishes the http port to the host
    elixir-in-action/todo
```

You can now interact with the system locally:

```
$ curl -d "" \
  "http://localhost:5454/add_entry?list=bob&date=2023-12-19&title=Dentist"
OK

$ curl "http://localhost:5454/entries?list=bob&date=2023-12-19"
2023-12-19 Dentist
```

Like the build stage, the production image is overly naive. In particular, it doesn't support clustering via distributed Erlang, or establishing a remote shell (via the --remsh switch). This can be addressed with some work, but for the sake of brevity, it's not discussed here. If you want to establish an Erlang cluster from multiple containers, especially if they are running in a Kubernetes cluster, take a look at the libcluster library (https://hexdocs.pm/libcluster/).

This concludes the topic of releases. Once you have your system up and running, it's useful to see how you can analyze its behavior.

13.3   Analyzing system behavior

Even after the system is built and placed in production, your work isn't done. Things will occasionally go wrong, and you'll experience errors. The code also may not be properly optimized, and you may end up consuming too many resources. If you manage to properly implement a fault-tolerant system, it may recover and cope with the errors and increased load. Regardless, you'll still need to get to the bottom of any issues and fix them.

Given that your system is highly concurrent and distributed, it may not be obvious how you can discover and understand the issues that arise. Proper treatment of this topic could easily fill a separate book—and an excellent free book is available, called *Stuff Goes Bad: Erlang in Anger*, by Fred Hébert (https://www.erlang-in-anger.com/). This chapter provides a basic introduction to some standard techniques of analyzing complex BEAM systems, but if you plan to run Elixir or Erlang code in production, you should at some point study the topic in more detail, and *Stuff Goes Bad* is a great place to start.

13.3.1 *Debugging*

Although it's not strictly related to the running system, debugging deserves a brief mention. It may come as a surprise that standard step-by-step debugging isn't a frequently used approach in Erlang (which ships with a GUI-based debugger; see https://www.erlang.org/doc/apps/debugger/debugger_chapter.html). That's because it's impossible to do classical debugging of a highly concurrent system, where many things happen simultaneously. Imagine you set a breakpoint in a process. What should happen to other processes when the breakpoint is encountered? Should they continue running, or should they pause as well? Once you step over a line, should all other processes move forward by a single step? How should timeouts be handled? What happens if you're debugging a distributed system? As you can see, there are many problems with classical debugging, due to the highly concurrent and distributed nature of BEAM-powered systems.

Instead of relying on a debugger, you should adopt more appropriate strategies. The key to understanding a highly concurrent system lies in logging and tracing. Once something goes wrong, you'll want to have as much information as possible, which will allow you to find the cause of the problems.

The nice thing is that some logging is available out of the box in the form of Elixir's `logger` application (https://hexdocs.pm/logger/Logger.html). In particular, whenever an OTP-compliant process crashes (e.g., `GenServer`), an error is printed, together with a stack trace. The stack trace also contains file and line information, so this should serve as a good starting point for investigating the error.

Sometimes, the failure reason may not be obvious from the stack trace, and you'll need more data. At development time, a primitive helper tool for this purpose is `IO.inspect`. Remember that `IO.inspect` takes an expression, prints its result, and returns it. This means you can surround any part of the code with `IO.inspect` (or pipe into it via `|>`) without affecting the behavior of the program. This is a simple technique that can help you quickly determine the cause of the problem, and I use it frequently when a new piece of code goes wrong. Placing `IO.inspect` to see how values were propagated to the failing location often helps me discover errors. Once I'm done fixing the problem, I remove the `IO.inspect` calls.

A richer experience can be obtained with the dbg macro (https://hexdocs .pm/elixir/Kernel.html#dbg/2). Similarly to IO.inspect, this macro generates the code that returns its input argument. As a result, any expression can be safely wrapped in dbg, as long as it's not binding any variables. The dbg macro prints more detailed information, such as intermediate results of the pipe chain.

Another useful feature is *pry*, which allows you to temporarily stop execution in the iex shell and inspect the state of the system, such as variables that are in scope. For detailed instructions, refer to the IEx.pry/0 documentation (https://hexdocs.pm/ iex/IEx.html#pry/0). An overview of typical debugging techniques is also available on the official Elixir site at https://elixir-lang.org/getting-started/debugging.html.

It goes without saying that automated tests can be of significant assistance. Testing individual parts in isolation can help you quickly discover and fix errors.

It's also worth mentioning a couple of useful benchmarking and profiling tools. The most primitive one comes in the form of the :timer.tc/1 function (https://erlang.org/doc/man/timer.html#tc-1), which takes a lambda, runs it, and returns its result together with the running time (in microseconds).

In addition, a few profiling tools are shipped with Erlang/OTP: cprof, eprof, and fprof. Elixir includes mix tasks for running these tools:

- mix profile.cprof (https://hexdocs.pm/mix/Mix.Tasks.Profile.Cprof.html)
- mix profile.eprof (https://hexdocs.pm/mix/Mix.Tasks.Profile.Eprof.html)
- mix profile.fprof (https://hexdocs.pm/mix/Mix.Tasks.Profile.Fprof.html)

Finally, there are various benching libraries available, such as Benchee (https://hexdocs .pm/benchee). I won't explain these in detail, so when you decide to profile, it's best to start reading the official documentation as well as the Erlang documentation at https://www.erlang.org/doc/efficiency_guide/profiling.html.

13.3.2   Logging

Once you're in production, you shouldn't rely on IO.inspect or dbg calls anymore. Instead, it's better to log various pieces of information that may help you understand what went wrong. For this purpose, you can rely on Elixir's logger application. When you generate your Mix project, this dependency will be included automatically, and you're encouraged to use logger to log various events. As already mentioned, logger automatically catches various BEAM reports, such as crash errors that happen in processes.

Logging information goes to the console, by default. If you start your system as a release, the standard output will be forwarded to the log folder under the root folder of your release, and you'll be able to later find and analyze those errors.

Of course, you can write a custom logger handler, such as one that writes to syslog or sends log reports to a different machine. See the logger documentation for more details (https://hexdocs.pm/logger/Logger.html). The logger application is mostly a wrapper around Erlang's :logger module, so it's also worth studying the Erlang logging guide (https://www.erlang.org/doc/apps/kernel/logger_chapter.html).

13.3.3 *Interacting with the system*

A substantial benefit of the Erlang runtime is that you can connect to the running node and interact with it in various ways. You can send messages to processes and stop or restart different processes (including supervisors) or OTP applications. It's even possible to force the VM to reload the code for a module.

On top of this, all sorts of built-in functions allow you to gather data about the system and individual processes. For example, you can start a remote shell and use functions such as `:erlang.system_info/1` and `:erlang.memory/0` to get information about the runtime.

You can also get a list of all processes using `Process.list/0` and then query each process in detail with `Process.info/1`, which returns information such as memory usage and the total number of instructions (known in Erlang as *reductions*) the process has executed. Such services make way for tools that can connect to the running system and present BEAM system information in a GUI.

One example is the `observer` application, which you've seen in chapter 11. Being GUI-based, `observer` works only when there's a windowing system in the host OS. On the production server, this usually isn't the case. But you can start the `observer` locally and have it gather data from a remote node.

Let's see this in action. You'll start your system as a background service and then start another node on which you'll run the `observer` application. The `observer` application will connect to the remote node, collect data from it, and present it in the GUI.

The production system doesn't need to run the `observer` application, but it needs to contain the modules that gather data for the remote `observer` application. These modules are part of the `runtime_tools` application you need to include in your release. You can easily do this via the `:extra_applications` option in mix.exs.

Listing 13.4 Including `runtime_tools` in a release (todo_release/mix.exs)

```
defmodule Todo.MixProject do
  ...

  def application do
    [
      extra_applications: [:logger, :runtime_tools],     ⊲┘ Includes runtime_tools
      ...                                                       in the OTP release
    ]
  end

  ...
end
```

The `:extra_applications` option specifies Elixir and Erlang stock OTP applications you depend on. By default, Elixir's `:logger` OTP application is included as a dependency when you generate a new project with the `mix` tool.

NOTE Notice that `:extra_applications` serves a different purpose than the `deps` function in the mix.exs file. With `deps`, you list third-party dependencies that must be fetched and compiled. In contrast, with `:extra_applications`, you list Elixir and Erlang stock applications that are already compiled on your disk, as a part of Erlang and Elixir installations. The code of these dependencies doesn't have to be fetched, and nothing needs to be compiled. But you still need to list these dependencies to ensure applications are included in the OTP release.

With this change, `runtime_tools` is included in your OTP release, and now, you can remotely observe the production system. Let's see this in action. First, you need to start the to-do system in the background:

```
$ RELEASE_NODE="todo@localhost" \
  RELEASE_COOKIE="todo" \
  _build/prod/rel/todo/bin/todo daemon
```

Note that the `RELEASE_COOKIE` OS environment variable is set to configure the secret node cookie.

Now, start the interactive shell as a named node, and then start the `observer` application:

```
$ iex --hidden --sname observer@localhost --cookie todo

iex(observer@localhost)1> :observer.start()
```

Note how you explicitly set the node's cookie to match the one used in the running system. Also, just as with the earlier `remsh` example in section 13.1.1, you start the node as hidden. Once the observer is started, you need to select Nodes > todo@localhost from the menu. At this point, `observer` is presenting the data about the production node.

It's worth mentioning that `observer` and `runtime_tools` are written in plain Erlang and rely on lower-level functions to gather data and present it in various ways. Therefore, you can use other kinds of frontends or even write your own. One example is observer_cli (https://github.com/zhongwencool/observer_cli), an observer-like frontend with a textual interface, which can be used via the command-line interface.

13.3.4 *Tracing*

It's also possible to turn on traces related to processes and function calls, relying on services from the `:sys` (https://www.erlang.org/doc/man/sys.html) and `:dbg` (https://www.erlang.org/doc/man/dbg.html) modules. The `:sys` module allows you to trace OTP-compliant processes (e.g., `GenServer`). Tracing is done on the standard output, so you need to attach to the system (as opposed to establishing a remote shell). Then, you can turn on tracing for a particular process with the help of `:sys.trace/2`.

Let's see it in action. Make sure that the node is not running, and then start it in the background with `iex` started:

```
$ TODO_SERVER_EXPIRY=600 \
  RELEASE_NODE="todo@localhost" \
  RELEASE_COOKIE="todo" \
  _build/prod/rel/todo/bin/todo daemon_iex
```

For the purpose of this demo, the todo server expiry time is increased to 10 minutes.

Now, you can attach to the running node and trace the process:

```
$ _build/prod/rel/todo/erts-13.0/bin/to_erl _build/prod/rel/todo/tmp/pipe/

iex(todo@localhost)1> :sys.trace(Todo.Cache.server_process("bob"), true)
```

This turns on console tracing. Information about process-related events, such as received requests, will be printed to the standard output.

Now, issue an HTTP request for Bob's list:

```
$ curl "http://localhost:5454/entries?list=bob&date=2023-12-19"
```

Back in the attached shell, you should see something like this:

```
*DBG* {todo_server,<<"bob">>} got call {entries,
  #{'__struct__' => 'Elixir.Date', calendar => 'Elixir.Calendar.ISO',
    day => 19,month => 12, year => 2023}} from <0.983.0>}

*DBG* {todo_server,<<"bob">>} sent [] to <0.322.0>,
  new state {<<"bob">>, #{'__struct__' => 'Elixir.Todo.List',
    next_id => 1, entries => #{}}}
```

The output may seem a bit cryptic, but if you look carefully, you can see two trace entries: one for a received call request and another for the response you sent. You can also see the full state of the server process. Keep in mind that all terms are printed in Erlang syntax.

Tracing is a powerful tool because it allows you to analyze the behavior of the running system. But be careful because excessive tracing may hurt the system's performance. If the server process you're tracing is heavily loaded or has a huge state, BEAM will spend a lot of time doing tracing I/O, which may slow down the entire system.

In any case, once you've gathered some knowledge about the process, you should stop tracing it:

```
iex(todo@localhost)1> :sys.trace(Todo.Cache.server_process("bob"), false)
```

Other useful services from :sys allow you to get the OTP process state (:sys.get_state/1) and even change it (:sys.replace_state/2). Those functions are meant to be used purely for debugging or hacky manual fixes—you shouldn't invoke them from your code.

Another useful tracing tool comes with the `:erlang.trace/3` function (https://www.erlang.org/doc/man/erlang.html#trace-3), which allows you to subscribe to events in the system such as message passing or function calls.

Additionally, a module called `:dbg` (https://www.erlang.org/doc/man/dbg.html) simplifies tracing. You can run `:dbg` directly on the attached console, but it's also possible to start another node and make it trace the main system. This is the route you'll take in the next example.

Assuming the to-do node is still running, start another node:

```
$ iex --sname tracer@localhost --cookie todo --hidden
```

Now, on the `tracer` node, start tracing the main `todo` node, and then specify that you're interested in all calls to functions from the `Todo.Server` module:

```
iex(tracer@localhost)1> :dbg.tracer()          Starts the tracer process
iex(tracer@localhost)2> :dbg.n(:"todo@localhost")    Subscribes only to events
iex(tracer@localhost)3> :dbg.p(:all, [:call])        from the todo node
iex(tracer@localhost)4> :dbg.tp(Todo.Server, [])   Subscribes to function
                                                    calls in all processes
Sets the trace pattern to all functions
from the Todo.Server process
```

With traces set up, you can make an HTTP request to retrieve Bob's entries. In the shell of the `tracer` node, you should see something like the following:

```
(<12505.1106.0>) call 'Elixir.Todo.Server':whereis(<<"bob">>)
(<12505.1106.0>) call 'Elixir.Todo.Server':child_spec(<<"bob">>)
(<12505.1012.0>) call 'Elixir.Todo.Server':start_link(<<"bob">>)
(<12505.1107.0>) call 'Elixir.Todo.Server':init(<<"bob">>)
(<12505.1107.0>) call 'Elixir.Todo.Server':handle_continue(init, ...)
(<12505.1106.0>) call 'Elixir.Todo.Server':entries(<12505.1107.0>, ...)
(<12505.1107.0>) call 'Elixir.Todo.Server':handle_call({entries, ...})
```

Each output line shows the caller process, the invoked function, and the input arguments.

Be careful about tracing in production because huge numbers of traces may flood the system. Once you're finished tracing, invoke `:dbg.stop_clear/0` to stop all traces.

This was, admittedly, a brief demo; `:dbg` has many more options. If you decide to do some tracing, you should look at the `:dbg` documentation. In addition, you should take a look at the library called Recon (https://github.com/ferd/recon), which provides many useful functions for analyzing a running BEAM node.

We're now finished exploring Elixir, Erlang, and OTP. This book covered the primary aspects of the Elixir language, basic functional programming idioms, the Erlang concurrency model, and the most frequently used OTP behaviors (`GenServer`, `Supervisor`, and `Application`). In my experience, these are the most frequently needed building blocks of Elixir and Erlang systems.

Of course, many topics have been left untreated, so your journey doesn't stop here. You'll probably want to look for other knowledge resources, such as other books, blogs, and podcasts. A good starting place to look for further material is the "Learning" page on the official Elixir site (https://elixir-lang.org/learning.html).

Summary

- To start a system, all code must be compiled. Then, you must start a BEAM instance with properly set up load paths. Finally, you need to start all OTP applications.
- The simplest way to do this is to rely on Elixir tools such as `iex` and Mix.
- An OTP release is a standalone system consisting only of runtime artifacts—compiled OTP applications and (optionally) the Erlang runtime system.
- OTP releases can be easily built with the `mix release` task.
- Once the release is running, you can connect to it via a remote shell or attach to its console. Then, you can interact with the system in various ways and find detailed information about the VM and individual processes.

index

RELATED MANNING TITLES

F# in Action
by Isaac Abraham

ISBN 9781633439535
331 pages *(estimated)*, $59.99
March 2024 *(estimated)*

Functional Programming in Scala, Second Edition
by Michael Pilquist, Rúnar Bjarnason, and Paul Chiusano
Foreword by Martin Odersky and Daniel Spiewak

ISBN 9781617299582
488 pages, $59.99
May 2023

Grokking Simplicity
by Eric Normand

ISBN 9781617296208
592 pages, $49.99
April 2021

Data-Oriented Programming
by Yehonathan Sharvit
Foreword by Michael T. Nygard and Ryan Singer

ISBN 9781617298578
424 pages, $59.99
July 2022

For ordering information go to www.manning.com

A new online reading experience

liveBook, our online reading platform, adds a new dimension to your Manning books, with features that make reading, learning, and sharing easier than ever. A liveBook version of your book is included FREE with every Manning book.

This next generation book platform is more than an online reader. It's packed with unique features to upgrade and enhance your learning experience.

- Add your own notes and bookmarks
- One-click code copy
- Learn from other readers in the discussion forum
- Audio recordings and interactive exercises
- Read all your purchased Manning content in any browser, anytime, anywhere

As an added bonus, you can search every Manning book and video in liveBook—even ones you don't yet own. Open any liveBook, and you'll be able to browse the content and read anything you like.*

Find out more at www.manning.com/livebook-program.

*Open reading is limited to 10 minutes per book daily